Why Globalization Works

Why
Globalization
Works

Martin Wolf

Yale University Press New Haven and London

For Alison
and in memory of Edmund and Rebecca Wolf

Copyright © 2004 by Martin Wolf

For information about this and other Yale University Press publications, please contact:
U.S. Office: sales.press@yale.edu   yalebooks.com
Europe Office: sales@yaleup.co.uk   www.yalebooks.co.uk

Set in Minion by Northern Phototypesetting Co. Ltd, Bolton
Printed in the United States of America

Library of Congress Cataloging-in-Publication Data
Wolf, Martin, 1946–
   Why globalization works/Martin Wolf.
      p. cm.
   Includes bibliographical references and index.
   ISBN 0–300–10252–6 (cl.: alk. paper)
      1. Globalization—Economic aspects. 2. International economic relations.
   I. Title.
   HF1359.W6534 2004
   337—dc22   2004000475

A catalogue record for this book is available from the British Library

The paper in this book meets the guidelines for permanence and durability of the Committee on Production Guidelines for Book Longevity of the Council on Library Resources.

Contents

List of Tables and Figures

Tables

Figures

Acknowledgements

My intellectual debts are acknowledged in the Preface, but in writing a book one also accumulates many personal debts. The writing of this book took place in the summers of 2002 and 2003. This would have been impossible without the forbearance and encouragement of Richard Lambert and Andrew Gowers, successive editors of the *Financial Times*, who put up with two lengthy absences without complaint. I am grateful to them both. I also owe much to Chrystia Freeland, the *FT*'s deputy editor, who read and commented on large parts of the draft. I would like to thank my brother, Daniel, for having been an unfailingly good listener over a lifetime. But I owe most of all to my immediate family and, above all, to my wife, Alison, who tolerated the anxiety this project caused and the months it took. I thank them all and promise, in return, not to start on another book for at least a year or two.

Preface – Why I Wrote This Book

Free trade, one of the greatest blessings which a government can confer on a people, is in almost every country unpopular.
Thomas Macaulay, 1824[1]

Ideas matter. That is perhaps the most important of the lessons I learned from my father, the late Edmund Wolf. He was an Austrian Jewish refugee from Hitler who came to Britain before the Second World War. A playwright and passionate intellectual, he taught me how the insane ideas of the Nazis and the almost equally insane ideas of the communists had destroyed, or were still destroying, civilized life in large parts of the world. Since I was born just after the Second World War, in 1946, these dangers were not ancient history. Germany had been defeated only a year before my birth. By the time I was aware of the outside world, I already knew that ideas mattered a great deal. I understood, for example, that both my parents were refugees from an armed idea. I learned that, although the immediate families of both my parents had survived by fleeing Europe, the great majority of their relatives had perished in what is today called the Holocaust, though I think of it by its Hebrew name – the Shoah, or destruction. My mother, who came from a Dutch-Jewish family, told us that nearly thirty of her aunts, uncles and cousins perished under the Nazis. I also soon discovered that communist dictatorships had divided Europe and still threatened the freedom and tranquillity of the country in which I was growing up.

Because my father was an honest man and writer, he thought and wrote of people not as they might be but as they were. He was, for this reason, never attracted to communism, unlike so many of his contemporaries. He condemned communism as a Procrustean bed upon which ideologically motivated despots tortured people in the name of humanity. He was always pro-democracy and anti-communist. Many intellectuals then considered anti-communism to be more than a little shameful. His opinion was the exact opposite. But, as was true of most intellectuals at that time, he was inclined towards socialism, though of a moderate and cautious kind. Social democracy was then his natural intellectual home. I do not know what he would have thought of Tony Blair, the man. But he would have liked his politics. Throughout a lengthy career as a journalist, broadcaster and writer (he was, among other things, programme organizer for the German service of the British Broadcasting Corporation in the 1950s, London correspondent and later columnist for the distinguished German weekly, *Die Zeit*, and a documentary film-maker and author of prize-winning plays for German television between the 1960s and 1980s) he returned repeatedly to the importance of liberal democracy. This, it should be remembered, was at a time when many German intellectuals flirted with varieties of radical Marxism.

My father was the most important influence upon me, both intellectual and moral. I also learned from my no less remarkable mother the abiding value of simple human decency. I have never rebelled against the values of my parents, though I became more of a classical liberal – what I mean throughout this book by a 'liberal' – and less of a social democrat or 'social liberal', as time passed.[2] I learned that enlightenment ideals of freedom, democratic government and disinterested search for truth were infinitely precious and frighteningly fragile. I discovered, too, that these values had many enemies, some open and some covert. Worst among them were those intellectuals who benefit from the freedom only liberal democracies provide, while doing everything they can to undermine it. These, I later discovered, were the kind of people George Orwell had attacked before, during and after the Second World War. But they return in every generation, spreading their havoc upon the innocent young. In the 1960s the most influential pied piper was probably Herbert Marcuse. More recently, it seems to have been Jacques Derrida.

In October 1965, I went up to Corpus Christi College, Oxford University, to read classics. This was just before a wave of protest swept across my generation. Some of those protests – particularly against the war in Vietnam – seemed then and still seem now justified. The demand for personal liberalization I sympathised with, though now I feel that it did both great good and great harm, as is often the case with revolutions. But many of the protests took the form of an infantile leftism against which I had been inoculated. I met many sub-species of Marxist. They seemed to believe the differences among them were important. I was reminded of what Samuel Johnson said when asked to distinguish the merits of two minor poets: there is no point in settling the point of precedency between a louse from a flea. I already knew that all the varieties of Marxism were both wicked and stupid. The hostility to liberal – or 'bourgeois' – democracy they shared I found contemptible. History has since more than vindicated my responses, learned so early from my parents.

Fortunately, I discovered more positive things at Oxford, especially when I switched from the study of classics to politics, philosophy and economics in 1967. The chief lesson relevant to this book concerned the damage caused by the collapse of liberalism in the late nineteenth and early twentieth centuries under the assault of assorted collectivist ideologies – imperialism, militarism, socialism, communism and, finally, fascism. But I also learned that good economic policy – then thought, wrongly, by many Oxford economists to consist of little more than a wise Keynesianism – could help sustain a liberal society and economy against such attacks. Political stability and social harmony were in great danger once an economy failed, as it had done in the 1930s. Economics was about far more than prosperity, significant though that was. It was also important if we were to sustain civilization. Once people are deprived of hope of a better life for themselves and their children, societies based on consent are likely to founder.

When I went up to Oxford I was, under the influence of my father, still a social democrat in the tradition of the then recently deceased leader of the Labour Party, Hugh Gaitskell. I had been active as a staunch anti-Marxist in the Labour Party's Young Socialists since I was sixteen. In Oxford, I joined the Labour Club. At the end of my first term, I was involved in forming a breakaway club, the Oxford University Democratic Labour Club, since Marxists opposed to the then Labour government of Harold Wilson dominated the old Labour Club. In 1967 I became chairman of the Democratic Labour Club, which we had founded in early 1966. I continued to be an active supporter of the Labour Party until the early 1970s.

In 1969 I went to Nuffield College, Oxford, to study for what is now called the Master of Philosophy in economics. There I learned, principally from three teachers – Ian Little, Maurice Scott and Max Corden – the importance of international trade for prosperity, above all for developing countries. Max Corden had then completed his important work on effective protection and was teaching trade theory in a way particularly valuable to the mathematically challenged (such as myself).[3] The other two men (together with Tibor Scitovsky of Yale University) published in 1970 one of the most influential books on economic development of the past half-century, *Industry and Trade in Some Developing Countries*.[4] This brilliant book – a *Wealth of Nations* for our time – summarized a multi-country study of trade policy and economic development organised by Professor Little for the Development Centre of the Organization for Economic Co-operation and Development. It was a counter-revolutionary manifesto, arguing for the importance of outward-looking trade regimes, against import substitution, and for the market economy, against *dirigisme*. Subsequently, this approach became the conventional wisdom. At the time, it challenged a damaging orthodoxy.

This book cemented my conversion to belief in the superiority of the market economy over any available alternative. It was, to apply Winston Churchill's wise words about democracy, the worst of all economic systems, except all the other forms that have been tried from time to time. That shift in perspective was strengthened by my writing a short thesis on British housing policy. From this I discovered the disastrous consequences of rent control and the growth of council (or public) housing. I was persuaded by Colin Crouch, then also at Nuffield College, subsequently at the London School of Economics, to write a short pamphlet on this topic for the Young Fabians. The pamphlet was rejected out of hand by an anonymous reader. I later learned he was the former cabinet minister Richard Crossman. This helped persuade me that the Labour Party had become intellectually moribund, wedded to an out-of-date and unworkable statism. This conviction was subsequently strengthened by my failure to persuade the vastly more intelligent Anthony Crosland of the need for a radical change in the country's calamitous housing policies.

Subsequently, the works of Friedrich Hayek, particularly *The Road to Serfdom* and *The Constitution of Liberty*, convinced me that a market economy was also a necessary condition for a stable and enduring democracy. The market may not be a sufficient condition for such a democracy. But it was a necessary one, because the concentration of power inherent in a planned economy was incompatible with effective pressures from below. Markets also allowed people to express their personal choices. They were a dimension of freedom.

This set of convictions shifted me from social democracy to classical liberalism. I remain such a liberal today, not only because of my belief in the supreme value of personal freedom, but because of an abiding scepticism about the wisdom and capacity of an intrusive government. Today, however, I would consider my differences from social democrats (or, in the United States, liberals, as they call themselves) to be small. This is partly because the death of socialism has killed all sane people's belief in the planned economy and state ownership. Liberals, social democrats and moderate conservatives are on the same side in the great battles against religious fanatics, obscurantists, extreme environmentalists, fascists, Marxists and, of course, contemporary anti-globalizers. This book is addressed to all those who fall within these broad categories, and will, I hope, largely convince them that a global market economy is highly desirable. The big issue is not that, but how best to govern and regulate it.

In my last year at Nuffield, I applied to join the World Bank as a young professional. The then head of the Bank's economics department, David Henderson, strongly influenced this decision. Ironically, he was to fall out with the Bank's president, Robert McNamara, shortly afterwards. He then left the Bank to return to the United Kingdom. He was subsequently to be the chief economist of the Organization for Economic Co-operation and Development in the 1980s. Another warrior in the liberal cause, whom I met at the same time, was Deepak Lal, then research fellow in the college.

I started my professional career at the World Bank in 1971 in the division run by a remarkable British economist, Stanley Please. I did so because this seemed a fascinating and rewarding opportunity, but also because I believed then, as I do now, that raising the incomes of the poor countries was the most important contemporary challenge for economists. It turned out to be a superb education. I also made many lifelong friends. Some of them went on to play important roles in their home countries. Among my earliest colleagues were Montek Singh Ahluwalia, later a reforming finance secretary of India, and Shankar Acharya, later India's chief economic adviser, both of whom played significant roles in India's market-oriented reforms of the 1990s.

Working as an economist on east Africa between 1972 and 1974 and then on India between 1974 and 1977, I learned first-hand of the damage done by *dirigiste*, inward-looking economic policies. This was not only because of the grotesque inefficiency, but also because of the epidemic of corruption they caused. Throughout my ten years at the Bank, I was principally engaged in arguing for greater reliance on the market mechanism and trade.

My first big report for the World Bank was on the private sector in Kenya. Shortly afterwards, I worked on the anti-agricultural bias of policies adopted in Zambia. Both experiences depressed me greatly, since these countries were going over an economic cliff with the support, more or less enthusiastic, of the World Bank. But my longest period was spent working on the inordinately anti-trade and interventionist policies of India, which World Bank assistance also sustained, albeit to a smaller extent, because of the size of the country. I have never forgotten the consequences of a licensing system dedicated to telling companies what to produce and with what technologies and inputs. This work culminated in a book on India's exports.[5] During my time working on India, I had the opportunity to make a number of friends. The most impressive of these was Dr Manmohan Singh, then the government of India's chief economic adviser and later India's reforming finance minister.

My work at the World Bank also included a year as a team member for the very first World Development Report, published in 1978. This was one of the most imaginative initiatives of the then Bank president, Robert McNamara, and was run by Ernest Stern, who had by then been selected to be the operational head of the Bank, a role he played for almost two decades. Again, my personal focus was trade. During my time at the Bank, an important influence was the late Bela Balassa, of Johns Hopkins University and the World Bank, who worked tirelessly to promote export-oriented trade policies.[6] Other important intellectual influences were Jagdish Bhagwati, then at the Massachusetts Institute of Technology and now at Columbia, and Anne Krueger, then at the University of Minnesota and now first deputy managing director of the International Monetary Fund. Both of these scholars published summary volumes of a classic study of foreign trade regimes and economic development in the late 1970s.[7]

By the late 1970s, I had concluded that, for all the good intentions and abilities of its staff, the Bank was a fatally flawed institution. The most important source of its failures was its commitment to lending, almost regardless of what was happening in the country it was lending to. This was an inevitable flaw since the institution could hardly admit that what it could offer – money – would often make little difference. But this flaw was magnified by the personality of Robert McNamara, former US Defence Secretary, who was a dominating president from 1967 to 1981. McNamara was a man of ferocious will, personal commitment to alleviating poverty and frighteningly little common sense. By instinct, he was a planner and quantifier. Supported by his chief economic adviser, the late Hollis Chenery, he put into effect a Stalinist vision of development: faster growth would follow a rise in investment and an increase in availability of foreign exchange; both would require additional resources from outside; and much of these needed resources would come from the Bank. Under his management, the Bank and Bank lending grew enormously. But every division also found itself under great pressure to lend money, virtually regardless of the quality of the projects on offer or of the development programmes of the countries. This undermined the professional integrity of the staff and encouraged borrowers to pile up debt, no matter what the likely returns. This could not last – and did not do so. As Montek Ahluwalia once told me, the Bank was a growing business in a dying industry. It was certain to reach the limit to its growth. It did so soon after McNamara's departure.[8]

By that time I had had enough. I had worked on India as senior divisional economist for three years. During that time, my chief function, so far as the Bank was concerned, was to justify the provision of significant quantities of aid, even though this money was helping the government of India avoid desperately needed policy changes. As it turned out, those changes were made in the midst of a deep foreign exchange crisis in 1991, almost two wasted decades later. The changes were made under the direction of Manmohan Singh, then finance minister, with the assistance of Montek Ahluwalia as economic secretary and later finance secretary. This experience confirmed three lessons: policy changes could make a huge difference to economic performance; such changes could be put into effect by relatively small teams of intelligent, motivated and well-disciplined individuals; and, most important of all, those changes could not be imposed from outside.

Unfortunately, lending too much was not the Bank's only fault. It also had to lend to governments. This had two undesirable consequences: it had to assume that the government represented the interests of the country; and it reinforced an unjustifiably collectivist view of that national interest. Bank lending made it easier for corrupt and occasionally vicious governments to ignore the interests and wishes of their peoples. By the end of my time at the Bank, I came to the conclusion that its borrowers fell into three categories – those that did not need the help; those that would not use the help; and those that needed the help and would use it. The Bank was constitutionally incapable of concentrating its efforts on this third, often quite small group. As a result, its efforts were often either unnecessary or wasteful. I therefore came to agree with most of the criticisms of aid that had long been made by the late Peter (Lord) Bauer.[9]

The realization that the institutions designed to oversee aspects of the global economy might fail, even though integration was an important element in successful development, has stayed with me to this day. To defend a liberal world economy is not to defend the International Monetary Fund, the World Bank, the World Trade Organization or any specific institution. These must be judged – and reformed or discarded – on their merits. At that stage, this realization persuaded me to leap from the cocoon of the Bank to the comparatively uncertain world of think tanks. In September 1981, I joined the

London-based Trade Policy Research Centre, as director of studies, a post once held by the late Harry Johnson, a giant of post-war international trade theory. The Centre, under its energetic director Hugh Corbet, had won a deserved reputation for its work on trade liberalization and the multilateral trading system. I had first come into contact with it during my last two years at the Bank. With a colleague, Donald Keesing, I wrote a substantial study of the system of quotas operated by advanced countries against the textiles and clothing exports of developing countries.[10] It was an invaluable lesson not only in the hypocrisy with which the world's richest countries have responded to the comparative advantage of the poor, but also in the mixture of complexity with irrationality of some trade policy regimes.

I was director of studies at the Centre for six years. During that time, most of the work was aimed at promoting an eighth round of multilateral trade negotiations, subsequently known as the Uruguay Round, which finally began in 1986. The Centre played a substantial role in developing the agenda for trade negotiations on services. But my most important contribution was a programme of studies on the role of developing countries in the trading system. The aim of these studies was to question the long-standing reluctance of developing countries to negotiate on a reciprocal basis, insisting, instead, on 'special and differential treatment'. The most important study on this theme was by the late Robert E. Hudec, a distinguished scholar of international trade law, then working at the University of Minnesota.[11]

Alas, the finances of think tanks are chronically fragile, at least in the UK. By 1986, it was becoming evident that the Centre was likely to fold, as was to happen not so long afterwards. As I was looking for new work, in 1987 I was invited, out of the blue, by the then editor of the *Financial Times*, Geoffrey Owen, to become chief economics leader writer. This was a heroic gamble on his part. Although I had written several articles for the paper, I had never been – or intended to become – a journalist. But it seemed an irresistible challenge. So I joined the *FT* in September 1987.

By this time, the conventional wisdom on economic policy had undergone many revolutionary changes. The naive Keynesian faith in the ability to fine-tune economies to achieve given real outcomes had been shattered by the stagflationary 1970s. It was replaced by the search for monetary stability. This was to result in widespread adoption of inflation targeting – an idea I first heard from Maurice Scott in the 1970s. *Dirigisme* and protectionism had gone out of favour almost everywhere. Exchange controls had been abolished by the Thatcher government in the UK in 1979. Privatization began in the UK in the early 1980s and then swept the world. The so-called 'Washington consensus' of the 1980s – a term invented by the British economist John Williamson – emphasized the importance of sound fiscal and monetary policies and greater reliance on market forces in economic development. Most directly relevant to me was the widespread acceptance of the failure of inward-looking trade policies and the wisdom of trade liberalization. Partly for this reason, developing countries did play a greater role in the Uruguay Round than in any previous one. This culminated in the creation of the World Trade Organization in January 1995.

It appeared then that the idea of an integrated world economy, founded on market relationships, had been reborn after a long collectivist hiatus.[12] The collapse of the Soviet empire between 1989 and 1991 – the most pleasurable surprise of my life – appeared to confirm the global transformation in politics and economic policy. Socialism was dead. The American analyst, Francis Fukuyama, even proclaimed the end of history. This viewpoint has been condemned by those who have unfairly caricatured it. What Fukuyama argued was that liberal democracy had proved to be the only way to run an advanced economy and society. He was right in this. But the enemies of liberalism could still threaten its survival, so putting to an end what historians will almost certainly view as a golden age. Nor did this thesis mean that the follies and crimes which mar most of human history would not be repeated, in one form or another, in the centuries to come. At worst, disorder could again engulf the world. If history teaches anything, it is that we have choices. We can choose a better world – or a worse one.

This book is therefore a work not of academic scholarship, but of persuasion. It starts from the proposition that a world integrated through the market should be highly beneficial to the vast majority of the world's inhabitants. The market is the most powerful institution for raising living standards ever invented: indeed there are no rivals. But markets need states, just as states need markets. In a proper marriage between the two, one has contemporary liberal democracy, incomparably the best way to manage a society. Its blessing need to be spread more widely. The problem today is not that there is too much globalization, but that there is far too little. We can do better with the right mix of more liberal markets and more co-operative global governance. I am not arguing for the replacement of states. That would be both senseless and damaging. I am arguing for a better understanding by states of their long-run interest in a co-operative global economic order. Justifying these propositions is the kernel of the book.

The ruin of the first liberal order led to the thirty years of catastrophe from which my parents' generation suffered so much. The lives of billions of people were blighted by those mistakes. Now we all – or almost all – know better. The ideas which undermined faith in the liberal order were wrong. Socialism does not work. Communism and fascism were crimes, as well as blunders. Imperialism was a blind ally. Militarism and nationalism destroyed European civilization. Now we have, by luck as much as by judgement, recreated a better liberal international order – one that extends opportunities to the world as a whole. It is our duty to our descendants not to throw away this golden opportunity once again.

Part I **The Debate**

Chapter 1 **Enter the 'New Millennium Collectivists'[1]**

What is the market? It is the law of the jungle, the law of nature. And what is civilization? It is the struggle against nature.

Edouard Balladur, former prime minister of France, 1993[2]

Who imagines that the welfare of Americans would be improved if their economy was fragmented among its fifty states, each with prohibitive barriers to movement of goods, services, capital and people from the others? Who supposes that Americans would be better off if every state had its own capital market, or GE, Microsoft and IBM could operate in only one of these states? In such a Disunited States, without inter-state direct investment, capital markets or trade, the decline in standards of living would be precipitous. Some states would become prisons, with desperately unhappy populations locked inside. A similar disaster would befall Europe if policymakers once again fragmented the European economy into the isolated national economies of 1945.

Yet this is precisely the current fate of large swathes of the world. If some critics of globalization had their way, still more would be in the same state. Why, however, would humanity be better off for having its economy broken up into more than 200 entirely self-sufficient pieces? Maybe continental economies, such as the United States, would remain reasonably prosperous. But what would happen to small economies such as Hong Kong, Ireland, Taiwan or South Korea?

Furthermore, why should one stop at 200 pieces? Why not break the world economy up into 10,000 countries, 600,000 tribes or 6 billion self-sufficient human beings? There is no point at which one reaches just the 'right' degree of self-sufficiency of just the 'right' collective selves. The view that the present political division of humanity is natural and inevitable is nonsensical. The parallel idea that each unit should be economically self-sufficient is equally absurd. Today's states are arbitrary products of recent history. The logical destination of a movement dedicated to self-sufficiency must be the atomization of humanity, perhaps into family bands. This would be back to the future with a vengeance – back to the mesolithic period.

It cannot make sense to fragment the world economy more than it already is but rather to make the world economy work as if it were the United States, or at least the European Union. Is this impossible? No. Is it undesirable? Again, no. The failure of our world is not that there is too much globalization, but that there is too little. The potential for greater economic integration is barely tapped. We need more global markets, not fewer, if we want to raise the living standards of the poor of the world. Social democrats, classical liberals and democratic conservatives should unite to preserve and improve the liberal global economy against the enemies mustering both outside and inside the gates. That is the central argument of this book.

Introducing antiglobalization.com

Proponents of economic integration will find that they confront many opponents. In the course of the 1990s, it became impossible to hold a sizeable meeting of business people, international organizations or heads of western government in any relatively accessible place without the attendance of an army of angry, often violent protesters. The Canadian observer Sylvia Ostry has called this movement 'dissent.com'.[3] I think of it as 'antiglobalization.com'. Organizers had to consider cancelling or truncating meetings or moving them to remote or well-policed places, such as Qatar, site of the World Trade Organization's ministerial meeting in 2001. After the collapse of the Soviet Union, the idea of a global market economy seemed all-conquering. Just a decade later it was again on the defensive. The disappearance of the Soviet Union and, with it, the collapse of attempts to run a non-market economy seems to have liberated utopians to dream, no longer constrained by anything that is happening in the world.

The intellectual clash between liberal capitalism and its opponents is the chief theme of this book. It is not that concerned with the social and intellectual origins of the protest movement itself.[4] It focuses, instead, largely on the arguments advanced by those who want to halt or reverse market-driven globalization and destroy the international institutions that promote and oversee it. These members of antiglobalization.com fall, broadly, into two groups: old-fashioned economic interests on the one hand, and, more important today, single-issue, non-governmental organizations, often with mass memberships, on the other.

The economic interests include many trades unions, concerned with jobs at home and labour standards abroad; and farm lobbies and other producer groups, determined to protect their vulnerable economic positions. While no longer the only important groups engaged in lobbying and protest over trade policy, these groups still matter. Members of trades unions provided much of the muscle at the protest against the ministerial meeting of the World Trade Organization in Seattle in the autumn of 1999. The influence of the trades unions was also behind the unscripted comments of President Clinton, during the Seattle meeting, on the desirability of imposing sanctions against countries or companies that violate labour standards – remarks that virtually ended hopes of a productive outcome. The American Federation of Labor – Congress of Industrial Organizations (AFL-CIO), the central organization of the American labour movement has played a decisive part in shifting the Democratic Party of the US against trade liberalization and the WTO. The need to keep organized labour happy also lay behind the flirtation with protectionism of Vice President Albert Gore in his presidential campaign in 2000. Similarly, industrial lobbies, particularly the steel industry, play a dominant role in maintaining support for protectionist anti-dumping laws, while agricultural lobbies have great weight in determining the trade policies of the European Union, the United States, Japan and elsewhere.

These groups are economically rational. The labour movement of the United States, for example, quite properly reflects the interests of its members, many of whom work in import-threatened industries, such as steel and textiles and clothing. The fact that unions represent only 9 per cent of US private-sector workers, almost entirely in the 'old economy', means that they are bound to be a voice against liberal trade. As the late Mancur Olson – the great theorist of the logic of collective action – pointed out, only an 'encompassing organization', namely, one that represents most of the economic interests in society, is likely to campaign for policies that raise overall incomes rather than increase the incomes of their members at the expense of others.[5] It is not surprising therefore that Scandinavian trades unions – indeed most European trades unions – have views on trade that better reflect the general economic interest of their countries, since they represent a wider spectrum of the work-force.

Yet these traditional producer interests are no longer dominant in opposition to liberalization. In the period between the end of the Second

World War and the 1980s, high-minded free-traders and economic liberals thought of themselves as pitched against narrow-minded sectional interest groups. Increasingly, they find themselves opposed by groups at least as dedicated to an ideological cause as they are. As that distinguished defender of free trade, Jagdish Bhagwati of Columbia University, has noted:

> The proponents of free trade . . . started from, or at least could always claim, the higher moral ground. But today's challengers of free trade often fight our general interest with theirs; and the most vociferous among them even claim the higher moral ground. And since our case is more taxing on the mind and theirs is plainer to the view, the public policy debate has put the proponents of free trade into a battle that is harder than ever to wage.[6]

These new actors are idealistic, not narrowly self-interested. Their goals are also generous, not narrow. They include conservationists and environmentalists, fearful that the liberal world economy will sweep away hard-won domestic regulations or exacerbate perceived global environmental damage; lobbies for development, concerned about the overhang of debt or the devastation allegedly caused by the structural adjustment and liberalization imposed by the International Monetary Fund and World Bank under the so-called 'Washington consensus'; consumer groups, worried about product safety and consumer health; human rights groups, troubled by exploitation and the oppression in mainland China, Burma and other parts of the developing world; Church groups of all denominations; women's groups; and campaigners for indigenous groups and traditional ways of life. These organizations are often put under the convenient, if presumptuous, label of 'civil society'.[7] But civil society is a name for all social activity that lies outside the operation of the state. It should not be appropriated by a limited subset of pressure groups. In a recent analysis, David Henderson, formerly chief economist of the Organization for Economic Co-operation and Development, calls these activists 'new millennium collectivists' instead.

Antiglobalization.com is organized into what Professor Ostry calls 'mobilization networks'. 'The main objectives of these networks', she argues, are to heighten public awareness of the target international institution's role in globalization and, by doing so, to change its agenda and mode of operation – or, in the case of the more extreme members, to shut it down. While these networks are loosely knit coalitions of disparate groups, analysis shows that a significant proportion consist of environmental, human and gender rights non-governmental organizations (NGOs).

To these groups should be added a more traditional assortment of old-fashioned socialists and neo-Marxists and, probably far more dangerous in the long run, mercantilists, nationalists and assorted anti-liberal groups of the right that played such a big role in bringing down the liberal regime of the late nineteenth century. Today such groups can be found supporting Patrick Buchanan in the United States or Jean-Marie Le Pen in France.[8] As Henderson has observed, many in business and government believe in a mild version of mercantilism and economic nationalism. He has called these widely shared views about the economy and, in particular, international commerce 'do-it-yourself-economics'.[9] The popularity of many of these views is one reason the more extreme versions are still dangerous.

In all, anti-liberal attitudes that had foundered in the shipwreck of twentieth-century nationalism and totalitarianism are bubbling up, like flotsam, on to the surface of political life. Old preferences for the comforts of community over individual striving, for traditional ways over rapid change, for the beneficence of the state over the cold logic of the market, for collectivism over freedom and for the nation over the global economy have been reborn. Marxist, nationalist and fascist opponents of liberal capitalism had aspired to a post-enlightenment form of tribalism. Today's demands appear more atavistic, albeit less dangerous. The guiding ideas still come from the eighteenth and early nineteenth centuries. But instead of Hegel's philosophically based nationalism or Karl Marx's post-enlightenment ideology of scientific socialism, the sources are more likely to be Jean-Jacques Rousseau's myth of the noble savage or William Blake's hostility to Newton's science and 'dark Satanic mills'.

The complaints of antiglobalization.com

The protest movement is fractured into many different and often discordant communities of ideas. What they share is only what they are against. As the British journalist John Lloyd argues, many in the movement share 'the belief that globalization is essentially Western/American capitalism, which is an oppressive and impoverishing force'.[10] Their shared enemy is called 'neo-liberal globalization' or, for those less enamoured of neo-Marxist jargon, 'corporate globalization'. The enemy is, in short, liberal internationalism, using the word 'liberal' in its traditional British rather than its contemporary American meaning. Antiglobalization.com can best be defined not by what it is for, but by what it is against.

The critics make the following more or less specific charges against market-driven globalization.

It destroys the ability of states to regulate their national economies, raise taxes and spend money on public goods and social welfare.

In the process, it undermines democracy, imposing in its place the rule of unaccountable bureaucrats, corporations and markets.

It amounts to an abdication of power by benevolent democratic governments in favour of predatory private corporations.

It has caused – and is causing – mass destitution and increased inequality within and between nations.

It is destroying the livelihood of peasant farmers.

It is depriving the poor of affordable medicines.

It is also lowering real wages and labour standards and increasing economic insecurity everywhere.

It is destroying the environment, eliminating species and harming animal welfare.

It is causing, in these various ways, a global race to the bottom, in which low taxes, low regulatory standards and low wages are imposed in every country.

It is permitting global financial markets to generate crises that impose heavy costs particularly on the less advanced economies.

It enshrines greed as the motive-force of human behaviour.

And it is destroying the variety of human cultures.

By now, an immense literature of complaint, on these lines, has grown up, almost all of it distinguished by disregard for facts and professional economic analysis. The area that is clearly an exception to this is finance, on which a number of top-class professional economists, foremost among them the Nobel-laureate Joseph Stiglitz, have added their criticisms.[11] Another influential critic on finance is the billionaire financier and speculator George Soros, a fascinating example of fox turned guard dog.[12] Another academic opponent of globalization is Dani Rodrik of Harvard University.[13] These are serious critics. But Professors Stiglitz and Rodrik, though important voices, are exceptions to the general view of professional economists. In addition, there is, by now, a mountainous literature of protest designed to make the reader's flesh creep, stretching from the French author Viviane Forrester, at the hysterical end of the debate, to the British historian of ideas John Gray, at the more sober one.[14] Strung out in between are such authors as the British journalists Larry Elliott and Dan Atkinson, the American commentator William Greider, the Cambridge academic Noreena Hertz, the Canadian journalist Naomi Klein, the American expert on defence Edward Luttwak, and the British journalist George Monbiot.[15] Not to be forgotten are the political aspirants, such as Patrick Buchanan.[16]

Arrival of mega-terrorism

Into the comparatively cosy world of those for and against economic globalization arrived, on the eleventh of September 2001, something horrifyingly new. A small group of terrorists brought down the twin towers of the World Trade Center in New York and damaged the Pentagon. A fourth hijacked aeroplane was brought down by its passengers before it hit its target. This was a moment that changes the world. What remains unclear is only how it will do so. That must depend on how the rest of the world, particularly the United States, responds.

We can view this event as an episode in the resistance of the Islamic world to westernization, as witness to the abiding force of human evil, as the end of liberal optimism and as an assault on liberal globalization. All are valid, not excluding the last. The attack on the US was also an assault on globalization. It was carried out by men suffused with hatred of the liberal west's impact on their sacred territories and values. It was, as such, an extreme reaction to 'cultural globalization'.[17] It was also likely to encourage internationally integrated states to close their borders to the free movement of goods and people. Observers, some sympathetic to international economic integration and some critical, leaped to precisely this conclusion.

Among those sympathetic to globalization, Stephen Roach, the chief economist of Morgan Stanley, noted in the *Financial Times* immediately after the attack that movement of people and goods, though not of information, would become somewhat more difficult.[18] This can indeed be thought of as a tax on commerce, but it need not be a prohibitive one. Similarly, there would be pressure to increase spending on defence. In theory, this could crowd out private investment. But the threat of low-technology terrorism is not similar to that posed by the old Soviet Union. It is not through vast armies, navies and air forces that it can be contained but through superior intelligence and better security. This need not cost a fortune.

Among those hostile to globalization, John Gray, a professor at the London School of Economics, argued that its end was not only inevitable but desirable.[19] Globalization, he argued, is a deluded secular creed, similar to Marxism. 'For market liberals', he declared, 'there is only one way to become modern. All societies must adopt free markets.' This comparison of a belief in liberty and democracy with Marxism – the ideology of totalitarian despots that, on some calculations, cost 100 million lives – is grotesque. More importantly, Professor Gray indulges in caricature. Globalization is no fanatical ideology, but a name for the process of integration, across frontiers, of liberalizing market economies at a time of rapidly falling costs of transport and communications.

A collapse in international economic integration is unnecessary. It is certainly undesirable. But both Roach and Gray were right on one point: the outrage was planned and executed by people who are profoundly hostile to global integration.[20] Osama Bin Laden's terrorists are passionate anti-liberals. Theirs is the latest of the totalitarian and authoritarian ideologies to have opposed liberalism over the past two centuries. Because of where they come from, these ideologues dress their objectives in the garb of religion, not of class or nation. But their objective is power, just as was true of Mussolini and Hitler, Lenin and Stalin, Mao Zedong and Pol Pot. To obtain power, they wish first to define the world by their enemies. Come, they say to the Muslim masses, march under our banner against our hated foe. America is our enemy. To their credit, these fanatics have identified a genuine power as their chief enemy, not, as Hitler once did, the Jews. Yet the differences are not so great. Where Hitler promised a Third Reich, they offer a restored caliphate. These fanatics are weaker, for the moment, but would not remain so if they seized control of a state in possession of nuclear weapons, such as Pakistan.

The eleventh of September was an attack on modernity by people who believe the world should be forced back to the seventh century. These are dangerous enemies of civilized modernity. They help define who we are and what we believe in. The same is not true of anti-globalization protesters. They fall rather in the category of spoiled children. But they are 'our' children. If we fail to persuade the idealistic young of the merits of a liberal global economic order, it may founder before the certainties of its enemies. A house divided cannot stand.

Argument of the book

There are, by now, a number of excellent books that answer the specific criticisms of international economic integration by anti-globalizers.[21] This book sets these replies in a wider context. It attempts to show that the anti-liberal views of the critics put them on the wrong side of a great debate. When the ideologically impassioned left last took full command, it produced the monstrosities of Soviet and Maoist communism. If anything, its grasp on reality has worsened since then. The mood was captured in a banner seen at an anti-capitalist protest in London: 'replace capitalism with something nicer', it said. It is easy to indulge in such fantasies. But fantasies are not the route to a tolerable future.

The reason for rejecting most, though not all, of the charges of the critics is not that the world is perfect, but that it would be worse if they had their way. They would throw away half a century of progress in reconstructing a liberal international economic order.

The book starts, in the next chapter, with the definition of economic globalization. It proceeds, in the second main part, with arguments for a liberal market economy in terms of its long-run contributions to prosperity, democracy and personal freedom. It looks at the mutually reinforcing and interdependent relationship between the market and the democratic state. Finally, it examines what happens when markets cross frontiers.

In the third part, the book looks at the long history of globalization. It argues that while globalization has proceeded further than ever before in some respects, in others it is much more limited than before, even though the technological basis for integration has advanced substantially. The biggest failure by far is in the transfer of capital and ideas to the developing world. These opportunities need to be seized.

Then, in the fourth part, the book looks in detail at the arguments of the critics. Most of their arguments turn out to be wrong. They are wrong about global impoverishment, corporate domination, the threat to the sovereignty of the democratic state and the so-called race to the bottom in environmental and social regulation. But they are not wrong on all points. Critics are right about the hypocrisy of the developed world on liberalization. Alas, many in the movement are trying to make this hypocrisy even worse. Critics are right, too, that the institutions set up to manage the global economy do not work as well as they might, particularly in finance.

Finally, in the fifth part, the book looks at how serious the threats to globalization now are. On this, it takes a guardedly optimistic position. But it also focuses on the chief obstacle to making the world work better. This is not its limited economic integration, as critics of economic globalization argue, but its political fragmentation. It is the deep-seated differences in the institutional quality of states that determine the persistence of inequality among individuals, across the globe. The big challenge, it concludes, is to reconcile a world divided into states of hugely unequal capacities with exploitation of the opportunities for convergence offered by international economic integration. In short, if we want a better world, we need not a different economics, but better politics.

Edouard Balladur was wrong. The market is not a jungle, but among the most sophisticated products of civilization. It requires for its successful working a complex mixture of constraints, both internal and external to the market itself.[22] The most dangerous jungle is politics. It is there, above all, that we must focus our efforts.

Chapter 2 What Liberal Globalization Means

A 'neo' is someone who pretends to be something, someone who is at the same time inside and outside of something; it is an elusive hybrid, a straw man set up without ever identifying a specific value, idea, regime or doctrine. To say 'neoliberal' is the same as saying 'semiliberal' or 'pseudoliberal'. It is pure nonsense. Either one is in favor of liberty or against it, but one cannot be semi-in-favour or pseudo-in-favour of liberty, just as one cannot be 'semipregnant', 'semiliving', or 'semidead'.

Mario Vargas Llosa[1]

Globalization is a hideous word of obscure meaning, coined in the 1960s, that came into ever-greater vogue in the 1990s.[2] For many of its proponents it is an irresistible and desirable force sweeping away frontiers, overturning despotic governments, undermining taxation, liberating individuals and enriching all it touches. For many of its opponents it is a no less irresistible force, but undesirable. With the prefixes 'neo-liberal' or 'corporate', global-ization is condemned as a malign force that impoverishes the masses, destroys cultures, undermines democracy, imposes Americanization, lays waste the welfare state, ruins the environment and enthrones greed. Many of these beliefs are wrong. Globalization is, on balance, resistible. But globalization is also, on balance, highly desirable. Precisely how desirable depends on the choices that are made.

Before trying to elucidate these propositions, one must start by defining what we mean by globalization. This is no trivial task. For, as Paul Hirst of Birkbeck College and Grahame Thompson of the Open University note, 'globalization has become the new grand narrative of the social sciences. We say this less out of any commitment to the sensibilities of postmodernism – we have none – than because we feel the concept offers more than it can deliver.'[3]

The works of third-way theorists, such as Anthony Giddens, adviser to Tony Blair, the British prime minister, fall into this trap. For Professor Giddens, globalization is an irresistible force, transforming all aspects of contemporary society, politics and the economy.[4] Globalization, thus defined, becomes unmanageably broad. It becomes, as Professors Hirst and Thompson remark, a catchphrase for 'often very different cultural, economic and social processes'.[5]

We can avoid these murky waters, for this book has a narrower focus, in economics. This is not only because the economics of globalization are important in themselves, but because they are the driving force for almost everything else.

Defining liberal globalization

What then might be meant by economic globalization? The simplest of all definitions comes from Anne Krueger, the first deputy managing director of the International Monetary Fund. In the John Bonython lecture, delivered in Australia in 2000, she defined globalization as: 'a phenomenon by which economic agents in any given part of the world are much more affected by events elsewhere in the world' than before.[6] There is, however, another more technically precise version of this process: the integration of economic activities, across borders, through markets. Thus, David Henderson, former chief economist of the Organization for Economic Co-operation and Development, defines globalization as: free movement of goods, services, labour and capital, thereby creating a single market in inputs and outputs; and full national treatment for foreign investors (and nationals working abroad) so that, economically speaking, there are no foreigners.[7]

A related definition is offered by Brink Lindsey of Washington's Cato Institute, in his book *Against the Dead Hand*. There, Lindsey defines the word:

> in three distinct but interrelated senses: first, to describe the economic phenomenon of increasing integration of markets across political boundaries (whether due to political or technological causes); second, to describe the strictly political phenomenon of falling government-imposed barriers to international flows of goods, services, and capital; and, finally, to describe the much broader political phenomenon of the global spread of market-oriented policies in both the domestic and international spheres. Since I contend that globalization in the first sense is due primarily to globalization in the second sense, and that globalization in the second sense is primarily

due to globalization in the third sense, I do not think it unduly confusing to use the same word to mean three different things.[8]

This is a useful definition of the kind of globalization – let us call it 'liberal globalization' – the protesters condemn. It clarifies its elements in a relatively precise manner. And it does so by showing that what we are talking about is *movement in the direction of greater integration,* as both natural and man-made barriers to international economic exchange continue to fall. A necessary consequence of such a process of integration is the increased impact of economic changes in one part of the world on what happens in the others.

The process of economic integration discussed here could have two conceivable end points. In one, technology remains roughly as it is today, but there are no policy barriers whatsoever to the movement of goods, services, information, capital or people. For reasons of history, the world would still contain distinct cultures and languages, and different legal systems. These would add to the barriers that distance and difficulties of communication continued to impose. Companies would still tend to be national or multi-national, not global. The political preconditions for such a global economy could be either the unilateral abolition of barriers by what remained sovereign states, a structure of restricted national sovereignty, similar to that of today's EU members, or a global federation. In other words, a globalized economy, so defined, could be combined with a number of different structures for global governance. This form of integration is conceivable, though it is immensely far from where we are today. We are most unlikely to get there this century, let alone the next decade.

A second and much more radical definition of a global economy would be one in which, in addition to the abolition of politically imposed barriers to economic integration, costs of transport and communications were zero. This form of a global economy is conceivable, but practically impossible. In this world distance would no longer matter. It would be the end of geography. There would no longer be services that are intrinsically non-tradable, such as haircuts, hospital operations and looking after children or old people. The world would be like London or New York today, with almost every conceivable culture effectively cheek by jowl. Economically, the world would be reduced to a point, something that cyberspace has come close to achieving; but only for information.

The value of this more extreme thought-experiment lies in forcing us to appreciate the abiding and enormous importance of costs of transport and communications. While these costs may continue to fall, they will never come close to zero, except for things that can be completely dematerialized – essentially information. If people want to participate fully in Swedish culture, enjoy a wide choice of Swedish schools for their children, have predominantly Swedish neighbours and partake of the full range of benefits offered by the Swedish welfare state, then they have to live in Sweden. Again, most people will continue to work or go to school within a relatively modest radius of where they live. This would remain true even if all policy barriers to movement of goods, services, capital, information and people were eliminated. Indeed, as the share of services in consumption and gross domestic product rises, geography may come to matter more and more, not less and less.

The point is that distance will always matter, because we are physical. Because distance always matters, so does space. Because space always matters, so does territorial control. Because territorial control matters, so do states. For this simple reason, economic processes will not compel the death of states, unless a state is expunged, whether voluntarily (as in a decision to merge with some other state or states) or forcibly (as in conquest). Indeed, the policies and capacities of states remain central to any understanding of how economic globalization works.

Against technological determinism

Some authors write as if technology were decisive for globalization on its own. The most influential author to come close to this line is Thomas Friedman, foreign affairs columnist for the *New York Times*, in his lively and illuminating book *The Lexus and the Olive Tree*.[9] He defines three democratizations – of technology, information and finance. Behind all three is an unquestioned technological revolution, namely, the immense increase in our capacity to communicate and access information, symbolized by the mobile phone and the Internet. Because of the three democratizations, argues Friedman, traditional top-down organizations – companies and governments – are vulnerable to 'Microchip Immune Deficiency Syndrome'. This:

> is the defining political disease of the globalization era. It can strike any company or country, large or small, East or West, North or South. . . . MIDS is usually contracted by countries and companies that fail to inoculate themselves against changes brought about by the microchip, and the democratizations of technology, finance and information. . . . The only

known cure for countries or companies with MIDS is 'the fourth democratization'. This is the democratization of decision-making and information flows, and the deconcentration of power, in ways that allow more people in a country or company to share knowledge, experiment and innovate faster. ... MIDS can be fatal to those companies and countries that do not get appropriate treatment in time.[10]

Technological determinists argue that the only alternatives today are full openness to the world economy or marginalization and poverty. Furthermore, they add, if a country is a little bit open to modern communications, political pressures from a better-informed population will, on their own, force governments to liberalize their economies and democratize their polities. If this were so, liberalization would no longer be an independent policy choice. It would be the necessary consequence of the technological changes of our time. If technology dictated policy, liberalization would be not an option but a destiny.

Technological determinism is not absurd. It is merely exaggerated. The colossal recent falls in the costs of communicating information must have radical effects on economies, by lowering the cost of making transactions and increasing information about available opportunities to transact. The lower the costs of communications, the higher and more ruthlessly enforced policy barriers must be if economies are to remain as closed to flows of information as they used to be. For this reason, technological determinists are right to believe that the innovations of the past one or two decades have made globalization more difficult to prevent.

Yet one must avoid exaggerating what follows. First, it is not the case that complete liberalization must follow the decline in costs of communications. Governments can continue to control movement of physical things if they wish. Indeed, modern technology makes this easier than before. Governments can oversee and regulate the movement of people even more easily; they can impose barriers upon movement of capital, by failing to recognize or enforce contracts with foreigners; and they can limit international flows of services by controlling the convertibility of domestic means of payment into foreign exchange. Whether they will choose to do any of these things is another question.

Second, even if technology did dictate greater liberalization, it would not follow that governments were helpless. This is because even in a liberal world there would remain, as argued above, both costs of transport and communications and cultural obstacles to mobility. The argument that technology dictates liberalization and this, in turn, renders governments helpless before global economic forces is an intellectual swindle used by many left-of-centre governments to confuse what they choose to do with what they are compelled to do. As Clive Crook of *The Economist* has argued in his survey of globalization, 'when governments claim that globalization ties their hands, because politically it makes their lives easier, they are conning voters and undermining support for economic freedom. Whatever else this may be, it is not good governance.'[11]

On wider aspects of globalization

The definitions above concern only the economic aspects of globalization. Yet changes in technology and the economy also have complex cultural, social and political effects. Changes in how people are able to earn their living, in what they can buy, in how readily they can move from place to place, in how easily they can transport things, in how they can disseminate and access information and ideas necessarily transform human societies and the individual human beings who live within them.

Some scholars have attempted to define such non-economic aspects of globalization relatively precisely. The sociologist Peter Berger, of Boston University, has argued, for example, that there are four facets of cultural globalization: business values – or the impact of 'Davos man', named after the location of the annual meeting of the World Economic Forum; intellectual values – or the influence of the 'faculty club'; popular commercial culture; and the spread of religious movements – particularly evangelical Protestantism, now thought to embrace some 250 million people world-wide.[12] He argues that '[G]lobalization is, *au fond*, a continuation, albeit in an intensified and accelerated form, of the perduring challenge of modernization. On the cultural level, this has been the great challenge of pluralism: the breakdown of taken-for-granted traditions and the opening up of multiple options for beliefs, values and lifestyles. It is not a distortion to say that this amounts to the great challenge of enhanced freedom for both individuals and collectivities.'[13]

Changes in technology and economic policy do have such political, social and cultural effects. How could they not do so? Today, a regime that wants its people to be fully engaged in the global economy cannot prevent them from gaining access to the extraordinary range of information, including that about their own country. This may make despotic regimes unsustainable. But, important though they are, these changes are not part of the definition of globalization employed here. They are treated, instead, as consequences or concomitants.

Conclusion

Globalization is defined in what follows as integration of economic activities, via markets. The driving forces are technological and policy changes – falling costs of transport and communications and greater reliance on market forces. The economic globalization discussed here has cultural, social and political consequences (and preconditions). But those consequences and preconditions are neither part of its definition nor a focus of our attention.

Part II   Why a Global Market Economy Makes Sense

Prologue

Most critics of globalization are fervent opponents of a market economy that embraces the world as a whole. Some of them are against any sort of market economy. Others are merely against one that includes foreigners (though they may not admit it). This raises an obvious question. Why does anyone believe such an economy is a good idea? If the critics were right, supporters of the global market economy would be in favour of mass poverty, grotesque inequality, destruction of state-provided welfare, infringement of national sovereignty, subversion of democracy, unbridled corporate power, environmental degradation, human rights abuses and much more. Naturally, they are not. To demonstrate this, such criticisms need to be confronted. But it is necessary first to explain what a market economy is, why it has a close and supportive relationship with democracy, why and how it raises living standards, in what ways it depends on support from the state, how the market moves naturally and beneficially across frontiers and, not least, how such a global market economy brings both great benefits and challenges for global political relations. The purpose of Part II of this book is to provide just such an explanation.

Chapter 3 **Markets, Democracy and Peace**

There has been no country with a democratic political sphere, past or present, whose economy has not been dominated by private ownership and market co-ordination.
János Kornai[1]

The force of the protests against globalization derives from a now age-old hostility to the liberal market economy. But what are the underlying features of a liberal economy? What does such an economy imply for democracy and for international relations?

Freedom and property

The fundamental value that underpins a free society is the worth of the active, self-directing individual. It is a belief in individual freedom. This is not a belief that the individual is somehow outside or above society. The individual, being human, is always embedded within society. Human beings are cultural animals. But the particular characteristic of the free society is that the forms of social engagement are as much chosen as imposed, at least for adults. The central feature of such a society is voluntary action – the freedom to choose.

It has long been argued that such a society requires a distinct culture – one that puts intrinsic value on all individuals, equally, and moulds them to accept personal responsibility for their actions and fate. The German sociologist Weber famously argued that Protestantism was a powerful contributory cause to the success of the countries of north-west Europe in making a free society and economy work. This no longer seems quite so plausible now that Catholic Europe and east Asian countries have also been successful in promoting a modern economy.[2] Nevertheless, it is easy to accept that some cultures are more readily adapted to making a success of a free economy and society than others.[3] Unfortunately, culture changes slowly.

The bedrock of a liberal society is, as John Locke argued in the seventeenth century, the right of all individuals to own and use property freely, subject to well-defined, law-governed constraints.[4] A liberal society is therefore a commercial society. But freedom to seek one's own way in life, outside the boundaries of caste, class, community or, more recently, of gender, cannot be restricted to economic activities alone. The culture of a liberal society is, for this reason, inimical to established hierarchies of power or opinion.[5] It is no accident that commercial societies came to consider freedom of thought and expression of great value. A merchant is a practical man who must make rational judgements about the world, not least of the risks he runs.[6] He learns from experience, not from authority, and relies on his own judgement, not those of others. The combination of practicality, rationalism and freedom of inquiry became the basis for the west's greatest achievement – modern science. It is, again, no accident that science reached its greatest flowering in a commercial west.

A liberal society is endemically restless and, for those who treasure the unchanging and the traditional, consequently insecure, however wealthy it may become. It does not merely accommodate novelty, but welcomes it. The merchant makes profits by seizing an unperceived opportunity for gain, thereby changing the economic world. The intellectual makes a reputation by arguing something new, thereby changing the beliefs of the world. Traditional hierarchies, deference, ways of life and beliefs are all subject to the solvent action of liberty. Liberalism means perpetual and unsettling change. Most of its enemies have, at bottom, hated it for that reason.

If individuals are to be free, they need protection both by – and from – the state. The importance of the combination of a strong and beneficent government cannot be exaggerated. In his last book, published posthumously, Mancur Olson argued that 'we know that an economy will generate its maximum income only if there is a high rate of investment and that much of the return on long-term investments is received long after the investments are made'.[7] Perhaps the most important single difference then between the societies that became rich and those that did not was the ability of people in the former to make long-term contractual arrangements. They need a high level of trust in one another and, still more important, in the political author-ities.[8] People will make such investments only if they are reasonably sure that the fruits will not be seized. All modestly complex societies have a wide range of markets for immediate transactions. The bazaar is a developed feature of Middle Eastern societies, for example. But the bazaar does not make countries rich. Only rather special societies have markets with a rich web of long-term, prosperity-enhancing contracts. These are the defining feature of what Karl Marx called 'capitalism' – a society in which people can make and own long-term investments with reasonable safety through a web of abstract paper claims.

The condition for such confidence is normally expressed as freedom under the law or, more simply, as the rule of law. Anarchy and liberty do not border one another, but are polar opposites. Under anarchy every man's liberty is bounded by the predatory activity of everybody else – the world where life is 'nasty, brutish and short', as described by Thomas Hobbes in his classic book *Leviathan*. Under liberty, the state protects everybody from predators, not excluding itself. But this seems to be a contradiction. If the state succeeds in establishing a monopoly of force over a given territory, why should it accept a rule of law that curbs itself? This is a question that the Chinese party-state asks itself today. So far, it can see little reason why it should, which may prove a decisive hindrance to China's long-term development. Why then would any state be simultaneously potent enough to protect its citizens from one another and restrained enough to protect them from itself? This is Gulliver bound by Lilliputians. It looks to be a miracle – and historically it has been a rare event.

Towards a beneficent state

In a famous fresco in the town hall of the Italian city of Siena, the medieval artist Ambrogio Lorenzetti painted allegories of good and bad government. The Italians of his era had experienced both, as do the peoples of the world today. In the Allegory of Good Government, a figure of the Common Good presides, with Wisdom, Peace, Justice, Faith, Charity, Magnanimity and Concord. Where then were these virtues to come from? Historically, a strong and beneficent state has emerged from a combination of three forces – regulatory competition, internal representation and moral reform.

Regulatory competition

One of the reasons why Europe outstripped China, India and the Islamic world, all of which were considerably more advanced a thousand years ago, was competition among rulers or, as it would now be called, 'regulatory competition'. In his classic analysis of western technological advance, *The Lever of Riches*, Joel Mokyr of Northwestern University argues that,

> from its modest beginnings in the monasteries and rain-soaked fields and forests of western Europe, Western technological creativity rested on two foundations: a materialistic pragmatism based on the belief that the manipulation of nature in the service of economic welfare was acceptable, indeed, commendable behaviour, and the continuous competition between political units for political and economic hegemony.[9]

Similarly, in a lecture delivered in 2001, Charles Calomiris of Columbia University summarized this view as follows:

> political fragmentation in medieval Europe decentralized authority and spurred continuing competition among rulers. European civilization was unique in this respect – a fact that reflected climactic and geographic factors peculiar to Europe. That political fragmentation and competition, combined with the cultural inheritance of Roman, Christian and Germanic traditions, fostered the concepts of private property and individual rights.[10]

Regulatory competition is an important (and controversial) force today, not least because it is one of the complaints of critics of globalization that the beneficent plans of governments are being undermined by such competition, via capital flight or emigration of labour. The most telling answer to this worry is that governments are not necessarily wise and beneficent. In medieval and early modern Europe, competition among rulers kept freedom alive. In China, in contrast, there was no such competition: the state was a monopolist and behaved as one.[11] But when the French king decided to drive out the Protestants in the late seventeenth century, the English were happy to accept these hard-working people, to the benefit of their country. Similarly, when the Church suppressed Galileo, his ideas promptly took root elsewhere. Earlier, princes gave charters to cities to encourage commerce, aware that the communities of merchants might otherwise move to the realm of some rival. These merchants were particularly useful to monarchs, because they paid taxes in money. With this money, kings could afford armies of their own, freeing themselves from dependence on their unreliable feudal vassals.

As the Nobel-laureate Douglass North notes:

> there was continuous interplay between the fiscal needs of the state and its credibility in its relationships with merchants and the citizenry in general. In particular, the evolution of capital markets was critically influenced by the

policies of the state because, to the extent that the state was bound by commitments that it would not confiscate assets or in any way use its coercive power to increase uncertainty in exchange, it made possible the evolution of financial institutions and the creation of more efficient capital markets.[12]

Regulatory competition continues to be a powerful force today. Indeed, it is one of the chief reasons for the spread of economic liberalization in the 1980s and 1990s. Deng Xiaoping was influenced by the economic successes of Hong Kong, Singapore, South Korea and Taiwan in his decision to introduce market reforms into China. Similarly, the success of Chile in the 1980s and 1990s influenced reformers throughout Latin America. Back in the 1970s, when I worked at the World Bank, we were influenced by the successes of the more market-oriented and outward-looking economies of east Asia.

Constitutional democracy and the rule of law

Regulatory competition is not enough. An absolute monarch may still seize the wealth of his subjects or default on his debts when his dynasty is threatened. Secure freedom requires governments interested in the long-term health of their countries. The best solution is a constitutional democracy with representative parliaments – government accountable to the governed. Such a democracy must be constitutional, that is, law-governed. It is not enough to move from the tyranny of one person to tyranny of the majority. A constitutional democracy entrenches individual freedoms and the rules of the democratic process. As Olson points out, a big step was taken in the seventeenth century when two revolutions created a special form of government in the United Kingdom, one in which, for the first time, the state's creditors, through parliament, controlled government. They were interested in their debtor's credit-worthiness and, by creating a sound structure for the national debt, both strengthened the state and established sound financial markets.[13]

This emergence of parliamentary government built upon earlier progress in both parliamentary representation and the rule of law. From the seventeenth century English settlement emerged the idea of the division of powers subsequently embodied in the American constitution. This was transmitted from England to the nascent United States by a Frenchman – Charles Montesquieu – in his classic, *L'Esprit des Lois*, published in 1748. As an intriguing recent paper observes:

both the English and the American conception of freedom are based on a common notion that the will of the sovereign – even a democratically elected sovereign – must be restrained. Both reject the idea – articulated most clearly by Rousseau – that the democratically elected sovereign can, on behalf of the people, legitimately act without constraints. Both the English and the American conceptions of freedom deal with the limits on government, but refer to different limits.[14]

The English version of freedom started from the independence of the judiciary in applying the law. The common law itself was ancient, while trial by jury went back to the twelfth century. From this foundation and the seventeenth-century parliamentary revolution, the Americans built the idea of checks and balances. It grants the courts the right to review the constitutionality of legislation. As one would expect, analysis of today's world shows that the independence of the judiciary on the English model contributes to both the economic and political freedom of a country, while American institutions, on their own, contribute mainly to political freedom.[15]

Usually, though not always, a democratic electorate has (if they understand this) an interest in choosing institutions and policies that make society as a whole richer rather than in seizing wealth from a minority. Where pre-tax inequalities in incomes and wealth are large, however, this may cease to be true. If a large majority earns much less than the average income, it may be easy to obtain a majority in a universal (or wide) suffrage democracy in favour of seizing the wealth or incomes of the rich minority. Democracy then becomes populist, as it has long been in much of Latin America. The outcome over time has been lower average post-tax incomes than would have been the case if less predatory policies had been chosen.[16] This is an important reason why the stability of a democracy requires some limits on the extent of inequality. This is likely to be particularly important when, as the American academic Amy Chua observes, the wealthy are members of an easily identifiable ethnic minority. Under such circumstances, she argues, democracy may prove inconsistent with sustained economic liberalism.[17]

As Olson notes, 'the establishment of a democracy and the conduct of an election do not necessarily bring secure contract or property rights'.[18] Internal faction-fighting or external enemies may destroy the democracy. Historically, this has happened to many republics, the outcome being oligarchy or despotism or, more often, a move from the former to the latter, as in the Medicis' Florence and in Rome in the first century before the common era. But if there is a lasting democracy, there must be a rule of law, by definition, because the government must both accept free speech and political competition and abide by the results of elections. Thus 'the only societies where individual rights to property and contract are confidently expected to last across generations are the securely democratic societies'.[19]

Private property is also a necessary condition for political pluralism. A political entity (be it an individual, family or party) that controls all a country's resources, through the state, is unlikely to allow any opposition access to the means of campaigning against it. Worse, if all economic decisions are political, loss of power threatens a loss of livelihood. Power becomes the only route to wealth. This is not just lethal for the economy. It is also lethal for democratic politics, which become a form of civil war. It is only when politics are not a matter of personal survival that a stable democracy is conceivable. For democracy to function, therefore, the domain of the political has to be circumscribed. The market economy, based on private property, achieves this.

It is possible for countries to offer economic but not political freedoms – to have market economies, but not democracy or civil and human rights. But the correlation between these freedoms is strong.[20] If the individual's autonomy is respected in one sphere, it will normally be respected in another. In the long run, market economies tend to become democratic, as recent experience in east Asia has made plain.[21] Moreover, even if all market economies are not democracies, stable democracies have market economies, as Professor Kornai says.[22] Social democrats too often ignore this intimate link between economic liberalism and political democracy, between the values of the merchant and those of the citizen. The market underpins democracy, just as democracy should normally strengthen the market.

The market supports democracy in another way – via growth. A modern market economy has, as the discussion in the following chapter shows, been the only system to have generated large and sustained rises in real incomes per head over lengthy periods. These rises have made the shift to a democratic system from what were, traditionally, more repressive regimes immeasurably easier. This shift followed only once the market economy had generated what has long been called the 'industrial revolution'. When the economy's output per head is rising, a society's life is 'positive-sum' – everybody can become better off. In a static society, however, social life is 'zero-sum': if anyone is to receive more, someone else must receive less. The politics of zero-sum societies are fraught in a way those of positive-sum societies are not. The difference is large. Over a generation a society in which income per head rises at, say, 1.5 per cent a year, has over 50 per cent more income per head to spread around, if it wishes to do so. A safe bet is that if environmentalists imposed a zero-growth society, it would swiftly become authoritarian (even if it had not become so to impose the zero growth). Authority would presumably be exercised by priest-kings, worshippers of Mother Nature in her guise as Queen of Ecology.

It was no accident therefore that it was only in the early twentieth century that franchises became universal in the modern advanced economies. Economic freedom and a degree of political representation predate mass democracy. But there are strong pressures upon successful market economies to move towards universal suffrage and, with rising incomes and wider education, limited obstacles to it as well. The emergence of an educated, middle-class society interested in politics and desiring influence over political life is also decisive. So is increased acceptance of broadly liberal ideas, itself made easier by a growing economy. If one accepts the equality of citizens before the law, it is difficult to deny equality of citizens in making the law as well.

Moral reform

The third element in moving from a predatory state to a liberal 'service state' and a successful market economy can best be described as moral. Values matter. The rule of law is dependent on honest judges and policemen and soldiers who obey civilian leaders, however much they may despise them. There can be no Praetorian Guard in a stable liberal democracy. Today, any list of the states in which the army is most completely subject to civilian control is headed by the advanced liberal democracies. But how does an unarmed population achieve service from those with power over it? A part of the answer is that it pays them reasonably well, because it is prosperous enough to do so. A second part of the answer is that it provides a government made legitimate by popular consent. But the third part is moral. As the Canadian journalist and writer Jane Jacobs has noted, the symbiosis between state and market that is the basis of civilized society is matched by a symbiosis between two cultures or moral syndromes – commercial culture and guardian culture. Both are necessary. Together, they are sufficient.[23]

The essence of the commercial syndrome is voluntary agreement, honesty in dealings, openness to strangers, respect for contracts, innovation, enter-prize, efficiency, promotion of comfort and convenience, acceptance of dissent, investment for productive purposes, industry, thrift and optimism. This is the attitude of the merchant through the ages. Guardians, on the other hand, shun trading, control territory, show obedience, bravery and discipline, follow precedent, respect tradition, are loyal, admire leisure and treasure honour. This is the ethos of the warrior. Today, guardians are servants of the state. Merchants are servants of the market. Because both are necessary and each is suspicious of the other, there is a permanent tension. But the symbiosis has proved fruitful. At its heart is the distinction in behaviour between business people who know they are entitled to sell their wares to the highest bidder, but not to use force, and judges and soldiers who know that they are not allowed to sell their wares to the highest bidder, but are entitled to use force. These patterns of behaviour are complex and tacit. That is just one of the reasons why it has been so difficult to spread the way of life of advanced liberal democracies.

The achievement

The relation between the state and the market, democracy and individual freedom, the sphere of the merchant and that of the guardian is complex and difficult and has been subject to constant renegotiation. One reason has been changing views on the role of governments. The fundamental role of the governments of free societies is to protect the liberties of the citizens. But they are also, increasingly, required to provide other public goods: health, education, infrastructure and environmental regulation. Democratic politics have also, inevitably, led to a huge expansion of the redistributive functions of the state. The revenues of the governments of members of the Organization for Economic Co-operation and Development have, on average, increased from about 10 per cent of gross domestic product a century ago to an average of just under 40 per cent today. In some European countries, the share is over 50 per cent.

The collapse of state socialism between 1989 and 1991 has shown that liberal democracy is the only political and economic system capable of generating sustained prosperity and political stability. This is the sense in which the American analyst Francis Fukuyama was right to argue that this is the end of history.[24] As Leo Tolstoy might have said, all rich countries are rich in much the same way, but all poor countries are poor in their own different ways. This does not mean that all advanced democracies are identical. On the contrary, there is much legitimate discussion of the differences among them, some of which will be considered further below.[25] But these difference – even those between the United States and Sweden – pale into insignificance next to the diversity shown by the full range of human societies, past and present.

Consider the characteristics of the advanced liberal democracies. They are constitutional democracies, subject to the rule of law; they respect private property and the ability to make contracts; they protect freedom of speech and inquiry; they recognize fundamental human rights; they have elected governments; and they have independent and honest judiciaries, rational bureaucracies and armies subject to civilian control.[26] These are remarkably rare features of human societies, both in history and today.[27]

International relations of liberal democracy

Liberal democracy does not only have domestic virtues. It is also the only system of governance for which harmonious and co-operative inter-state relations are a natural outcome. This important proposition was put forward by the German philosopher Immanuel Kant in his tract *Perpetual Peace*. Liberal democracies may fight with other states, but have no reason to fight with one another. When Norman Angell, the British liberal, wrote in his subsequently derided masterpiece, the *Grand Illusion*, published in 1909, that a war among the great powers could only prove mutually ruinous, he was correct. That the war happened and was the disaster he foresaw merely show that stupidity is infinite, particularly among naive collectivists and self-proclaimed realists.

Liberal democracy is conducive to harmonious international relations because the prosperity of a nation derives not from the size of the territory or population under its direct control, but from the combination of internal economic development with international exchange. This insight is the heart of Adam Smith's *Wealth of Nations*. It was not just a point about economics, but an equally original and important point about international relations. Mercantilism – the view that the aim of trade is the accumulation of treasure – was worse than bad economics. It was also lethal politics, because it led to conflict where conflict was unjustified. The rapid growth generated by industrialization should have helped instil Smith's lesson quickly. Unfortunately, it took almost two centuries:

> Wealth based on land is a zero-sum game, so violent conflicts over turf were inevitable. Wealth based on industry, by contrast, is a positive-sum game – despite the fact that mercantilist and Marxist notions about competition for markets obfuscated this message for almost a century. It took two world wars to teach the lesson, but the notion that more territory equals more power has been firmly relegated to intellectual history, at least in the advanced industrialized nations.[28]

A country with secure property rights, scientific inquiry and technological innovation will become richer. But, since division of labour is limited by the size of the market, it will also benefit from trade, not just in goods and services, but in ideas, capital and people. The smaller a country is, the greater the benefits. Trade is far cheaper than empire, just as internal development is a less costly route to prosperity than plunder. This was the heart of Angell's argument. Germans would become no richer, individually, if they controlled Alsace. In similar vein, when promoting free trade in Britain in the first half of the nineteenth century, Richard Cobden, father of the Anti-Corn Law League, argued that unilateral free trade would promote prosperity and peaceful relations with other countries.

Peaceful international commerce and the market economy can generate a standard of living far above that of huge, economically closed and ill-governed countries. In 2000, for example, Hong Kong, with a population of 7 million and no natural resources to speak of, had a GDP per head, at purchasing power parity (PPP), of $25,600, Singapore, with 4 million people, had one of $24,900 and Denmark, with 5 million, had one of $27,300. Against this, China's 1.26 billion had an average GDP per head of $3,900, India's 1 trillion one of $2,300, Indonesia's 207 million one of $2,800, Brazil's 168 million one of $7,300, and Russia's 146 million, sitting on a sixth of the world's land surface, one of $8,000.[29] Power does not beget wealth. That was a great collectivist delusion of the late nineteenth and first half of the twentieth centuries. But, in order to achieve high standards of living, small countries do need a great deal of trade. Hong Kong's gross trade (exports plus imports of goods) was 259 per cent of GDP at PPP in 2000; Singapore's was 294 per cent and Denmark's was 69 per cent. China's, in contrast, was 9 per cent, while India's was only 4 per cent.

Yet the interests of the country in peaceful development and international commerce are not necessarily those of all its inhabitants. A monarch or military class may benefit from plunder, at the expense not just of the plundered, but of its own society. This is far truer in pre-industrial societies. The king or tyrant of 50 million people can build bigger palaces than the king of 5 million and strut more magnificently on the world stage. But a Russian serf was no better off for the grandeur of his Tsar. Similarly, a military class can obtain big estates at the expense of its defeated rivals. But the costs of war fall on ordinary people. Russians were conscripted for 25 years. If such hapless people have no voice in public affairs, the state may be happy to go to war. But if those who will lose the most from fighting are in political control, they are likely to be unwilling to fight and particularly unwilling to suffer vast casualties for mere national aggrandizement. For this reason Kant predicted that war would cease once all countries had become republics or, as we would now say, democracies. Today, this idea, known as the 'democratic peace', has received a great deal of scholarly support. Stable liberal democracies that trade freely with one another are indeed pacific, at least with one another.[30]

When Thomas Friedman put forward his Golden Arches theory of international peace, that no two countries with a McDonald's restaurant had ever gone to war, he was advancing this thesis – that liberal democracies did not fight each other – in particularly graphic terms. Subsequently, Nato bombed Serbia. But, as he points out in the latest edition of his book, *The Lexus and the Olive Tree*, he was proved right by the outcome. The Serbs had to decide whether they want 'to be part of Europe and the broad economic trends and opportunities in the world today' or whether they 'want to keep Kosovo and become an isolated, backward tribal enclave'.[31] The Serbs chose the former. They disposed of Milosevic to do so.

The basis for peaceful relations derives not only from the objectives and internal political structure of a liberal democracy, but from its nature. A law-governed state is the only sort of state that can be securely bound by international treaties, because those affected can appeal to the courts against their government. A tyrant will repudiate an international obligation whenever that seems convenient. A law-governed state will find this far harder to do. Today, as one group of scholars writes, 'there is no longer a strict separation between domestic and international legal rules'.[32] The chief reason for this is that the agreements made by governments have become part of their domestic laws and, as such, are binding upon them. Many of these express conventions on how the state may treat its citizens. As such, they are an expression of the basic principle of liberal democracy – that the state exists to serve its citizens and is duty bound to protect them from harm, *including from itself.* The extent of the resultant treaty activity is extraordinary. Between 1946 and 1975 alone, the number of international treaties in force between governments more than doubled, from 6,351 to 14,061, while the number of such treaties embracing inter-governmental organizations expanded from 623 to 2,303.[33] Between 1909 and 1996 the number of inter-governmental organizations expanded from 37 to 260.

The second reason for peaceful relations of liberal democracies is the associations formed across borders among private citizens and organizations of private citizens. As the great French liberal of the early nineteenth century Alexis de Tocqueville observed, one of the most remarkable features of

American democracy was then – and still is – the number of associations. These have now spread world-wide. In 1909, there were 176 international non-governmental organizations. In 1996, this number had risen to 5,472.[34] The growth of the anti-globalization movement is itself a testimony to the capacity for forming associations of citizens of liberal democracies. So is the creation and spread of the corporation and the private partnership in such activities as law, accounting, consultancy and investment banking.

Collectivist challenges to a liberal order

Liberalism is therefore far more than a purely economic creed. It is the bedrock of democracy at home and peaceful relations abroad. But liberalism is also fragile, as was proved towards the end of the nineteenth century and in the course of much of the twentieth. It is vulnerable to collectivist ideas – nationalism, socialism, communism, fascism and, last and worst, the creed that brought all horrors together in one disgusting package – national socialism. The connection between nationalism, mass violence and an intense sense of the people as a collective emerged with the French revolution. But it reached its full fruition more than a century later.

In his classic *Nations and Nationalism*, the philosopher Ernest Gellner argued that nationalism emerged for a practical reason.[35] The modern state needs a shared high culture, because it requires skilled, interchangeable people. That culture will normally (though not always) be rooted in a single language. Languages create a sense of nationhood in the people that speak them and that sense of nationhood, in turn, creates the demand for a state of their own.

Nationalism supports the modern state and economy: it increases the authority of the state; it enhances the state's ability to mobilize resources; and it increases the ability of the state to break down divisions that impede mobility and economic efficiency. The primary loyalty to the nation makes a nation state an extraordinarily potent form of social organization.

That nationalism exists because it is useful does not make the feelings it evokes less genuine. Human beings are gregarious, capable of extraordinary devotion to the social unit that claims their loyalty. Nationalism taps into these instincts. It offers us the idea of an extended family – a nation. At its limits, it promises the dissolution of the pangs of individuality in the broth of collective harmony. It is obvious therefore that nationalism is both useful and dangerous. It can be exploited by groups in society with a pre-liberal or anti-liberal ideology of plunder and force to turn liberal democratic societies towards war.

In practice, this happened among the European great powers – particularly in Germany – in the late nineteenth century. But extreme militaristic nationalism and later still its bastard child, fascism, did not emerge in the most advanced and stable liberal and democratic states, such as the United Kingdom, but in those in which pre- and anti-liberal ideas and interests were most powerful, partly because the shift to liberal ideas was recent and superficial. Germany had, after all, been united by the Prussian military caste under the direction of Otto von Bismarck. Thus the Marxist-Leninist argument that imperialism, militarism and fascism are a natural consequence of liberal democracy or of capitalism and bourgeois democracy is one of many big lies.[36]

Nineteenth-century nationalism coincided with a resurgence, in the last three decades of that century, of pre-modern imperialistic and protectionist ideas. The aim of countries became to create a protected sphere of their own. From the point of view of promoting prosperity, these shifts were an error. This is particularly true of the late nineteenth-century scramble for new empires in Africa. But, worse than that, the emergence of protectionism and imperialism changes the calculus of international relations: suddenly, being small and weak begins to look rather a bad choice, because one might be locked out of opportunities for peaceful exchange and prosperity. In a protectionist world, countries will try to become part of trading blocs or create empires. Imperialism and protectionism are, for this reason, self-fulfilling prophecies – they create the dog-eat-dog world their proponents believe justifies them. It is for this reason that, in recreating the liberal world order, the Americans, led by Franklin Delano Roosevelt's long-serving secretary of state Cordell Hull, placed great weight on the principle of non-discrimination, alongside that of liberalization. This was an attempt to leave behind the world of hostile trading blocs. It is an understanding that the United States now seems to have almost lost.

Just as the dog-eat-dog world of nineteenth-century nationalism went naturally with resurgent imperialism and protectionism, so did it blend smoothly with socialism, notwithstanding the supranational values of the latter. International socialism was a slender reed. Nationalists argued that citizens shared a common blood and destiny. Socialists claimed that all property should be owned and managed in common. These two visions came together where they were forced, willy-nilly, to do so – in the state, the locus of power. The socialist state made the state a pseudo business enterprise. What was more natural then than for that enterprise to be thought of as the nation's family business? In multi-ethnic socialist states, the authorities tried to create pseudo nationalities – or even more pseudo nationalities than usually created by nationalists: the Soviet Union and Yugoslavia were the important examples.

These two western ideologies, nationalism and socialism, swept across the developing world in the post-Second World War era, for much the same reason that they had swept across Europe in the nineteenth century. Socialism, in particular, had the advantage that it was an intellectually fashionable creed in the west but was not practised by it to its fullest extent. Thus it was possible for leaders of developing countries to be both modern and anti-western at the same time. But socialism did not work, while nationalism became an excuse for grubby tyranny. Saddam Hussein was an Arab Hitler. These are dead ends. By the 1980s, this had become obvious to all. An era of renewed liberalism was at hand.

Challenge ahead

Since the Second World War, the advanced economies have all become liberal democracies. Today's globalization is ultimately a consequence of that choice. Their governance has not been the same as nineteenth-century *laissez-faire*. States are far more interventionist. But acceptance of the basic logic and values of liberal democracy – elections, property rights, liberal trade and, increasingly, liberal movement of capital – has been common to all the advanced market economies. They have differed, however, on the role of the state in income redistribution, regulation of private transactions and provision of certain public services. All such differences within countries are negotiable, just as differences among them are manageable. Sweden, France, the US and Japan are all liberal democracies. As I will show, there is no overwhelming force inherent in globalization that will oblige them all to become identical. There is still room for difference, and such room must be protected.

The issue of today is whether liberal democracy can be as securely established in much of the developing world. It is going to take time. The democracies being established are, inevitably, highly imperfect. They often fail to respect the rights of minorities or the rule of law. Impoverished majorities are particularly threatening to the stability of liberal democracies. But movement has broadly been in a better direction. Yet one would never imagine this from the criticisms of the protesters against globalization. One might even suppose that the move to economic liberalization and democratization since the early 1980s has been a political and economic catastrophe. The opposite is the case. Not only has there been great economic advance among developing countries that have successfully integrated in the world economy, but a huge spread of democracy – a form of governance that was unheard of three centuries ago, was rare a century ago, existed in only thirty-five out of 147 countries in 1975, but had reached eighty-four countries by 1995.[37] Today is the first time in human history that a majority of the world's population lives in democracies. In 2000, the share of the total population in democracies reached 57 per cent. The collapse of the wasteful and oppressive Soviet socialist tyranny was a milestone in this desirable direction.

Against this background, the despair and anger of the critics of market-led globalization is unbalanced. If they succeed in halting the movement towards international integration, much of this progress is likely to be lost, as prosperity falls, a corrupting web of controls on economic transactions grows, resentments over barriers to commerce increase and international ill will expands. The task ahead is, instead, not to halt global economic integration, but to make it work for more people than ever before.

Chapter 4   The 'Magic' of the Market

Though my heart may be left of centre, I have always known that the only economic system that works is a market economy. This is the only natural economy, the only kind that makes sense, the only one that leads to prosperity, because it is the only one that reflects the nature of life itself. The essence of life is infinitely and mysteriously multiform, and therefore it cannot be contained or planned for, in its fullness and variability, by any central intelligence.

Vaclav Havel[1]

The enemies of globalization are opponents of the market economy. That is the heart of this debate. But what is such an economy? Where has it come from? How does it work, both within a country and across frontiers? It is impossible to assess the critique of globalization without trying to examine these fundamental questions. This chapter looks at the market itself. The next looks at the role and limits of government.

Rise of the market economy

'Trade and market-regulated behaviour, though present from very early times, remained marginal and subordinate in civilized societies' until about a thousand years ago.[2] Thus did the American historian William McNeill describe the gathering revolution of the past millennium. Prior to that period, he argued, command systems were the principal way of mobilizing resources in complex societies.[3] Civilization – by which I mean large-scale hierarchical societies, with a complex internal division of labour – was the fruit of the agrarian revolution, which seems to have begun in the fertile crescent of West

Asia some 10,000 years ago and arose not much later in the valleys of the Indus and the Yellow River.[4] The vast majority of people in these societies were tillers of the soil, feeding themselves and those in power over them, with their lives and livelihoods perennially vulnerable to the weather, disease and the stationary and roving bandits described by Mancur Olson.[5] Beyond the limits of complex civilizations were nomads of steppe and sand, mountain-dwellers and, remoter still, the hunter-gatherers. In the Americas a parallel evolution occurred, though some thousands of years later.[6]

Throughout the agrarian era of human history, commerce and trade, albeit significant, remained marginal activities.[7] The merchant and, still more, the moneylender were distrusted and despised. In many of the value systems of civilized society they came below the tillers of the soil, particularly in Confucian China.[8] Occupants of the highest social places were the ever-recurring figures of the warrior-ruler and the priest-scribe-bureaucrat. The power they held was also the most effective route to wealth. For the warrior-ruler, the two came naturally together. The highest position of all was held by those who combined the two aspects of authority in one – priest-kings, such as the Byzantine emperors, or, loftier still, god-kings, such as the pharaohs of ancient Egypt. The moral and mental machinery of contemporary revolutionaries harks back to those pre-modern times. The party-state of the communist era was a ruthless priest-kingdom. In contemporary North Korea, it even turns out to be a hereditary one.

Only when the commercial spirit – and its concomitant rationalistic approach to technological innovation and scientific inquiry – seized control of powerful states (as outlined in the previous chapter) did the market economy comprehensively transform ways of life. In the beginning its impact was fitful. In China, after a remarkable technological and commercial flowering under the Sung dynasty (960–1279), advance slowed sharply. It was on the western promontory of Eurasia that the commercial revolution broke through the crust of tradition and repression that lay over agrarian hierarchical societies. It gathered strength, albeit fitfully, over several centuries, before bursting into astonishing life in the nineteenth century.

From a technological view, the decisive shift was towards use of inanimate energy – wind, water and, most important, fossil fuels – from the old reliance on animate energy – human and animal power. What is called the industrial revolution is better named the energy revolution. Some economists refer to the growth of the past two centuries as 'Promethean', after the legendary titan who brought fire to man.[9] This distinguishes that form of growth from the

'Smithian', which works via the division of labour and economies of scale, as described in the *Wealth of Nations*, published in 1776. The arrival of Promethean growth was the most important event since the agrarian revolution. But adjusting to its onset has been painful. Never before have ways of life changed so much and so quickly. The agrarian revolution spread across the globe over thousands of years, not two centuries. In no more than six or seven generations, the Promethean revolution has brought in its train urbanization, industrialization, global economic integration, two world wars, the spread of democracy and a global commercial culture. The proportion of people working in British agriculture halved between 1780 and 1870. Not surprisingly, such upsetting changes have repeatedly brought a backlash by millenarians promising a perfect future and romantics longing for a more natural past.[10]

The liberating technological changes of Promethean growth did not emerge from nowhere. They reflected a new way of organizing the economic activities of society as a whole – a sophisticated market economy with secure protection of property rights. Unshackled from the constraints of tradition and driven by hope of gain, economic actors were tied by competition to the wheel of what the great Austrian economist Joseph Schumpeter called 'creative destruction'. To achieve success in their battles with their competitors, businesses have been driven to exploit and nurture the ever-burgeoning power of technology and science. Within a market economy the hope of gain and the fear of loss drive inventors and innovators to apply new ways of doing things or to produce new products.[11]

As Professor Mokyr notes:

> for a society to be technologically creative, three conditions have to be satisfied. First, there has to be a cadre of ingenious and resourceful innovators who are both willing and able to challenge their physical environment for their own improvement. . . . Second, economic and social institutions have to encourage potential innovators by presenting them with the right incentive structure. . . . Third, innovation requires diversity and tolerance.[12]

The second and third of these was as important as the first. Happily, the environment of eighteenth- and nineteenth-century enlightenment Europe, particularly of Britain, provided all three.

To describe what happened in the early nineteenth century as an 'industrial' or even as an 'energy' revolution is misleading. It would be more accurate to describe it as a culmination and acceleration of a market revolution that became far more powerful with the mass application of physical energy. The active force of profit-seeking business people exploited and drove the economic transformation, as it continues to do to this day. It is they who choose the investments and make the technological innovations. The market economy is, as a result, the only human institution that generates a 'permanent revolution'.

Growth during the market millennium

If the last thousand years have, as Professor McNeill argues, been the millennium of the market, what have been the consequences? The short answer is that the world has undergone an unprecedented transformation. According to the economic historian Angus Maddison, the population of the world rose twenty-two-fold over the last millennium, but world gross domestic product (at purchasing power parity) rose thirteen times as fast.[13]

This astonishing increase in population, output and incomes per head has no earlier parallels. The world's population barely increased in the first millennium, while the average standard of living in 1000 was also much the same as it had been a thousand years before, at a bare subsistence level. Today, however, very few countries have living standards close to the world average of a thousand years ago: Chad or Sierra Leone might be examples.

Moreover figures for economic growth in the second millennium under-state the true increase in the standard of living. Life expectancy was twenty-four in England between 1300 and 1425. It had probably been much the same in the Roman Empire. By 1801–26, the English level had reached forty-one. By 1999 it had reached seventy-seven. Two centuries ago or more, nobody, however powerful and rich, had access to dentistry, medicine or sanitation worthy of the name. Nathan Rothschild, founder of the Rothschild dynasty in England, died in 1836 of an infected boil. Today, antibiotics would have cured him with ease. Anne, Queen of England, bore fifteen children, not one of whom survived to maturity. Even in 1900 one in ten children in the United States died before his or her first birthday. By the late 1990s the rate was down to seven in a thousand.

Growth accelerated enormously after 1820. But something important had already started to happen before then. World population rose nearly four-fold between 1000 and 1820. World GDP rose perhaps six-fold. This meant a 50 per cent rise in real incomes per head. This aggregate conceals very different performances by western Europe and the rest of the world. Between 1000 and 1820, European real incomes per head rose about three times. In the most successful market economies in Western Europe, the United Kingdom and the Netherlands, average incomes per head were about four times as high as they had been in 1000.[14] But, prior to the early nineteenth century, sustained rises in living standards were largely limited to western Europe and, from the seventeenth century onwards, the British colonies of North America.

In the period after 1820, the rate of global growth greatly accelerated. Between 1820 and 1998, world population rose almost six-fold, its GDP forty-nine-fold and its GDP per head almost nine-fold. Between 1820 and 1998, real GDP per head rose nineteen-fold in western Europe, the former British colonies of North America and Australasia. In Japan, which was relatively poor in 1820, standards of living had risen thirty-one-fold by 1998. In the rest of the world, real GDP per head rose only five-fold. Almost every economy is richer than it was two centuries ago, but some have done much better than others.

The historically unprecedented economic dynamism of the last two centuries and the divergence in performance across countries are the two most important features of the world we inhabit. The *dynamism* was the product of institutions, practices and attitudes that emerged in western Europe over an extended period. These cultural, social and political advantages combined with favourable resource endowments, particularly the proximity of coal and iron.[15]

The *divergence* was the result of the uneven spread of this form of rapid growth. In the course of the nineteenth century, rapid growth – what the Nobel-laureate Simon Kuznets called 'modern economic growth' – spread swiftly from Britain to the rest of western Europe and the former British colonies overseas. Incomes converged strongly among these countries.[16] Rapid growth also jumped from one end of Eurasia to the other once the United States forced Japan to open up its economy in the mid-nineteenth century. At the present stage in human history, all the successful economies are rooted in European or Sino-Japanese culture.[17]

In 1820, the richest country in the world had a real income per head about four and a half times as high as the poorest. The ratio was fifteen to one by 1913, twenty-six to one by 1950, forty-two to one by 1973, and seventy-one to one by 2000.[18] Not all is gloom. Africa's average real income per head is perhaps three times higher than it was a century or so ago. Asia's as a whole is up six-fold since 1820 and Latin America's nine-fold. In 1900 life expectancy was a mere twenty-six in today's developing world. It was sixty-four by 1999. This is much the same as the sixty-six achieved by today's advanced countries as recently as 1950.

Yet the overall picture of a world in which some countries have economies that grow more or less consistently while others do not is correct. A few countries have already caught up on the leaders of the nineteenth century, while some are growing very rapidly, including the world's biggest, China. India, the world's second biggest country, is also beginning to sustain reasonably rapid growth, at last. But many countries have been failing. As Lant Pritchett of the World Bank has noted, out of a sample of 108 developing countries for which data are available, 'sixteen developing countries had negative growth over the 1960–90 period. . . . Another 28 nations . . . had growth rates of per capita GDP less than 0.5 per cent per annum . . . and 40 developing nations . . . had growth rates less than 1 per cent per annum.'[19] So what explains successful economies? The answer is that they have dynamic market economies. But what does this mean? That is the question to which we now turn.

How an advanced market economy works

Think for a moment about what our economy achieves. We can buy food produced all over the world, which is then bought, processed, distributed and sold though a long chain of wholesalers and retailers to satisfy our varying tastes. The food will be extraordinarily safe.[20] One can buy clothing made by workers in China, India, Italy or Mexico, in a staggering number of different fabrics and styles. For personal transport, one can choose from many varieties of motor car; for entertainment, one can select a DVD player and flat-screen television; for work, leisure or personal bureaucracy, one can buy a personal computer. An army of competing inventors, designers, producers and distributors try to meet all these and many other demands. A host of intermediaries takes money from households and supplies it to those who persuade them they can use it productively. In the process, they create an endless array of financial instruments, including bank deposits, bonds, equities and assorted derivatives, and package and repackage risk, allowing savers and investors to diversify and hedge their portfolios.

We take all this for granted. Yet it is extraordinary. What makes it far more extraordinary – and to many quite scary – is that nobody is in charge. Adam Smith's metaphor of the invisible hand remains as illuminating as ever. Self-interest, co-ordinated through the market, motivates people to invent, produce and sell a vast array of goods, services and assets.

As a way of satisfying the material wants of mankind, self-interest exceeds the power of charity as the Amazon exceeds a rivulet. This is what Ronald Reagan called 'the magic of the market'. But 'the market process', as Friedrich Hayek called it, is not magic. It is far cleverer than that.

In his book *Reinventing the Bazaar*, John McMillan of the University of California, at Berkeley, indicates the nature of this institution by comparing an 'absolutely free market' to 'folk football'. But 'a real market is like American football, an ordered brawl'.[21] To a large extent, the rules governing markets evolve with markets themselves. The result today, in advanced economies, is a system of extraordinary complexity and efficiency.

Every society has some markets. Equally, in no society are markets ubiquitous. In contemporary advanced economies, three categories of transaction occur largely or entirely outside markets: those within households; those with the government and within it; and those inside corporations. Yet markets are significant institutions virtually everywhere. They emerge in prisons and concentration camps; they emerged in communist dictatorships even though the participants, condemned as 'speculators', were often shot out of hand; and in almost all developing countries they emerge as the informal sector where people trade outside the purview of foolish regulations and corrupt regulators.[22]

Yet many societies today and virtually all societies historically had only very limited markets. Those markets dealt only in immediately available goods and services. These transactions are self-enforcing: one buys a fruit or a carpet and pays for it. The constraint on development is the absence of markets for transactions that take a long time to reach fruition: borrowing, lending, investing and insuring. In such transactions trust and confidence matter a great deal. In many developing countries, these longer-term or complex transactions are limited to dealings with family or close friends, where misbehaviour carries credible sanctions.

If a sophisticated market economy is to work, it has to solve five problems: first, information must flow smoothly, giving people confidence in what they are buying; second, it must be reasonable to assume people will live up to their promises, even if these promises are to be executed decades into the future; third, competition must be fostered; fourth, property rights must be protected; and, finally, the worst side effects on third parties must be curtailed.[23]

The flow of reliable *information* and the ability to *trust* are the life-blood of markets. As James Q. Wilson, formerly professor at Harvard, puts it: 'trust must exist in a society for it to be a capitalist society because people who do not trust their neighbors, do not trust other groups, do not trust distant people, cannot trade with them; and, unable to trade with them, capitalism remains at the level of a bazaar economy'[24] Sometimes, obtaining information on what is available is too expensive to allow any market to emerge. To this the rise of the information economy is providing some answers. At other times, the difficulty is 'asymmetric information'. If one thinks that the person one is dealing with not only knows more about what is being sold than one does oneself, but has an incentive to deceive one as well, the transaction may well not occur. Happily, there are solutions. People in business can provide guarantees or create reputations for honest dealing; they can invest in a brand that associates the company with the quality of what it sells; and they can employ more or less credible professionals (such as accountants) to certify the truth of what they are saying. Regulators can help by certifying the quality of a company's processes or products, their financial soundness or whatever else may be relevant. The law and other forms of recourse provide penalties for deceit or the breaking of contracts. Finally and perhaps most important, the values of a society can support honesty: if cheating and stealing are regarded as normal, a society will possess no more than a shallow and undeveloped market economy. If high levels of personal probity and honest dealing are encouraged, the market economy will work well.

Competition is essential to good performance. A private monopoly may be more efficient than a public one, largely because it has clearer objectives, but it is likely to be more exploitative and less innovative than competitive businesses. In principle, sound competition policy can remedy anti-competitive behaviour. Some actions – making price-fixing and other forms of cartel behaviour illegal, for example – are self-evident. But imposing competition by administrative or legal fiat can be tricky. There is often a temptation to use competition policy as a way of protecting competitors instead of competition or consumers.

Protection of *property* is the necessary condition for a sophisticated market economy. Indeed, it is the most important single condition. People need to be able to own things. What does ownership mean? It means, first, that people have a right to the residual income, over and above that committed to other parties – suppliers, lenders, employees and so forth. This gives them an incentive to use the asset productively or, if they cannot do so, to sell it to someone who can. Second, the owner also possesses residual control rights. Not only does the owner have the incentive to use the asset productively. He or she has the right to do so as well. In a sophisticated modern economy, such rights of ownership are complex. They rest in mere pieces of paper and may be exercised through chains of agents.[25]

The protection of property links to what economists call *externalities*, the production of 'goods' or 'bads' whose positive or negative value is not included in the calculations of those making the transactions themselves. They are in some way or another outside the market, usually because there is an incomplete specification of property rights. Where externalities exist, property rights may well need to be qualified. The right to make use of a river passing through one's land may exclude the right to take more than a certain proportion of the water it contains, or to pollute it. Sometimes, as the Nobel-laureate Ronald Coase has argued, such externalities can be addressed through bargaining among those affected.[26] Often, however, the costs of reaching and policing such bargains will be excessive or the costs (and benefits) may be distributed too widely for those affected to have an adequate incentive to coalesce to 'internalize' the externality. A solution will then have to be imposed by a coercive power – usually the state.[27]

Central features of a modern market economy

A modern market economy is therefore about as far from Edouard Balladur's jungle as can readily be imagined. The market is a complex and sophisticated piece of institutional machinery that has evolved over centuries on the basis of the broad principles of freedom of contract, secure property rights and a service-providing state. Four interconnected features of the modern market economy are of decisive importance, especially for any discussion of global economic integration. These are: the corporation; innovation and growth; intellectual property; and the role and functioning of financial markets. All depend on institutional arrangements underpinned by the state as creator and enforcer of the law. All are focal points for the criticisms of protesters against globalization. Yet, without them, we would not have the economic dynamism we take for granted. They are at the heart of a modern market economy.

Corporations[28]

The Nobel-laureate Kenneth Arrow has remarked that 'truly among man's innovations, the use of organization to accomplish his ends is among both his greatest and his earliest'.[29] The private corporation is the most extraordinary organizational innovation of the past two centuries. Today's economy would be unimaginable without its dynamism and flexibility. The corporation is a hybrid institution: it is hierarchical, but embedded in markets. Before the modern corporation, commerce was largely the province of individual merchants, while big hierarchical institutions, both civil and military, were the province of rulers.[30] Today, there exists an institution that combines the two. This required the merging of two distinct forms of social organization and value systems, that of the merchant and that of the administrator. Making such organizations entrepreneurial remains an abiding challenge.

The modern multi-unit business enterprise emerged in the 1840s, almost at the beginning of the era of Promethean growth. This was the point at which technological advance combined with an enlarging economy 'to make administrative co-ordination more productive and, therefore, more profitable than market co-ordination'.[31] The modern corporation also required the invention of limited liability, which occurred in 1856. Otherwise the immense capital needed would have remained unavailable.

Corporations are crucial to a modern economy. In the United States transactions in the market account for well under a third of total incomes.[32] Yet the corporation is not above or outside the market. Shifts in market conditions, including technology or trade, will alter the boundaries of corporations, force them to merge, impose fundamental changes in strategy or maybe bankrupt them. Companies are servants of market forces, not their overlords. If they do not meet the terms of market competition, they will disappear.

Why do companies exist? The simple reason, first proposed in a classic 1937 article by Ronald Coase, is that transaction costs can make hierarchical structures more efficient than market transactions.[33] For such an organization to work, it must be possible to form relationships of trust. As one might expect, therefore, large companies are far more prevalent in advanced countries with high levels of trust than in less developed ones: in the United States plants with fifty or more employees account for 80 per cent of manufacturing employment; in Indonesia, the proportion is only 15 per cent.[34]

The corporation is a wonderful institution. But it contains inherent drawbacks, the core of which are conflicts of interest. Control over the company's resources is vested in the hands of managers who may rationally pursue their interests at the expense of all others. Economists call this the 'principal-agent' problem. In the modern economy, where shares are held by fund managers, there is not just one set of principal-agent relations but a chain of them.[35] Asymmetric information and obstacles to collective action exacerbate the principal-agent problem. Corporate managers know more about what is going on in the business than anybody else and have an interest in keeping at least some of this information to themselves. It is hard to create incentives that ensure management acts in the interests of others. Equally, dispersed shareholders have a weak incentive to monitor management, because they would share the gains with others but bear much of the cost themselves.[36] The upshot is the vulnerability of the corporation to managerial incompetence, self-seeking, deceit or malfeasance.

In practice, there are six (interconnected) ways of reducing these risks. The first is market discipline: financial failure will ultimately find managers out, provided governments can be dissuaded from bailing failed companies out. The second is internal checks, with independent directors, requirements for voting by institutional shareholders and internal auditing. The third is private regulation, such as listing requirements of stock exchanges. The fourth is official regulation that covers the composition of boards, structure of businesses and reporting requirements. The fifth is transparency, including accounting standards and independent audits. The last is, once again, values of honest dealing.

Economists are very uncomfortable with the notion of morality. Yet it seems to have rather a clear meaning in the business context. It consists of acting honestly even when the opposite may be to one's advantage. Such morality is essential for all trustee relationships. Without it, costs of supervision and control become exorbitant. At the limit, a range of transactions and long-term relationships becomes impossible and society remains impoverished. Corporate managers are trustees. So are fund managers. The more they view themselves (and are viewed) as such, the less they are likely to exploit opportunities created by the conflicts of interest within the business.

Innovation[37]

Rising standards of living and their uneven spread have been, as noted above, the most remarkable features of a global market revolution. The source of this sustained growth has been technological innovation. Of that there is no doubt. In technological innovation modern market economies found the economist's free lunch. A brilliant book by William Baumol of New York University sheds light on this revolution.[38] He builds on the insights of the Austrian economist Joseph Schumpeter to expose the machine that drives capitalism. Professor

Baumol argues that innovation rather than price competition is the central feature of the market process. Competition forces companies to invest in innovation. Otherwise, they risk falling behind and, ultimately, being driven out of their markets.

In Schumpeter's model of the capitalist economy, the engine of innovation was the extraordinary profits offered to the lone entrepreneur. Yet, as Baumol makes clear, the bulk of the innovation that drives economies occurs within existing companies. It is a routine aspect of their behaviour. Overall, such innovative activity will not be particularly profitable: some companies will be lucky; others will not. But the motivation is no longer the hope of exceptional profit. It is the certainty of failure if one is not in the race. Innovation then does not come from outside the market. It is hard-wired into capitalism.

Intellectual property

Given the role of innovation, intellectual property is not a marginal feature of the property-rights regime of a modern market economy, but its core. It is the most important example of property that only a powerful state can protect. The reason such action is needed is that ideas are public goods. Put plainly, this means that a person can enjoy the fruits of an idea without depriving anyone else of its benefits. But also, once divulged, they are available to everybody. Yet if ideas are freely available, nobody can make money out of creating them.

The solution has been intellectual property – patents, copyright and trade-marks. For innovation, patents are the most important. But they are also a legally sanctioned restraint of trade.

Intellectual property protection requires striking a delicate balance. It is essential, but can easily go too far. There will be strong pressure from powerful and self-interested producer lobbies to make intellectual property protection too tight. Protection must also not be granted too freely. In the United States, that now seems to be happening, with protection granted to genes with unknown use and trivial business methods – such as 'one-click' purchasing on the Internet.[39] Over-liberal granting of intellectual property rights is a restraint on trade and should be viewed as such.

Financial markets

Financial intermediation is as central a feature of a modern market economy as the corporation, innovation and intellectual property. It is its bloodstream, taking resources from people who do not need them or cannot use them and supplying them to people who do need them and can use them. Overwhelming evidence links the depth and sophistication of financial markets to levels of output per head. As a World Bank report on finance stated, 'there is now a solid body of research strongly suggesting that improvements in financial arrangements precede and contribute to economic performance. In other words, the widespread desire to see an effectively functioning financial system is warranted by its clear causal link to growth, macroeconomic stability, and poverty reduction.'[40] The Bank noted, for example, that developing countries with relatively deep financial markets in 1960 subsequently grew far faster than those with relatively shallow ones.

Financial systems perform four essential functions: they mobilize savings (for which outlets would otherwise be far more limited); they allocate capital (to finance productive investment and permit people to spend temporarily above their current incomes); they monitor managers (to ensure funds will be spent as promised); and they transform risk (by pooling risk and distributing it to those best able to bear it). These are vital functions. It is absolutely impossible to imagine a successful market economy without a dynamic, competitive and flexible financial system.

Yet market-driven financial arrangements, though irreplaceable, are liable to well-known difficulties.

First, financial markets suffer from inadequate supplies of information and obstacles to monitoring performance.

Second, financial markets are, partly for this reason, fragile. This is particularly true of banks. Their fragility comes from the fact that their liabilities are short term, in domestic or, occasionally, in foreign currency, usually payable at par and on demand, but their assets are long term, with values that are vulnerable to interest rate, credit and macroeconomic risks.

Third, financial markets are liable to wild swings in prices, both upwards and downwards, because of the instability of valuations of uncertain streams of income.

Fourth, financial markets tend towards herd behaviour. This is particularly true when ill-informed players believe they lack information available to others. When classes of assets are unfamiliar to a large number of investors, herding behaviour may be very powerful.

Fifth, financial markets may generate self-fulfilling expectations and so what economists call 'multiple equilibria'.

Financial markets are fragile because of the inherent challenge of orienting economic activity to an unknowable future. It would be quite wrong to conclude that the 'imperfections' underlying such fragility mean either that such markets should be abolished or that there exist some evident cures. Without financial intermediation, market economies would be unable to perform. As for eliminating market 'failures', one must remember that one can never do better than one's best. So-called imperfections are irrelevant, therefore, if the costs of eliminating them exceed the benefit of trying to do so.

Conclusion

The world of full information and perfect competition is an illusion. If it did exist, the dynamism of the modern market economy would not occur. Indeed, it would be ruled out, by assumption. The modern corporation, perpetual innovation, intellectual property and sophisticated financial markets imply a substantial degree of monopoly and instability. But they also are what make the modern market economy astoundingly successful.

Morality of market economies[41]

Intelligent critics are prepared to accept that a sophisticated market economy works far better than any other economic system. But they would proceed to complain that markets encourage immorality and have socially immoral consequences, not least gross inequality. These views, albeit common, are largely mistaken.

Inequality

All complex societies are unequal. In all societies people (generally men) seek power and authority over others. But, among sophisticated societies with an elaborate division of labour, societies with market economies have been the least unequal and the inequality they generate has been the least harmful. To many this may seem a shocking statement. It should not be.

Remember that in agrarian kingdoms or feudal societies, kings and lords had the power of life and death. The rich and powerful could seize the labour, the possessions and even the lives of subjects, serfs and slaves, at will. Perhaps the most unequal societies of all were the state-socialist and national-socialist regimes of the twentieth century. A Stalin or a Mao possessed absolute control over the resources of vast countries and their inhabitants. When, on a whim, Mao decided on the Great Leap Forward in the 1950s, 30 million people died.

The irony is that such tyranny was justified by the alleged horrors of capitalist inequality. To eliminate market-driven inequality, all power was concentrated in the hands of the state, which then promptly and inevitably generated non-market-driven inequalities for the benefit of those who controlled it.

In all that matters – in the ability to lead one's own life and the legal rights one possesses – the modern liberal democracy is unprecedentedly equal. Virtually all citizens have access to a range of goods and services unavailable even to the wealthiest a century or even half a century ago. Wealthy people have more influence over the life of a democracy than do the majority of its citizens. But, compared to the power and influence that accrued to the wealthy in traditional societies, the power of today's wealthy is highly circum-scribed. Politicians have more power and intellectuals more influence than men with big cheque books. Who has made more difference to the way Americans live their lives today, Ronald Reagan, Milton Friedman or Warren Buffett?

No rich man or corporation can ignore the law, as a number of corporate scoundrels discovered in 2002. Even Bill Gates, the world's richest man, discovered he could not ignore the low-paid lawyers of the Department of Justice when it went after Microsoft's alleged monopolistic abuses. A few centuries ago, the richest man in a European country could create a private army capable of defying the state. Today, Gates would exhaust his fortune in less than three months in trying to rival the spending of his country's defence department. In a competitive market economy subject to the rule of law, Gates or Warren Buffett can tyrannize over their bank balances, not over people. They can support politicians, not coerce them.[42] They can cajole customers, not compel them. They can give money to charity, not create armies. They can order their businesses, not buy their workers. Gates and Buffett are citizens, entrepreneurs, investors and philanthropists. They are neither tyrants nor overlords. A competitive market economy neither ends inequality nor eliminates the desire for power and prestige. It tames them instead.

Freedom, democracy and the permanent opposition

A competitive market economy is a reflection – and a source – of freedom. It is also a necessary condition for democracy. In a society where political power determines the allocation of wealth, it is impossible to be independent without being powerful. But in a market society that combination is possible and this, in turn, provides a basis for competing political parties. As Vaclav Havel explained, 'a government that commands the economy will inevitably command the polity; given a commanding position it will distort or destroy the former and corrupt or oppress the latter'.[43]

Liberal democracies with market economies are, as Joseph Schumpeter argued in his classic book *Capitalism, Socialism and Democracy*, the only societies that create their own opposition. 'Capitalism created both a parvenu class of rich plutocrats and corporate climbers and a counter-culture of critical intellectuals and disaffected youth.'[44] It continues to do so today. Take a look at the campuses, the publications and the protesters in western democracies. Only in a market economy could books condemning society's rich and powerful be published and promoted with such success. Only in a market economy would the wealthy give large sums of money to universities that provide comfortable homes to those who despise the wealthy and the system that made them so. The market economy does not merely support its critics, it embraces them.

Yet lauded and successful critics indulge in paranoid fantasies about

> corporate space as a fascist state where we all salute the logo and have little opportunity for criticism because our newspapers, television stations, Internet servers, streets and retail spaces are all controlled by multinational corporate interests. And considering the speed with which these trends are developing, we clearly have good reason for alarm. But a word of caution: we may be able to see a not-so-brave new world on the horizon, but that doesn't mean we are already living in Huxley's nightmare.[45]

So even Naomi Klein has to admit the limits of corporate power. In fact, anti-corporate books and television programmes are being published and produced with great commercial success. Klein's *No Logo* has become a brand all of its own. Capitalism nurtures its enemies. It also tries to make money out of them. But then they make money too.

Morality

Markets also require, reward and reinforce valuable moral qualities: trustworthiness, reliability, effort, civility, self-reliance and self-restraint. These qualities are, critics argue, placed in the service of self-interest. Yet, since people are self-interested, this is neither surprising nor shocking. But people are not completely self-interested. Happily, a wealthy society allows people to be far less driven by material objectives than one in which the vast majority of people are on the threshold of subsistence. A prosperous market economy also generates a vast number of attractive activities for those who are not motivated by wealth alone. People can work for non-governmental organizations or charities. They can work in the public sector, as doctors, teachers or policemen. They can even live off the welfare state and devote their lives to campaigning against the iniquities of capitalism. It is only the wealth generated by successful market economies that has made a welfare state possible. Poor countries today and all societies historically lacked the means to provide economic security to their citizens. Moreover, if people do make a great deal of money, they can use it for any purpose they wish. They can give it all away – and some have.

Over the last two centuries in the advanced market economies, the value placed on eliminating pain and injustice and on human and, more recently, animal life and welfare has also hugely increased. This is partly because a liberal society places such heavy weight on individuals. It is partly because people, being richer and far more secure, can afford concern with deeper moral ends. It is partly because people are better informed about what goes on across the world. It is partly because premature death and pain have been so much reduced, making life seem far more precious. The savage punishments and casual injustices in the judicial systems, military services and educational institutions of two centuries ago are gone. It took militarists, extreme nationalists, communists and fascists – the anti-liberals – to bring these horrors back, indeed to glory in violence and cruelty. Now, with the passing of these creeds, advocacy of human and animal rights has gone global, ironically as part of the litany of anti-globalization.

Again, consider environmentalism. Business is supposedly indifferent to the environment. That, indeed, is one of the principal criticisms of a market economy. Yet we now know that the supposedly benevolent state-socialist economies were environmental catastrophes. The market economy has avoided these disasters for at least four reasons: first, it provides the means for independent critics of environmental abuses to flourish; second, it generates the prosperity that makes people concerned about the environment; third, it implies a separation between companies and the government that makes independent regulation possible; and, finally, companies are concerned about their reputations and will act to protect them, in response to campaigning against them. For these reasons, effective environmental pressure groups have emerged only in market democracies.

Conclusion

The liberal market economy is morally imperfect, because it reflects the tastes and desires of people, who are also imperfect. A market economy satisfies the desires of the majority more than the tastes of a refined minority. It rewards the hustler more than the sage. But it is also the basis of freedom and democracy. It encourages valuable moral virtues. It makes people richer and more concerned about environmental damage, pain and injustice. It makes the welfare state possible.

Those who condemn the immorality of liberal capitalism do so in comparison with a society of saints that has never existed – and never will. This, it appears, can be a literal truth. At the end of *Empire*, a tedious neo-Marxist tome on globalization, the authors compare the communist militant to St Francis of Assisi. 'Once again', conclude the authors, 'in postmodernity we find ourselves in Francis's situation, posing against the misery of power the joy of being. This is a revolution that no power will control – because biopower and communism, cooperation and revolution remain together, in love, simplicity, and also innocence. This is the irrepressible lightness and joy of being communist.' This is the absurdity one must embrace, in the wake of the collapse of state-socialism, if one is to envisage a society better than the liberal democracies.[46]

Markets matter

The arrival of an economy dominated by sophisticated markets with secure property rights, long-term investment and constant innovation has brought about a revolution in human life. These benefits have not been equally shared. But there is almost no part of the globe where standards of living are not significantly higher than they were two centuries ago. Most opponents of the market economy compare the worst of today with the best. That may seem fair enough. But it makes as much sense to compare the worst of today with the normal in the past. By those standards, we have already come a long way.

Yet if markets matter, so do governments. What are the role and limits of government in a liberal market democracy? This is the topic of the next chapter.

Chapter 5 **Physician, Heal Thyself**

*What this war has demonstrated is that private capitalism –
that is an economic system in which land, factories, money and
transport are owned privately and operated solely for profit –
does not work.*

George Orwell[1]

Not so very long ago, economic planning and public ownership of the means
of production were the wave of the future. Even a man as wise as George
Orwell believed in both these bad ideas. That faith did not end with the 1940s.
When I worked at the World Bank during the 1970s every developing country,
however limited its intellectual resources, was expected to produce a five-year
economic plan in pale imitation of the Stalinist model. Sophisticated developing countries, such as India, produced sophisticated plans. Less sophisticated countries produced less sophisticated plans. All these plans had one
thing in common, however: they were fictions. But they were not harmless
fictions. They inflicted grave damage on the economies and people of these
supposedly 'planned' societies.[2] Anti-capitalists of today talk as if these experiments with planning had never happened or, if they did, have no significance
now that state-socialism has collapsed. They are wrong. The experience with
national economic planning has important lessons. It helps us understand
what a state can usefully do – and is obliged not do – if it is to see a rise in the
living standards of the people for whom it has responsibility.

What the state cannot do: the death of central planning

In the twentieth-century heyday of the anti-liberal counter-revolution, an
extraordinary belief grew up.[3] This faith held that the entire national economy

not only could – but should – be brought under central control and direction. This was the faith that failed. It was an example of what the late Friedrich Hayek called the 'fatal conceit' – the belief in our ability to plan and control human destiny.

The belief that central planning was possible emerged partly from the success of the modern business corporation, partly from a realization that it would be easier to manage an industry with a few large players than one with many smaller ones, and partly from the experience of economic mobilization for war. People found it increasingly natural to think of a country as a large company. Even today, the notion lives on in metaphorical discussions of 'UK plc' or 'America Inc'. But for the better part of a century people who considered themselves progressive did not think of this as a metaphor. They considered the planned economy logical, necessary and desirable. They were wrong.

First, planners cannot find out what needs to be done to co-ordinate the production of a modern economy. As Professor McMillan points out, there are 20,000 different job categories in the United States. A central plan cannot begin to cope with such complexity.[4] Worse, the information planners need about the possibilities of production is locked away in their underlings' heads. The planned will want to tell planners not the truth, but what they find personally convenient. It is in the interests of factory managers to tell planners the levels of production that would be easy for them to achieve, since they are far more likely to be penalized for failure to achieve targets than for over-achieving them.

Second, even if a technically feasible plan could be drawn up, there is no reason to believe it will be implemented. It is in the interests of factory bosses to produce what they find personally beneficial and, wherever desirable and feasible, deceive their superiors. Maybe factory managers will meet the purely quantitative targets, but they can easily evade targets for quality, even where such targets can be specified. Planners can only inspect part of the production. Only users in markets automatically inspect all of the production.

Third, it is impossible for planners to know what hundreds of millions of different people desire. So the technically feasible plan, even if implemented, will bear no relation to what people actually want. Think, for a moment, of cosmetics. How could a central planner know better than the consumers what the individual woman wants? Planners can only provide users with what they believe they *should* want, which is quite another matter.[5]

Fourth, because prices bear no relation to costs, there is no way to calculate what production needs to increase and what production needs to be reduced.

A technically feasible plan can, quite easily, be wealth-destroying. Without prices generated in a market, rational calculation of what needs to be produced is impossible.

Fifth, the comparison with a war effort is completely misguided. The salient feature of war is that the state defines the goals. The salient feature of peace is that individual consumers define them. In peacetime, production's function is to satisfy consumers. The objectives of production in war and peace are opposites.

Sixth, even if all such problems can be resolved, planners do not know the possibilities for production of new things or of old things in new ways. Worse, they find such novelties – the fruits of innovation – inconvenient. Any innovation disrupts the plan automatically. It also brings additional uncertainties, since nobody can know with reasonable confidence how to produce completely new products or how successful a new technique may turn out to be. In practice, therefore, the planned economy is as innovation-resistant as the market economy is innovation-prone.

Finally, foreign trade cannot be integrated successfully into the plan since, by definition, foreigners cannot be planned, unless the planners control those foreigners. Planning is hierarchical by its nature, because it turns a country into a single company. It can be stretched across borders only if there is a clear hierarchy among countries. For this reason, independent planned countries pursue autarky, so far as they can. At the same time, they always need trade since there are some things they cannot make. But planners do not know what it makes sense for them to trade, since they do not know what anything costs.

The idea of comprehensive national planning is not just mistaken. It is ludicrous. It ignores everything we know about the role of incentives and information in economics. Output per worker in the Soviet Union and eastern Europe was about a third below that in the west even when they had the same equipment. The productivity of Chinese peasants doubled once the communes were abolished.[6] Planning would fail even if the planners were benevolent and competent. Alas, there is every reason to expect the people who reach the top of a bureaucratic hierarchy to possess neither of these virtues. Central planning could not have succeeded in a long-run race against market economies. Yet developing countries were cajoled into doing it. Sometimes they desperately wanted to. That was, if anything, more ludicrous, since these governments did not possess the powers of coercion over factory managers possessed by a Soviet planner.

What the state needs to do for the economy

If central planning is unworkable, the market is inescapable. There is no third way of running a complex modern economy based on an extensive division of labour. The alternative of customary behaviour is feasible only in simple economies where changes in economic conditions are rare. Some contemporary anti-market romantics imagine that it would be possible to escape from the market in this way. Often they add to this the idea that the economy should be fragmented into small 'local' pieces. They are dreaming. They should also remember that customary behaviour of this kind was usually enforced by oppressive social hierarchies.

So what role does the state have to play to make a market economy work? At the broadest level, it has three functions: first, to provide things – known as public goods – that the market cannot provide for itself; second, to internalize externalities or remedy market failures; and, third, to help people who, for a number of reasons, do worse from the market or are more vulnerable to what happens within it than society finds tolerable.

The discussion above of the link between the market and politics, in Chapter 3, and of the workings of a modern sophisticated economy, in Chapter 4, already indicates the public goods the government must provide. It starts with *security of property* from predators. This necessitates armies, police, judges and prisons. Drawing up and implementing legislation is a central function of the state. But these functions need to be separated. Independence of the judiciary from both the government and legislature is the most important single way to protect citizens from the predatory activities of the government.[7]

A fundamental requirement for the protection of property is, therefore, the impartial *rule of law*. The Nobel-laureate Amartya Sen has argued, that 'legal and judicial reform is important not only for legal development, but also for development in other spheres, such as economic development, political development, and so on, and these in turn are also constitutive parts of development as a whole'.[8] As one might expect, indicators of the quality of the rule of law are highest in members of the Organization for Economic Co-operation and Development, followed by east Asia. The lowest levels are in sub-Saharan Africa and the former Soviet Union – the last being a good indicator of the impact of central planning and the party-state regime over more than seventy years.[9]

A second public good the state needs, under present arrangements, to provide is *sound money*. Over the past three centuries, monetary systems have evolved dramatically. Initially, most money was still in metallic form;

subsequently, most money was in paper form, though still convertible into metal. Finally, in the twentieth century, money became purely government-created, or fiat money. At each stage new challenges have arisen.

A currency will be stable only if governments manage their debts sustainably or if the central bank is able to stand aside when the government is driven into default. Throughout history, sovereign defaults have been a leading cause of economic disruption, either because they undermine the currency, through some form of debasement or inflation, or because they destroy the solvency of financial institutions that lent to the government, or, more often, both.

This is both an old story and a new one. A recent example is the Argentine government's default at the end of 2001. Philip II of Spain brought a famous banking house, the Fuggers, to its knees by his debt repudiation of 1575.[10] William III created the Bank of England to manage the country's debts during its wars with France at the end of the seventeenth century. So successful was the English – later British – state in establishing sound finance that it was able to pay for long conflicts without defaulting, overtly or covertly (through debasement or inflation). Honest money, credit and public finance, together with taxes more or less honestly paid, were (along with the sea and the Royal Navy) the decisive advantages of Great Britain in a series of long wars against France in the eighteenth and early nineteenth centuries.[11] They were also central to the development of the British economy in the eighteenth and nineteenth centuries.

After the 1930s and the Great Depression, it was widely accepted that the government's responsibility for sound money and public finances came together in the obligation to fine-tune the macroeconomy. This was a development of the economics of John Maynard Keynes, in his *General Theory of Employment, Interest and Money*, published in 1936. After the stagflationary débâcle of the 1970s, this idea went out of fashion. Today, inflation-targeting and sustainable public finances are generally believed, among economists, to provide as much macroeconomic stability as is reasonably attainable. There is, however, a substantial debate over the responsibilities of central banks for reducing the amplitude of financial bubbles.

Other important examples of goods with public goods characteristics are *infrastructure* and *basic research*. Roads have, historically, been a salient example of infrastructure the state alone can provide. Road space is not a pure public good, since it is unquestionably rival in consumption: two cars cannot occupy the same space at the same time. But it has been hard to charge users sensibly, though modern technology may make wider use of road charging possible. Fundamental research is close to being a pure public good. Governments are important financiers, therefore, though charitable donations and corporate support are also likely to be forthcoming in a free society.

When government acts to internalize *externalities*, it is also providing public goods. Every advanced society has some form of planning regulation, to preserve environmental amenities. Similarly, every society has some form of control over pollution. These are cases in which what is rational for the transactors can lead to sizeable costs for innocent bystanders. As population densities grow, economic output increases and the world population becomes more urbanized, neighbourhood effects of this kind become more significant. These environmental spillovers can be local, national or global. Where they are global, environmental externalities also have to be internalized at the global level.

In addition to providing public goods, governments directly finance or provide certain *merit goods*. Such goods are consumed individually. But society insists on a certain level or type of provision. This may be either because these goods have public goods characteristics (my good health or education benefits others, for example, and vice versa), because a certain level of consumption is deemed a necessary condition for participation as a citizen, because of insufficient information about the nature of the goods or services in question, because a market failure makes it impossible to secure an adequate supply, or maybe for all of these reasons.

Obvious examples of merit goods are health and education, which are financed by governments everywhere. In the case of health, for example, it is impossible for the ordinary consumer to know what he or she needs. There are also important public goods aspects to health: your infectious disease is a threat to me. Similarly, it is hard to finance education, particularly basic education, against income that will accrue decades hence without some government assistance. For fundamental reasons of both equity and efficiency, governments end up financing education and health in every advanced society. But such finance does not imply that government needs to supply the service in question. It could buy health and education services from competing private sector suppliers and would probably do better if it did.

Governments implement *regulatory policies* for private enterprise. One important example is *competition policy*. Sometimes, governments also feel the need to create specific regulatory regimes for industries with monopoly power, such as water, electricity or telecommunications, because general competition policy is insufficiently effective. Sometimes the creation of a market is so complex that governments find themselves engaged directly in its design or act through independent agencies to achieve the same result. This has applied, in recent decades, to markets in electric power and to sales and use of the radio spectrum. The débâcle with Californian electricity deregulation, where wholesale prices shot up after liberalization, shows what happens when such designs go wrong. Governments are also responsible for policy levers with powerful economic effects, such as the structure and level of *barriers to trade or investment*. In addition, governments raise taxes and spend money to achieve their goals. *Taxation* and the pattern of *public procurement* have powerful effects on the operation of the private sector, especially on incentives for economic activity and competition among providers of the goods and services that governments buy.

Where there is difficulty in organizing private sector monitoring, where contracts are too long term to be effectively monitored or where governments feel obliged to protect people from themselves, governments often directly regulate economic activities. For reasons discussed in the previous chapter, financial sectors are particularly heavily regulated. Governments also increasingly find themselves regulating the health and safety of processes and products.

Markets generate a certain distribution of rewards. In response, political processes are likely to try *redistribution*. All advanced democracies redistribute income to some extent. Much of that redistribution is associated with the provision of *security* to individuals deemed unlucky or deserving in some way: the old, single parents, families with children, the disabled or the unemployed. In addition, most governments interfere in market processes directly to achieve what they consider, for some reason or another, more desirable outcomes: minimum wages and anti-discrimination legislation fall into this category.

Making interventions effective

The role of the state in a modern market economy is, in short, pervasive. The difference between poor countries and richer ones is not that the latter do less, but that what they do is better directed (on the whole) and more competently executed (again, on the whole). States have some functions they must perform: above all, protection of property and management of the government's own finances. States also have functions they must at present perform, such as the provision of sound money (though one could conceive of worlds in which this would be unnecessary). They have functions they feel compelled to perform by virtue of potential or actual market failure: the provision of infrastructure, basic research and merit goods; regulation of competition and of utilities with monopoly power; and internalization of externalities, particularly environmental externalities. Finally, they have functions they feel compelled to perform by pressure from their electorate: income redistribution, provision of security and action against discrimination.

While some of the state's activities are unquestionably essential, even well-run liberal democracies do far more than they can do well and almost certainly far more than they need to do.[12] There are strong pressures for governments to 'do something' where doing nothing might be far better. In any given area, government will hear only from those who want it to act. No politician or bureaucrat benefits from saying that he thinks it is better to leave ill alone, on the view that intervention is likely to make the position still worse. They also have their own interest in making concerned citizens dependent upon them.

Yet even if there is an agreement that states should act, this does not indicate how they should do so. For, as experience with state planning shows, governments are under big handicaps in designing interventions, even if their intentions are good. What then are the implications for good policy? They are mostly just common sense. Unfortunately, sense is far from common.

The first requirement of effective policy is a range of qualities that come under the headings of *credibility, predictability, transparency and consistency*, both over time and across activities. Private sector actors will not behave in the desired way if they do not know what is wanted. They must also know that they have no alternative. In other words, policy must be predictable and credible. If implementation is negotiable, the regulated industry will act in ways that makes persisting with the policy more difficult. In the process, it will make the policy more costly than it would otherwise be.

A good example of the value of credibility is trade liberalization. If business people know that a barrier to imports will disappear some years hence, they will adjust relatively smoothly. That will, in turn, reduce the economic costs for all concerned: workers will know that the industry is likely to contract and will, accordingly, seek other jobs; and investment will also go elsewhere. But suppose the policy change lacks credibility. Then it would be in the interest of businesses and workers not to make the adjustment, in the hope that the government will fail to do what it has promised. Because of the resistance to adjustment, the costs of implementing the policy become higher than they needed to be. So the government may, indeed, back off. In that case, the lack of credibility becomes self-fulfilling, with untoward consequences not just for credibility in this area, but more generally. Weak governments impose unnecessary costs.

This is one of the most important justifications for making binding international agreements to liberalize. By making policy more credible, they make adjustment more inescapable, and so reinforce credibility. Similar arguments apply to environmental policies.

The second set of requirements comes under the heading of *directness*. Assume that there is some identifiable market failure. Then the right policy is the one that is most directly targeted at that failure and does the minimal amount of collateral damage.

For this reason, as will be shown further below, a trade policy measure is unlikely to be the best way to deal with, for example, an environmental concern. Again, even if one accepts that agricultural policy should have economic, social, food quality and environmental objectives, it is inconceivable that a set of policies aimed at raising production through higher prices will be the best for meeting all these objectives. There is an excellent chance that one policy intended to hit three separate objectives will fail to hit any of them. The EU's common agricultural policy is a superb example of just this: it promotes economically costly production; it fails to preserve rural activities; it worsens food quality; and it inflicts damage on the environment.

Another example can be drawn from policies to reduce greenhouse-gas emissions. The least costly policy is one that makes the marginal cost of reducing greenhouse-gas emission the same in all economic activities. If that were not the situation, one could obtain more valuable output, with the same emissions, by increasing production (and emissions) where the marginal costs of reducing emissions are relatively high and vice versa. It follows that there should be no exemptions from a tax on emissions.

The third requirement is going with the *grain of incentives*. Policy should elicit the behaviour one wants, at least cost. This involves two layers of analysis. The first is that market incentives – ones that work through prices – are usually the most effective means. If one has the knowledge to decide on the right tax on an undesirable activity or right subsidy to a desirable one, such taxes or subsidies are almost always better policies than quantitative targets and commands. They are market-compatible measures.

The second and deeper level is to consider market failures the result of incomplete property rights. If that failure can be corrected, the market should generate the best possible response. Professor McMillan gives the example of tradable pollution licenses in the United States.[13] In the Clean Air Act of 1990, the Environmental Protection Agency created a market in tradable rights to pollute. It transpired that the degree of abatement desired was much less costly than people had expected. This was shown by the fact that the average market price for cleaning up a ton of sulphur dioxide turned out to be $150. The EPA had initially estimated that the cost would be five times as high.

Market failures need to be addressed if sufficiently serious. But this raises a fourth and final point: *remediability*. Remedies are costly. They need to be credibly better than the ailments. For government action to be justified, the world must be credibly better after the action than before it. In making that judgement, one must also take into account the inherent failures of government. As is argued further below, one must avoid what the economist Harold Demsetz once called 'the nirvana approach', a comparison between the actual market outcome and the ideal, but unattainable, alternative that might be produced by omniscient, benevolent and omnipotent government intervention.[14]

Why government fails

We know there are some things states cannot do – plan an entire economy. We know there are some things states must do – protect property rights. This is a 'must have' if there is to be a sophisticated market economy. There are also 'nice to haves'. Unfortunately, the mechanism of the state is at least as defective as that of the market. In fact, throughout most of history and in most countries today, it has been far more so. Governments do not only fail to provide 'nice to haves', they fail to provide 'must haves'. Often the most important violator of the conditions needed for markets to generate prosperity is government itself. It does not offer a remedy for market failures, but is a source of greater failures itself. This is not an accident. It is inherent in any political process, but it is truest, inevitably, in the poor countries that most need better government.

Flaws of good governments

Think of an advanced democracy, such as the United Kingdom or the United States. These have stable political regimes, entrenched civil and political rights, elections, a well-defined legal system, an independent judiciary and modest levels of corruption. States like these are, quite simply, the best in history. Some will say that Sweden, Switzerland or maybe France is even better. So they may be. But these distinctions are modest. The advanced economies of today have, as one might expect, the most sophisticated, responsive and law-abiding states ever.

For some observers, including critics of economic globalization, this is suffi-cient to establish the superiority of political processes over all others, above all the market. Professor Benjamin Barber has just such a romantic view of the democratic political process. '[T]he self-interested motives on the basis of which consumers spend their pennies have nothing to do with who runs anything, let alone with the kind of civil society these same consumers hope to live in or the civic objectives they forge together as citizens in democratic political arenas in order to control the public and political consequences of their private consumer choices.'[15] The first part of Barber's statement is nonsense. He should try to stay in business when nobody is prepared to buy what he wishes to sell. The statement about democracy is more serious. Indeed, it is fundamental to the debate on the global market economy. For Barber is unquestionably correct on his central point: governments are extremely important.

The difficulty lies in his description of the political process of a modern mass democracy as one in which citizens come together to forge common objectives. This is a naive account of how politics do – or can – work in a modern complex representative democracy. The United States of close to 300 million people with very divergent backgrounds, ways of life and experiences is not the world described by Aristotle in his discussion of the polis of Ancient Greece. Pericles' Athens is gone for ever (if, in fact, it ever existed).

What then are the problems? One is that modern governments are, like modern economies and societies themselves, enormously complicated. They rest, as today's world does, on an elaborate division of labour. The decisions they make are highly technical. It is impossible for an outside observer to observe, let alone sensibly judge, more than a tiny proportion of the decisions being made. This is a statement that I can make with some confidence, since doing precisely that has been my job since 1987 at the *Financial Times*.

Not only is it very difficult to know what is going on, but most citizens have no interest in doing so. They are 'rationally ignorant'.[16] What makes their ignorance rational is that the probability of their individually affecting a policy outcome is zero. So why would one expect them to invest prodigious efforts in analysing the options, even if it were in an area in which they have a chance of doing so? Consequently, the majority of voters also have no basis on which to form a rational view of genetically modified foods, to take one contemporary example.

Three (overlapping) classes of people are relatively well informed: first, people who are paid to be, such as newspaper columnists, academic experts in a relevant field, bureaucrats and politicians; second, people whose livelihood depends on specific political decisions, such as doctors on health policies, teachers on education policy, farmers on agricultural policy, steel workers on trade policy, corporations on policy towards intellectual property, and so forth; and, finally, people who find a specific area of policy of absorbing interest. The first group tends to the cynical, the second to the self-interested, and the last to the fanatical. There is no reason to expect what emerges from this process to be a reflection of anything one could reasonably call the common interest. Not only is influence on the process extremely unequal, but it is also vitiated by the very partial nature of the influences at work. One person, one vote looks more egalitarian than the widely divergent wealth that influences a market. Wealth always brings disproportionate political influence, not just greater purchasing power. But there are others who also wield disproportionate political influence, above all, people who specialize in being opinion formers.[17] It is not an accident that opinion formers are, in general, strongly in favour of more politics and fewer markets.

In elections, one votes for a candidate or party that makes some broad promises over a long list of issues. One does not expect many of these to be implemented even if one's candidate or party wins – and often one is not disappointed in these expectations. So far as most voters are concerned, that is the end of the matter. Then, in the period between elections, policy is made in a hugger-mugger of special-interest lobbies, self-proclaimed 'public-interest' groups, journalists, assorted experts, bureaucrats, politicians, particularly more influential ones, and anybody else with a big enough axe to grind.

Most people would accept that those with economic interests are far from objective pursuers of the common weal. But what about some of the other actors in this play? One might hope that Greenpeace, Oxfam and the rest are impartial and disinterested. But many non-governmental organizations are heavily dependent on public funding. Others depend for fund-raising on the more or less plausible manufacture of photogenic crises. Again, bureaucrats are supposed to represent a broad public interest. But they too have interests, most important of which are to stay in business. It is no surprise to discover that the direction of public spending in every advanced country has been consistently upwards as a share of GDP over the last century.[18] Only economic collapse is likely to reverse this trend.

Advanced democracies do at least a tolerable job of providing the things needed for such a society and economy to function. But much of the detail of policy is horrendously bad. Institutions capable of the farm policies of today cannot be defined in the terms that Barber attempts to employ. The same is true of most trade policy, much environmental policy, the treatment of risk across different activities, energy policy, labour market policy in much of continental Europe and so on and so forth. Government is essential. Of that there is no doubt. But to rely on it to do a sensible job of remedying so-called market failures when it busily introduces so many failures of its own is absurd.

Catastrophe of bad governments

Yet the advanced representative democracies are impressive governmental systems by both contemporary and historical standards. If one raises one's eyes and looks at the rest of the world or at the history of the last century, one sees corrupt, incompetent, brutal and, depressingly often, murderous governments everywhere. A big part of the history of the twentieth century is a story of the crimes inflicted by those in power upon innocent people.

Alas, this era of mal-government is not over. Consider Rwanda or Serbia in the early 1990s. Look at Russia's brutality in Chechnya, at Burma's soldier-thugs, at the Taliban's brutal and regressive Afghanistan, or at Saddam Hussein's Iraq. Look, too, at the kleptocrats: Mobutu Sese Seko in the former Zaire, the Suharto family in Indonesia or Robert Mugabe in Zimbabwe.[19] War, civil war, massacre, political instability, autocracy, state failure, public sector profligacy, constant interference in markets, default, inflation and corruption have been salient features of the developing world over the last half-century. The notion that one can rely on governments, particularly in the developing world, to make an honest and disinterested effort to protect property, provide other public and merit goods and so raise national economic welfare, is mostly laughable. In the 1990s, at last, even the World Bank admitted the seriousness of bad government as a constraint on development. Indeed, that is probably the most important development of the era of James Wolfensohn as the World Bank's president.

Consider, for a moment, just the more obvious policy failures. As William Easterly, formerly at the World Bank, points out, a recurrent feature of the developing world has been high black-market premia on exchange rates. These are a symptom of suppressed inflation. Governments have attempted to finance public spending through the monetary printing press (thus violating a fundamental public goods function of the state). This creates inflationary pressure, which is partially suppressed through an artificially fixed exchange rate. But the pressure emerges in rising domestic prices of non-tradable goods and services and declining competitiveness of exports (which may well shrink). The balance of payments worsens and citizens desperately try to get their money out. Thus emerges the black market. But this black market is not merely economically damaging. It is corrupting. There is an overwhelming temptation to buy domestic currency at the black-market rate rather than the official one. As Easterly notes, premia can reach insane levels: 'Ghana had a world-record 4,264 per cent black market premium in 1982 and had consistently had the premium above 40 per cent for eighteen of the previous twenty years.'[20]

Take a look at Mexico: between 1970 and 1982, two bad presidents destroyed the country's proud record of macroeconomic stability in the name of helping the poor. In 1976, a crisis forced a devaluation and a sharp slowdown in growth. Then came oil. But President López Portillo managed to waste even this surge in wealth. The country devalued again in 1982 and defaulted, triggering the Latin American debt crisis. Then painful reforms began, but the government failed to regulate the banking sector (another fundamental government role in an insured banking system). This led to a third foreign exchange crisis in two decades, in 1994–5.[21]

Fiscal, monetary and financial policies have certainly not been the only areas of government failure. Government monopolies have repeatedly failed to provide reliable electricity, telephone services, water, education or health services. 'In Nigeria, the government has failed almost completely to provide basic services, despite $280 bn in government oil revenues since the discovery of reserves in the late 1950s. The government has preferred to spend its money instead on things like the $8 bn steel complex that has yet to produce a bar of steel and a new national capital built from scratch, not to mention the breath-taking amount of money stolen by the rulers.'[22] In many developing countries, it has been easy to find examples of negative value-added production – enterprises whose inputs were worth more than their outputs – because of the enormous protection given to final products in the name of self-sufficiency and infant-industry development. Then consider India's public spending. A meticulous analysis by the National Council for Applied Economic Research concluded that 10 per cent of GDP – roughly 40 per cent of all public spending – went on subsidies for power, water and food to relatively prosperous people. Meanwhile, the national average literacy rate was only 57 per cent in 2002.[23]

There is also pervasive corruption. Hernando De Soto, the Peruvian economist, once registered a small clothing factory in Lima as an experiment. It took ten months. In that time, he was asked for bribes ten times by government officials. On two occasions, he had to pay them, since the experiment would otherwise have ground to a halt.[24] Remember what corruption means: it is the abuse of a position of public trust for personal gain. How can a state rife with such corruption provide what the market needs to achieve prosperity? The answer, of course, is that it cannot do so.

Corruption exists everywhere. But it is far worse in poor countries than in rich ones. Transparency International has a well-known index with a scale of zero to ten that rates corruption by the perceptions of those affected. Among advanced countries, almost all were above seven in 2001, with Denmark top on 9.5. The lowest among the advanced liberal democracies were France (6.7), Belgium (6.6) and Italy (5.5). At or below two were Bangladesh (0.4), Nigeria (1.0), Uganda (1.9), Indonesia (1.9), Bolivia (2.0), Kenya (2.0) and Cameroon (2.0). Meanwhile, Russia and Pakistan were on 2.3, India on 2.7, China on 3.5, Brazil on 4.0.[25]

There is, as one might expect, strong evidence that corruption impairs economic growth. Nobody wants to invest or do the other growth-promoting things discussed in Chapters 2 and 3 in a highly corrupt country.[26] Yet all corruption is not equal in its effects. Analysts distinguish centralized from decentralized corruption. Under centralized corruption, one person determines the size of the take. Call this Suharto's Indonesia. Under decentralized corruption, officials and politicians compete for the take. Call this India.

Centralized corruption should be less damaging, provided the ruler is enlightened. It is against the ruler's interests to let the rate of 'taxation' imposed by corruption become too high. But, under competing decentralized corruption, it is a case of grab while you can. Such destructive competition for loot can create an economic implosion, as in Nigeria. Government is a natural monopoly for good reason. Competing bandits are bad news.

A significant subset of such corruption is state capture by private interests.[27] An important example of this was the role of the so-called 'oligarchs' in Boris Yeltsin's Russia. Where the economic élite is competing for favours, the impact will be to corrupt policy-makers and bureaucracy. Vladimir Putin told Russia's business leaders in 2000 that 'you have yourselves formed this very state, to a large extent through political and quasi-political structures under your control, so perhaps what one should do least of all is blame the mirror'.[28] The economic effects of such capture are powerfully negative, since this élite is interested in favours for itself and not in an impartial rule of law. Only a wide business community of competing producers has an interest in the rule of law. But such a community is difficult to organize politically.

A society in which it is deemed normal for judges, bureaucrats or politicians to accept bribes creates a trap for those trying to achieve reform. In a society in which everyone cheats and takes or pays bribes, there is little incentive not to join in. It is rational for each individual to participate in this destructive game and, given the prevalence of such misbehaviour, little incentive for anybody to cease doing so, since the chances of being caught and punished are small. In a society in which cheating and bribery are rare, however, there is far less incentive to act dishonestly, since there is a far greater chance of being caught and punished as well as of obtaining what one wants honestly. Moving from the first sort of society to the second is difficult, however.

Conclusion

Good markets need good governments. This is just as true of global as of purely domestic markets, if not more so. Indeed the former grow out of the latter, as will be shown in the next chapter. Unfortunately, good governments are not easy to find. Even in advanced liberal democracies, where governments work relatively well, political and bureaucratic processes are as flawed as markets, if not far more so. In general, it is a case of balancing defective markets against defective political processes. In developing countries, however, governments are generally still worse. Many governments are grossly incompetent, corrupt, or both. This is both a cause and a consequence of poor policy performance. Decentralized, competitive corruption, including state capture by corrupt private interests, is particularly damaging. Improvements will not occur unless and until these constraints are at least partially lifted. One important way of doing so, it happily turns out, is to open up economies to global competitive forces.

How to reform the state

Even good and relatively uncorrupt governments are highly imperfect, by their nature. But they are also absolutely essential. So a central question is how to obtain the best governments one can. The answer to this question can be divided into two parts: internal reform and regulatory competition.

Internal reform

Reforms in the governance of the advanced liberal democracies have been designed to make them more effective. An important element in those reforms has been the mirror image of the observation above that good markets need good governments. Good governments also need good markets. More precisely, the more the government focuses on its essential tasks and the less it is engaged in economic activity and regulation, the better it is likely to work and the better the economy itself is likely to run. Good markets protect governments, just as good governments protect markets. They have a symbiotic relationship.

This is an important part of the argument for privatization. In the case of ordinary productive enterprizes, nationalization tended to mean political interference and waste, but also a diversion of attention and effort by governments. In the case of utilities, privatization allowed the creation of a far more transparent and rule-governed regime than that in place beforehand. Again, this has important economic benefits. But it also improves the quality of regulation. It is almost impossible to be both a producer and a regulator at the same time. The two activities are inherently different.

All this is important and valuable everywhere. But in the developing world much more needs to be done. A start has to be made by reducing the opportunities for corruption. Critics of the market and of global economic integration seem to be entirely unaware that a control, regulation or restriction creates an opportunity for corruption. Wherever there is a gap between the market value of something and an official price or the price government is prepared to allow, there is an incentive to cheat and to bribe. If the black-market price of foreign currency is twice the official rate, people will bribe officials to let them sell on the black market. Similarly, if imports of certain much desired commodities are restricted or under a very high tariff, business people will bribe officials to let them take the commodities in or evade the tariff. Again, if one needs a large number of bureaucratic permissions to do something in business, the officials have an opportunity to demand bribes. But there is worse: once it is known that a government is prepared to create such exceptional opportunities, there will be lobbying to create them. Then there is not just the corruption of the government, but the waste of resources in such 'rent-seeking' or 'directly unproductive profit-seeking activities'.[29]

In the early 1970s I worked on Kenya when the import-control regime was coming into place. I watched it corrupt the civil service in front of my eyes. Then in the mid-1970s I worked for the World Bank on India. The corrupting import-control regime operated for so long by its government went back to the late years of the British Raj. But, unlike in Britain, the restrictions were never liberalized after the Second World War. On the contrary, a twisted ingenuity went into elaborating the regime. Progressively, these and similar regulations in other areas corrupted the public administration. If the control regime of 1945 had remained in place for a further forty-five years, how far would the British civil service have remained non-corrupt? Not that far, would be my guess.

Regulatory competition

Predation is lucrative and attractive. Historically, the most important constraint has been external regulatory competition as much as internal pressure. Too often it is only when states fall far behind their competitors, when every enterprising person tries to leave, when capital goes enthusiastically anywhere else, when default threatens and capital outflow becomes a flood that governments are driven to reform. Such competition for people, capital and the development and application of ideas was, as argued in Chapter 3, a crucial element in the explanation for the rise of Europe.

Governments are natural monopolies over a given territory. Competitive government over a given territory means civil war. But we know that monopolies tend to become exploitative, oppressive, slothful and indifferent.[30] So one of the strongest arguments for an open economy is that it puts a degree of competitive pressure on government. If one believes governments are always benevolent, wise and caring, one may well object to that pressure. But the great irony of the anti-globalization critics is that most of them believe in none of those things. They are then in the paradoxical situation of wanting governments to intervene more, which will create corruption, and to close off markets, which will relieve bad governments of competitive pressure, while expecting governments to become more devoted to the weal of the mass of the public. Yet both theory and experience show that the more interventionist the state and the more closed the economy, the more likely the government is to be captured by powerful interests. To be illiberal and opposed to state-capture by special interests, including corrupt politicians, is incoherent.

Conclusion – your humble public servant

Good government is essential. It is a good in itself and essential for the working of a sophisticated market economy, which is, in its turn, the cradle of prosperity and freedom. There is a symbiosis between the market and the state. But it is a subtle one. The role of government is to be a humble and honest servant. How many humble and honest governments can we find? Not enough, is the answer. That matters in all circumstances. But, as we shall see in subsequent chapters, this is even more important when markets cross borders. Bad governments are a huge obstacle to gaining the benefits of economic integration across borders. Indeed, they are the most important obstacle of all.

Chapter 6 **The Market Crosses Borders**

> *What is prudence in the conduct of every family can scarce be folly in that of a great kingdom. If a foreign country can supply us with a commodity cheaper than we ourselves can make it, better buy it of them with some part of the produce of our own industry, employed in a way in which we have some advantage.*
>
> Adam Smith.[1]

I perform a specialized function – commentary on the world economy – within the global division of labour. I work for a publication that sells more than three-fifths of its copies outside what was once its home market. These copies are published on the same day in some twenty different places around the world. It is also possible to subscribe to the Internet version of the newspaper. Moreover, my personal transactions do not stop at the seas surrounding Britain. I am not limited to British cameras, computers and vegetables or to sightseeing and investing only in Britain. I, as is true of the *FT* itself, am part of an internationally integrated economy. Here then are two realities of the contemporary marketplace: it crosses borders, ably assisted by modern technology; and it allows people to perform specialized functions.

Behind these realities is a more important one: I make my transactions because, given my resources and opportunities, I expect to benefit from them. As Adam Smith said more than two centuries ago, what is beneficial *within* a country is also beneficial *for* a country. People buy and sell with residents of their country because they expect to be made better off. They buy and sell with non-residents for the same reason.

When the statisticians add up transactions with non-residents, they call these a country's external transactions. But these are not a country's transactions, except statistically. Other than where a government is directly involved, a country's transactions are the aggregate of individual transactions by its residents. Moreover, because the motivation for such transactions is the same as for transactions with fellow residents, they are just as likely to contribute to the welfare of those who undertake them. This, in a nutshell, is the logic of global economic integration.

Yet there are also some important differences between transactions within jurisdictions and transactions across them. These differences fall under three categories: economic, jurisdictional and values.

The *economic* difference is that there are special obstacles – legal and non-legal – to activities that cross frontiers. Borders matter. Countries do not normally transact, but governments regulate transactions. Without exception, they regulate transactions between residents and non-residents differently from how they regulate transactions among residents. But policy and practice vary all the way from total prohibition (North Korea) to almost total freedom (Hong Kong).

The *political* difference is that more than one legal jurisdiction is unavoidably affected when transactions cross borders. Consequently, such transactions create an inescapable challenge – that of multiple jurisdictions.

The *value* difference is that economic analysis and political discourse generally proceed as if the welfare of foreigners or non-residents counts for nothing. It is one of the ironies of current debate that critics of globalization, who tend to present themselves as cosmopolitan, include many who take this assumption to extremes. But the assumption is not implausible: actual political institutions behave as if the welfare of foreigners counted for far less than those of nationals and residents.

Behind these differences between domestic and international transactions is one of the most obvious facts about the world: markets want to be cosmo-politan; states do not.[2] Technology permitting, a market for mutually enriching exchange will span the globe, because people will want to buy at the cheapest price (for any given quality) and sell at the highest. Jurisdictions, however, are territorial. Yet markets, as we have seen in Chapters 3, 4 and 5 above, are dependent on states, since states alone provide the legal order and regulatory structure they require. Some people, it is true, suggest that there are alternative ways of providing these conditions for productive commerce – through the active involvement of non-governmental organizations or through transnational institutions. But, significant though these new actors may become, they cannot replace states as repositories of power and authority.[3] This conflict between the natural tendency of markets to cross borders and the need for the states that define those borders to support markets is at the heart of all the challenges created by a global economy.

The world is not merely divided into states. It is divided into unequal ones. The richest country (the United States) has a real income per head seventy times that of the poorest (Sierra Leone). The biggest country (China) has a population of 1.26 billion, while the World Bank's latest World Development Indicators lists nineteen independent and semi-independent economies with populations of fewer than 100,000. The dollar purchasing power of the biggest economy (the United States) is 36,000 times bigger than that of St Kitts and Nevis. The reality of the world is one of states with very different standards of living, technological sophistication, populations and economic size. Only the United States is a heavyweight on all these scales.

Yet the difference in scale is not that fundamental. The contrast between Finland and the United States is trivial compared to the gap between both and, say, Nigeria or Pakistan. The first two are, by historical standards, effective and powerful states: the latter are defective in almost all significant respects. Alas, many of the world's states are incapable of providing the basic require-ments of a civilized existence, let alone of a dynamic market economy. Inevitably, given the role of the state in supporting the market, theirs are also the countries that neither develop successfully nor play a significant role in the world economy. Outsiders will not contract with people who live in countries that lack the rule of law and at least a basic infrastructure. Ultimately, the inequality in the capacities of states makes for black holes in the world economy, countries from which little but desperate people and capital flight emerge.

Economics of integration

Economic transactions involve goods and services and what economists call 'factors of production' – labour, capital and land. By assumption, land cannot move. It is bound in space and, accordingly, provides a definition of a terri-torial state. But goods, services, labour and capital can and do move. So do people, as purchasers of goods and services in other countries, usually as tourists. What makes the notion of a country real economically is restrictions on the movement of one or more of these across frontiers. Today, virtually all countries have some restrictions on cross-border movement of goods and services. Restrictions on movements of people as tourists vary, with controls imposed by both sending and receiving countries. Restrictions on capital movement also vary. The advanced countries generally have no restrictions on movement of portfolio capital, but restrictions on foreign direct investment – ownership regulations, for example – as well as subsidies to inward investment remain. Restrictions on movement of labour are pervasive.

This makes the obvious point that liberalization is not an all-or-nothing proposition. Conceptually, it is possible to combine restrictions on trade and movement of capital and labour in eight different ways. At least five of these combinations have existed. The United Kingdom of the nineteenth century was close to freedom on all three dimensions. Within the European Union of today, all three are again free, in principle. Most developing countries were, until recently, highly restrictive on all three. Many still are. The Hong Kong of today has free trade and free movement of capital, but tight restrictions on movement of people, especially from China. The United States of the nineteenth century had restrictive trade policies, but movement of capital and labour was almost completely free. There are costs to any restrictions, in terms of freedom of choice, the emergence of black markets and corruption, and their effectiveness. But various combinations are certainly possible.

Trade[4]

Any analysis of trade starts from the assumption that movement of capital and labour is prevented. A country is a jurisdiction with a circumscribed pool of labour, capital and land. The argument for trade is that it increases opportunities for owners of these factors of production to engage in mutually beneficial transactions. It is an extension across frontiers of the division of labour. We need merely ask what our standard of living would be if we had to grow our own food, make our own clothes and shoes, build our own houses, make our own furniture, write our own books and newspapers, build our own vehicles or be our own doctors and dentists. But opportunities for the division of labour do not cease within a single national jurisdiction.

As Douglas Irwin of Dartmouth University argues, John Stuart Mill, one of the intellectual giants of the nineteenth century, divided the gains from trade into three categories. These were direct advantages, indirect advantages and intellectual and moral advantages.[5]

In the first category come the standard static gains from trade – exploitation of economies of scale and comparative advantage. David Ricardo propounded the latter idea, perhaps the cleverest in economics. The Nobel-laureate Paul Samuelson was once asked to name 'one proposition in all of the social sciences which is both true and non-trivial'.[6] His answer was comparative advantage. It is true and cannot be trivial, because author after author fails to understand the theory's most powerful implication.[7] Specialization makes sense, argued Ricardo, even if one country is more efficient at everything than its trading partners. Countries should specialize at what they are *relatively* most efficient at doing. Countries do not compete in trade, as companies do.[8] Rather, industries compete inside countries for the services of factors of production. Opening a country to trade moves output in the direction of activities that offer domestic factors of production the highest returns. The shrinking import-competing industry is not competing with imports from foreigners, but with what its own domestic export industry can pay.

Trade in accordance with comparative advantage is similar to a productivity increase. Instead of making a particular good, an economy can obtain more of it, indirectly, by exporting something else. These gains can be large. A classic example was the opening of Japan in 1858, under American pressure. Before opening, the prices of silk and tea were much higher in the world than in Japan, while the prices of cotton and woollen goods were far lower. After opening, Japan exported silk and tea and imported cotton and woollen goods. This is estimated to have increased Japan's real income by 65 per cent without considering the long-run productivity and growth impact of its joining the world economy.[9]

In the second indirect category come the dynamic gains from trade. Trade promotes competition and productivity growth. Companies innovate in response to competitive pressure. Widening the market to include more competitors increases this pressure.

Trade is also a conduit for foreign technology, via imports of capital and intermediate goods that embody significant innovations. Professor Irwin observes that even in the United States between a quarter and a half of growth in so-called 'total factor productivity', the part of productivity growth not explained by capital accumulation and improved skills, is attributable to new technology embodied in capital equipment. No developing country would have access to the world's advanced technologies without trade. This, as I discovered when I worked on India in the 1970s, was one of the reasons why its productivity growth was so low, even though it was operating far below the level of the world's best practice. Its imports were too restricted by the government to allow producers access to the world's best machinery.

It is virtually impossible to prove the correlation between trade liberalization and growth, beyond doubt. But as Professors Peter Lindert of the University of California, Davis and Jeffrey Williamson of Harvard state, there are *no* examples of countries that have risen in the ranks of global living standards while being less open to trade and capital in the 1990s than in the 1960s. 'There are', they continue, 'no anti-global victories to report for the postwar' developing world.[10] As one Indian observer has remarked of his own country's policies, 'by suppressing economic liberty for forty years, we destroyed growth and the future of two generations'.[11]

The third set of benefits are, claimed Mill, intellectual and moral. To the extent that trade facilitates growth, for example, as it has done in the most successful post-war developing countries, it has made a powerful contribution to the arrival of democracy. One of the most encouraging developments of the past two decades is that South Korea, Taiwan and Chile, all of which began their rapid outward-looking development under dictatorships, have now become stable and vibrant democracies. Even in China, market reforms, including trade liberalization, have brought an enormous reduction in the repressiveness of the political regime, compared to its totalitarian apogee under a Maoist dictatorship much admired by western leftists.

The bottom line then is that liberal trade is beneficial. The obstacles to it, largely created by governments, need to be reduced.

Capital

Recently, people have tended to argue for capital controls on the view that capital mobility has proved problematic for national economic management.[12] Against this should be set the strong arguments in favour of capital mobility. The most important of these is personal freedom. Controlling the ability of people to export their capital has been among the first steps of despotic or economically destructive regimes. It also imposes a constraint on the malfeasance of governments, particularly on the overt or covert theft of their people's savings or the all-too-frequent abuse of the financial system. From this point of view, freedom of movement of capital is even more important than that to buy and sell goods.

There are also efficiency reasons for being in favour of capital mobility, which allows shifting of consumption between periods, higher returns and risk-spreading. In particular, countries with surplus savings (such as today's Japan) or companies with a large stock of valuable knowledge (such as many of today's leading multinational companies) should be able to deploy what they own abroad, to mutual advantage. Placing a part of one's capital abroad is also a way to diversify risks. Since one is always heavily exposed to the country one lives and works in, it makes sense to diversify that risk away. Thus the suppliers and recipients of finance should both gain.[13]

Capital mobility also changes the analysis of trade, which is usually based on the assumption that capital and labour are immobile. But, as Ronald Jones of the University of Rochester has written:

> the idea of comparative advantage is linked to the notion that inputs are trapped by national boundaries, so that the only decision that needs to be made concerns the allocation *within* the country of these inputs. Ricardian theory stressed that a comparison of absolute productivities of such inputs between countries had no bearing on the allocation issue or on subsequent patterns of international trade. Instead, it was the *comparative* advantage of these inputs among sectors that matters. . . . However, once any input has the choice of country location, . . . [t]he doctrine of comparative advantage, with its emphasis on the question of what a factor *does* within the country, needs to share pride of place with the doctrine of absolute advantage guiding the question of where an internationally mobile factor *goes*.[14]

This is an important point. If capital moved freely to equalize expected returns across the world, only the relative abundance and productivity of human and natural resources would determine the pattern of trade. This is indeed one of the fears of many critics of globalization.

At present, however, this qualification to theory seems far less important than one might expect (and, with the welfare of poor countries at heart, also hope). As will be discussed further below (Chapter 8), the investible resources of the world are locked into already rich countries, with much the largest cross-border flow to the United States from other rich countries (especially Japan). Movement of capital from rich countries to poorer ones has been not only modest, but crisis-prone.[15] In 2000, for example, the gross dollar savings of the high-income developed countries were $5,600 billion. If a mere 10 per cent of these gross savings were to flow to the developing world, this would amount to $560 billion a year. But the highest net flow of long-term capital to developing countries in the 1990s was only $341 billion in 1997, just before the Asian crisis.[16] More than a decade ago, the Nobel-laureate Robert Lucas noted this low level of capital flow to developing countries, which is contrary to standard assumptions about where returns would be highest.[17]

Again, the multinational companies possess vast knowledge and experience in virtually every area of economic activity. In particular, as was asserted in Chapter 4, it is inside these institutions that much of the economically useful knowledge of the advanced countries is developed, retained and applied. It is in the interests of countries around the world, but especially of developing countries, to gain access to that knowledge via foreign direct investment. Now, many developing countries recognize that foreign direct investment brings benefits that foreign borrowing does not. The direct investor is locked in and cannot flee the country whenever trouble strikes. If investors make reasonable profits, they will consider themselves long-term participants in the host country's economy and often bring in more capital. Last and most important, direct investment brings substantial additional benefits that spill over into the domestic economy, including transfer of technology and managerial skills.[18] In many developing countries, multinational corporations have been the most important way to train nationals in modern management and technology. Some of these benefits, notably the last, are not restricted to developing country recipients. Ireland and the United Kingdom are two relatively advanced economies to have gained hugely from inward direct investment.[19]

One explanation for the modest flows of capital to developing countries is the shortage of complementary human skills. Another explanation would be external economies in the use of that capital: people are more productive if they work with other productive people. But it is also important to remember the discussion of financial fragility in Chapter 4. Difficulties exist within any financial system, because of asymmetric information, problems in foretelling the future, self-fulfilling panics and herd behaviour. But when funds cross borders, these vulnerabilities become still greater.[20]

In emerging market economies, difficulties over the design of the exchange rate and monetary regimes interact with the fragility of financial arrangements, to create a host of obstacles to stable and sizeable capital flows. First, ignorance of financial and economic conditions in foreign countries is greater than at home. This applies particularly to emerging-market economies. Second, confidence in the probity of the governments and legal systems of countries abroad is low. Third, important elements of the legal and regulatory systems malfunction or do not exist. Fourth, banking institutions often have comprehensive guarantees, while being used by governments or owners for their own purposes, which makes them fundamentally unsound.[21] Fifth, financial and accounting information is often lacking altogether, or is totally unreliable. Sixth, foreigners may expect to be discriminated against during a financial crisis, especially when the state or well-connected domestic interest is insolvent. Seventh, the government may have a long history of financial profligacy and default and so a poor reputation. Finally, when there is cross-border lending in a currency other than the borrower's, which is normal in lending to emerging markets, there is the additional foreign currency risk. All these problems are relatively small if, say, American banks lend in the United Kingdom. They are large if they lend to, say, Argentina. Their net effect is to make finance expensive, small in size and, worst of all, unstable.

The low level of foreign direct investment in many emerging market economies is explained by not dissimilar factors. Confidence in the probity and effectiveness of the governmental and legal systems is often very low. The economy is likely to be unstable, as may be the politics. The risk of national-ization or some other form of expropriation may well loom. The market may be modest in size, while the inputs needed to use the country as an export platform could well be lacking. It is not surprising, for all these reasons, that foreign direct investment in Africa is so low, to take just one example. It is also unsurprising that the profit requirements on investments there are so high.

Yet none of these difficulties, real though they are, is sufficient reason for giving up on the aim of greater net capital flows to poorer countries. These should be treated as constraints to be lifted, not ones to be accepted. For if they are treated as binding and reinforced with capital controls, the world's poorest people will find it still more difficult to escape their plight.

People and geography

Traditional economic theory suggests that if trade is free and, still more, if capital flows freely, people should not need to move to gain higher incomes. Trade and capital mobility should equalize returns to labour across the world. Unfortunately, the assumptions underlying these orthodox models have turned out to be very far from true. We see the surplus capital of some rich countries pouring into the richest country in the world. In terms of purchasing power, a bus driver in Germany receives thirteen times one in Kenya, though his skills are much the same.[22] Workers with given skills earn vastly more in rich countries than in poor ones. Yet the rich countries that pay these higher wages for the same skills do not offer lower returns on capital than poor ones. If anything, the reverse is the case. Apparently capital-scarce countries have dismally low returns on capital, while apparently capital-abundant ones offer high returns. Similarly, free trade does not equalize wages, because productive efficiency diverges immensely across countries.

This paradoxical situation has two powerful – and disturbing – implica-tions. The first is that the simplest thing we can do to alleviate mass human poverty is to allow people to move freely or their labour services to be traded freely, though perhaps temporarily. This is not a cause critics of globalization have embraced. That is not surprising, since it would kill support for their cause in high-income countries. Yet the US could fit in another billion people. There is even much empty space in Europe, too. This is not a recommendation. It is an observation of human hypocrisy.

The second implication is that there is no end of geography. Geography combined with jurisdiction matters more today than ever before in history. The quality of one's life depends even more on where one is born than on the class into which one is born. This means, in turn, that free trade and capital movement, albeit beneficial, will not, on their own, equalize global incomes. The big question then is why the productive possibilities of different jurisdictions differ to such an extent. Beyond the financial failings already mentioned above, there are three additional reasons.

The first is that richer countries can invest far more in the skills of their people. A large supply of human skills not only raises returns to capital and unskilled labour, but allows all productive processes to be run more efficiently, for it is the skilled who understand how things need to be done.

The second reason is that there are increasing returns to activities in specific locations.[23] Agglomerations of skill raise returns on all those skills. But skill also begets knowledge, which begets more knowledge, which then begets more skill. These increasing returns are location specific. We are indeed social animals: our incomes depend on the skills of those around us.

The last reason is that different jurisdictions differ in their ability to offer the requirements of productive market activity – property-rights protection, an honest and effective bureaucracy, judicial independence, good-quality infrastructure, decent health and education services, and so forth.[24] This is the hand of history at work: some places may have started from a poor resource endowment or geographical isolation; they may then have suffered predatory forms of colonization; they may be afflicted by cultural handicaps; and they may have made serious policy errors.[25] Quite possibly, they may have experienced all these things. This unhappy past may then have cumulated over time into a vicious circle of poor government, low growth, low skill formation and so back to poor growth.

The notion of such poverty traps can be overdone. Few imagined four decades ago that South Korea would be among the most successful developing countries. But history matters and so, therefore, does geography.

This is not the end of the story of human mobility. Assume the increasing-returns story is right. Then skilled people in poor countries will earn less than they could in rich ones. They will want to move and, given their skills, may well be allowed to do so. Assume also that skilled people raise the wages of the unskilled where they live. Then free movement of skilled people from poor countries benefits rich countries and the skilled migrants, but harms the poor they leave behind. This is a reverse-aid programme. It is also one in which the rich countries are deeply engaged at present. The British National Health Service, for example, could not function without imports of skilled staff from developing countries.

Getting policy right

The ability of a country to take advantage of opportunities offered by inter-national economic integration depends on the quality of the state and the policies it follows. What is necessary for a well-functioning domestic economy is just as necessary, if not more so, for a smooth engagement with international commerce. Indeed, they must be the same, since commerce is commerce, regardless of whom it is with. If anything, these conditions are more important for transactions with foreigners, since they always have more alternatives.

The second important policy conclusion is that, in keeping with the principles of good policy outlined in the previous chapter, the best interven-tions are direct ones. This is why modern trade theory insists that the case for free trade is stronger than that for *laissez-faire*. The reason for this is that market failures are nearly, though not always, domestic in origin. The best policy is one targeted directly at that failure.[26]

Consider, for example, one of the best-known arguments for protection – the infant-industry argument. The argument for infant-industry protection is that there is learning-by-doing or other network benefits that are not captured by a company, but benefit an entire industry. If these benefits are large, a potentially profitable industry may never even be started. This, it is argued, is a justification for protecting the nascent industry from foreign competition. But protection is an indirect and ineffective policy for promoting infants. Apart from the cost it imposes on consumers, it has two other seriously negative side-effects: first, it limits the new industry to the domestic market, since protection, by definition, raises returns only on domestic sales; and, second, it provides protection from the world's most potent competitors. The first limitation may not matter much for countries with relatively big and rapidly growing domestic markets (such as the United States in the nineteenth century), but it is significant for most developing countries, which have tiny markets: Nigeria's dollar purchasing power in 2000 was less than a tenth of London's. The second limitation means that, protected from effective competition, the infants almost always fail to grow up.[27]

Is an intervention at the border ever the most direct one? The answer is yes. National security is a reason for such protection. A country also has the right to decide who lives within its borders. One might describe this as a country's defining right. That is also why controls on the movement of people across borders are universal. There are also arguments for imposing either tariffs on imports or taxes on exports where a country has monopoly power in trade. In this way, a country can drive down the prices of its imports or raise the prices of its exports. The strategic trade policy literature of the 1980s and 1990s, which examined trade policy for oligopolistic industries, was a more sophisticated application of the same basic notion. But the underlying idea of exploiting foreigners is disturbing. There are also big problems with applying strategic trade policy: knowledge of the degree and sustainability of monopoly power is quite limited; results of strategic trade policy models are also extraordinarily unstable; and governments can be 'gamed' by the companies to obtain undeserved and costly protection.

The conclusion then is that the principle of directness rules out almost all use of trade policy as a way of dealing with defects in the domestic economy. Similarly, the same principle makes controls on financial transactions with foreigners generally undesirable, since most (though not quite all) of the problems that arise in financial markets reflect failures that are just as relevant for the domestic economy. But directness does justify control on the movement of people at the border.

The third important policy objective is to be wary of costly interactions among policies. Among the most important is the danger of attracting inward direct investment by offering protection. Think of a simple example of a car company that is enticed by protection against imports into setting up an assembly plant that uses completely knocked down kits. It is perfectly possible for the foreign currency cost of each kit to be the same as a complete car. Then the profit that is exported comes from a tax on domestic consumers, as does the bill for wages and other raw materials. The foreign currency balance of the country is now worse than before, since the kits cost the same as cars used to do, but it expatriates profits as well. This is not an imaginary example. It is an often repeated case of stupidity, justified on infant-industry grounds.

Conclusion

Trade in goods and services is helpful for the performance of the economy. More trade in capital would help as well, particularly greater direct investment in poor countries. But there is too little of it, while flows of debt creating capital are unstable. Movement of people and trade in labour services are, in the present circumstances, probably the best thing one could do for the poor of the world. But the political obstacles are mountainous.

Politics of integration – liberal unilateralism versus liberal internationalism[28]

The most obvious difference between domestic and international transactions is that more than one government has the capacity to interfere. It is possible for either or both to do so. The difficulty arises with all forms of trade and capital flows, along with the payments that relate to these transactions (remittances of dividends and interest receipts, repatriation of capital, and payment for imports). The question is what needs to be done about the potential for conflict in such situations. Should a government ignore what another government does, even if that includes expropriation of the assets of their nationals or exclusion of their exporters from the latter's markets, or not?

Historically, liberals have been split on this issue. Some take the view that it is in the interest of a country to follow liberal policies unilaterally, whatever other governments may do. The point has been put by the late Joan Robinson in her well-known remark that if others throw rocks into their harbour, there is no reason to throw rocks into our own. That seems obvious enough. At worst, if everybody in the world prohibited transactions, one would end up in the same situation as if one chose to do this to oneself. But even if many countries restrict trade or capital mobility, one can allow one's citizens to benefit from transactions with those that do not do so. The liberal countries will, inevitably, then dominate these international transactions.

Unilateral liberalization would be less beneficial in an illiberal world than if more governments followed liberal policies, but it would still be better than nothing. The point is not theoretical. In the post-war era, liberalization by the high-income (first) world and a few exceptional less developed economies (Hong Kong and Singapore) unquestionably benefited those who liberalized, even though most of the developing (third) world and all the communist (second) world decided not to follow suit. The same argument was made by the British free-traders, Richard Cobden foremost among them, in the 1840s. Following Adam Smith and David Ricardo, they argued that it was in the country's interest to follow free trade, regardless of what others did. If the latter followed their example, that was all well and good. If not, so be it. The argument is a good one. The prosperity of Hong Kong and Singapore shows that it is valid today.

Liberal unilateralism has, however, been fairly rare, especially for strong powers. This is partly because it is hard to persuade the public at large of the virtues of unilateral liberalization. To many this looks like unilateral disarmament, in keeping with the general (and mistaken) view that trade is a form of war. Most people – and most governments – are mercantilists: they believe, mistakenly, that exports are the aim of trade and imports the cost. The United States has always been mercantilist in this sense, unlike the United Kingdom in its heyday as the world trade leader. Liberal unilateralism is also rare because some activities of foreign governments – expropriation of the property of one's own citizens, for example – are highly objectionable to powerful domestic interests.

Yet there are more positive reasons for what should be called 'liberal internationalism' – reliance on agreements with other governments to establish a securely liberal environment. Such agreements help countries to be liberal, since they engage economic interests in favour of greater access to foreign markets, including for investment, thereby creating powerful coalitions against protectionist special interests. In the United States, use of the administration's powers to reach agreements with foreigners has also been a way of bypassing the constitutionally mandated, but historically catastrophic, logrolling in congressional legislation on trade policy, which culminated in the calamity of the Smoot–Hawley tariff of 1930. Such agreements create a framework of international law that provides more security for all participants in international transactions. Last, but not least, reciprocated liberalization multiplies the benefits.

These are powerful arguments. There is, therefore, a long history of international treaties of commerce. Indeed, Richard Cobden himself negotiated and signed the Cobden–Chevalier commercial treaty with France in 1860. With the most-favoured-nation clause at its heart – the principle of non-discrimination – this treaty became the basis for the *système des traités* that spread liberal trade throughout western Europe in the 1860s and 1870s. The intellectual roots of the General Agreement on Tariffs and Trade and, since 1995, the World Trade Organization were these treaties. Again, the

International Monetary Fund has, as a basic objective, convertibility of currencies on current account, since exchange controls are always an alternative to import controls. Similarly, countries have signed many bilateral investment treaties. In 1990, a total of about 400 such treaties were in effect. By 1997, as the case for inward investment became increasingly well accepted in developing and former communist countries, the number had jumped to 1,300, with more than 160 countries participating in at least one treaty.[29]

Once a large number of bilateral agreements has been agreed, the move to a single multilateral agreement makes sense: it reduces complexity for countries and, still more, for private agents. This is one of the arguments against the current explosion of regional trade agreements. Once there is a multilateral agreement among countries, there must be a dispute-settlement mechanism. That cannot be left in the hands of one party, since the agreement would then not be worth the paper it is written on. Equally, it cannot be left to the parties to the dispute, since they are, by definition, in disagreement. For a multilateral agreement to amount to anything, its dispute-settlement system must be out of the direct control of any party or parties to a dispute. By definition, therefore, an international agreement represents an infringement on the sovereignty, narrowly defined, of a member. The member accepts that infringement because it believes that it gains thereby. There are, as we have seen, good reasons for it to believe so. It can always choose not to change its behaviour and accept the legally imposed penalty instead.

The countries that gain the most from strong and enforceable international agreements are weak ones with poor reputations. They gain from the constraints on the actions of stronger partners. But they also gain from the acceptance of constraints on their own behaviour (as do all members), which make their liberal intentions towards trade and investment more credible. Ulysses, too, saw the value of binding himself to the mast. Constraints on sovereignty are, therefore, the aim of the exercise. In a world of international transactions and multiple jurisdictions, constraints on sovereignty are also desirable. Otherwise, the potential for conflict and unpredictability seems almost limitless.

While powerful arguments can be made for international agreements on trade, one must also recognize their drawbacks. In the first place, the logic of reciprocal bargaining is mercantilist. The GATT was a disarmament treaty for mercantilists. Import liberalization is seen as a concession. Over the years, negotiators and their publics, particularly in the most powerful trading nations, have learned to believe this is actually true. In the second place, reciprocal bargaining creates a serious dilemma for weaker countries, since they can offer little. Do they wait to liberalize until their trading partners agree to do so, which may mean for ever? Finally, people will complain about lost sovereignty. Yet in all such agreements, sovereignty ultimately remains. Countries can repudiate treaties. But they cannot then gain the benefits.

There is a tension between liberal unilateralism and liberal internationalism, with good arguments to be made on both sides. The best choice is to limit international agreements to the essential and mutually beneficial, while making participation voluntary, though with the proviso that one cannot gain from the restraints accepted by others unless one is prepared to accept some restraints oneself. The more these agreements are voluntary, the less likely they are to proceed in directions hostile to the interests of any member. A tension exists between unbridled discretion by governments and a predictably liberal global economy. Since democracy operates at the level of states and is likely to do so for the foreseeable future, international agreements also appear to be constraints on democracy. But, again, such constraints can be accepted if they bring with them constraints on the autonomy of others or, for that matter, of oneself.

Conclusion

Markets want to cross borders. There are overwhelming arguments for letting them do so. Unfortunately, bad jurisdictions, of which the world has far too many, create difficulties not just for international transactions, but for almost all productive transactions. Success always begins at home. It can, however, be supported by international agreements that are wisely designed and focused. Such agreements often appear to constrain sovereignty and democracy, but also contribute to the valuable goals of credibility, predictability and comity among countries.

Part III   **Why There Is Too Little Globalization**

Prologue

It is close to a conventional wisdom that over the past two decades a group of ideological fanatics, called 'neo-liberals', have succeeded in imposing their creed on an innocent humanity, at the expense of democracy, prosperity, equality, the environment, human rights, decent treatment of labour and, indeed, everything that is good and wholesome. This view of the history of the past two decades is almost entirely mistaken.

First, while liberal ideas (not 'neo-liberal', since that is an incomprehensible piece of neo-Marxist jargon) have made progress over the past two decades, they have not done so through the offices of passionate liberals. On the contrary, the policy changes that go under the heading of 'neo-liberal' have been introduced as often by long-standing socialists and communists as by parties that would be considered on the political right. The principal reason for this transformation was failure of the alternatives, symbolized so powerfully by the collapse of the Soviet empire between 1989 and 1991.

Second, globalization is considerably more limited than critics suppose. In some respects the global economic integration is no more than it was a century ago, before the breakdown that occurred between 1914 and 1945. In some ways, it is considerably less. The pity is not that there has been too much globalization, but that there is too little. Too many people are effectively outside the world market, largely because the jurisdictions in which they live fail to offer them and outsiders the conditions in which productive engagement in the world economy is possible.

Chapter 7 Globalization in the Long Run

As man advances in civilization, and small tribes are united into larger communities, the simplest reason would tell each individual that he ought to extend his social instincts and sympathies to all the members of the same nation, though personally unknown to him. This point being once reached, there is only an artificial barrier to prevent his sympathies extending to the men of all nations and races.

Charles Darwin[1]

In the very long run, where the long run consists of many centuries, the trend towards globalization – or integration of markets for goods, services and factors of production – is almost certainly irreversible. The proviso is that we avoid blowing up the planet. But in the 'short' run – where that run may be a century, or even more – it is not inevitable at all. Whether the opportunities for international economic integration afforded by technological advance are exploited depends, as we know from experience in the twentieth century, on policy choices that can be made – but also can be unmade. Today, we are living in an age of globalization, by which, as was explained in Chapter 3, is meant economic integration. To say so has become a cliché. But the same was also true a century ago. Then, as now, most observers assumed that the trend towards integration would prove unbreakable. We, however, know better. The liberal international economy of the late nineteenth and early twentieth centuries foundered. By 1945, it had disappeared. It has taken half a century to restore.

Logic of global integration

The American author Robert Wright has put the case for the long-run progress of economic and political globalization in his brilliant book

Nonzero.[2] His argument is contained in the title. There are almost limitless opportunities for positive-sum interaction among human beings, in the language of game theory. Human beings are also unique among animals in their ability to create the world in which they live. Thus the opportunities they identify stimulate invention and innovation and these, in turn, create further opportunities. As Wright argues, 'several trends span all of human history: improvement in the transport and processing of matter, improvement in the transport and processing of energy, improvement in the transport and processing of information'.[3]

As the technologies of travel, transportation and communication have improved, so inevitably have returns to exploiting these opportunities. If the means exist to transmit information, people, goods or services cheaply, someone, somewhere will exploit them. Over time, the result has been an ever-denser web of exchange spreading over an ever-wider geographical area. Contemporary globalization is merely a stage upon a long journey that is, in all probability, not yet close to its end.

Wright suggests, furthermore, that these technological changes, themselves inevitable given the restless and innovative nature of humanity, bring with them not just economic but political integration. Political structures have tended to grow in extent, along with dense webs of mutual economic inter-dependence. In 1500 BCE, says Wright, there were around 600,000 autonomous polities on the planet (how he counted them, I do not know, but the number seems plausible enough). Today, there are 193.[4] As Wright notes, 'the reason to expect the eventual triumph of global governance lies in three observations. (1) Governance has always tended to expand to the geographic scope necessary to solve emerging non-zero-sum problems that markets and moral codes can't alone solve. (2) These days many emerging non-zero-sum problems are supra-national, involving many, sometimes all, nations. (3) The forces behind this growing scope of non-zero-sumness are technological and, for plain reasons, bound to intensify.'[5]

It is not hard to see examples of such growing mutual interdependence. Among other things we need to bring the many poor-quality jurisdictions in the world up to a reasonable standard, for both economic and security reasons, to internalize regional and global environmental externalities, to deal with global health threats and to ensure consistent global treatment of trade and investment. The emergence of mega-terrorism on 11 September 2001 is a compelling argument for some form of global security structure (whether the United States likes this or not), as is the proliferation of nuclear weapons. The emergence of AIDS is, similarly, an argument for an effective global health regime. The failure of peripheral countries to provide stable monetary and financial systems is an argument for a global monetary and financial regime. One can give many further examples. None of these developments is inevitable. But the non-zero-sum logic is quite compelling.

As Wright also observes, this political evolution has a long history. As exchange developed, states have tended to become bigger. It would not be surprising, therefore, if a global market economy were to lead to some form of global governance, just as the rise of a more integrated European economy over the past two or three centuries has coincided with a series of attempts to impose a political superstructure, the European Union being far and away the most benign and successful. It is even probable that, were it not for the accident of history that placed a large and powerful island off the west coast of Europe, either France or Germany would have succeeded in that aim long ago.

Yet monopolistic political entities also create grave threats to human progress, as was argued in Chapter 5, since such structures choose hierarchical order and control over individual initiative and fluidity. Nevertheless, Wright's point is perceptive. Many of the contemporary criticisms of the global market economy are calls to confine the market within a state. Some critics wish to confine a global market within a global state of some kind, though they may not realize how radical the implications would be. These are the political *globalists*. At the opposite end are those who envisage matching market to state (or sub-state) by fragmenting the market. These are *localists*. Their vision seems most unlikely, barring a catastrophe (nuclear war, for example). Most plausible of all, in the short run, are *nationalists*, such as Patrick Buchanan or Jean-Marie Le Pen, who would confine the economy to existing states. (Intriguingly, Ralph Nader is also a nationalist in this sense: left meets right at the edge of the political spectrum.) Since the United States is economically already the biggest of these states, Buchanan can reasonably expect that his country would fare least badly in such a fragmented world economy. That is, no doubt, his aim.

Whichever way their preferences go, many critics want to align the domain of the market with that of political power. That was also the aim of the seventeenth- and eighteenth-century mercantilists against whom the early liberals struggled.[6] It is, once again, the subtext of the debates of our time. The contemporary (largely unjustified) intellectual hero-worship of Karl Polanyi by critics of the global market economy fits well into this perspective, for his widely cited 1944 book *The Great Transformation* has as its theme political resistance to the 'utopian' ideal of a liberal market economy and the need for far greater social regulation and control. At the present stage of human development, that would entail either some form of global authority, in charge of a global society, or a deliberate fragmentation of the world economy into national or local components.

Globalization in long-run perspective

Since globalization is a fuzzy term in its general use, it is impossible to say when it began. Maybe it was with the departure of homo sapiens from Africa some 100,000 years ago and the subsequent slow colonization of the world. But it is possible to say things that are somewhat more up to date about human interaction across the globe over the past few thousand years. To put our present era in better context, it will be helpful to start with what is being said about the shocking novelty of the Internet era. Then the discussion will look at four aspects of globalization in the long run: the sense of ourselves as part of a global community; global transmission of ideas and culture; global transmission of technology; and, finally, globalization of the economy, prior to the industrial revolution.

Nothing altogether new under the sun

The idea that there once were happy little local communities untouched by the outside world, living in ecological harmony and cultural isolation, is a fantasy. Human societies have always interacted intensely, through trade, intermarriage, war, conquest, plunder, the transmission of ideas and technological diffusion. The only thing special about our era is that we interact more intensely and more quickly than ever before, across the globe.

Thus almost all the widely cited aspects of contemporary globalization are old. The difference is only one of degree, not of kind. As Wright observes, none of the following is new: the declining relevance of distance; the 'ideas' economy; the 'weightless' economy; liberation by 'microchip'; 'Jihad vs. McWorld' – the tension described by the political scientist Benjamin Barber between global market and local identities – and the twilight of sovereignty.[7] Compared to what was available in, say, 1000 BCE, the naval technology of 1500 had killed distance: it made the world one. Again, long-distance trade has always concentrated on high-value-to-weight items: think of silk or cloves. The book had a revolutionary impact: neither the Reformation nor the scientific revolution of the sixteenth and seventeenth centuries would have been feasible without it. Let us see whether the Internet proves as important. Again, printing made possible a strong sense both of the world as a whole and of nationalism as an intellectual enterprise (McWorld and Jihad respectively). Think of the newspaper or the magazine. Financial crises have spread across borders ever since lending has. Nor is the impact of faraway events a new phenomenon either. The Mughal empire was the victim of political, military and technological progress half a world away. Earlier, the Persian empire was overthrown and the Byzantine empire greatly diminished as a result of events in the Arabian peninsula in the early seventh century.

Rise of a global consciousness

The development of a consciousness of the world as a whole is also a long journey, with two big landmarks along the way. The first came with the conquest of most of Eurasia, the biggest and long the most populous and culturally and technologically advanced continent, by the Mongols in the thirteenth century.[8] As the Columbia University economist Ronald Findlay has argued,

> for the first and indeed only time in history, a single regime presided over the entire length of the overland trade routes linking China and the Near East. This made it possible for merchants and goods to move safely over these vast distances, facilitating the transmissions of ideas and techniques. Since China was substantially ahead of both Islam and the West in the general level of its technology this flow chiefly benefited the lands at the western ends of the trade routes and beyond.[9]

> Alas, the bad comes with good: among the things the Mongols globalized was the Black Death, which seems to have been transmitted by their empire, possibly by their cavalry.[10]

In answering the question when globalization started, Professor Findlay argues that 'it began with the unification of the central Eurasian land mass by the Mongol conquests and the reactions this aroused in the sedentary civilizations that they were launched against'.[11] Among other things, it brought awareness to the Europeans of the civilizations of east Asia and a stronger desire to reach them by going around the Islamic world that had for so long stood in between. That, in turn, brought forth the effort to improve naval technology which enabled the European voyages of discovery of the fifteenth and sixteenth centuries. That was the second, and decisive, stage on the way to a global consciousness (and, indeed, globalization) – first Eurasia, then the world.

These European voyages and their dramatic impact on the world (not least on Europe itself) graphically illustrate the momentum of integration, over the long run. The Chinese possessed the means of transoceanic navigation by the early fifteenth century. Their fleets sailed all the way to Africa. But they then decided to beach their ocean-going junks.[12] A Chinese mandarin might have concluded, if he had thought in such terms, that the scrapping of the Ming dynasty fleet meant the end of globalization. He would have been wrong. For the Europeans took up the opportunity abandoned by the Chinese. Needier and free from central control, the inhabitants of the western prom-ontory of the Eurasian landmass sailed to China instead. The opportunity was there. Someone was bound to exploit it. It was the Europeans who, as a result, created the largely western-dominated world of today.

In the last decade of the fifteenth century, Christopher Columbus reached the Americas and the Portuguese entered the Indian Ocean. Since then, peoples that were previously isolated have become increasingly closely inter-connected. This has been true of relations among the civilizations of the Eurasian landmass. It has been still truer of relations between Eurasia and the hitherto largely – or entirely – isolated continents of Africa, the Americas and Australasia. Humanity became aware both of itself and of the globe as a whole.

Cultural globalization

Many of the complaints of today are about the cultural impact of global capitalism. But long-distance cultural impacts are hardly new. The great religions of humanity emanated either from the Middle East or from India. Jesus Christ was a Jew of the first century. The Roman Catholic Church, perhaps the most significant European cultural institution, emerged from a marriage of Jewish religion, Greek philosophy and Roman power. Islam has been an equally successful cultural export, to the point of eradicating the pre-Islamic cultures of the countries it has engulfed. But the spread of ideas and the clerisies that attend them is not just an old phenomenon. The most successful European religious export of the twentieth century was Marxism-Leninism. No better example of cultural globalization can be found than the communist revolution in China. In that most enduring of empires, Mao Zedong triumphed in the name of an ideology developed just a century earlier by a German of Jewish origins. Now the Chinese are trying to find a way to undo that dreadful error.

Relatively thin contact between places previously not in touch may well have a cultural impact greater than deeper impacts later on. The conversion of the Germans to Christianity, for example, changed the culture ineradicably (even though Adolf Hitler did his best to reverse it). But, at that stage, economic exchange was necessarily limited. It is true that, today, western ideas of democracy and the market economy, including business culture (and the intellectual counterculture to business culture) are spreading quite rapidly across the globe. But it was always so. Human beings imitate, or are absorbed by, the ideas of others on what to believe and how to live. Sometimes, they are forced to do so.

Technological globalization

Cultural and religious ideas transmitted comfortably across long distances centuries ago. So did scientific and technological knowledge. It is widely believed, though impossible to prove, that the technologies which transformed Europe in the late middle ages – movable type, gunpowder, the mariner's compass – came from China. We know that China possessed these long before the west. So 'Chinese influence is certainly possible and plausible. Direct evidence, however, is mostly lacking.'[13] Medieval Europe made advances of its own, notably in clockwork, which were transmitted to China, rather unsuccessfully, in their turn.[14]

Among the most important global exchanges occurred shortly after the European conquest of the Americas, with the introduction of the crops of the Americas to Eurasia (and later Africa) and the crops and livestock of Eurasia to the Americas. The arrival of the tomato, potato, tobacco and maize in Eurasia was as significant as the arrival of coffee, wheat and the horse in the Americas. China received maize, peanuts and the sweet potato in this exchange. Subsequently rubber went to Malaya and coffee to Brazil. This was globalization indeed. Compared to the impact of the post-Columbian exchange on Europe (and, for that matter, of its import of coffee, tea, sugar and the croissant), what is significant about Starbucks or McDonald's?

Economic globalization

Last but not least comes our topic, economic globalization. Long-distance trade is also far from new. During the middle ages, Venice imported spices, medicines, perfumes and silk from the east, while, in the Black Sea, Genoa traded grain, fur and slaves with southern Russia. There was both a land-route from China and the Indian Ocean sea-route, which transited via Egypt. In terms of volume of trade, the latter seems to have been more significant. This was presumably because of the higher cost of overland than maritime transport, which remained true until the coming of the railways in the nineteenth century. Genoan ships, writes Professor Findlay, 'took raw materials such as alum and cotton, as well as spices and other luxury products from the East, to the ports of the English Channel and the North Sea, bringing back wool and woollen cloth for Italy as well as re-export to the East. The Venetians, not to be outdone, followed suit.' In sum, 'the period from 1260 to 1350 saw the emergence of a genuine "world economy" '.[15]

Yet this was a modest beginning. The European voyages of discovery of the fifteenth to the eighteenth centuries were the most significant economic events of the last millennium, after the move to Promethean growth in Britain in the course of the eighteenth and early nineteenth centuries. A number of peripheral European countries – Portugal, Spain, the Netherlands, Britain and France – exploited superior military organization and technology, developed in intra-European conflict, to achieve control over much of the world. They sought wealth through plunder and trade. Out of their quest came great empires. In the long run, however, commerce proved more enduring and more fruitful: empires came and then went, as the costs of control rose and the rewards fell; but trade and investment remained. The result was the incorporation of much of the world into an economic system whose centre was, until the twentieth century, Europe, then Europe and North America, and today, though dominated by the west, includes advanced east Asian countries, particularly Japan.

The European conquest of the Americas was the big event. It gave the Europeans what Eric Jones has called the 'ghost acreage' of two new continents. From a population of 100 million and an area of 3.75 million square miles, the Europeans suddenly found themselves with an additional 20 million square miles. If the Chinese had discovered it first, the world would now look very different. As Professor Jones has said, 'what had happened was that the Europeans had discovered an unprecedented ecological windfall. Europe was sufficiently decentralized and flexible to develop in response, and not merely to consume the raw gains. This conjunction of windfall and entrepreneurship happened only once in history.'[16]

This is not quite true. In the long run, their vast possessions did rather little for Spain or Portugal, except give them an opportunity for slumber. Nor did Spain and Portugal do much for their vast possessions, which they treated as sources of plunder. The decisive shift was from imperial exploitation by the Iberians in Latin America to colonization and trade, under British legal and political institutions, in North America. That was, in time, to engender a new power, the United States, whose rise was to be the decisive geopolitical event of the nineteenth century. Today, the economy of erstwhile British North America (the United States and Canada) is three times bigger than that of Latin America and the Caribbean, at purchasing power parity, and more than five times bigger in current US dollars. This is a reversal of the situation three centuries ago and reflects the triumphant success of British America with industrialization and the equally striking failure of Latin America.

In addition to straightforward plunder, primarily the search for silver, the possession of both the Americas and maritime power created the basis for a trade in sugar, tobacco, indigo (an important natural dye) and, in the nineteenth century, cotton. African slaves were brought to the New World to produce these commodities, after the Europeans had succeeded in wiping out the indigenous inhabitants by disease and cruelty. Out of this grew the 'triangular trade' of the seventeenth and, above all, eighteenth centuries, which linked Europe to Africa and the New World, with the exchange of manufactures from the first to slaves from the second and commodities from the third.

Eric Williams argued that the profits from this exploitation of African labour financed the industrial revolution.[17] This remains controversial. A well-known study concluded that the profits from the slave trade were about half a per cent of British national income in 1770, 8 per cent of total investment and about 39 per cent of commercial and industrial investment.[18] Whether this was crucial is a matter of judgement. Certainly, such profits were not a sufficient condition for the industrial take-off. As Findlay remarks, none of this debate about the role of trade 'should be taken to imply that the Industrial Revolution could simply have occurred as a natural outcome of the expansion of overseas trade, however profitable. The acceleration of technical progress and productivity growth that has been sustained ever since depended upon a fortunate combination of circumstances and creative response that was unique to the northwestern corner of Europe.'[19] Opportunities do not create wealth. Only seizing them does.

For all these important economic developments, the direct impact of long-distance commerce on the economies of the world was relatively minor until the nineteenth century, because of the cost of transport and communications. This did not make it in any way irrelevant. It afforded an excellent living to Venice, for example. It generated the celebrated Silk Road. Most important, perhaps, the search for luxuries in the east Indies – spices, in particular – drove the Europeans of the fifteenth and sixteenth centuries towards their successful experiment with long-range naval commerce, backed by force, that ultimately transformed the entire world. The political economy of the seventeenth-century Netherlands and Britain would have been quite different without the role of an enriched mercantile class. London's support for parliament was decisive in the civil war and without trade there would have been no London.

Conclusion

Broadly defined, globalization is a long-run process with powerful forces behind it. Economics, conventionally defined, is a crucial component of a wider range of positive-sum activities that drive ever-wider exchanges and, with those exchanges, create bigger and more complex political institutions. Hunter–gatherer bands become chiefdoms, which become kingdoms, which become empires, just as local exchange added long-distance exchange, by land and sea, with a specialized class of voyagers and merchants to serve and develop both. People traded everything from which they could hope to make a profit. Together with these developments came a long series of cultural and technological exchanges that disseminated ideas about both how to live and how to make a living. The impact was often shattering. Religions submerged traditional cultures. New technologies – printing and gunpowder, for example – transformed ways of life. Disease laid waste communities. This exchange reached its highest level in Eurasia in the course of the late middle ages. Then, with the European voyages of discovery of the fifteenth to the eighteenth century, it came to incorporate the world. By the eighteenth century, complex webs of global domination and exchange had developed. At the centre of those webs were the Europeans. The time was ripe for the next stage of globalization – the global impact of Promethean growth.

Chapter 8 **Rise, Fall and Rise of a Liberal Global Economy**

For over two hundred years English ideas had been spreading eastward. The rule of freedom which had been achieved in England seemed destined to spread throughout the world. By about 1870 the reign of these ideas had probably reached its easternmost expansion. From then onward it began to retreat, and a different set of ideas, not really new but very old, began to advance from the East. England lost her intellectual leadership in the political and social sphere and became an importer of ideas. For the next sixty years Germany became the center from which ideas destined to govern the world in the twentieth century spread east and west. . . . Although most of the new ideas, and particularly socialism, did not originate in Germany, it was in Germany that they were perfected and during the last quarter of the nineteenth and the first quarter of the twentieth century that they reached their fullest development.

Friedrich A. Hayek[1]

The last two centuries have been incomparably the most dynamic in world history, with the twentieth far more dynamic even than the nineteenth. The world has been transformed. Among the many ways in which it has been transformed are in global economic integration, driven by revolutions in technology and changes in policy. Yet, while technology has moved in one direction only – towards lower cost of transport and communications overall – policy has not. After a long upswing of liberalism in the nineteenth century, there was a long reaction that began in the 1870s and reached its crescendo in the first half of the twentieth century. Since then there has been a slow recovery of liberalism. The fall of the Soviet empire and the shift of China and India from socialism and self-sufficiency to liberalization and international exchange were the most important events of the last two decades of the twentieth century for the world economy. At the beginning of the twenty-first century, we see the world from the vantage point of this tide towards liberalization, the question being whether this is another high-water mark for liberalism or still an early stage in a new advance.[2]

Growth and economic integration in the nineteenth and twentieth centuries

With the nineteenth century, the entire rhythm of the world economy changed, as has been pointed out in Chapter 4. It grew rapidly in the late nineteenth and early twentieth centuries. But anti-liberal pressures, two wars and huge policy mistakes by the United States in the 1920s and 1930s brought about a catastrophic implosion between 1914 and 1945. Subsequently, a liberal world economy was restored, initially in the high-income countries, later on in most of the world. Meanwhile, changes in technology, particularly communications technology, proceeded apace.

These four periods can be clearly seen in Tables 8.1 and 8.2, which come from Angus Maddison. Since 1820 there have been three periods of rapid growth in real income per head in the world as a whole: 1870–1913, 1950–73 the so-called 'golden age' – and 1973–98. These are also the periods of fastest

Table 8.1 Growth in GDP per head 1820–1998 (annual average compound growth rates, per cent)

Region	1820–1870	1870–1913	1913–50	1950–73	1973–98
Western Europe	0.95	1.32	0.76	4.08	1.78
Western offshoots*	1.42	1.81	1.55	2.44	1.94
Japan	0.19	1.48	0.89	8.05	2.34
Eastern Europe and former USSR	0.64	1.15	1.50	3.49	−1.1
Latin America	0.10	1.81	1.42	2.52	0.99
Asia (excluding Japan)	−0.11	0.38	−0.02	2.92	3.54
Africa	0.12	0.64	1.02	2.07	0.01
World	0.53	1.30	0.91	2.93	1.33

Source: Angus Maddison, *The World Economy: A Millennial Perspective* (Paris: Development Centre of the Organization for Economic Co-operation and Development, 2001), Table 3–1a.

* The United States, Canada, Australia and New Zealand. These should have been called British offshoots, to differentiate them from Latin America.

Table 8.2 Growth in volume of merchandise exports: world and major regions, 1870–1998 (annual average compound growth rates, per cent)

Region	1870–1913	1913–50	1950–73	1973–98
Western Europe	3.24	−0.14	8.38	4.79
Western offshoots*	4.71	2.27	6.26	5.92
Eastern Europe and former USSR	3.37	1.43	9.81	2.52
Latin America	3.29	2.29	4.28	6.03
Asia	2.79	1.64	9.97	5.95
Africa	4.37	1.90	5.34	1.87
World	3.40	0.90	7.88	5.07

Source: Maddison, The World Economy: A Millennial Perspective, Table 3–2a.

* The United States, Canada, Australia and New Zealand. These should have been called British offshoots, to differentiate them from Latin America.

growth in the history of the world. In each there was also rapid growth of world exports, in volume terms: 3.4 per cent a year between 1870 and 1913, then 7.9 per cent between 1950 and 1973, and 5.1 per cent between 1973 and 1998. Between 1913 and 1950, however, exports grew at only 0.9 per cent a year, while global GDP per head also grew at just 0.9 per cent. This was the worst period for world trade and the worst period for growth in standards of living of the past 130 years. It is also worth noting that the liberal market economy produced, in the years 1870–1913, the fastest growth the world had ever known up to that point.

The lesson of this experience is quite simple. Periods of fast economic growth are also periods of fast growth in world trade. This is true not just for the world as a whole, but for the dynamic parts of the world. Between 1870 and 1913, the world's most dynamic countries were the former British colonies: the United States, Canada, Australia and New Zealand. Incomes per head grew at 1.8 per cent a year, while exports grew at 4.7 per cent a year. Between 1950 and 1973, western Europe was the most dynamic big region of the world economy (though Japan's was the fastest-growing individual economy), with growth of real incomes per head at 4.1 per cent a year, while exports grew at the extraordinary rate of 8.4 per cent a year. Finally, between 1973 and 1998, the fastest-growing part of the world economy was non-Japan Asia, where real incomes per head rose at 3.5 per cent a year. Total exports from Asia (including Japan's) grew at 6 per cent a year over this period.

World markets for goods, capital and labour in the nineteenth and twentieth centuries

The consensus of contemporary opinion is that there has never been a more rapidly integrating world economy than that of the 1990s. The evidence is against this, however. According to Kevin O'Rourke of Trinity College, Dublin, 'the most impressive episode of international economic integration which the world has seen to date was not the second half of the 20th century but the years between 1870 and the Great War. The nineteenth century, and in particular the late nineteenth century, was the period that saw the largest decline ever in intercontinental barriers to trade and factor mobility.'[3]

Trade

Prior to the nineteenth century, there seems to be no evidence of systematic price convergence for commodities or capital across the globe. Data put together by two distinguished economic historians, for cloves, black pepper and coffee, going back to 1580, show no convergence of prices between Amsterdam and east Asia before the early nineteenth century.[4] Similarly, there seems to have been no evidence of Anglo-Indian price convergence before the nineteenth century. The nineteenth century changed all that: prices of cloves, pepper and coffee converged after the 1820s. The price gap for wheat between Britain and the United States was about 100 per cent in the early 1800s. It began to fall from about 1840, reaching negligible levels by the 1880s and disappearing altogether just before the First World War. By the late nineteenth century commodity price convergence was strong for virtually all standard commodities: bacon, cotton and rice. While the evidence is incomplete, it appears there was no significant further commodity-market integration in the twentieth century.[5]

Because of the incompleteness of data on commodity-market integration, much attention has been paid to trade volumes and ratios of trade to GDP. 'Once again, the nineteenth century emerges as the canonical period of increasing world trade.'[6] World trade grew at a little over 1 per cent a year between 1500 and 1800 but has grown at around 3.5 per cent a year (in real terms) since 1820, with nineteenth- and twentieth-century overall growth rates much the same.[7] European trade multiplied forty-fold in the nineteenth century.[8] But the world economy grew roughly twice as fast in the twentieth century as in the nineteenth (entirely because of its unprecedented dynamism in the second half of the twentieth century). So the world economy integrated faster in the nineteenth than in the twentieth century.

According to the data in constant prices in Table 8.3, the ratio of world merchandise exports to GDP rose from just 1 per cent in 1820 to 7.9 per cent in 1913. It fell back to 5.5 per cent in 1950, as a result of the 1914–45 calamity, reaching 17.2 per cent in 1998. Western Europe became far more open in the post-Second World War period than it ever had been before, though this was less dramatically true for the United Kingdom, which was already highly trade-dependent by 1913. The United States became vastly more open than before, with ratios of exports to GDP at 10.1 per cent in 1998, against 3.7 per cent in 1913 and 3 per cent in 1950. This helps explain the hysteria about the novelty of globalization in that country. A number of developing countries – Argentina, Brazil, India – had no greater exposure to trade in the 1990s than in 1913 or even 1870. They are not among the developing world's successes, of course! China is certainly more open than ever before, with a ratio of exports to GDP at 4.9 per cent in 1998, up from 2.6 per cent in 1950. South Korea is dramatically more open: in constant prices the ratio of merchandize exports to GDP rose from 0.7 per cent in 1950 to 36.3 per cent in 1998. The data for Taiwan are similar. In the post-war period, all successful developing countries have had faster growth of trade than GDP.

Table 8.3 Merchandise exports as a share of GDP (constant prices, per cent)

Region	1820	1870	1913	1929	1950	1973	1998
France	1.3	4.9	7.8	8.6	7.6	15.2	28.7
Germany	n.a.	9.5	16.1	12.8	6.2	23.8	38.9
UK	3.1	12.2	17.5	13.3	11.3	14.0	25.0
Western Europe	n.a.	10.0	16.3	13.3	9.4	20.9	29.7*
US	2.0	2.5	3.7	3.6	3.0	4.9	10.1
Japan	n.a.	0.2	2.4	3.5	2.2	7.7	13.4
Argentina	n.a.	9.4	6.8	6.1	2.4	2.1	7.0
Brazil	n.a.	12.2	9.8	6.9	3.9	2.5	5.4
Latin America	n.a.	9.0	9.5	9.7	6.2	4.6	6.2*
China	n.a.	0.7	1.7	1.8	2.6	1.5	4.9
India	n.a.	2.6	4.6	3.7	2.9	2.01	2.4
Asia (including Japan)	n.a.	1.3	2.6	2.8	2.3	4.4	7.2*
World	1.0	4.6	7.9	9.0	5.5	10.5	17.2

Source: O'Rourke, 'Europe and the Causes of Globalization, 1790 to 2000' in Henryk Kierzkowski (ed.), *Europe and Globalization* (Basingstoke: Palgrave Macmillan, 2002), p. 70

* 1992

In constant prices (that is, in terms of volume), the world as a whole and most of the large economies appear to be far more open to trade today than ever before. Yet, surprisingly, this is not so true in current prices. This contrast needs explaining. Table 8.4 shows that, at current prices, ratios of trade to GDP in many advanced countries were not that much higher in the mid-1990s than in 1910. In the UK, for example, the ratio of trade to GDP, in current prices, was 57 per cent in 1995, against 44 per cent in 1910. In France the ratio was 43 per cent, against 35 per cent. The US stands out among the group of seven leading industrial countries for the big increase in its trade ratio, from 11 per cent in 1910 to 24 per cent in 1995. Japan stands out in the opposite direction: its trade ratio was 17 per cent in 1995, against 30 per cent in 1910.[9]

Why have ratios of trade to GDP risen so little in current prices in the high-income countries despite more than half a century of rapid growth in world trade? And why have these ratios grown so much more in constant than in current prices? The answer is that the trade-intensity of the goods-producing sectors of most economies is far greater than ever before, as intra-industry trade and intra-firm trade in inputs has exploded.[10] In the case of the United States, for example, the proportion of merchandise production exported has risen from less than 10 per cent in 1950 (and about 15 per cent in 1910) to over 40 per cent in 1997.[11] Meanwhile, GDP in current prices has become increasingly dominated by services, many of them publicly provided. In 1913 about two-thirds of GDP in advanced countries, in current prices, consisted of the production of goods; today, services make up the same proportion. Services remain far less tradable (and traded) than goods, even though, as communications technology has improved, they have also become more tradable than

Table 8.4 Total trade to GDP (current prices, per cent)

	1870	1910	1950	1995
UK	41	44	30	57
France	33	35	23	43
Germany	37	38	27	46
Italy	21	28	21	49
Denmark	52	69	53	64
US	14	11	9	24
Canada	30	30	37	71
Japan	10	30	19	17

Source: Richard E. Baldwin and Philippe Martin, 'Two Waves of Globalization: Superficial Similarities, Fundamental Differences', National Bureau of Economic Research Working Paper 6904, www.nber.org, January 1999.

ever before. In 1997, US exports of services were 3.4 per cent of GDP, against 8.5 per cent for merchandise exports. In the 1960s, in contrast, service exports were only 1 per cent of GDP. Between 1960 and 1997, the ratio of services exports to services value added in the United States rose from 1.7 per cent to 5.1 per cent – a big increase. Even so, services remain vastly more domestically oriented than merchandise production.[12]

The chief cause of the divergent trends between trade ratios in current and constant prices is, in fact, the same as that for this rise in the share of services in GDP in current prices – the fall in the relative prices of goods. This is the result of sustained increases in productivity in the goods-producing sectors of the economy. Trade has thus grown most in the broad sectors of the economy where prices have fallen most and so shares in GDP, in current prices, have failed to increase as much as shares in constant prices.

One other change is noteworthy. In the pre-First World War period, developing countries exported commodities in return for manufactures. Now they export manufactures (and some services) as well. The most successful developing countries over the past half-century have been the exporters of manufactures, virtually all from east Asia. 'In 1980, only 25 per cent of the exports of developing countries were manufactures; by 1998 this had risen to 80 per cent.'[13]

On balance, the steepest rise in trade and in integration of markets for goods was in the nineteenth century. After the 1914–45 disaster, trade has grown faster than output throughout the post-Second World War period. Inevitably, it has grown fastest for countries with liberal trade policies. The share of trade in global output increased from about 7 per cent in 1950 to over 20 per cent by the mid-1990s. Between 1950 and 1998, the volume of world production rose by 530 per cent and of world output of manufactures by 820 per cent. Over the same period, the volume of world merchandize exports rose by 1,840 per cent and the volume of world exports of manufactures by 3,500 per cent. As a result, on most measures the world economy trades more intensively today than ever before. This is dramatically true of the goods-producing sectors of the economy.

There have also been important changes in the nature of trade – the rise of intra-industry and intra-company trade, the increasing trade-intensity of services, though from a low level, and the rise of developing countries as exporters of manufactures. Finally, the weightlessness of trade must not be exaggerated. Distance still matters. Standard analyses suggest that at a distance of 4,000 kilometres trade volumes are 82 per cent less than at 1,000 kilometres.[14] In trade at least, the death of distance is much exaggerated.

Capital

Capital markets became more integrated in the course of the nineteenth century than ever before, reaching very high levels of integration by 1913. While there is little doubt that markets for goods are more integrated today than ever before and those for labour substantially less so, the position of capital is more confused. As with trade, there was a U-shaped pattern in the twentieth century, first a decline in integration, as shown by ratios of current accounts to GDP, real and nominal interest rate differentials and in applications of standard tests of the correlation between domestic savings and investment.[15] As with trade, it appears that at the beginning of the twenty-first century the world has returned to where it was a century earlier. Indeed, if one looks at gross foreign assets over world GDP (see Table 8.5), it appears that capital is more international than ever before. But this is misleading, since it largely reflects the enormous short-term positions in foreign assets. There are, in fact, big differences between the two periods, not all of which are favourable to the present. Four stand out.

First, the pre-1913 period did a much better job of transferring resources abroad. As a share of GDP the capital outflow from the UK – at an average of 4.6 per cent of GDP between 1870 and 1913 – has no contemporary parallels among the larger economies, even Japan.[16] (See Table 8.6 on the size of current accounts.) At its peak, British net overseas investment ran at 9 per cent of GDP, well over half its capital accumulation at the time, while British claims on the rest of the world were equal to two times GDP.[17] To put these numbers in contemporary terms, if the United States behaved the same way, it would be investing $1,000 billion a year more abroad than it has been receiving in inward capital flows and its net foreign assets would now be $20,000 billion,

Table 8.5 Foreign assets over world GDP (per cent)

1870	6.9
1900	18.6
1914	17.5
1930	8.4
1945	4.9
1960	6.4
1980	17.7
1995	56.8

Source: Nicholas Crafts, *Globalization and Growth in the Twentieth Century*, IMF Working Paper WP/00/44 (Washington DC: International Monetary Fund, 2000).

Table 8.6 Capital flows since 1870 (average absolute value of current account as per cent of GDP)

	UK	USA	Argentina	Australia	Canada	France	Germany	Italy	Japan
1870–1889	4.6	0.7	18.7	8.2	7.0	2.4	1.7	1.2	0.6
1890–1913	4.6	1.0	6.2	4.1	7.0	1.3	1.5	1.8	2.4
1919–1926	2.7	1.7	4.9	4.2	2.5	2.8	2.4	4.2	2.1
1927–1931	1.9	0.7	3.7	5.9	2.7	1.4	2.0	1.5	0.6
1932–1939	1.1	0.4	1.6	1.7	2.6	1.0	0.6	0.7	1.0
1947–1959	1.2	0.6	2.3	3.4	2.3	1.5	2.0	1.4	1.3
1960–1973	0.8	0.5	1.0	2.3	1.2	0.6	1.0	2.1	1.0
1974–1989	1.5	1.4	1.9	3.6	1.7	0.8	2.1	1.3	1.8
1989–1996	2.6	1.2	2.0	4.5	4.0	0.7	2.7	1.6	2.1

Source: Alan M. Taylor, 'International Capital Mobility in History: The Savings–Investment Relationship', National Bureau of Economic Research Working Paper 5743, www.nber.org, 1996.

appreciably more than the peak value of the US stock market in 2000. But, far from being a net creditor, at the end of 2001 the United States had net liabilities of about $2,000 billion.

Net capital imports were also on an extraordinary scale before 1914. Argentina, for example, ran a current account deficit averaging 18.7 per cent of GDP between 1870 and 1889 and 6.2 per cent of GDP between 1890 and 1913.[18] More revealing perhaps, the correlation between domestic investment and savings – a measure of self-sufficiency in savings – was lower between 1880 and 1910 than in all subsequent periods, up to 1990.[19] Today, however, much of the capital flow is two-way, and net positions are much smaller in relation to GDP. For aggregates of significant creditor and debtor countries, put together by Professors Maurice Obstfeld of the University of California, Berkeley and Alan Taylor of the University of California, Davis, the combined net asset position of the creditors was below 10 per cent of GDP in 1995, as was the combined liability position of the debtors.[20]

Second, the high-income countries, collectively, are now net *importers* of capital, not net exporters, with an aggregate current account deficit, in 2001, of nearly $200 billion (because the US deficit of over $400 billion more than offset the Japanese and European surpluses).[21] The fact that there were no aggregate net capital flows to developing countries also has powerful implications for the distribution of global investment. In 2000, measured at purchasing power parity, investment per head in the high-income countries, with 900 million people, was just over $6,000. In the middle-income countries, with 2.7 billion people, it was only $1,350. In the world's low-income countries, with

2.5 billion people, it was just under $400.[22] Rich people living in rich countries do much of the world's saving and invest most of it at home.[23]

Third, in the words of two knowledgeable analysts, 'globalized capital markets are back, but with a difference: capital transactions seem to be mostly a rich–rich affair, a process of "diversification finance" rather than "development finance" '.[24] In 1900, developing countries (on today's definition) in Asia, Latin America and Africa accounted for 33 per cent of global liabilities. Today, that figure is only 11 per cent.[25] In 1913, recipients were either land rich countries (such as the United States, Canada and Argentina) or labour-surplus countries, in equal measure: close to half of all direct investment and portfolio equity flows went to countries whose incomes per head were less than 40 per cent of the US level. Today, even though a far bigger fraction of the world's population is located in such low-productivity regions, the share of the cross-border flows of direct and equity investment that go to such countries is little over 10 per cent.[26]

In 1995, the inward stock of foreign direct investment in developing countries averaged 18 per cent of GDP, up from 13 per cent in 1970. Yet this was still far below the 30 per cent of the 1950s, the 51 per cent of the 1930s and the 40 per cent in 1914.[27] Seventy-four per cent of all foreign direct investment went to the high-income countries in 1999 and just 24 per cent to developing countries. Africa received 1 per cent and the least-developed countries half a per cent of the total, which was also just under 11 per cent of what China received. Edward Graham of the Washington-based Institute for International Economics notes, similarly, that the share of the high-income countries in equity flows abroad from US direct investors (which omit retained earnings and intra-company loans) was close to 80 per cent in the 1990s. The share of low-income countries was negligible.[28] The problem of the world's poorest countries, it appears, is not that they are exploited by multinationals, but rather that they are ignored by them.[29]

Fourth, the composition of capital flows has changed. Capital mobility is today much bigger for short-term instruments than it was in the earlier period and the stock of short-term assets is vastly larger. This is demonstrated by the turnover of the foreign exchange market, at several hundred trillion dollars a year. The composition of long-term flows was also somewhat different in the earlier period from today's: investment was more in tangible assets than in intangible ones; by far the largest part of the earlier flows took the form of bonds, while today stocks and bonds are of roughly equal importance; portfolio flows predominated over direct investment in the earlier period, while direct investment has exceeded portfolio investment since the Second World War; and, finally, before 1914 direct investment was largely undertaken by free-standing companies, particularly in mining and transportation, while today transnational companies predominate, with a large proportion of their investment in production of services.[30] The narrowness of British investment abroad was striking. Pre-1914 data on bond flotations suggest that '40 per cent of British overseas investment in quoted securities was in railways, while 30 per cent was in the issues of national, state and municipal governments, 10 per cent was in resource-extracting industries (mainly mining) and 5 per cent was in public utilities. Commercial, industrial and financial activities that are so prominent today tend to be absent from this list.'[31]

Migration

Peter Lindert of the University of California, Davis and Jeffrey Williamson of Harvard have concluded that 'all of the real wage convergence before World War I was attributable to migration, about two-thirds of the GDP per worker convergence and perhaps one half of the GDP per capita convergence'.[32] They conclude that, in contrast, capital mobility had virtually no impact. Yet today migration has been largely removed as a mechanism for convergence of wages and living standards. As with difficulties over foreign direct investment, but in reverse, this is a reflection of national sovereignty as an obstacle to globalization. Electorates in rich countries want to preserve their privileged access to the world's predominant stock of human and physical capital and know-how. As a result, obstacles to migration are the biggest single difference between today's globalization and that of the late nineteenth century.

Paul Hirst of Birkbeck College and Grahame Thompson of the Open University note that 'the greatest era for recorded voluntary mass migration was the century after 1815. Around 60m people left Europe for the Americas, Oceania, and South and East Africa. An estimated 10m voluntarily migrated from Russia to Central Asia and Siberia. A million went from Southern Europe to North Africa. About 12m Chinese and 6m Japanese left their homelands and emigrated to East and South Asia. One and a half million left India for South East Asia and South and West Africa.'[33]

During the 1890s, a high point for population movement, the inflows of people into the US were equal to 9 per cent of the initial population – equivalent to an immigration of 25 million today. In Argentina, the comparable figure was 26 per cent; in Australia, it was 17 per cent. In the same decade, the

UK's outflow was 5 per cent of the initial population, Spain's was 6 per cent and Sweden's was 7 per cent. In the 1990s, immigration into the US was equal to about 4 per cent of the initial population.[34] The stock of migrants was just 2.3 per cent of the world population in both 1965 and 1990 and 2.9 per cent in 2000. Within western Europe, the share of migrants in the population rose from 3.6 to 6.1 per cent between 1965 and 1990. In the US it rose from 6 to 8.6 per cent. In 1911, however, the foreign born were 14.7 per cent of the population of the United States and 22 per cent of Canada's.[35]

While trade and some capital flows may be more liberally treated and bigger in relation to global economic activity than a century ago, the reverse is unquestionably true for movement of people. All the high-income countries operate controls on immigration that vary between tight and very tight. The exception is the freedom of movement of labour within the European Union. The biggest movement of people takes the form of refugees moving among (or even within) relatively poor countries. An exception to this is the movement (largely illegal) of Mexicans into the United States. These controls on migration create the world's biggest economic distortion – the discrepancy in rewards to labour. The market for labour is certainly the world's most unintegrated. That is why critics of globalization find the rewards to labour in poor countries shockingly unjust. But nobody seems to be suggesting the obvious answer: free migration.

Today, real wages for an unskilled person in the world's poorest countries are a small fraction of the wage he or she could earn in a rich one. These controls have locked a large part of humanity into failed states and economies, with inevitably adverse consequences for their incomes and so for global inequality. The emergence of a global market for skilled people may be making this even worse since the wages of the unskilled depend heavily on the presence of the skilled.

Explaining the ups and down of economic integration

Professors Lindert and Williamson have summarized what happened to market integration since 1820, as follows.[36]

First, from 1820 to 1914, price gaps in commodity markets between continents were cut by 81 per cent, 72 per cent of which was because of cheaper transport and 28 per cent was due to the pre-1870 tariff reductions. Then, between 1914 and 1950, the gaps doubled again, due to new trade barriers. Finally, between 1950 and 2000, they were cut again by 76 per cent, to end up lower than in 1914. Of this cut 74 per cent was due to trade liberalization and 26 per cent due to cheaper transport. Over the entire 1820–2000 period, price gaps were cut by 92 per cent, 18 per cent due to policies and 82 per cent due to cheaper transport.

Second, between 1820 and 1914, shares of migrants in populations of recipient countries rose (from 9.6 per cent in the United States, for example, to 14.6 per cent), entirely because of falling transport costs. Then, between 1914 and 1950, the migrant share was cut back (from 14.6 per cent to 6.9 per cent in the United States) entirely because of more restrictive immigration policies. Finally, between 1950 and 2000, shares rose again (from 6.9 per cent to 9.8 per cent in the United States), because of lower transport costs, with no net change in immigration policies. Overall, argue Lindert and Williamson, there was no clear change in migrant shares between 1820 and 2000, with policy restrictions fully offsetting transport improvements. But, it should be stressed, the global labour market disequilibrium exploded from a situation in which real wages in the richest countries were at most three times those in the poorest (for equivalent skills) to one in which they could be at least fifteen to one.

Finally, the world's capital market became significantly more integrated between 1820 and 1914, largely because of improvements in communications technology and institutional developments (the gold standard, accounting, joint-stock company, and development of equity and bond markets) rather than changes in policy. Between 1914 and 1950, the capital market became totally disintegrated into self-sufficient national markets. Finally, between 1950 and 2000 the disintegration was reversed, leaving things roughly where they had been in 1914. The reversal was partly due to improved technology and institutional developments (twenty-four-hour capital markets and growth of multinational companies) and partly due to liberalization of capital controls, particularly over the past three decades.

Overall, then, these scholars conclude that falling costs of transport and communications were more important sources of global integration in the nineteenth century, while policy was more important in the twentieth, first by closing national economies between 1914 and 1945 and then by slowly reopening them. Technology has consistently tended to lower costs of integration, but policy offset it between 1914 and 1945. It is now time to look at these two elements more closely: first, transport and communications technology and, second, changes in policies affecting international economic exchange.

Technological change

Changes in technology of transport and communications create opportunities for commerce and are, in turn, created by them. There is a strong argument to be made that the century which saw the biggest revolution in these technologies was the nineteenth, not the twentieth.[37] The railway, the steamship, the refrigerator and the telegraph created the opportunities for the integration of the nineteenth and early twentieth centuries. The railway made the shipping of commodities in bulk over land feasible for the first time in history. This, in turn, made it possible for the United States to become the world's first continental economy after the end of its civil war. The cost of shipping a bushel of wheat from New York to Liverpool halved between 1830 and 1880 and then halved again between 1880 and 1914.[38] For the first time, not only luxuries, but staple products, even perishables, could be transported, in bulk, from one end of the globe to the other. Prior to the steamship, poor people could not cross the oceans *en masse* looking for a better life. With the steamship, tens of millions of people could cross the oceans with ease.

The first transatlantic cable was laid in 1866. This, argues Professor O'Rourke, was 'the most important breakthrough of the last 200 years' for the capital markets. Before its introduction, it took ten days for information to travel between London and New York: arbitrageurs had to place orders on the basis of information ten days old, which would be executed only ten days later. With the cable, the twenty days were reduced to one. The result was an immediate 69 per cent decline in average price differentials for the same financial assets between the two cities. 'No other innovation, including the late nineteenth-century invention, the telephone, or its late twentieth-century equivalent, the Internet, has had comparable impact on the speed of information flows and capital market integration.'[39]

The twentieth century added radio, television, transcontinental telephony, the satellite, the computer and the Internet to the list of enabling technologies. It also added the container ship, the giant tanker and the airliner. In 1995, the World Bank reported that between 1920 and 1990, the cost of oceanic freight fell by 70 per cent, but subsequent work has challenged this. Today, however, some scholars believe that ocean freight rates may not have fallen since 1910.[40] But air transport was invented. Its availability has exploded since the Second World War, while the unit cost of air transport fell by more than 80 per cent between 1930 and 1990.[41] The cost fell by about 15–20 per cent between 1975 and 1993 alone.[42] The cost of a three-minute telephone call from New York to

London fell from about $250 in 1930 to a few cents today, in current prices.[43] With the Internet, the cost of global communication is now close to zero. This is proving particularly important for the global delivery of services and the organization of intra-company trade.

New opportunities have been created and, again, they have been exploited. They are to be seen in twenty-four-hour financial markets, mass tourism and the global interconnection of production that has spawned the multinational corporations of today. The share of United States imports carried by air rose from 8.8 per cent in 1974 to 19 per cent in 1996. Nearly a third of its exports go by air.[44] Increased speed and security of sea transport has lowered costs to users, even if freight rates may not have fallen. More rapid transport was, according to one researcher, equivalent to a reduction in the tariff on United States imports of manufactures from 32 to 9 per cent between 1950 and 1998.[45] People living in 1900 could not have imagined these changes, just as people living in 1800 could hardly have imagined the railways and steamships, let alone the telegraph cables, that knitted together the world of the Victorians.

In the long run, the world seems bound to become more globalized, because opportunities have grown enormously. Yet this certainly does not mean the death of distance. Distance will always matter, because we are physical beings located in a specific place. As the former director general of the Confederation of British Industry, Adair Turner, has argued in his book *Just Capital*, many valued activities are 'high-touch' – looking after babies and old people or serving meals.[46] As we become richer and the cost of material things falls, we demand more of these services. It is even possible to imagine a world in which there is far more intensive trade in commodities and in information, but the share of GDP and employment affected is far smaller than today, because productivity rises rapidly in these tradable activities and so their relative prices continue to fall. Meanwhile, an ever-higher proportion of income is spent on personal services.

Yet our ability to transport goods, services, people and information has increased so vastly over the past two centuries that the opportunities for growing exchange cannot be suppressed. Perhaps the most important change is simply the information people possess about what is happening elsewhere and their ability to interact with foreigners. George Orwell's dystopia, *1984*, turned out to be the reverse of the truth: modern computer and telecommunications technology liberates rather than imprisons. In the end, even the communist gangster-state of the Soviet Union collapsed under the strain of trying to suppress its people. The Soviet Union's autarkic regime foundered not because it was physically impossible to control cross-border movement of knowledge and ideas, but because the costs of so doing became unbearably high.

Politics and policy

If it was not transport and communications technology that created the great collapse of the liberal world in the 1914–45 disaster, what did? The answer is the interactions between politics and policy, themselves driven by profound economic and social forces. Yet, quite as important as the purely material forces, in Marx's sense, were ideas, his among them. In the second half of the nineteenth century and with increasing force in the twentieth, collectivist ideas of various kinds became dominant, from the benign democratic socialism that turned into contemporary social democracy, to the far more menacing creeds of Marxism-Leninism, imperialism, nationalism, social Darwinism, fascism and Nazism.

A concoction of anti-liberal ideas was ingested by an ever-wider circle of thinking people. Thomas Mann's masterpiece *The Magic Mountain*, set at the time of the First World War, describes the assault on liberalism by more malevolent creeds. In the end, the United States, a liberal democracy through and through, brought liberalism back almost from the dead. The collapse of the Soviet empire between 1989 and 1991 marked the triumph of these ideas and the end of late-nineteenth-century collectivism.

Naturally, this was not the end of anti-liberalism. On the contrary, liberalism's triumph was brief. But, as utopian and nationalist forces have regrouped in the high-income countries in the 1990s, they have had to approach liberalism in a different way, partly by opposing the thrust of modern economic growth. Meanwhile, parts of the developing world, until relatively recently captivated by socialism, have developed indigenous forms of fascism. Such forces are evident within militant Hinduism and, still more, within extreme forms of contemporary Islam.

The liberal heyday[47]

The integration of the European and so, given the political dominance of the European powers in the world during the nineteenth century, of almost all the world economy was the international manifestation of the Promethean revolution. But it also rested on three signal political developments.

First, there was almost a century of relative peace after the end of the Napoleonic Wars in 1815. That peace was based on the idea of the concert of nations and a more or less implicit acceptance of the dominance of Great Britain in the rest of the world and of Russia in eastern Europe. The United States did not figure in these calculations, largely because its energies were devoted to internal development and the expansion of the frontier westwards. This geopolitical equilibrium was to be undermined and then destroyed by the rise of Prussia and then of Germany in the second half of the century.

Second was the establishment of liberal trade and sound money. Liberal trade spread from the United Kingdom to France, through the Cobden–Chevalier treaty in 1860, and then to most of Europe through a series of bilateral treaties based on the most-favoured-nation, or non-discrimination, principle. Sound money, internal and external, was established through the gold standard. (See Table 8.8 for the complex monetary history of the past 130 years.) Until the First World War, the resistance of organized labour to the necessary corrections in money wages was sufficiently feeble to make this possible.

Finally, there was a broad acceptance of liberal ideas among the increasingly influential middle classes, at least in economics. These ideas underpinned the other features of the system: a desire for peaceful international relations, liberal trade and the gold standard. Their influence was tied to the prestige of Great Britain, which reached its European zenith at the time of the Great Exhibition in 1851.

Not so strange death of nineteenth-century liberalism[48]

This liberal universe collapsed under a series of pressures, internal and external to the European powers. Why did it do so?

The starting-point must be with the internal changes brought about by industrialization. The biggest question, particularly in the old countries of Europe, became how to accommodate the pressures and harness the energies of the new and rapidly growing working class. Among the most successful answers was nationalism, reinforced by a more or less explicit alliance between the old ruling classes and the working class, against the liberal middle classes. At the same time, élites saw the economic and military value of a literate population and so created, or promoted, national and largely nationalized systems of education. These, in turn, became vehicles for the propagation of new nationalist ideologies.[49]

Mass literacy and nationalism were closely connected to the new military realities. Power rested increasingly upon the mobilization of mass armies of motivated and obedient citizens, as the French state had demonstrated in the Revolutionary and Napoleonic Wars. Creating such armies became a central task of the state. As all male citizens were mobilized, the need to establish a unifying ideology became still more important. Nationalism served this turn as well. The literate citizen–soldiers of the nineteenth century could hardly be denied the vote. The mobilization of women in the First World War similarly made further extension of the suffrage unavoidable. As the suffrage spread and the need to secure the loyalty of a mobilized population became more pressing, demands also emerged for protection against the winds of economic change. Welfare states were born. It was no coincidence that the starting-point was in Bismarck's conservative and nationalist Germany.

The development of social security, which became, in time, the basis for European social (and Christian) democracy coincided with the first age of global economic integration.[50] It was not just a tactic by a conservative élite to embrace the working class, though such considerations were important in a number of countries. It also mattered greatly to the working class. Together with the rise of the trades unions, social security was to be a potent legacy to modern Europe. It came to the more individualistic United States only in the 1930s.

Social security, for all its evident benefits, also imposed – and still imposes – a largely disregarded cost: it makes it far less attractive to share the benefits of citizenship with outsiders. That was already becoming less pleasing as real wages began to rise in the industrializing states.[51] In the rich societies of the world, citizenship became, for those without significant personal property, the most valuable asset they owned. Residence gives access to work in the countries with the highest wages. Universal suffrage gave the adult population the ability to vote for exclusion of immigrants from the domestic labour market. It also gave them the right to vote for parties that promised to redistribute wealth from richer members of their societies to the less successful. A widening suffrage established socialist or, at the least, radical parties in the domestic politics of advanced countries. It made control over immigration inevitable, while the nationalist ideology made such restrictions natural. Immigrants, after all, were foreigners and, as such, people who could not be trusted to share in the community of values required by citizen armies.

Equally natural were imperialism and protectionism. Imperialism had many benefits for the new militarily mobilized nation states. It gave a *raison d'être* for the old military élites in a new age. It was the old ethic of feudal plunder in an up-to-date guise. It was a way of binding the working class into a great national endeavour. It could also be presented to the middle classes as a way of securing access to natural resources or markets or just jobs for their children. Imperialism was a self-fulfilling prophecy. The imperialism of others made imperialism rational for oneself.

Meanwhile, protection against imports of manufactures was an obvious way to reward the industrial working class. Protection could also be justified for militarily essential products, such as steel. Policy-makers wanted an economy capable of fighting long wars. This led to government involvement in the development of the 'national economy' – an entity that belonged to the nation state collectively, not to its people individually. The German empire, the most powerful and threatening of the new European nation states, was particularly successful in developing its economy in these ways. That success shook faith in *laissez-faire* elsewhere, including in Britain, where imperial preference and industrial protection became powerful causes by the end of the nineteenth century. Infant-industry protection was adopted in many New World economies, notably the United States. Interests of class and concepts of national survival were behind the pressure for protection of agriculture once the steamship and the railway brought grain and beef from the New World in large quantities.[52]

Bismarck's tariffs of 1879, which supported both industrial and agricultural products, were a decisive moment: the most dynamic and the biggest economy on the European continent had rejected liberalism. France finally followed with the Meline tariff of 1892. Tariffs also rose in Sweden, Italy and Spain during the 1880s and 1890s. In the United States, meanwhile, tariffs were high after the civil war and stayed high. They were raised still further in 1890. As Princeton University's Harold James argues, protection could be provided one product at a time. It was (and is) a good way for US legislators to provide services retail to their voters.[53] In Latin America, tariffs rose throughout the late nineteenth century. Tariffs in Russia were and remained high. Of the significant economic powers only Britain clung to the old faith, though with diminishing fervour.

The end of *laissez-faire*, liberal trade and unchecked immigration were almost inevitable consequences of the movement in the developing European countries towards the universal-suffrage, militarily mobilized, industrialized nation state. Equally inevitable were privileges for trades unions, legal protections in labour markets and the emergence of welfare states. The United States was different because its population arrived to take advantage of the unique benefits of a free country with effectively limitless resources to exploit and no immediate enemies. But it remained true to the staunch protectionism of its industrial north throughout the late nineteenth century and the first half of the twentieth.

Animating these shifts towards nationalism and protectionism was the anti-liberal current of ideas: the rise of collectivist ideologies of which nationalism was just one. As Lindsey remarks: 'A new prospect came . . . to the fore – one of rival nations, rival races, pitted in fundamental and irresolvable conflict, and engaged in a grim and merciless struggle for supremacy or submission. This radical and ruinous shift of perspective did not merely coincide with the spreading enthusiasm for centralization and top down control: rather the two developments were interconnected and mutually reinforcing.'[54]

Collectivism and nationalism were brought together most completely in Germany. Gustav Schmoller, an influential state socialist, wrote that 'all small and large civilized states have a natural tendency to extend their border to reach seas and large rivers, to acquire trading posts and colonies in other parts of the world. And they constantly come into contact with foreign nations, with whom they must, quite frequently, fight. Economic development and national expansion, progress in trade and an enhancement of power are in most cases inextricably connected. . . .'[55] What the German ideology offered was tribalism allied to modern science and technology. It was both reactionary and modern. It was, apparently, almost infinitely seductive. In 1915, Werner Sombart, who started as a Marxist and ended as a Nazi, wrote that war 'is necessary in order to prevent the heroic outlook from falling prey to the forces of evil, to the narrow, abject spirit of commerce'.[56]

The glorification of war, the collective and the national and contempt for peace, the individual and the cosmopolitan were to become *Leitmotifs* of late nineteenth- and early twentieth-century German thought. Kant and the other great German liberals of the late eighteenth and early nineteenth century were forgotten. German strength and assertiveness then awoke a powerful response in the imperialism and protectionism of Joseph Chamberlain in Britain. In turn, the threat of British imperial protection, especially when the United States was also protectionist, inevitably strengthened Germany's belief that it needed an empire and, later, *Lebensraum* of its own.

Whether this transformation in perspective and political realities was certain to lead to war is an open question. But this outcome became highly probable. The struggle *for* empire turned into the life-and-death struggle *among* empire-builders that we know as the First World War.

Yet the global economy continued to function relatively smoothly until war broke out. There were many financial crises in peripheral countries.[57] But these did not shake the gold standard in the core countries. Trade grew rapidly, though this was entirely because of declining transport costs, since trade barriers were generally rising. But trade barriers were relatively modest by the standards of what was to follow, particularly since there were no quantitative restrictions on imports.

From world war to world war

The First World War was a crime and a blunder. But it was no accident. It shook the liberal global economic system to its foundations. The war directly caused an enormous increase in the power and responsibilities of states. It also produced the first systems of national economic planning, later imitated by Stalin's Russia and the combatants of the Second World War. Lenin explicitly recognized the German war economy as 'a complete material preparation for socialism'.[58] This new form of planned economy subsequently became the model for all the developmental states of post-colonial developing countries.[59] The war also greatly increased the sense of obligation to the citizen–soldier. Welfare states were bigger in the inter-war years than they had been before the war, just as they were bigger in the 1950s than before the Second World War.[60]

By the time of the First World War, nationalism was not the only collectivist ideology. Socialism and communism were both well established. More broadly, doubt was expressed by intellectuals in the free-market orthodoxies of the high Victorian period. Capitalism was increasingly viewed as unjust, unstable and inefficient. The new achievements of the state in mobilizing resources for war could, it was argued, be as readily adapted to peacetime. Socialists and communists were not alone in believing this. Many on the right also accepted that collectivist solutions, which inevitably meant national solutions, were right for the new time.

The First World War led to the imposition of controls on trade. Protectionism was strong in Europe throughout the 1920s as well. Tariff rates drifted upwards. Efforts were made to reverse this trend, notably at the 1927 World Economic Conference. They failed.[61] The First World War also directly caused the subsequent monetary disorder. Huge public debts were run up to finance the preparations for the war and then the war itself. Inflationary finance was universal. So was inflation. After the war, the creation of new states in central and eastern Europe and the weakness of some of the old made public finances unmanageable. Almost everybody had expected someone else to pay for their war. They were all disappointed, including the French who had some reason to believe the peace settlement would deliver vast German reparations. In the words of the late Rudi Dornbusch, 'governments who could do virtually nothing could do that one thing: printing money. And that is what marked the early 1920s: phenomenal money creation and even more extreme inflation throughout central Europe and eastern Europe, from Germany to Russia, from Austria to Greece. France, to its own surprise, did not go quite as far, Britain and the US not at all.'[62]

The failure to re-establish monetary stability in the 1920s, after the disruption of the war, strengthened doubts about economic liberalism. The Great Depression confirmed them. The Smoot–Hawley tariff in the United States, in 1930, which raised the average tariff on manufactures in the world's chief creditor nation to the offensive level of 48 per cent (see Table 8.7), was the last straw. Italy and France reacted at once. Britain finally abandoned free trade and the gold standard, for ever, in 1931. This collapse in trade was a huge spur to the search for autarky and *Lebensraum*, most of all for Germany and Japan.

In just three years, from 1929 to 1932, world trade fell by 70 per cent in value terms and 25 per cent in real terms. Prices in world trade collapsed, and trade restrictions were mounted around the world, as 'beggar-thy-neighbor' policies became the rule. Tariffs were escalated, quantitative restrictions and selected preferences became the rule, exchange controls soon followed. The open economy had given way to protection of national markets and an

Table 8.7 Average tariffs on imported manufactured goods (per cent)

	1875	1913	1931	1950	Pre-Uruguay Round	Post-Uruguay Round
France	12–15	20	30	18	–	–
Germany	4–6	17	21	26	–	–
Italy	8–10	18	46	25	–	–
UK	0	0	n.a.	23	–	–
EU	–	–	–	–	5.7	3.6
US	40–50	44	48	14	4.6	3.0

Source: Michael D. Bordo, Barry Eichengreen and Douglas A. Irwin, 'Is Globalization Today Really Different than Globalization a Hundred Years Ago?', National Bureau of Economic Research Working Paper 7195, www.nber.org, June 1999, Table 3.

overwhelming presumption that economics stops at the border. If these were the policies at the center, the periphery responded in kind. Debt default was common and industrialization behind protective barriers became the rule in those countries where commodity [price] collapses no longer afforded a living. Latin America is a case in point.[63]

Mass unemployment was unbearable in universal-suffrage democracies. *Laissez-faire* capitalism was finished. On this almost everybody agreed. The question was whether the market mechanism could be allowed to survive, as Keynes hoped. Those on the left rejected even this. True, there were a few holdouts against the interventionist trend – notably, the Austrians and the Chicago school. But even there doubts were expressed. The great Austrian economist Joseph Schumpeter published his classic, *Capitalism, Socialism and Democracy*, a brilliant declaration of surrender to the victorious forces of socialism, during the Second World War.[64]

By the 1930s the combination of collectivist ideas, protectionist interests, universal suffrage, war, monetary disorder and economic depression had destroyed the assumptions, beliefs, policies and practices that had underpinned the liberal world economic order. The great powers created economic systems that reinforced their own power and shielded them from the power of their rivals. Multilateralism was replaced by bilateralism, non-discrimination by discrimination, free trade by comprehensive protection, freedom for capital flows by exchange controls, fixed by floating exchange rates, and free movement of labour by rigorous restrictions (see Table 8.8). National socialism, fascism, militarism and communism were seen as the waves of the future, loathed by some and loved by others. This was a new world, if hardly a brave one.[65]

Yet the catastrophe might not have been as deep if the transition from Britain to the United States as liberal hegemon had not so signally failed. By the end of the First World War, an exhausted and shrunken Britain no longer had the means to stabilize the global order. But the continental colossus made almost every conceivable mistake between its entry into the First World War and Pearl Harbor. It imposed an unworkable peace, but refused to enforce it; it exacerbated the reparations crisis by insisting upon payment of the inter-allied war debt; it failed to abide by the monetary rules of the restored gold standard; it triggered the Great Depression; its central bank neglected to halt the monetary collapse that spread world-wide via the gold standard; it accelerated the rush into world-wide protectionism with the Smoot–Hawley tariff; and it did nothing to resist the fascist and Nazi threats. Britain no longer had the means or the morale. The US lacked the will and the wisdom. The disasters

Table 8.8 History of monetary and exchange rate regimes

Regime	Period
I. International Gold Standard	1879–1914
II. Inter-war instability	1918 1939
— Floating	— 1918–1925
— Return to gold	— 1925–1931
— Return to floating with controls	— 1931–1939
III. Semi-fixed-rate dollar standard	1945–1971
— Establishing convertibility	— 1945–1958
— Bretton Woods system proper	— 1958–1971
IV. Floating-rate dollar standard	1971–1984
— Failure to agree	— 1971–1974
— Return to floating	— 1974–1984
V. EMS and greater D-Mark zone	1979–1993
VI. Plaza-Louvre intervention accords	1985–1993
VII. Towards renewed floating and Emu	1993–
— Broad multilateral surveillance	— 1993–1997
— End of dollar pegs	— 1997–
— Monetary union in the EU	— 1999–

Source: Paul Hirst and Grahame Thompson, *Globalization in Question: The International Economy and the Possibilities of Governance*, second edition (Cambridge: Polity Press. 1999), p. 33, updated.

of those years would have been avoided if the US had understood in 1917 what it had learned by 1941.

A world restored – from post-war reconstruction to China's membership of the WTO

The first and most important condition for restoration of a liberal global order was an engaged US. A second was Europe's desire to restore the internal and external commerce on which its prosperity had always depended. Yet in moving towards a liberal international economy, the legacy of the previous half-century could not be ignored. The most important inheritances in the advanced countries, particularly in western Europe, were the commitment to domestic economic stabilization, above all full employment, to the welfare state, to various forms of the 'mixed economy' and to control over immigration. What resulted, therefore, was a successful process of liberalization, but one that focused on trade and currency convertibility on current account. This was a period in which fixed exchange rates were combined with domestic monetary autonomy by means of controls on convertibility, principally on capital account.

The United States liberalized its economy relatively swiftly after the end of the Second World War. Its volte-face on trade had already tentatively begun in 1934 with its Reciprocal Trade Agreements Act which incorporated unconditional most-favoured-nation treatment. This was to bear fruit after the war, in the General Agreement on Tariffs and Trade negotiated in 1947, this being the commercial policy chapter of the stillborn International Trade Organization. Over eight trade negotiations, the last being the Uruguay Round, barriers to imports of manufactured goods in the high-income countries were lowered to negligible levels (see Table 8.7). But relatively substantial tariff and non-tariff barriers remained in the high-income countries to imports of labour-intensive goods, especially clothing, and on agricultural products. These barriers fell particularly heavily on exports from developing countries.[66]

In the early post-war years, the United States also supported discriminatory liberalization within the western part of a divided Europe, partly in response to the growing fear of communism, brought to eastern Europe by Soviet bayonets, but popular in much of the west as well. The liberalization began under the auspices of the Marshall Plan (orchestrated by the Organization for European Economic Co-operation, which later became the Organization for Economic Co-operation and Development) and subsequently within the European Community and, to a lesser degree, the European Free Trade Area. Currency convertibility on current account and the shift away from bilateral clearing of payments was finally achieved in western Europe on 31 December 1958.

Meanwhile, the empires of the weakened European powers disintegrated over the succeeding three decades after the end of the Second World War. The newly independent countries (along with the depression-scarred commodity exporters of Latin America, and communist China) followed, with few exceptions, the path of inward-looking industrialization and the planned economy that had been trodden by the Soviet Union.[67] Most came to regret this choice. Not only was it to prove costly economically, but the massive expansion of the state, the economic distortions it created and the extent of its interference in everyday economic life were corrupting. Most developing countries are trying, with varying success, to undo the damage.

Yet, in terms of economic growth, the 1950–73 period was the most successful ever. Only one region – developing Asia – has done better since then (see Table 8.1), though that is a crucial exception, since that region contains over half the world's population. Some argue that this success was due to the controls, particularly on capital flows. But it is more plausible that the rapid growth of the period was driven by three special factors: the exceptional opportunities for catch-up growth, especially in western Europe and Japan after the disruptions of the inter-war period; the stimulus of what was initially a mild, but ultimately destabilizing, global inflationary process; and the initial benefits of industrialization in newly independent developing countries oriented towards import substitution. As the later collapse of the Soviet empire suggests, inward-looking development runs into the sand, however, as the economy falls further behind leading-edge technologies, competition is weak, returns fall, export growth sags, the balance of payments becomes chronically fragile, and governments find it increasingly difficult to manage their finances. This era of somewhat illusory growth came to an end in most developing countries either in fiscal, monetary and debt crises or in a disturbing slowdown in growth, or, frequently, in both.

The 1970s and 1980s also created a crisis for the partial liberalization of the advanced countries. First, perceived conflicts between domestic stabilization and a fixed exchange rate, above all in the US, led to the breakdown, after 1971, in the Bretton Woods system of fixed but adjustable exchange rates. The abandonment of pegged exchange rates then allowed a period of monetary expansion that, coupled with the oil shocks of the 1970s, ended in exceptionally high inflation. This led, equally naturally, to the world of domestic monetary control or, subsequently, inflation control with which the world is increasingly familiar. Free capital movement and domestic stabilization (see Table 8.8) were chosen, at the price of a floating exchange rate. In this sense, today's economic order is quite different from that of 1870–1914.

Countries that could not tolerate floating rates, however, notably in Europe, decided that there was a need for a new exchange rate arrangement based on the principle of Europe-wide stabilization. Thus began, also in the early 1970s, the drawn-out process that led three decades later to currency union. Developing countries meanwhile clung as long as possible to their exchange rate pegs, almost all against the dollar. Combined with excessive borrowing by governments and incompetent liberalization of controls on capital flows, the result was to be a series of shattering exchange rate and financial crises in the 1980s and 1990s.

The move to floating rates and domestic monetary stabilization made it easier to contemplate the abolition of exchange controls. But this move, which was to become universal among the advanced countries by the early 1990s, was also consistent with the advance of information technology and the general move towards reliance on market forces. For the high unemployment, high inflation and lower growth of the 1970s did more than destroy faith in naive

Keynesianism; it also created increased interest in market solutions. There began what amounted to a market counter-revolution in the advanced economies.

Meanwhile, developing countries also changed course, for not entirely dissimilar reasons to those of the advanced countries. The success of outward-looking trade policies became recognized in the course of the 1970s, largely as the result of the work of economists, notably Oxford University's Ian Little, Jagdish Bhagwati, then at the Massachusetts Institute of Technology but now at Columbia University, Anne Krueger, then at the University of Minnesota but now first deputy managing director of the International Monetary Fund, and the late Bela Balassa of the World Bank and Johns Hopkins University.[68] The long-standing opposition of Peter Bauer of the London School of Economics to planning and foreign aid was, in substantial measure, vindicated.[69]

Meanwhile, the brutality and poverty of the Soviet system had robbed socialism of its intellectual and moral prestige in the west in the 1960s and 1970s. In the 1970s and 1980s, the failures of import substitution and the collapse of the Soviet Union destroyed the credibility of the inward-looking planned economy in developing countries. The debt crisis of the early 1980s and chronic stagflation also brought about a revolution in concepts of macro-economic policy. The result was a reunification of economic policy, as developing countries adopted regimes similar to those of the advanced countries – trade liberalization, relaxation of exchange controls, fiscal stability and low inflation.[70] Developing countries, too, increasingly abandoned fixed exchange rates, adopted inflation targets and liberalized exchange controls. Between 1975 and 1997, the proportion of developing countries with flexible exchange rates rose from 10 per cent to over 50 per cent.[71] Today, the proportion would be still higher. The exceptions moved towards currency boards or outright use of another country's currency, usually the dollar, as their own.

Developing countries also participated in trade negotiations that, with the Uruguay Round and establishment of the World Trade Organization, became comprehensive in scope and deep in their domestic implications. In 2002, China, less than three decades previously in the grip of Mao Zedong's tyranny, joined the WTO – a symbolic moment in the reunification of the world economy. With 144 members by 2003, the WTO is close to being a universal organization. The most important country to remain outside was Russia. But its membership, too, is now only a matter of time.

To many critics, the last two decades of the twentieth century were the age of a manic 'neo-liberalism' imposed by ideological fanatics on a reluctant world. This picture is false. The change in policies was, with very few exceptions, introduced by pragmatic politicians in response to experience. The stagflation of the 1970s discredited naive Keynesianism; the return of inflation discredited the view that monetary policy does not matter; the failure of nationalized industries discredited state ownership; the revolt of organized labour discredited wage controls; the distortions evident in the economy discredited price controls; the superior performance of outward-oriented, market-friendly developing countries (such as Singapore and Taiwan) and the equally evident relative failure of the inward-looking colossi of China and India discredited self-sufficiency; the high inflation and external debt cum fiscal crises of Latin America discredited populism; and, most important of all, the weakening and collapse of Soviet state-socialism discredited faith in allegedly rational central planning.

Some of the politicians who brought in the changes of the 1980s and 1990s were, up to a point, ideologically convinced economic liberals: Ronald Reagan and Margaret Thatcher come to mind. Yet even these two leaders came to power only in response to a demand for change. But many of the leaders who made the most difference were far from being committed liberals. Many were on the left. Indeed, economic liberalism has never been exclusively or even mainly a conservative creed. The list of important reformers includes Jacques Delors, with the single-market programme in Europe, Deng Xiaoping in China, Narasimha Rao in India, Enrique Cardoso (erstwhile dependency theorist) in Brazil, and the Labour Party's Roger Douglas in New Zealand. No French government privatized more than the socialist one of Lionel Jospin. The Democrats under Bill Clinton agreed to the World Trade Organization. Tony Blair's government made the Bank of England independent. The Bretton Woods institutions – the World Bank and the International Monetary Fund – supported policies of macroeconomic stabilization and liberalization in developing countries on largely pragmatic grounds as well.[72]

Assessment

If we look at the history of the last century, two points stand out. First, if we are to understand the limited increase in the extent of globalization and the ups and downs, we must look at policy. In the first half of the twentieth century, governments closed down international economic interdependence. Then, in the second half, there was opening of barriers to movement of goods, services and capital, though far less so of people. That opening began with trade in the high-income countries and spread to capital flows slowly. Many European countries liberalized capital flows only about 1990. The opening spread to much of the rest of the world, in both trade and capital flows, in the 1980s and 1990s.

The second point is that the degree of international economic integration remains limited. The high-income countries are more open on trade and capital flows than ever before. But they continue to protect labour-intensive, resource-processing and agricultural activities. In so doing, they inflict substantial harm on developing countries. The high-income countries also operate tight controls on inflows of immigrants. Many developing countries still remain more closed to trade, capital and movement of people than they were a century ago. Net flows of capital and direct investment to developing countries are, in all, also very modest. Globalization is not rampant. It remains remarkably limited.

Part IV   **Why the Critics are Wrong**

Prologue

Now that we know why a global market economy makes sense and how, after the crimes and blunders of the early 20th century, one has been, at least partially, restored, let us turn to those who think it has all been a huge mistake. Critics of economic globalization make many charges. In this section, the most important ones are divided under five headings: first, global economic integration has worsened inequality and poverty, everywhere; second, liberal trade undermines prosperity and thwarts development; third, economic globalization serves only the interests of predatory multinational corporations; fourth, financial liberalization is a threat to economic development; and, finally, integration undermines democracy, sovereignty, the welfare state and environmental regulation, creating, instead, a headlong race to the bottom.

Chapter 9 **Incensed about Inequality**

> *Globalization has dramatically increased inequality between and within nations, even as it connects people as never before. A world in which the assets of the 200 richest people are greater than the combined income of the more than 2bn people at the other end of the economic ladder should give everyone pause.*
>
> Jay Mazur, president of the Union of Needletrades, Industrial and Textile Employees.[1]

Jay Mazur is not alone. Ignacio Ramonet has written on similar lines, in *Le Monde Diplomatique*, that:

> the dramatic advance of globalization and neoliberalism ... has been accompanied by an *explosive growth in inequality* and a return of mass poverty and unemployment. The very opposite of everything which the modern state and modern citizenship is supposed to stand for.
>
> The net result is a *massive growth in inequality*. The United States, which is the richest country in the world, has more than 60 million poor. The world's foremost trading power, the European Union, has over 50 million. In the United States, 1 per cent of the population owns 39 per cent of the country's wealth. Taking the planet as a whole, the combined wealth of the 358 richest people (all of them dollar billionaires) is greater than the total annual income of 45 per cent of the world's poorest inhabitants, that is, 2.6bn people.[2]

Let us, for a moment, ignore the assumption that the number of poor (how defined?) in two of the richest regions in the world tells one anything about global inequality, or about poverty for that matter, or even about inequality within the US and the European Union. Let us also ignore the comparison between the *assets* of one group of people, the richest, and the *incomes* of another, the poor, which is a comparison of apples and oranges. (In order to obtain the permanent incomes of the rich, one would need to divide the value of their assets by at least twenty.) These absurdities merely make Ramonet's diatribe representative of the empty rhetoric of many critics of globalization. But the questions that underlie his remarks need to be tackled. Here are seven propositions that can be advanced about what has happened in the age of so-called 'neo-liberal globalization' over the past two decades

First, the ratio of average incomes in the richest countries to those in the poorest has continued to rise.

Second, the absolute gap in living standards between today's high-income countries and most developing countries has also continued to rise.

Third, global inequality among individuals has risen.

Fourth, the number of people in extreme poverty has risen.

Fifth, the proportion of people in extreme poverty in the world's population has also risen.

Sixth, the poor of the world are worse off not just in terms of incomes, but in terms of a wide range of other indicators of human welfare.

Seventh, income inequality has risen in every country and particularly in countries most exposed to international economic integration.

In the rest of this chapter I will consider what we know about these propositions and how the answers relate to international economic integration. Before examining them, however, we need to ask what matters to us. Most of the debate has been either about whether inequality has risen between the world's rich and poor or about whether the number of people in income poverty has risen. But critics of globalization have themselves often rightly argued that there is more to life than income. What is most important must be the living standards of the poor, not just in terms of their incomes, narrowly defined, but in terms of their health, life expectancy, nourishment and education.

Equally, we need to understand that rises in inequality might occur in very different ways. Three possibilities come to mind at once: a rise in incomes of the better off, at the expense of the poor; a rise in the incomes of the better off, with no effects on the welfare of the poor; or rises in incomes of the better off that, in various ways, benefit the poor, but not by proportionately as much as they benefit the better off. It seems clear that the first of these is malign, the second desirable, unless the welfare of the better off counts for nothing, and the third unambiguously desirable, though one might wish more of the gains to accrue to the poor. True egalitarians would differ on these judgements, of course. Indeed, an extreme egalitarian might take the view that a world in which everybody was an impoverished subsistence farmer would be better than the world we now have, because it would be less unequal. Most people – including, I imagine, many protesters against globalization – would regard this as crazy. Few are that egalitarian. Most people are not even as egalitarian as the late philosopher John Rawls, who argued that inequality was permissible only to the extent that it benefited the poor.

We need to be equally careful in considering the role of globalization in relation to inequality and poverty. International economic integration may affect global inequality in several different ways. Here are a few possibilities: it may increase inequality by lowering the incomes of the poor; it may raise the incomes of the better off, without having any impact on the incomes of the poor; it may raise the incomes of the poor by proportionately less than it raises the incomes of the better off; or it may raise the incomes of the poor by proportionately more than it raises those of the better off. Only the first is unambiguously bad, but all of the first three would be associated with increasing inequality. Yet both of the last two mean higher living standards for the poor.

Again, it may not be globalization, as such, that delivers these outcomes, but a combination of globalization with non-globalization. Globalization may raise incomes of globalizers, while non-globalization lowers the incomes of non-globalizers. Then an era of globalization may be associated with rising inequality that is caused not by globalization, but by its opposite, the refusal (or inability) of some countries to participate.

The most important questions to bear in mind in the discussions below are, therefore, these. Is human welfare, broadly defined, rising? Is the proportion of humanity living in desperate misery declining? If inequality is rising, are the rich profiting at the expense of the poor? Is globalization damaging the poor or is it rather non-globalization that is doing so? To answer all these questions, one must start at the beginning, with economic growth.

Economic growth and globalization

In the mid-1970s I was the World Bank's senior divisional economist on India during the country's worst post-independence decade. After a spurt of growth in the early phase of its inward-looking development, growth in incomes per head had ground virtually to a halt. Hundreds of millions of people seemed, as a result, to be mired in hopeless and unending poverty. In a book published in 1968, a well-known environmentalist doomsayer, Paul Ehrlich, had written the country off altogether.[3] For a young man from the UK, work in India as an economist was both fascinating and appalling: so much poverty; so much frustration; so much complacency. Yet I was convinced then, as I am now, that, with perfectly feasible policy changes, this vast country could generate rapid rates of economic growth and reductions in poverty. No iron law imposed levels of real output (and so real incomes) per head at only 10 per cent of those in high-income countries.

Since those unhappy days, India has enjoyed the fruit of two revolutions: the green revolution, which transformed agricultural productivity; and a liberalizing revolution, which began, haltingly, under Rajiv Gandhi's leadership, in the 1980s and then took a 'great leap forward' in 1991, in response to a severe foreign exchange crisis, under the direction of one of the country's most remarkable public servants, Manmohan Singh, the then finance minister. Slowly, India abandoned the absurdities of its pseudo-Stalinist 'control raj' in favour of individual enterprise and the market. As a result, between 1980 and 2000, India's real GDP per head more than doubled. Stagnation has become a thing of the past.

India was not alone. On the contrary, it was far behind a still more dynamic and even bigger liberalizing country – China, which achieved a rise in real incomes per head of well over 400 per cent between 1980 and 2000. China and India, it should be remembered, contain almost two-fifths of the world's population. China alone contains more people than Latin America and sub-Saharan Africa together. Many other countries in east and south Asia have also experienced rapid growth. According to the 2003 *Human Development Report* from the United Nations Development Programme, between 1975 and 2001, GDP per head rose at 5.9 per cent a year in east Asian developing countries (with 31 per cent of the world's population in 2000). The corresponding figure for growth of GDP per head for south Asia (with another 22 per cent of the world's population) was 2.4 per cent a year. Between 1990 and 2001, GDP per head rose at 5.5 per cent a year in east Asia, while growth rose to 3.2 per cent a year in south Asia.

Never before have so many people – or so large a proportion of the world's population – enjoyed such large rises in their standards of living. Meanwhile, GDP per head in high-income countries (with 15 per cent of the world's population) rose by 2.1 per cent a year between 1975 and 2001 and by only 1.7 per cent a year between 1990 and 2001. This then was a period of partial convergence: the incomes of poor developing countries, with more than half the world's population, grew substantially faster than those of the world's richest countries.

This, in a nutshell, is why Mazur and the many people who think like him are wrong. Globalization has not increased inequality. It has reduced it, just as it has reduced the incidence of poverty. How can this be, critics will demand? Are absolute and proportional gaps in living standards between the world's richest and poorest countries not rising all the time? Yes is the answer. And is inequality not rising in most of the world's big countries? Yes, is again the answer. So how can global inequality be falling? To adapt Bill Clinton's campaign slogan, it is the growth, stupid. Rapid economic growth in poor countries with half the world's population has powerful effects on the only sort of inequality which matters, that among individuals. It has similarly dramatic effects on world poverty. The rise of Asia is transforming the world, very much for the better. It is the 'Asian drama' of our times, to plagiarize the title of a celebrated work by a Nobel-laureate economist, the late Gunnar Myrdal.

What, the reader may ask, has this progress to do with international economic integration? In its analysis of globalization, published in 2002, the World Bank divided seventy-three developing countries, with aggregate population, in 1997, of 4 billion (80 per cent of all people in developing countries), into two groups: the third that had increased ratios of trade to GDP, since 1980, by the largest amount and the rest.[4] The former group, with an aggregate population of 2.9 billion, managed a remarkable combined increase of 104 per cent in the ratio of trade to GDP. Over the same period, the increase in the trade ratio of the high-income countries was 71 per cent, while the 'less globalized' two-thirds of countries in the sample of developing countries experienced a decline in their trade ratios.

The average incomes per head of these twenty-four globalizing countries rose by 67 per cent (a compound rate of 3.1 per cent a year) between 1980 and 1997. In contrast, the other forty-nine countries managed a rise of only 10 per cent (a compound rate of 0.5 per cent a year) in incomes per head over this period. As Table 9.1 shows, these more globalized countries did not have particularly high levels of education in 1980. At that time, they were also a little poorer, as a group, than the rest. Subsequently, the new global-izers, as the World Bank calls them, cut their import tariffs by 34 percentage points, on average, against 11 percentage points for the other group. They also achieved a better reading on the rule of law than the others. The World Bank's conclusion is that, 'as they reformed and integrated with the world

Table 9.1 Characteristics of more globalized and less globalized developing economies (population-weighted average)

Socioeconomic characteristics	More globalized (24)	Less globalized (49)
Population, 1997 (billions)	2.9	1.1
Per-capita GDP, 1980	$1,488	$1,947
Per-capita GDP, 1997	$2,485	$2,133
Compound annual growth rate of GDP per head, 1980–1997	3.1%	0.5%
Rule of law index, 1997 (world average = 0)	−0.04	−0.48
Average years primary schooling, 1980	2.4	2.5
Average years primary schooling, 1997	3.8	3.1
Average years secondary schooling, 1980	0.8	0.7
Average years secondary schooling, 1997	1.3	1.3
Average years tertiary schooling, 1980	0.08	0.09
Average years tertiary schooling, 1997	0.18	0.22

Source: World Bank, Globalization, Growth & Poverty: Building an Inclusive World Economy (Washington DC: World Bank, 2002), Table 1.1.

market, the "more globalized" developing countries started to grow rapidly, accelerating steadily from 2.9 per cent in the 1970s to 5 per cent in the 1990s'.[5]

While what the Bank says is both true and important, it should be observed that its notion of a group of twenty-four countries is something of a fiction. China and India contain, between them, 75 per cent of the group's combined population. With Brazil, Bangladesh, Mexico, the Philippines and Thailand, one has 92 per cent of the group's population. Moreover, Asian countries dominate: they make up 85 per cent of the population of this group of globalizing countries.

What then do we learn from the success of the countries picked out as globalizers by the World Bank? We can say, with confidence, that the notion that international economic integration necessarily makes the rich richer and the poor poorer is nonsense. Here is a wide range of countries that increased their integration with the world economy and prospered, in some cases dramatically so. A subtler question, to which we shall return in subsequent chapters, is precisely what policies relatively successful developing countries have followed. Critics are right to argue that success has not required adoption of the full range of so-called 'neo-liberal' policies – privatization, free trade and capital-account liberalization. But, in insisting upon this point, critics are wilfully mistaking individual policy trees for the market-oriented forest. What the successful countries all share is a move towards the market economy, one in which private property rights, free enterprise and competition increasingly took the place of state ownership, planning and protection. They chose, however haltingly, the path of economic liberalization and international integration. This is the heart of the matter. All else is commentary.

If one compares the China of today with the China of Mao Zedong or the India of today with the India of Indira Gandhi, the contrasts are overwhelming. Market forces have been allowed to operate in ways that would have been not just unthinkable but criminal a quarter of a century ago. Under Mao, economic freedom had been virtually eliminated. Under the Indian control system, no significant company was allowed to produce, invest or import without government permission. From this starting-point, much of the most important liberalization was, necessarily and rightly, internal. Given where it was in the 1970s, liberalizing agriculture alone started China on the path towards rapid development. Similarly, eliminating the more absurd controls on industry permitted an acceleration in Indian economic growth. In both cases then these initial reforms and the abundance of cheap and hard-working labour guaranteed accelerated growth.

Yet in neither case can the contribution of economic integration be ignored. This is spectacularly true of China. The volume of China's exports grew at 13 per cent a year between 1980 and 1990 and then at 11 per cent between 1990 and 1999. Between 1990 and 2000 the ratio of trade in goods to Chinese GDP, at market prices, jumped from 33 to 44 per cent, an extraordinarily high ratio for such a large economy. The ratio of merchandise trade to output of goods in the economy rose from 47 per cent to 66 per cent over the same period.[6] In 2001, China's gross merchandize exports of $266 billion amounted to 4.3 per cent of the world total, up from a mere 0.7 per cent in 1977.[7] By that year, China was the world's sixth largest merchandise exporter (including intra-European Union trade in the total), just behind the UK, but already ahead of Canada and Italy. Meanwhile, private capital flows into China jumped from 3 per cent of GDP in 1990 to 13 per cent in 2000. By 2001, the stock of inward foreign direct investment in China was $395 billion, 6 per cent of the world's total, up from $25 billion in 1990. In 2000, inward direct investment financed 11 per cent of the giant's gross fixed capital formation, while foreign affiliates generated 31 per cent of China's manufacturing sales and, more astonishingly, 50 per cent of its exports.[8] It is possible to argue that China's dramatic economic growth somehow had nothing to do with its headlong rush into the global market economy. But it would be absurd to do so.

India's integration was much less spectacular. So, not coincidentally, was its growth. Yet here, too, the change was palpable. India's volume of merchandise exports fell in the 1980s, which contributed mightily to the foreign exchange crisis that brought to an end its overwhelmingly inward-looking liberalization of the 1980s. But export volume rose at 5.3 per cent a year between 1990 and 1999, after external liberalization had begun. India's share in world merchandise exports had fallen from 2.1 per cent in 1951 to a low of 0.4 per cent in 1980. But by 2001 this share was modestly back up, to 0.7 per cent, putting it in thirtieth place globally. Between 1990 and 2000, the share of trade in goods also rose from 13 to 20 per cent of GDP. India did achieve a significant success in exports of commercial services (particularly software). By 2001, its exports of such services were $20 billion, almost half as much as its $44 billion in merchandise exports. Its share in world exports of commercial services was 1.4 per cent, double its share in exports of goods, while its rank in the world was nineteenth, though even here it was behind China's exports of $33 billion (2.3 per cent of the world total). India also lagged in openness to inward direct investment, which only reached $3.4 billion in 2001. But even this was close to revolutionary in a country that had, for decades, discouraged all inward FDI. In 1990, the total stock of inward FDI was a mere $1.7 billion. By 2001, it had reached $22 billion. The 1990s were, in all, India's most economically successful post-independence decade. They were also the decade in which the country liberalized both internal and external transactions and increased its integration into the global economy. An accident? Hardly.

Now consider an even more fascinating example in the Bank's list of globalizing economies – Bangladesh, certainly the poorest sizeable country in the world in the 1970s and, as I remember well, almost universally deemed a hopeless case. Even this country has benefited from international economic integration. The GDP per head of Bangladesh rose at 2.3 per cent a year between 1975 and 2001, generating a 60 per cent rise in real income per head over more than a quarter of a century. Between 1990 and 2001, GDP per head grew considerably faster, at 3.1 per cent a year, as the economy opened. In 1975, Bangladesh's real GDP per head (measured at purchasing power parity) was roughly half that of sub-Saharan Africa. By 2000, its real GDP per head was close to the average level of sub-Saharan Africa. In the 1980s, Bangladesh's volume of merchandise exports barely rose. In the 1990s, it rose at a remarkable 15 per cent a year. Between 1990 and 2000, the ratio of exports to GDP jumped from 18 to 32 per cent. The volume of trade also grew 6 percentage points a year faster than GDP in the decade. Bangladesh did not suddenly become a magnet for foreign direct investment. That is hardly surprising, since it has been ranked bottom of seventy-five countries in the cost of corruption.[9] But the stock of inward direct investment did reach $1.1 billion by 2001, up from $150 million in 1990. Even for Bangladesh, international economic integration has paid off. It is only a start. But it is, at least, that.

If a successful move to the market, including increasing integration in the world economy, explains the success stories of the past two decades, what explains the failures, that is, those which have failed to take advantage of the opportunities for global economic integration? Failure to develop has involved a complex interplay of institutions, endowments and policies.

Emphasis on institutions and their evolution has, quite properly, become a dominant focus of analysts of development. It is discovered, not surprisingly, that poor performers have corrupt, predatory or brutal governments or, sometimes even worse, no government at all, but rather civil war among competing warlords.[10] The failure of the state to provide almost any of the services desperately needed for development is at the root of the African disaster. This reflects both the artificiality of the states and the weak – if not non-existent – sense of moral responsibility of Africa's 'big men'. Mobutu's Zaire was perhaps the most catastrophic example. But he was also one of many. Today, Robert Mugabe's destruction of once-prosperous Zimbabwe is almost equally horrifying.[11] An even more depressing case is that of sub-Sahara's giant, Nigeria. Today, Nigeria's GDP per head, at PPP, is the same as it was in 1970, despite three decades of abundant oil revenues, all of which has been wasted in foolish public spending and capital flight. The proportion of Nigeria's population in extreme poverty (real incomes of less than a dollar a day, at PPP) has doubled over this period. The élite has been predatory in the extreme: in 2000, the top 2 per cent had the same income as the bottom 55 per cent.[12] Much of Nigeria's wealth has been squirrelled away abroad. Alas, Nigeria is merely an extreme case. It is estimated that about 40 per cent of Africa's private wealth was held overseas by 1990. But bad governments have also failed to provide the infrastructure on which development depends. As a result, African countries trade even less with one another and the rest of the world than would be predicted from their adverse locations.[13]

The second obstacle to development is a country's natural endowments. There is much evidence that location in the tropics is a handicap, though whether this is only via the impact on the evolution of countries' institutions, or independently, remains controversial. The probability is that it is a bit of both. Debilitating diseases have long been rife in the tropics. But it is also true that colonial regimes tended to create predatory institutions in their tropical possessions.[14] Distance from the sea is also a handicap and particularly being landlocked. The disadvantages faced by the landlocked – a natural form of protection against foreign trade – also underline the costs of non-globalization.[15]

Endowments enter into development in another way, as resources. Natural resources, especially mineral wealth, seem to be an obstacle not a spur, to economic development. This 'resource curse' has many dimensions: resources tend to corrupt politics, turning it into a race to seize the incomes produced by resources, often generating debilitating civil wars; they generate unstable terms of trade, because prices of natural resources or agricultural commodities fluctuate widely; and they produce a high real exchange rate that, among other things, hinders development of internationally competitive manufacturing.[16]

Data on real GDP per head show that developing countries with few natural resources grew two to three times faster between 1960 and 1990 than countries with abundant natural resources. The World Bank demonstrates that no fewer than forty-five countries experienced 'unsustained growth' over the past four decades: they matched their 1999 level of real income per head in a previous decade, many as far back as the 1960s. All but six of these countries possess 'point-source natural resources' – oil or minerals. Nigeria is one example of a country ruined by an abundance of oil. Angola is another: its GDP per head is lower today than it was in 1960.[17] So much, by the way, for the view that what countries need for successful development is more aid. If foreign resources were all that was needed to make a country rich, Angola and Nigeria would not be in the state they are in.[18]

Even where natural resources do not generate corrupt, rent-seeking societies, they can be an obstacle to sustained development. In the post-war era, the most successful route to development seems to have been via the export of labour-intensive manufactures, the route on which China has followed Hong Kong, Singapore, Taiwan and South Korea. The success of developing countries with exports of manufactures has been astonishing: in 1980 only 25 per cent of the merchandise exports of developing countries were manufactures. By 1998, this had risen to 80 per cent. The old view in which developing countries exported commodities in return for manufactures is entirely outmoded. Today, they are just as likely to export manufactures (and services, too, since their share in total exports of developing countries has risen to 17 per cent, from 9 per cent in the early 1980s) in return for commodities.[19]

The path of manufactures offers a number of significant advantages. World markets for manufactures, while not free, have been relatively open and dynamic. Markets for agricultural commodities have either been slow-growing and price-insensitive (as for the classic tropical commodities – cocoa, tea and coffee), highly protected in the world's most important markets (as for temperate agricultural commodities), or both (as for sugar). Manufactures also offer a natural ladder up the chain of comparative advantage. A country that has specialized in natural-resource exports will find it hard to shift into competitive manufactures as it must break into world markets after having already achieved quite high real wages and, correspondingly, must do so at relatively high levels of productivity. Since there is learning-by-doing (and other spillovers) in manufacturing, achieving this transition to exports of manufactures can be tricky at relatively high-wages. The transition can be thwarted altogether by policies of blanket protection used, as they were in Argentina and other resource-rich countries, to spread resource rents to a politically influential working class. The task is not hopeless: the US itself is an example of such a transition, successfully completed a century or so ago. More recently, Chile has had great success with a path based on commodity exports.

A final aspect of resources is human resources, both latent and overt. Under latent resources are the underlying cultural and behavioural assumptions of a society – its software, so to speak. Under overt human resources is the level of education achieved by the population. It cannot be altogether an accident that the most successful region of the world, after Europe and the British offshoots in the New World, is east Asia, long home to sophisticated agrarian states, with established bureaucratic cultures and developed mercantile traditions. From this point of view, sub-Saharan Africa has been doubly handicapped, long isolated from Eurasia, still enveloped in tribal traditions and lacking a sizeable number of highly educated people at the time of independence, when many mistakes were made.

Finally, there are policies. If all that mattered were endowments and institutions, one would never have seen sudden take-offs by some countries in response to policy changes. But the rapid growth of South Korea and Taiwan in the 1960s only followed a move to realistic exchange rates and export promotion. The mistakes repeatedly made by other countries have included overvalued real exchange rates, often used to suppress the inflationary consequences of fiscal imprudence (as in Zimbabwe today), creation of corrupt and incompetent public sector monopolies in vital areas, such as electric power generation and distribution or marketing of export commodities; and high and variable protection against imports, often via corruption-fuelling controls. How much these mistakes matter tends to depend on a country's comparative advantage. If a country possesses a supply of very cheap and highly motivated labour, as China does today, it seems easier to survive mistakes (and institutional failings) that would cripple an Argentina or a Mexico. Nevertheless, it was only after a series of reforms that China began to integrate into the world economy. Countries without China's human resources must try even harder to get policy right.

Growth and inequality

Now what does the performance of those who have succeeded in growing through economic integration mean for inequality? Inequality is a measure of relative incomes. If the average real incomes of poor countries containing at least half of the world's population have been rising faster than those of the relatively rich, inequality among countries, weighted by population, will have fallen. This will be true even if the ratio of the incomes of the world's richest to the world's poorest countries and the absolute gaps in average incomes per head between rich countries and almost all developing countries have risen (as they have).

These two points may need a little explanation. First, compare, say, the US with China. Between 1980 and 2000, according to the World Bank, Chinese average real incomes rose by about 440 per cent. Over the same period, US average real incomes per head rose by about 60 per cent. The ratio of Chinese real incomes per head, at purchasing power parity, to those of the US rose, accordingly, from just over 3 per cent in 1980 to just under 12 per cent in 2000.[20] This is a big reduction in relative inequality. But the absolute gap in real incomes between China and the US rose from $20,600 to $30,200 per head (at PPP). The reason is simple: since China's standard of living was, initially, about a thirtieth of that of the US, the absolute gap could have remained constant only if China's growth had been thirty times faster than that of the US. That would have been impossible. If China continues to grow faster than the US, however, absolute gaps will ultimately fall, as happened with Japan in the 1960s and 1970s.

Second, while the *ratio* of the average incomes per head in the richest country to those in the world's least successful countries is rising all the time, the *proportion* of the world's population living in the world's poorest countries has, happily, been falling. Thirty years ago, China and India were among the world's poorest countries. Today, the poorest seems to be Sierra Leone, a country with a population of only 5 million. China's average real income per head is now some ten times higher than Sierra Leone's. The largest very poor country today is Nigeria, with a population of 127 million in 2000 and a real income, at PPP, just a fortieth of that of the US (and a fifth of China's). Again, this means that rising ratios between the average incomes of the world's richest and poorest countries are consistent with declining inequality among countries, weighted by their populations. Moreover, it is also perfectly possible for inequality to have risen in every single country in the world (as Mazur alleges, wrongly) while global inequality has fallen. Unless the increase in inequality among individuals within countries offsets the reduction in population-weighted inequality among countries, not only inequality among (population-weighted) countries, but also inequality among individuals will have declined.

Andrea Boltho of Oxford University and Gianni Toniolo of Rome University have computed population-weighted inequality among forty-nine countries that contain 80 per cent of the world's population, back to 1900.[21] To compute their measure of inequality, the gini coefficient, the authors weight the average income, at purchasing power parity (in order to compare standards of living), of each country by its population.[22] They conclude that inequality among countries, weighted in this way, reached its maximum in 1980, at a value of 0.54, but has fallen by 9 per cent since then, to 0.50, a level not seen since some six decades ago. This decline in inequality among countries, weighted by their population size, is exactly what one would expect.

The reason for weighting distribution among countries by population is that it is people who matter, not countries. Then the right thing to do must be to take account of changes in distribution of income within countries as well. A paper by François Bourguignon and Christian Morrison, for the World Bank, has attempted this heroic task for 1820 to 1992.[23] As Figure 9.1 shows, they reach five significant conclusions.[24]

First, global inequality among individuals rose progressively, from 1820 to a peak in 1980.

Second, all the increase in global inequality over those 160 years was the result of increases in inequality *among* countries, not *within* them. Within-country inequality was, they estimate (albeit roughly), lower in 1980 than 1820.

Third, back in 1820, only 13 per cent of the inequality of individuals was determined by differences in the average prosperity among countries. By 1980,

Figure 9.1 Decomposition of world income inequality (mean logarithmic deviation)

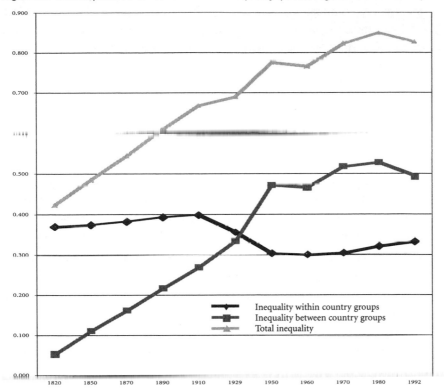

Source: François Bourguignon and Christian Morrison, 'Inequality among World Citizens' (*American Economic Review*, Vol. 92, No. 4 (September 2002), pp. 727–44).

however, just over 60 per cent of inequality among individuals was determined by differences in the average prosperity of countries. In the words of the authors, 'differences in country economic growth rates practically explain all the increase in world inequality'[25] By 1980, the most important determinant of one's prosperity was not one's class or profession, but where one lived.

Fourth, inequality within countries reached a peak in 1910, subsequently fell to a trough in 1960 and then started to rise, modestly, once again.

Finally, because of a fall in inequality among countries, which offset a modest rise in inequality within them, global inequality among individuals fell, at last, between 1980 and 1992.

The most important conclusion then is that, since the beginning of the nineteenth century, changes in inequality among the world's individuals have been driven by changes in the relative wealth of nations. In particular, the steeply

rising inequality among the people of the world in the nineteenth and first half
of the twentieth century was driven by the divergent performance of Europe and
the British offshoots, on the one hand, and Asia, on the other. What matters then
is relative rates of economic growth over extended periods. Consequently, Asia's
improved growth performance, and especially that of the Asian giants, has
started to reverse this picture of rising inequality over the past two decades.

This World Bank study suffers from two defects: to take the analysis so far
back, it had to rely on highly limited, indeed sketchy, data; and it ended in
1992, at the beginning of yet another decade of rapid growth in Asia, not least
in China. More recent studies, on similar lines, remedy these defects. These are
by another group of three authors at the World Bank, by Surjit Bhalla,
formerly a World Bank economist, and by Xavier Sala-I-Martin of Columbia
University (see Figure 9.2).[26] All three reach a very similar conclusion: global
inequality among households, or individuals, peaked in the 1970s, whereupon
it started to fall. This decline happened not because of greater equality within
countries, but because of greater population-weighted equality among them.

The three World Bank authors found, for example, that income inequality
increased within high-income countries between 1980 and 1995, but fell quite
sharply, world-wide, from its peak in 1965–9. This happened entirely because of
reductions in (population-weighted) inequality among countries. Bhalla's results
are similar, but even stronger. Global inequality in 2000 was lower, he argues,
than at any time since 1910. It had fallen from its peak in 1980 by 5 per cent (on
the gini-coefficient measure). He agrees that inequality rose among people living
in high-income countries after 1980, though it was well below levels in 1960.
Inequality had fallen sharply among the people of the developing countries, with
China and India included, but not with these two giants excluded. Finally,
Professor Sala-I-Martin concludes that global inequality peaked in the 1970s
(in 1978, to be precise). Between then and 1998, he, too, found inequality had
fallen by 5 per cent (also on the gini-coefficient measure). It fell substantially
more, however, on some of the other measures (see Figure 9.2).

Others contest this relatively sunny picture of global interpersonal inequality
in the age of globalization. Perhaps the most important challenge has come
from other World Bank researchers. Branko Milanovic, in particular, has
written an influential paper, assessing what he calls 'true world income distribution' for 1988 and 1993.[27] The important difference between this study (as
well as Bank analyses of changes in global poverty, to which I will turn below)
and the studies cited above is that it ignores data from national accounts. It
relies, instead, only on household surveys of income and expenditure. This has

Figure 9.2 Inequality among people in the age of globalization (mean logarithmic deviation)

Source: Xavier Sala-I-Martin, 'The World Distribution of Income (Estimated from Individual Country Distributions)' (May 2002, mimeo), Table 8

advantages: surveys include home consumption, which is important for poor people in poor countries, and exclude undistributed profits and increases in inventories, which do not affect the current welfare of a population. But it also has a significant disadvantage: the level and rate of rise of spending in such surveys frequently bear little relation to figures in national accounts. This is worrying. National accounts may be flawed, but they do have the virtue of being self-checking, since they are put together from independent evidence on output, income and expenditure. No comparable internal checks can be made on surveys of household incomes and spending.

Milanovic concluded from the evidence he uses that inequality rose substantially between 1988 and 1993. Measured by the gini coefficient, the rise was from 0.63 to 0.66 (a remarkably large 5 per cent jump over such a short period). He also concludes that 'The most important contributors were: rising urban–rural differences in China, and slow growth of rural purchasing-power adjusted incomes in South Asia, compared to several large developed market economies.'[28] The results, though significantly different from those of the other researchers cited above, do at least support them in one respect. Milanovic concludes that 'the difference between countries' mean incomes . . . is the most important factor behind world inequality. It explains between 75 and 88 percent of overall inequality' (depending on the measure used).[29] Milanovic also comes up with a number of additional statistics: the richest 1 per cent of people in the world receive as much (in PPP terms) as the bottom 57 per cent; and an American with the average income of the bottom decile (the bottom 10 per cent) is better off than two-thirds of the world's people.

Milanovic's conclusion that inequality increased sharply over five years was, subsequently, the basis of an influential article in *The Economist* newspaper by Robert Wade of the London School of Economics.[30] But are his results both credible and meaningful? A part of the answer is that this was an exceptional period, which makes the results more credible but less meaningful. Chinese economic growth slowed at the time of the Tiananmen Square massacre in 1989. Similarly, India suffered an economic crisis in 1991. Thus Milanovic's analysis was, accidentally, timed to coincide with the one period in the last two decades of the twentieth century when the two giant developing countries were growing quite modestly.[31] Even Sala-I-Martin found that global inequality rose between 1986 and 1989, before falling, once again, after 1990 (see Figure 9.2). It would, for this reason, be dangerous to generalize from an analysis that covers this period. All the same, the size of the increase in inequality estimated by Milanovic is remarkable. According to Bhalla, the relative incomes of the high-income countries would need to rise by 27 per cent to generate a 5 per cent increase in global income inequality (measured by the gini coefficient). That simply did not happen. So the question of credibility remains.

Milanovic's data indicate, for example, that there was no increase in rural incomes in China between 1988 and 1993. National accounts give quite a different picture. So what is going on? A part of the answer, as suggested above, is that average household incomes and spending generally rise much more slowly in surveys of household income and expenditure than in national accounts. To take a significant example, the survey data relied upon by two authoritative World Bank researchers for their estimates of changes in absolute poverty between 1987 and 1999 show a rise in real consumption in developing countries of just 11 per cent.[32] Over the same period, observes Bhalla, national accounts data (converted with PPP exchange rates) show rises in average real incomes of 24 per cent and in consumption of 21 per cent. This is not some small discrepancy – it is a yawning chasm.

Bhalla also observes that, between 1987 and 1998, the ratio of average incomes in surveys of incomes to those in national accounts fell from 56 to 46 per cent in east Asia, from 75 to 62 per cent in south Asia and from 69 to 63 per cent in sub-Saharan Africa. For consumption surveys, the ratio of average fell from 82 to 81 per cent in east Asia, 73 to 56 per cent in south Asia and 125 to 115 per cent in sub-Saharan Africa. On similar lines, Milanovic shows that, for Africa, average household income/expenditure in the surveys he used was 79 per cent of levels in national accounts in 1988, but only 70 per cent by 1993. For Asia, the ratio fell more modestly, from 61 to 59 per cent. Nevertheless, in Milanovic's study, growth in average incomes, between 1988 and 1993, in the developing regions with the largest number of poor people was lower than in national accounts (at PPP): 49 per cent, against 54 per cent, for Asia, and 19 per cent, against 33 per cent for sub-Saharan Africa. This, in turn, must be a part of the explanation for the discrepancy between Milanovic's results and those of researchers who use national accounts.

How then is one to explain this discrepancy between the growth shown in surveys and the growth shown in national accounts? Logically, there are three alternatives.

The first is that the surveys are correct in their estimate of the level of consumption and incomes, in which case economic growth has been far slower in many important developing countries than we have believed. The national accounts are not reliable estimates, but propaganda. The second possibility is that both national accounts and the surveys are correct, for what they cover. This would be possible if virtually all the spending (and income) under-recorded in the surveys was by (and of) the rich *and* if the true share of the rich in both incomes and spending in the economy was also rising rapidly. This would mean that in many developing countries income and spending were becoming more unequal, more quickly, than the standard estimates of inequality suggest. The third possibility is that household surveys have become ever less reliable as a way of estimating the rise in real incomes and spending over time (though they still remain all we have if we want to calculate changes in the distribution of income and spending over time).

The first possibility seems hugely implausible. If we did reject national accounts data for economic growth, we would be left with no idea of what has been going on in developing countries. Moreover, while there are questions about national accounts data, notably for China, they are probably the most carefully constructed national data in any country. This leaves the second and third possibilities. We cannot, on the evidence we now have, distinguish between them. In other words, either countries have been becoming more unequal more quickly than all the evidence suggests (because of rapid increases in unrecorded incomes and spending of the rich) or the household surveys themselves are unreliable.

This is not, however, the only difficulty. Converting incomes at average PPP exchange rates will itself create important distortions because the consumption of tradable goods and non-tradable services will vary across households. In general, the poor in developing countries will consume more of the former and the rich more of the latter. Every visitor from the west to a developing country must have been struck by the ability of the prosperous to employ hordes of servants, long vanished in the west, even though they cannot afford the latest high-technology machinery. If this were taken into account, the income distribution, properly measured at PPP, would be more unequal than the measured income distribution at domestic relative prices. The reverse side of this is that, in rapidly growing countries, the prices of services rise in relation to those of goods. If the poor consume goods more intensively than the rich, then they gain more from growth than the rich do. Thus, while the initial income distribution would be more unequal than calculations at domestic relative prices suggest, it would also be becoming more equal more quickly than they suggest. This reinforces the assumption that the poor are likely to have benefited substantially from growth in rapidly growing developing countries.

The bottom line is that it is plausible that inequality among individuals across the world has been falling over the past two decades, because of the relatively rapid growth of the Asian giants. This is consistent with rising inequality within many countries, rising relative gaps between the average incomes of the richest and very poorest countries, and increasing absolute gaps between the average incomes in the high-income countries, on the one hand, and virtually all developing countries, on the other. But the latter simply shows the tyranny of history. By 1980, inequality among countries was so large that it was impossible for absolute gaps to close, until there was much greater convergence of relative incomes.

Yet this ignores the fact that a great many countries have not enjoyed rapid growth, most notably in Africa, but also, to a lesser extent, in Latin America, the Middle East and, in the 1990s, the countries in transition from communism, especially the former Soviet Union. In the 1990s, for example, according to the

Human Development Report, fifty-four countries, with 12 per cent of the world's population, had negative growth rates in real incomes per head, while another seventy-one countries, with 26 per cent of the world's population, had growth of between zero and 3 per cent a year in real incomes per head.[33] Similarly, in the World Bank's study of globalization, countries containing 1.1 billion people had virtually stagnant real incomes between 1980 and 1997 (see Table 9.1). While the poor performance of so many countries may not have prevented global income distribution from improving (though it will tend to do so once China's average incomes rise above the world average), it has certainly had a significant impact on the scale and regional distribution of world poverty. To that topic, just as vexed as income distribution, we now turn.

Growth and poverty

On all measures, global inequality rose until about the early 1980s. Since then, it appears, inequality among individuals has declined as a result of the rapid growth of much of Asia and, above all, China. But it is also important to understand what drove the long-term trend towards global inequality over almost two centuries. It is the consequence of the dynamic growth that spread, unevenly, from the UK in the course of the nineteenth and twentieth centuries. In the process a growing number of people became vastly better off than any one had ever been before, but few can have become worse off. Such dynamic growth is bound to be uneven. Some regions of the world proved better able to take advantage of the new opportunities for growth, because of superior climates, resources and policies. In just the same way, some parts of countries, particularly huge countries such as China or India, are today better able to take advantage of new opportunities than others. To bemoan the resulting increase in inequality is to bemoan the growth itself. It is to argue that it would be better for everybody to be equally poor than for some to become significantly better off, even if, in the long run, this will almost certainly lead to advances for everybody.

For this reason, it makes more sense to focus on what has happened to poverty than to inequality. Again, the statistical debate is a vexed one. But some plausible conclusions can be reached.

The World Bank has, for some time, defined extreme poverty as an income of a dollar a day at 1985 international prices (PPP). Bourguignon and Morrison also used that figure in an analysis of extreme poverty since 1820, on the same lines as their analysis of inequality (see Figure 9.3).[34] It comes to three intriguing conclusions. First, the number of desperately poor people rose from

Figure 9.3 Extreme poverty in the long run (less than a dollar a day at PPP, in 1985 prices, millions and world population share)

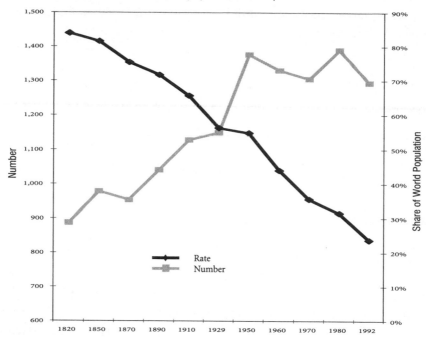

Source: François Bourguignon and Christian Morrison, 'Inequality among World Citizens' (*American Economic Review,* Vol. 92, No. 4 (September 2002), pp. 727–44).

about 900 million in 1820 to a peak of from 1.3 to 1.4 billion between 1960 and 1980, before falling, modestly, to just under 1.3 billion in 1992. Second, the proportion of the world's population living on less than a dollar a day fell dramatically, over time, from over 80 per cent in 1820, a time when living on the margins of subsistence was the norm, to about two-thirds at the beginning of the twentieth century, to close to 50 per cent by 1950, then 32 per cent in 1980 and, finally, 24 per cent by 1992. The contrast between rising numbers and falling proportions of the world's population in extreme poverty reflects the race between higher output and rising population, particularly in poor countries. In 1820, the world's population was a little over a billion. By 1910 it was 1.7 billion and by 1992 it had risen to 5.5 billion.

Again, the results from Bourguignon and Morrison are cause for qualified optimism. From being universal, extreme poverty has become, if not rare, the affliction of less than a quarter of a vastly increased human population. But, again, it is necessary to look more closely at what has happened in the supposed period of globalization, the years since 1980. Here, the authoritative voice is that of the World Bank, the institution whose 'dream is a world without poverty'.[35] The numbers in Tables 9.2 and 9.3 come from two recent World Bank publications.[36] They reach the following conclusions.

First, the number of people in extreme poverty fell from 1.18 billion in 1987 to 1.17 billion in 1999, but not before jumping upwards to 1.29 billion in 1990, underlining the extent to which the 1988–93 period chosen by Milanovic was exceptional.

Table 9.2 Income poverty, by region (millions of people living on less than $1.08 a day at 1993 PPP)

Regions	1987	1990	1999
East Asia and Pacific	418	486	279
(Excluding China)	114	110	57
China	304	376	222
Europe and Central Asia	1	6	24
Latin America and Caribbean	64	48	57
Middle East and North Africa	9	5	6
South Asia	474	506	488
Sub-Saharan Africa	217	241	315
Total	1,183	1,292	1,169
Total, excluding China	880	917	945

Sources: World Bank, *World Development Report 2000/2001: Attacking Poverty* (Washington DC: World Bank, 2000), Table 1.1, and World Bank, *Global Economic Prospects and the Developing Countries 2003: Investing to Unlock Global Opportunities* (Washington DC: World Bank, 2003), Table 1.9.

Table 9.3 Regional incidence of income poverty (share of people living on less than $1.08 a day at 1993 PPP, in regional populations, per cent)

Regions	1987	1990	1999
East Asia and Pacific	26.6	30.5	15.6
(Excluding China)	23.9	24.2	10.6
China	27.8	33.0	17.7
Europe and Central Asia	0.2	1.4	5.1
Latin America and Caribbean	15.3	11.0	11.1
Middle East and North Africa	4.3	2.1	2.2
South Asia	44.9	45.0	36.6
Sub-Saharan Africa	46.6	47.4	49.0
Total	28.3	29.6	23.2
Total, excluding China	28.5	28.5	25.0
World total	23.7	24.6	19.5

Sources: World Bank, *World Development Report 2000/2001: Attacking Poverty*, Table 1.1, and World Bank, *Global Economic Prospects 2003*, Table 1.9.

Second, enormous declines in the number of people in extreme poverty have occurred in dynamic east Asia, from 486 million in 1990 to 279 million in 1999, including China, and from 114 million to 57 million, excluding China. In China itself, the decline, between 1990 and 1999, was from 376 million to 222 million. Rapid growth reduces poverty dramatically. This remains today, as it has been for two centuries, an abiding truth.

Third, the number of people in extreme poverty fell very modestly in south Asia between 1990 and 1999, while it rose sharply in eastern Europe and central Asia (the former Soviet empire) and, above all, sub-Saharan Africa, from 217 million in 1987 to 241 million in 1990, and then 315 million in 1999.

Fourth, the regional incidence of poverty fell dramatically in east Asia, from 30.5 per cent of the population in 1990 to just 15.6 per cent in 1999. Excluding China, it fell from 24.2 to 10.6 per cent. In China, it fell from 33 per cent of the population to just under 18 per cent over nine years. This was, without doubt, the most rapid reduction in the incidence of extreme poverty anywhere, ever.

Fifth, the incidence of poverty also fell sharply in south Asia (dominated by India) in the 1990s, from 45.0 per cent of the population in 1990 to 36.6 per cent in 1999. But it rose sharply in eastern Europe and central Asia and also increased in sub-Saharan Africa, from 47.4 per cent of the population to 49.0 per cent.

As with the numbers of inequality, so with those on poverty, controversy abounds. In the optimistic corner are, once again, Bhalla and Sala-I-Martin. A comparison between their results and those of the World Bank for the number of people in absolute poverty over the 1990s (on slightly different definitions) appears in Figure 9.4. All three show substantial declines between 1990 and the end of the decade. But the World Bank's is a 9.5 per cent decline over nine years; Sala-I-Martin has one of 13.1 per cent over eight years; and Bhalla one of 25.6 per cent over ten years.

What is one to make of these discrepancies? As Sala-I-Martin notes, the difference between his results and those of the World Bank, after some adjustments, are not large.[37] The big discrepancy is with the results of Bhalla. The most important source of those differences seems to be his use of national accounts data for the growth in average incomes and spending, along with household surveys for distribution of income and spending, against the Bank's use of surveys for both.

The implication of this difference is shown most clearly for what is, in many ways, the most surprising single case: India. For in India, as we know, real incomes per head rose by around a half in the 1990s yet the number of people

Figure 9.4 The fall in numbers in extreme poverty in the 1990s (millions)

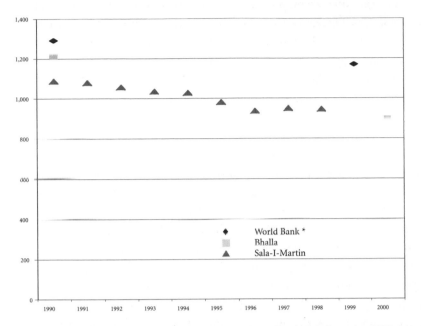

Source: World Bank, *Global Economic Prospects and the Developing Countries 2003: Investing to Unlock Global Opportunities* (Washington DC: World Bank, 2003), Table 1.9; Surjit S. Bhalla, *Imagine There's No Country: Poverty, Inequality and Growth in the Era of Globalization* (Washington DC: Institute for International Economics, 2002), Table 9.1; and Sala–I–Martin, 'The World Distribution of Income (Estimated from Individual Country Distributions)' (May 2002, mimeo), Table 3A.
* To make these data roughly comparable, those chosen are as follows: for the World Bank, the $1.08 poverty line, at 1993 PPP, which appears to apply to consumption; for Bhalla, a $1.30 poverty line, at 1993 prices and, for Sala-I-Martin, his consumption poverty rates (applied to world population, to derive levels) for a dollar a day (probably at 1993 PPP).

in extreme poverty appears, on the World Bank data, to have fallen quite modestly. In south Asia, as a whole, dominated by India, it fell only from 506 million to 488 million between 1990 and 1999. This, Bhalla suggests, does not look very plausible. Since the latter figure is 42 per cent of all the people in extreme poverty in the world, any significant error in calculating it is bound to create equally significant mistakes in the totals.

One thing we do know is that between 1987 and 1998 the proportion of the consumption shown in national accounts covered by the household surveys fell from 73 per cent to only 56 per cent in south Asia. It looks then as though the surveys missed a great deal of the rise in consumption in these countries. Moreover, as Bhalla points out, surveys of wages and unemployment in India indicate rises in rural wages that are far more consistent with consumption figures in the national accounts than in the household surveys of expenditure. In addition, India's official estimate of the poverty rate in 1999 (at a threshold rate of $1.25 a day, at PPP, in 1993 prices, which is higher than the Bank's $1.08 and should generate a significantly higher number of poor people) was 26 per cent, or 260 million. Yet the Bank apparently calculates this figure, on its own lower threshold, at around 360 million. It also calculates the level of poverty, on the Indian government's $1.25 line, at 470 million, which is 210 million more than the Indian government does itself. The government's estimates are themselves at the high end. Other estimates – from the respected National Council for Applied Economic Research, for example – give far lower numbers still for the population in extreme poverty in India, at 150 million in 1999.[38]

In short, there are good reasons to believe that the Bank has overestimated the number of people in extreme poverty – and underestimated its decline. If that is not so, then it must surely mean that the increase in inequality in India since the early 1990s has been very large indeed. That is logically possible, since so many of the poor live in the most backward states, such as Uttar Pradesh and Bihar. But it is not what India's own data show. One may not wish to go as far as Bhalla, who argues that the proportion of the developing world's population below $1.25 a day (at 1993 PPP) fell from 44 per cent in 1980 to 13 per cent in 2000. But the decline in poverty in India, and so the world, may well be substantially greater than the Bank suggests.

This, needless to say, is not universally accepted. Professors Thomas Pogge and Sanjay Reddy, also of Columbia University, like Professor Sala-I-Martin, argue that the Bank's numbers, if not necessarily too optimistic, are unsoundly based. They suggest, in particular, that this admittedly heroic attempt to compare poverty across the globe with the use of one measuring rod ($1.08 a day at PPP, in 1993 prices) is fundamentally flawed, in three ways. First, the international poverty line used by the Bank 'fails to meet elementary requirements of consistency'. As a result, 'the Bank's poverty line leads to meaningless poverty estimates'. Second, 'the Bank's poverty line is not anchored in any assessment of the basic resource requirements of human beings'. And third, 'the poverty estimates currently available are subject to massive uncertainties because of their sensitivity to the values of crucial parameters that are estimated on the basis of limited data or none at all'.[39]

Let us grant most of this. It is evident that converting national data with PPP exchange rates that are themselves both averages for economies and variable from year to year is a rough-and-ready procedure, to put it mildly. Equally, the dollar-a-day line is both inherently arbitrary and bound to mean different things in different countries. It is also true, as Pogge and Reddy argue, that PPP adjustments, which are largely for the relative price of non-tradable services, will create large, and growing, mismeasurement of the real incomes of the poor, since the latter consume commodities more intensively than the better off. That could well justify higher poverty lines. At the same time, it might mean that the rate of decline in poverty is higher than estimated by the Bank, since relative prices of commodities normally fall in fast-growing countries.

The big question, however, is whether it would be easy to do better. Pogge and Reddy suggest that the exercise should be conducted in terms not of arbitrary levels of income, but of capabilities – 'calories and essential nutrients'. They argue that 'the income persons need to avoid poverty at some particular time and place can then be specified in terms of the least expensive locally available set of commodities containing the relevant characteristics needed to achieve the elementary human capabilities'.[40] This sounds straight-forward. In fact, long experience suggests that reaching agreement on such poverty levels across countries is nigh on impossible.

Pogge and Reddy provide a warning. All poverty estimates are inherently arbitrary. Certainly, there is no good reason to believe in anybody's estimates of the levels of poverty at any moment. Trends are another matter. It is certain that the share of those in extreme (absolute, as opposed to relative) income poverty in the world's population has fallen enormously over the last two centuries, a decline that has, equally certainly, continued since 1980. It is almost equally certain that the numbers in extreme income poverty fell in east Asia over the past few decades and particularly over the past two. That is likely, though less certain, for India. Encouragingly, both China and India show enormous declines in estimates of numbers in extreme poverty on their different national measures (about 100 million for India, between 1980 and 2000, and 220 million for China, between 1978 and 1999, despite large increases in population in both countries over this period). Given these changes in east and south Asia, it is plausible, though not certain, that numbers in absolute income poverty declined world-wide. What is more than merely plausible is the proposition that, where numbers in extreme poverty have declined, the cause has been accelerated growth. This is as true of regions within countries (especially where mobility is hindered, as in China) as among them.

Poverty and human welfare

In the absence of any of the internationally comparable measures of capabilities that Pogge and Reddy call for, one has to look at other supporting evidence. It is here that we find unambiguous good news. For it is clear that human welfare has improved greatly in recent decades.[41] As an independent analyst, Indur Goklany, persuasively argues, it is possible, in addition, for people to enjoy better health and longer lives, at lower incomes, than before.[42] This is the result of technological and organizational improvements that have come from the world's rich countries. In 1913, life expectancy at birth in the US was fifty-two years. US GDP per head, at PPP, was then about 50 per cent higher than China's would be in 2000, and 150 per cent higher than India's.[43] Yet, in 2000, life expectancy in China was seventy and in India sixty-three. In 1900, Sweden seems to have had the world's highest life expectancy, at fifty-six. In 2000, only very poor countries, mostly in Africa, had life expectancy as low as (or lower than) this. As Goklany shows, the curve relating life expectancy to average GDP per head has shifted upwards over time. Similarly, the curve relating infant mortality to incomes has shifted downwards over time. Much the same desirable pattern can be observed for the relationship between other indicators of human welfare and income.

In the developing world as a whole, life expectancy rose by four months each year after 1970, from fifty-five years in 1970 to sixty-four years in 2000. It rose from forty-nine in 1970 to sixty-two in south Asia and from fifty-nine to sixty-nine in east Asia. Tragically, life expectancy fell in thirty-two countries in the 1990s, mostly because of the AIDS epidemic, or the gross incompetence (or worse) of governments, as in North Korea and Zimbabwe.[44] It also fell because of western hysteria about DDT, which removed the only effective way of controlling that dreadful curse, malaria. Improvements in life expectancy have meant a decline in global inequality as well. In 1950, average life expectancy in developing countries was two-thirds of the levels in high-income countries (forty-four and sixty-six years of age, respectively). By 2000, it was 82 per cent (sixty-four and seventy-eight).

Meanwhile, in the developing world as a whole, infant mortality rates have fallen from 107 per thousand in 1970 to eighty-seven in 1980 and fifty-eight in 2000. In east Asia, the region with the fastest-growing economy, they have fallen from fifty-six in 1980 to thirty-five in 2000. In south Asia, infant mortality fell from 119 in 1980 to seventy-three in 2000. In sub-Saharan Africa progress was, once again, slower. But infant mortality fell even there, from 116 in 1980 to ninety-one in 2000.

Losing a child must inflict the sharpest grief human beings can suffer. The decline in infant mortality is thus a tremendous blessing in itself. So, too, is the rise in life expectancy. But these improvements also mean that it makes sense to invest in education. The world increasingly produces smaller families with much better-educated children. On average, adult literacy in developing countries rose from 53 per cent in 1970 to 74 per cent in 1998. By 2000, adult male illiteracy was down to 8 per cent in east Asia, though it was still 30 per cent in sub-Saharan Africa and (a real scandal this) 34 per cent in south Asia. Adult female illiteracy was more widespread than that for men, but was also improving. Between 1990 and 2000, female illiteracy fell from 29 per cent to 21 per cent in east Asia. In south Asia, it fell from 66 per cent to 57 per cent (an even worse scandal than the low rate for men), while in sub-Saharan Africa it fell from 60 to 47 per cent. Illiteracy is much lower among the young. This guarantees that rates will continue to fall, as time passes.

The reduction in fertility rates has also been remarkable. In the developing world as a whole, births per woman (the fertility rate) have fallen from 4.1 in 1980 to 2.8 in 2000. In east Asia, the fertility rate, down from 3.0 to 2.1, is already at close to the replacement rate. In Latin America, the fertility rate has fallen from 4.1 to 2.6. Even in south Asia it has fallen from 5.3 in 1980 to 3.3 in 2000. Again, progress has been slowest in sub-Saharan Africa, where the birth rate has only fallen from 6.6 in 1980 to 5.2 in 2000. But, in all, these reductions tell us of improved control by women of their fertility, of fewer children with more parental investment in each and of far stronger confidence that children will survive to maturity. The demographic transition that is now under way in the developing world is immensely encouraging. It is also an indication as well as a source – of rising welfare.

Now, let us look at hunger. Growth in food production has substantially outpaced that of population. Between 1961 and 1999, the average daily food supply per person increased 24 per cent globally. In developing countries, it rose by 39 per cent, to 2,684 calories. By 1999, China's average daily food supply had gone up 82 per cent, to 3,044 calories, from a barely subsistence level of 1,636 in 1961. India's went up by 48 per cent to 2,417 calories, from 1,635 calories in 1950–1. According to estimates by the United Nations Food and Agricultural Organization, the average active adult needs between 2,000 and 2,310 calories per person. Thus the developing-country food supply has gone, on average, from inadequate to adequate. Hunger persists. But the FAO estimates that the number of people suffering from chronic undernourishment fell from 920 million in 1969–71 to 790 million in 1997–9, or from 35 to 17 per cent of the population of developing countries. Trends in sub-Saharan Africa, the continent that did not grow, were far worse. Between 1979–81 and 1997–9, the share of the population that was undernourished declined from 38 to 34 per cent, but absolute numbers, in a rapidly growing population, rose from 168 million to 194 million.[45]

Now, turn to what has become one of the most controversial indicators: child labour. One would expect that more prosperous parents, with fewer children, who are also expected to live longer, would wish to see their children being educated rather than at work. So, happily, it has proved. The proportion of children aged ten to fourteen in the labour force has, according to the World Bank, fallen from 23 per cent in all developing countries in 1980 to 12 per cent in 2000. The fall in east Asia has, once again, been astonishing, from 26 to 8 per cent. In south Asia, it has fallen from 23 to 15 per cent. In sub-Saharan Africa, the decline has been less impressive, from 35 to 29 per cent. China's transformation has been breathtaking, with a fall from 30 per cent in 1980 to just 8 per cent in 2000. In lagging India, the fall was from 21 to 12 per cent. Thus, just as one would expect, countries whose economies have done well in the era of globalization have been ones in which parents have chosen to withdraw their children from the labour force. Parents have never put their children to work out of indifference or malevolence, but only out of necessity.

Finally, let us remember some of the other features of the last two decades: the world-wide shift to democracy, however imperfect; the disappearance of some of the worst despotisms in history; the increase in personal economic opportunity in vast swathes of the world, notably China and India; and the improving relative position of women almost, although not quite, everywhere.

All these are very encouraging trends. People in developing countries and, particularly, in the fast-growing ones are enjoying longer and healthier lives than before. They are better fed and better educated. They treat their fewer children better. All these good things have not happened only because of rising incomes. Learning from the high-income countries has helped. Developing countries are reaching higher levels of social progress at lower levels of income than the high-income countries of today. But, as one would expect, social progress has been greatest where incomes have risen fastest. It remains 'the growth, stupid'.

Inequality within countries

If Mazur was wrong about global inequality, is he at least right about inequality within countries? For, as I have argued above, it is perfectly possible that globalization has worsened income distribution within every country, while improving it in the world as a whole. But has it done so? The answer is: up to a point. To be more precise, one needs to look at what has happened within developing and high-income countries separately.

Inequality within developing countries

Inequality has increased among what the World Bank calls the 'new global izers', its twenty-four countries with an aggregate population of close to 3 billion people, but only because of China.[46] The widening of inequality in China over the past two decades, almost entirely because of growing inter-regional inequality, was, however, inevitable, for four reasons: first, the distri-bution of incomes in Mao Zedong's gigantic prison was at least highly equal; second, the growth has been driven, since the initial surge in rural incomes, after abolition of the communes, by integration into the world economy, which has been dominated by the coastal regions of the country; third, in a country as enormous as China, as in the world as a whole, any imaginable growth process is certain to be regionally uneven (as is also becoming increas-ingly evident in India); and, last but not least, the Chinese authorities have done their best to limit migration from the rural hinterland to the booming coast. Thus, in many ways, today's China replicates, on a smaller scale, what has happened in the world as a whole over the past two decades. The reason for the growing internal inequality is, as it has been at the world level, the rising gap between the living standards of regions (countries) that are integrating successfully into the world economy and regions (countries) that are not. The poorest regions (countries) were not hurt by globalization. They just failed to be part of it. The challenge for China (as for the world) is to improve the ability of these lagging regions to participate, not to accept the clamour from some critics to separate itself from the world economy (hardly likely, as it happens).

If we look at other globalizing developing countries, we find they are as likely to have an improved distribution of income as a worsening one. David Dollar and Aart Kraay, in an already well-known paper, have argued that trade helps growth and that the poor tend to share in equal proportions with the rich in any rise in subsequent incomes. The paper, based on an analysis of 137 countries, finds that the poorest 20 per cent of the population does, on average, share equally in growth.[47] This, interestingly, is a contradiction of a previously accepted idea, originally proposed by the Nobel-laureate Simón

Kuznets, that inequality rises initially with growth, before declining once again. Bhalla, in his subsequent analysis, argues that in fact Kuznets was right and Dollar and Kraay are wrong. The evidence continues to suggest modest widening in inequality in growing economies.[48] But note that, even if the Kuznets hypothesis were true, growth would still be very much better for the poor than stagnation all round.

What seems clear is that the poor do share in growth. Viet Nam is an interesting example. Of the poorest 5 per cent of households in 1992–3, some 98 per cent had higher incomes six years later. Similar declines in income poverty were observed in Uganda in the 1990s.[49] Two qualifications, however, need to be made about this story. First, even if the poor do share equally in any proportionate increase in incomes, as Dollar and Kraay argue, the absolute increase in incomes they enjoy depends on their initial share. This is one sense in which growth can be more, or less, 'pro-poor'. Second, whether or not the poor share more or less equally in the benefits of the faster growth stimulated by greater trade depends on a country's comparative advantage. This is particularly important in understanding the contrasting experience with the moves towards outward-looking policies of the east Asian tigers and Latin American countries.

Standard theory (and experience) suggests that liberalization is good for the incomes of the relatively abundant factor of production. In east Asia, initial comparative advantage was based on cheap labour. One would expect international integration to be especially good for the relative incomes of the poor – and, on the whole, it was.[50] Latin America is, however, a land-abundant continent with relatively high wages and a history of protection aimed at distributing income from the agricultural sector to the industrial working class. In these cases, one would expect liberalization to create greater inequality. The negative impact on the wages of the unskilled in Latin America has also probably been exacerbated by the entry of China and the rest of east Asia into the world economy.[51]

Inequality within high-income countries

Let us turn, then, from the developing countries to the high-income countries. Here there seems to be less ambiguity: inequality has risen in most high-income countries. Where it has not risen, unemployment has tended to increase instead. In these countries, moreover, changes in inequality tend to be driven by changes in relative wages, while in developing countries wage-earners, especially in the modern sector, tend to be an élite. Widening of gaps in relative pay between the skilled and unskilled was substantial in the US and UK in the 1980s and early 1990s. In the US, in particular, 'the widening has been severe enough that lower-skilled groups had no gain and probably a slight loss, in real pay, over the whole quarter century 1973–1998, this despite a healthy growth of real earnings for the labor force as a whole'.[52]

This pattern of rising relative pay between skilled and unskilled workers does not seem to apply to other important high-income countries, however, such as Germany, France, Italy and Japan, at least for full-time workers. But when one takes work hours and unemployment into account, the same applies. Unskilled workers were more likely to be unemployed or to work part-time. As a result, from the mid-1980s to the mid 1990s, twenty out of twenty-one members of the Organization for Economic Co-operation and Development experienced a rise in inequality, largely because of rising inequality of labour earnings.[53]

If these are the facts, what are the causes? Logically, there could be several, some that work via the demand for labour and others that work on the supply. These include: trade, particularly rising imports of labour-intensive manufactures, partly as a result of growing outsourcing by multinational companies; a general growth in competition, eroding the monopoly position of industries (such as steel and automobile manufacture) that have, historically, granted large wage premia to trade-union-organized unskilled and semi-skilled labour; laws and other social and economic changes that have weakened the bargaining position of trades unions; technology, particularly skill-biased technological change or, less technically, innovations which raise the relative demand for skilled labour; a failure of the education system to improve the supply of skilled labour with sufficient speed; and immigration of unskilled labour.

Trade, reinforced by immigration, is then one of a number of possible explanations for the growth in inequality or, more precisely, the declining relative position of unskilled workers in high-income countries. Some would further argue that trade has caused the skill-bias in technical change – to save on what is, by world standards, relatively expensive unskilled labour, companies have developed technologies that save on its use. But, even if this were not true, a well-known economic theorem, the Stolper–Samuelson theorem, named after its two inventors, argues that prices of factors of production, including wages of labour, will be equalized in trade.[54] If so, since unskilled labour is enormously abundant in the world and a far higher proportion of that labour is engaged – actually and potentially – in the world economy than ever before, the wages of such labour in the high-income countries are bound to fall, relatively if not absolutely. To put this point more brutally, the working people of the high-income countries have historically benefited from the monopoly of their countries in manufacturing. Now, however, they are in competition with the unskilled of the world, with potentially devastating results.

I will return to some of these points in the next chapter, when considering the impact of trade, more narrowly. At this point, one must note that there are a number of powerful assumptions underlying the applicability of the Stolper–Samuelson theorem. Among others, productive efficiency must be the same in all countries, which it is not. Moreover, if this theorem applied, there would have been an improvement in the terms of trade (a reduction in the price of labour-intensive imports relative to exports), followed by a switch in methods of production towards those that use what had become redundant unskilled labour more intensively, everywhere. Yet, as Jagdish Bhagwati of Columbia University and others have argued, neither seems to have happened since the early 1980s.[55] Particularly striking is the shift to greater use of skilled labour in almost every industry. This suggests to most observers that skill-biased technological change has been the dominant force.[56] Professors Lindert and Williamson summarize the broad consensus among economists on the rise in inequality in the US (where the rise has been particularly large) that somewhere between 15 per cent and a third is due to trade.[57]

The bottom line then is that the increased inequality in high-income countries over the past two decades may have been caused, in modest part, by increased exports from the developing world. Even so, two essential qualifications must be made.

First, if this has been the case, it is the result of an economic process that has benefited both the exporting countries *and* the importing countries as a whole. The right response is to help those adversely affected by low-wage imports, through retraining, improved education, generalized wage subsidies for low-wage labour and, if all else fails, simple transfers of income. It would be immoral for rich countries to deprive the poor of the world of so large an opportunity for betterment merely because they are unable to handle sensibly and justly the distribution of the internal costs of a change certain to be highly beneficial overall.

Second, remember above all that this upheaval in the high-income countries is part of a benign broadening of global prosperity. Bhalla has a particularly telling way of illustrating this. He defines the global middle class as those earning between $3,650 and $14,600 a year, at PPP, in 1993 prices. On his analysis, in 1960, some 64 per cent of all the middle-class people in the world lived in the high-income countries. Today, this is down to 17 per cent, with 51 per cent living in Asia, the Middle East and North Africa, up from just 6 per cent in 1960 and 16 per cent in 1980. Only the most selfish westerners can complain about a transformation that has brought so much to so many so quickly.

Conclusion

Let us return then to the propositions with which this exploration of growth, poverty and inequality began. Here they are, together with what we now know.

First, the ratio of average incomes in the richest countries to those in the very poorest has continued to rise in the age of globalization. Response: correct.

Second, the absolute gap in living standards between today's high-income countries and the vast proportion of developing countries has continued to rise. Response: also correct and inevitably so, given the starting-point two decades ago.

Third, global inequality among individuals has risen. Response: false. Global inequality among individuals has, in all probability, fallen since the 1970s.

Fourth, the number of people in extreme income poverty has also risen. Response: probably false. The number of people in extreme poverty may well have fallen since 1980, for the first time in almost two centuries, because of the rapid growth of the Asian giants.

Fifth, the proportion of people in extreme poverty in the world's population has also risen. Response: false. The proportion of the world's population in extreme poverty has certainly fallen.

Sixth, the poor of the world are worse off not just in terms of incomes, but in terms of a wide range of indicators of human welfare and capability. Response: unambiguously false. The welfare of humanity, judged by life expectancies, infant mortality, literacy, hunger, fertility and the incidence of child labour has improved enormously. It has improved least in sub-Saharan Africa, partly because of disease and partly because of the continent's failure to grow.

Seventh, income inequality has risen in every country and particularly in countries most exposed to international economic integration. Response: false. Income inequality has not risen in most of the developing countries that have integrated with the world economy, though it has risen in China.

Inequality has apparently risen in the high-income countries, but the role of globalization in this change is unclear and, in all probability, not decisive.

We can also make some propositions of our own. Human welfare, broadly defined, has risen. The proportion of humanity living in desperate misery is declining. The problem of the poorest is not that they are exploited, but that they are almost entirely unexploited: they live outside the world economy. The soaring growth of the rapidly integrating developing economies has transformed the world for the better. The challenge is to bring those who have failed so far into the new web of productive and profitable global economic relations.

Chapter 10 **Traumatized by Trade**

The exploitation of the world market has given a cosmopolitan character to production and consumption in every country. . . . All old-established national industries have been destroyed or are daily being destroyed. They are dislodged by new industries, whose introduction becomes a life and death question for all civilized nations. . . . In place of the old local and national seclusion and self-sufficiency, we have intercourse in every direction, universal interdependence of nations. And as in material, so also in intellectual production. The intellectual creations of individual nations become common property. National one-sidedness and narrow-mindedness become more and more impossible.

Karl Marx and Friedrich Engels, *Communist Manifesto*, 1848

Obviously, any nation or community's security would be better enhanced if its own people could grow their own foods – at least ensuring thereby their survival free of market idiosyncrasies – and also manufacture as many of their other needs as possible before entering world markets. The goal of societies should not be to find cheaper prices for products but to find the means to ensure that all the needs of all people are met and that a satisfactory and stable life is perpetuated within a system that does not collapse from being part of the volatile global market. If people grow their own food, produce their own necessities and control the conditions of their lives, the issue of price becomes irrelevant.

A Report of the International Forum on Globalization[1]

Here are two views from the left of the integrating global economy – one reactionary, the other forward-looking. It can be little surprise to anybody who knows the tenor of their thinking to find today's opponents of 'corporate globalization' in the former camp. Karl Marx understood that the global market economy was an enemy of 'national one-sidedness and narrow-mindedness'. The aspiration of many of today's activists is national or, better still, local self-sufficiency. Although particularly noisy, such critics are not alone. Many complaints are made against liberal trade and the World Trade Organization. This chapter will address nine of them.

First, imports from low-wage developing countries hollow out the industries of high-income countries and make it impossible for high-wage rich countries to compete without a collapse in their wage levels.

Second, the rise of production in developing countries threatens a global glut, deflation and depression.

Third, the competitive advantage of developing countries is based on exploitation of their workers, including of children.

Fourth, global free trade is destructive of the environment.

Fifth, for all these reasons, liberal global trade should be replaced by 'localization'.

Sixth, free trade undermines the development strategies of developing countries, which cannot compete with the advanced technologies of the high-income countries.

Seventh, trade in commodities is unfair and unrewarding for the developing countries.

Eighth, the World Trade Organization is an anti-democratic organization, run in the interests of transnational corporations and threatening to national autonomy, the environment and human welfare.

Ninth, high-income countries are hypocritical in their imposition of free trade upon developing countries, since they remain protectionist themselves, particularly in areas of most interest to developing countries.

It should not escape the reader's attention that these complaints are inconsistent. It makes no sense to argue that everybody is uncompetitive everywhere (though everybody ought to be uncompetitive somewhere). Nor should one complain about barriers against developing-country exports to high-income countries while recommending localization. Nor, again, should one encourage developing countries to pursue their own development strategies *and* high-income countries to pursue self-sufficiency, if the strategy the former wish to pursue is exporting to the markets of the latter. Nor, yet again, should one aspire to freedom for each country or community to frame its own environmental rules *and* seek to impose higher environmental standards everywhere. But consistency is hardly to be expected, since these complaints come from very different sources. The task, instead, is to separate those that make sense from those that do not. That is what this chapter attempts to do.

Fear of pauper labour and the myth of de-industrialization

The scholarly debate on the impact of imports on the distribution of labour incomes in high-income countries, discussed in the previous chapter, has more simplistic counterparts in the popular debate. The 'pauper labour' argument is back. How can workers in high-income countries compete with Chinese workers? How can they find jobs when the ones they have go abroad? How is the world going to avoid a glut of manufacturing capacity, with deflation and mass unemployment? Happily, the answer to all these questions is: easily.

Start then with those overwhelmingly competitive Chinese workers. It is true that, on average, a worker in Chinese manufacturing cost only $730, annually, between 1995 and 1999, while a German worker cost $35,000, an American one $29,000 and a British one $24,000. Is it then not perfectly evident that German, American and British wages will be driven down to Chinese levels?[2] It is not merely not obvious; it is untrue. Chinese labour is cheap because it is unproductive (see Figure 10.1).[3] If an American worker produces $81,000 dollars of value added annually, a German worker $80,000 and a British worker $55,000, while a Chinese worker produces only $2,900, it is not at all difficult for the workers of the high-income countries to compete, even if their wages are vastly higher.

The evidence on the relationship between productivity and wages is overwhelming. Stephen Golub, for example, has analysed the index of unit labour costs, at PPP, which relates the cost of labour to productivity and changes in real exchange rates. Note that if wages rise in line with productivity (and real exchange rates remain unchanged), the unit labour cost remains constant. Looking at seven developing countries, Golub finds that the unit labour cost rose in five from 1970 to 1993 (India, Korea, Malaysia, the Philippines and Thailand) and fell in two (Mexico and Indonesia). In the first five, then, wages rose even faster than productivity. In the last two, they rose more slowly. These deviations could occur for a number of different reasons – initial (or terminal) overvaluation or undervaluation of the real exchange rate or

Figure 10.1 Labour cost and productivity per worker in manufacturing (1995–9 average)

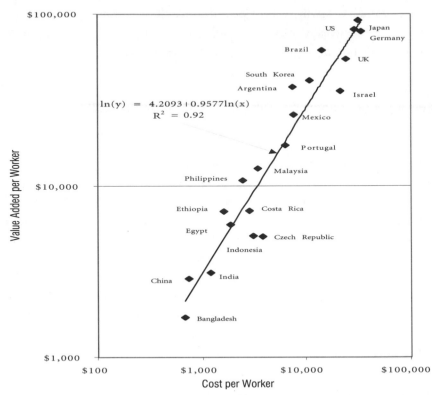

$$\ln(y) = 4.2093 + 0.9577\ln(x)$$
$$R^2 = 0.92$$

Source: World Bank, *World Development Indicators 2002* (Washington DC: World Bank, 2002), own calculations.

initial (or terminal) labour market disequilibria, for example. But the overall pattern is clear. Golub also analysed forty-nine countries at a point in time and found that productivity growth explained most of the variation in wage growth, again just as one would expect.[4]

Why are workers in high-income countries so much more productive than those in China (or other developing countries)? One explanation is that they have far more capital at their command than a Chinese worker. In 2000, Chinese gross capital formation per person was only about 4 per cent of US levels, at market exchange rates.[5] Moreover, because of China's rapid growth, its relative rates of investment were even lower just a few years ago. By comparison with high-income countries, therefore, China has very little capital to spread around. A second explanation is that Americans and Europeans are far better educated, on average, than Chinese. A third explanation is the

Chinese people's lack of experience with sophisticated modern management and manufacturing. A final explanation is the different composition of Chinese manufacturing. China specializes in relatively labour-intensive manufacturing, which makes value added per worker lower than in high-income countries. By exporting the products of its cheap but relatively unskilled labour, China gains access to the physical and human capital, and know-how, of high-income countries, embodied in their exports. China does not make Boeing aircraft and the US, by now, makes relatively few garments.

In future, the efficiency of Chinese workers and managers and the capital at their disposal will rise rapidly, generating correspondingly swift increases in productivity.[6] That will not make China invincibly competitive, because, in a competitive economy, wages will rise as well. They have done just that in other rapidly growing east Asian countries, such as South Korea. Today, South Korea's wages are fifteen times as high as China's. Fifty years ago, they would have been much the same. In time, China's wages and so its costs will also rise, together with its productivity. As they do so, its comparative advantage will also change. Today, South Korea has largely left garment manufacture behind. In time, so will China.

At this stage, a sophisticated critic would argue that China is different from South Korea. It has an enormous potential supply of labour, whose wages, in a competitive economy, will be determined not by rising productivity in manufacturing, but by low productivity back home in rural areas. If the latter rises slowly, as it is quite likely to do, then wages in Chinese industry must also rise slowly, if the labour market remains competitive. Since underlying productive efficiency is bound to grow in Chinese manufacturing, will this not make China invincibly competitive after all?

The answer, again, is no. Assume that the real wage does not rise at all, but 'total factor productivity' – the output that can be produced by a unit of capital and labour – does continue to increase. It will then become profitable to take advantage of this productivity increase through rapidly increasing employment of still cheap labour.[7] Increases in productivity per worker will then remain low, but the growth in industrial employment will be rapid. This is exactly as it ought to be in a country so early in its industrialization. Then, when the supply of labour begins to tighten, wages and labour productivity will both explode upwards. That also happened to South Korea after a decade or two of rapid growth.[8]

The same will happen in China, provided it is allowed to do so. If, however, the movement of labour into modern industry is controlled or wages are pushed up prematurely (as is, in fact, happening), China will end up with a dualistic economy instead, with higher wages for a relatively privileged few, but a smaller modern economy and a lower overall standard of living than would be desirable. Given the controls on labour mobility in China, that is quite likely to happen. These are also one of the reasons for the widening income gap between the people of the coastal provinces and the rest of the country. Either way, one can be confident that the relationship between real wages and productivity per worker will hold: either real wages *and* productivity per worker will rise slowly for a long time, or real wages will rise rapidly *and* so will productivity per worker.

If developing countries are not so overwhelmingly competitive in manufacturing, why have 'good' manufacturing jobs for unskilled or semi-skilled workers in high-income countries shrunk over the past three decades? Between 1970 and 2000, the US lost 2.5 million jobs in manufacturing, while the share of manufacturing in total employment fell from 26.4 per cent to 14.7 per cent. In the UK, the reduction in employment in manufacturing was 3.5 million between 1970 and 1998, while the share of manufacturing in employment fell from 34.7 to 18.6 per cent. The UK was extreme. But similar patterns can be seen elsewhere: 39.5 per cent of West Germany's workers were in manufacturing in 1970, an extraordinarily high share. By 1999, this had fallen to 24.1 per cent.[9]

To understand why absolute numbers employed and, still more, the share of employment in manufacturing fell in high-income countries over the past two or three decades, one has to go back to underlying causes. Logically, employment depends on output and productivity trends. If growth of labour productivity is higher than the growth of output, employment must shrink. If growth of productivity is sufficiently higher in manufacturing than in the rest of the economy, the employment share in manufacturing will fall, even if the employment level does not. Output, in turn, will depend on the growth in demand and changes in the trade balance. If the deterioration in the trade balance is big enough, positive trends in demand for manufactures can be consistent with a reduction in output.

What then are the facts? Paul Krugman, a well-known US trade economist, calculates that the increase in the US trade deficit in manufactures may have accounted for just a quarter of the decline of the share of manufacturing in US GDP, from 25.0 per cent in 1970 to 15.9 per cent in 2000. In 2001, the US ran a trade deficit in manufactures of $300 billion (approximately 3 per cent of GDP), of which $165 billion was with developing countries. The European

Union, however, ran an overall surplus in manufactures of $120 billion and a surplus with developing countries of $50 billion. In the US, therefore, trade created a modest gap between growth in demand for manufactures and in domestic output. But this is not true for the EU as a whole, where a negative impact of trade in manufactures with developing countries on jobs in manufacturing can only have come via differences in the labour intensity of what was exported and imported. In other words, balanced trade with developing countries will tend to raise productivity in manufacturing, since labour-intensive manufacturing will shrink and capital-intensive manufacturing rise. That is beneficial in itself, since it raises potential incomes, just as any other productivity increase does. The only requirement is a labour market capable of reallocating workers.

Now turn to output and productivity. Between 1973 and 1995, labour productivity in US manufacturing rose at 2.5 per cent a year, while it grew at only 1.5 per cent a year in the business sector as a whole. Similar gaps exist in every other high-income country. Inevitably, therefore, employment in manufacturing had to shrink, relative to that in the business sector as a whole, if output merely rose at the same rate in the two sectors. But people in high-income countries also tend to spend a declining share of their incomes on manufactures and an increasing share on services.[10] The combination of sluggish growth in demand for manufactures with rapid rises in productivity guarantees a steep fall in the share of employment in manufacturing in the years ahead, *regardless of what happens to trade balances.*

Consider the following simple example: an economy with an initial share of manufacturing in employment of 15 per cent; productivity growth at 2.5 per cent a year in manufacturing and 1.5 per cent a year in the rest of the economy; growth in demand for manufactures at 2 per cent a year (in real terms) and in demand for the rest of economic output (overwhelmingly services) at 2.5 per cent a year; and balanced trade in both manufactures and services. Then, after twenty-five years, the share of manufacturing in employment will be 11 per cent; after fifty years, it will be 8 per cent; after a hundred years, it will be 4 per cent. Manufacturing is, in short, the new agriculture.

To think this will be a disaster shows one is prey to the 'lump of labour fallacy' – the view that there exists a fixed number of jobs in an economy. Nobody with any knowledge of economic history could believe such a thing. Two hundred years ago, the share of the population engaged in agriculture in today's high-income countries was about three-quarters. Today it is 2 or 3 per cent in populations that have also increased many times over. Are all the people not required in the fields now unemployed? The answer is: of course not. They do a host of jobs, most of them far more amusing and less arduous than their ancestors could even have imagined in 1800. The same will be true in future.

So far, then, the notion of an insuperable tide of hyper-competitive production laying waste the jobs, industries and economic activity of the high-income countries can be seen as hysteria. But this leaves aside one last possible meaning to the notion of competition among countries. When a developing country, such as China, sends goods to the US or the EU, in line with its comparative advantage, the terms of trade – and so real incomes – of the importing countries improve. This means that the prices of their imports fall in relation to exports. That, in turn, means that the importing country can buy more with what it produces. It is better off. That, indeed, is why China's entry into world markets is beneficial for the high-income countries that make the sophisticated goods and services the Chinese wish to buy. Trade is not a zero-sum game. It is mutually enriching.

In a world with many countries, however, it is perfectly possible for the entry of new suppliers – particularly a huge country such as China – to hurt others. But this would come through competition not in the markets of importing countries, but in third markets. As China and other Asian countries continue to grow, the prices of what they export (manufactures, especially labour-intensive manufactures) may well fall relative to the prices of what they import (sophisticated manufactures, energy, other raw materials and food).

This could be quite important. As Figures 10.2 and 10.3 show, over the past three decades, the real prices of primary commodities have been very weak. The only exception is petroleum, whose real price exploded in the 1970s and then fell in the 1980s and 1990s. This has been wonderful for the high-income countries, which are net importers of commodities, and dreadful for many developing countries, which are net exporters. Now suppose that China becomes, in time, the world's largest importer of commodities. This seems rather likely. By doing so, it may reverse these trends in commodity prices. In addition, China will tend to drive down the relative prices of those manufactured goods in which it has a comparative advantage. Although a reduction in the relative prices of labour-intensive manufactures benefits high-income countries (which are net importers), while harming other developing country exporters, a reduction in the world prices of sophisticated manufactures, relative to commodities, would tend to worsen the terms of trade of the high-income countries.

Figure 10.2 Real prices of commodities (1980=100, deflated by US dollar unit value of manufactured exports from France, Germany, Japan, UK and US)

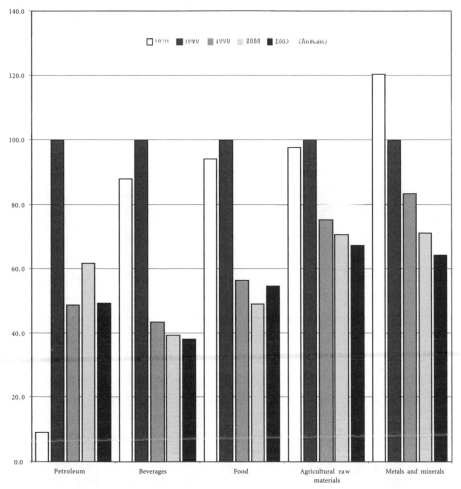

Source: World Bank, *Global Economic Prospects and the Developing Countries 2003: Investing to Unlock Global Opportunities* (Washington DC: World Bank, 2003).

As always, however, what matters is the size of these effects. Take an extreme possibility for the US. In 2001, US GDP was close to $10,000 billion, merchandise exports were $730 billion and merchandise imports were $1,180 billion. Net imports of manufactures were $300 billion and net imports of commodities were $150 billion. Now assume that China has no overall impact on the relative prices of different manufactures (though it is more plausible that it lowers the relative prices of US imports and raises those of US exports, which would make the US a bit better off). Assume also that China's rise

Figure 10.3 Real prices of selected agricultural commodities (1980=100)

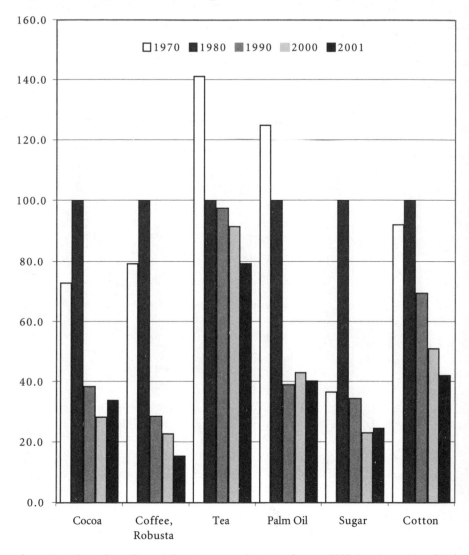

Source: World Bank, *Global Economic Prospects and the Developing Countries 2003: Investing to Unlock Global Opportunities* (Washington DC: World Bank, 2003).

doubled the relative prices of all commodities (with no differentiation, again, between those the US imports and those it exports), in relation to manufactures (whose price, in dollars, is assumed to remain unchanged). Roughly speaking, this would take the prices of commodities, in dollars, back to where they were in 1980. The net imports of commodities, which cost the US $150 billion in 2001, would now cost $300 billion. Thus the US would be worse off by just 1.5 per cent of GDP – about half a year's normal growth. In the case of the EU, the loss would be fractionally larger, because it is a slightly bigger net importer of commodities ($160 billion, instead of $150 billion). Yet the conclusion in both cases is the same. Even if the relative prices of commodities were to double, neither the US nor the EU would suffer a real income loss as big as 2 per cent of GDP. Moreover, this relative price assumption is, it should be stressed, an extreme one.

What then are the conclusions? First, an irresistibly competitive China is a figment of the fevered imagination, since the real cost of labour will tend to remain in line with its productivity. Second, the principal determinants of declining employment in manufacturing in the high-income countries have been sluggish demand and rapidly rising productivity, not trade. Third, even a dramatic impact on the terms of trade of high-income countries, via a huge rise in the relative prices of commodities, would have a modest impact on their real incomes. In short, worries about de-industrialization and global competition from pauper labour are nonsense.

Fears of global excess capacity

The prophets of doom are still not done. The next worry is that the rising productive capacity of Asian suppliers, particularly China, threatens global surfeit, deflation and depression. This thought is dear to the heart of William Greider, among the most influential critics of the new global market economy, who writes that 'the present regime is pathological fundamentally because it . . . destroys consumer incomes while it creates the growing surfeit of goods'.[11] This is a strange idea. Americans with close to the world's highest incomes succeed in spending, without apparent difficulty, virtually everything they earn. Yet one is asked to imagine that a world with billions of poor people cannot absorb additional production. The world we know cannot suffer from a surfeit of goods. It can only suffer from inadequate purchasing power.[12]

Consider the underlying economic mechanisms. Cheap imports of clothing from China replace production in the European Union or the US. This releases EU and US workers and so lowers inflationary pressures, which should allow the European Central Bank or the Federal Reserve to run an easier monetary policy, thereby expanding domestic demand. It also increases the real incomes of European and American consumers, since they do not have to spend as much on clothing as before. So they can spend their money on something else. Meanwhile, Chinese workers have increased incomes, which they also spend, invest directly or save. Because wages in China are lower than in the US, efficient companies producing in China, be they domestic or foreign, should be highly profitable. But, contrary to Greider's fears, profits are not a black hole. Their recipients will normally wish to invest and consume, if not there, then somewhere else. Finally, if the Chinese are unwilling to spend all their additional income, they can lend it. The world is not short of willing borrowers. So no obvious reason exists for a global glut.

It is true that some countries tend to save more than they invest at home (that is, they earn more than they spend), while others invest more than they save. Between 1997 and 2001, for example, Japan had an average gross national saving rate of 29.8 per cent against a gross national investment rate of 27.5 per cent. Similarly, the developing countries of east Asia and the Pacific ran a phenomenal average savings rate of 36.9 per cent, against an investment rate of only 33.9 per cent. On the other side, Latin America had a savings rate of only 17.9 per cent, against an investment rate of 21.7 per cent, sub-Saharan Africa had a savings rate of 13.9 per cent, against an investment rate of 17.6 per cent and, last but not least, the US had a savings rate of just 17.5 per cent, against an investment rate of 19.5 per cent.[13]

This pattern of surpluses and deficits will create difficulties only to the extent that the intermediation of the flows from the savings-surplus to the savings-deficit countries does not work smoothly. As it happens, that can be a problem, particularly for developing-country capital importers. That is why the US role as capital importer of last resort is, at present, an essential element in global macroeconomic stability. The US (and the EU, for that matter) are in a good position to import capital, however, since they possess relatively reliable financial systems and can also borrow in their own currencies. In the longer run, however, two further solutions can be envisaged: first, the capital-surplus countries – principally Japan and the developing countries of east Asia and the Pacific – should develop ways to lend and invest smoothly and safely in other parts of the world; and, second, they should encourage their people to spend just that little bit more of their rising incomes, partly by reforming their financial systems. But no insuperable difficulty should arise. If some people (Asians) wish to spend less than they earn today, then others need to be encouraged to spend more.

Worries about exploitation of labour in developing countries

Maybe people can be persuaded that imports of manufactures from developing countries, even China, do not mean the end of jobs in the high-income countries. But critics then argue that the competitiveness of the developing countries is built on gross exploitation of labour, including children. Is this not insupportable? The answer is that this is untrue and, being untrue, is not insupportable.

A cynic might wonder why so many people in high-income countries became conscious of the plight of exploited workers in developing countries in the 1990s. Could it be that they were beginning to compete? Yes, it could. In his excellent book on globalization, Philippe Legrain, a former speech writer to Mike Moore, reported a private comment uttered to him by a senior American trade-union leader: 'we don't give a damn about workers in the Third World. We just want to protect our members' interests.'[14] This has the merit of being honest. But it does not explain why so many young radicals adopted the exploitation of third-world workers by western multinationals as their cause. A charitable explanation is that they realized that many of the things they buy are produced in developing countries by poor people, for what they consider desperately low wages. This left many of them feeling guilty, whereupon they put two and two together and reached any number but four. They came to a conclusion that is the precise opposite of the truth, namely, that people who work in what people in the west naturally consider to be poor conditions and for dreadful wages are in this miserable condition because of their 'exploitative' jobs, not in such jobs because of their miserable conditions.

As was pointed out in the previous chapter, China's rapid growth over the past two decades has delivered more people from desperate poverty, more quickly, than ever before. That does not suggest exploitation. Moreover, the millions of young people, many of them women, who have fled rural China to work in factories along the coast were not forced to do so by anything other than their poverty at home. Inadequate though they seem to a prosperous westerner, the incomes they earn make an enormous difference to their prospects. This is especially true for women, whose status can be transformed in patriarchal societies by opportunities to earn incomes for themselves. As an informed observer of Bangladesh has noted, 'The income the women earn gives them social status and bargaining power. One very positive thing is that the average marriage age has increased.'[15]

Thoughtful critics may grant all this. But they will argue that the absence of enforceable labour rights guarantees that Chinese workers, and others similarly situated, will fail to gain the fruits of their labour. Trades unions can limit the ability of employers to exploit their bargaining power over the work-force, protect individuals against bullying and other forms of exploitation and insist on elementary standards of safety and health. All this is evidently desirable. But it is wrong to assume that activist trades unions or the panoply of worker rights treasured in Europe are inevitably appropriate for a labour-surplus developing country (or for a rich one, for that matter). They can also create injustice and waste.[16]

In China today, the proportion of the work-force employed in more or less modern activities is still small (perhaps an eighth). The wage for unskilled labour is set by its value in the rural hinterland. That, in technical terms, is its 'opportunity cost'. Critics – Greider, for example – complain that workers in countries such as China earn much less than the wages received by workers in comparable plants in high-income countries, even though those plants can operate just as efficiently there. That should be so. It makes no sense for workers with similar skills to be paid very differently in any given labour market. If employers are profit-maximizing, as Greider believes, they should employ more people instead, until the marginal product of labour equals its low cost. Any given plant would then employ substantially more people in China than it would in a high-income country. The average product of labour will be far higher than its marginal product, in such plants. Fortunately, this also makes China a profitable place in which to invest and so stimulates the country's economic growth.[17]

What might active trades unions achieve in this context? Suppose they were successful in raising wages and conditions for the lucky minority of workers employed in modern factories to levels closer to those westerners consider reasonable. The price of labour to modern enterprises would rise above its opportunity cost. The labour market would then be dualistic, with low incomes for the great majority and relatively high incomes for the organized few. Both profitability in the modern sector and the labour-intensity of production would be lower. The modern sector would then grow more slowly. People would queue for these high-paying jobs, creating more open unemployment. Migration from the countryside would also slow, delaying, perhaps indefinitely, the time when labour shortages began to raise rural wages rapidly. All these unions would have achieved is to have created an island of privilege in an ocean of misery.

Is this a progressive outcome? Hardly. Nor is it a theoretical possibility. It is exactly what has happened in India, where a combination of strong trades unions, job protection, reservation of production to small-scale enterprises and prohibition of closure of bankrupt plants has halted growth of employment in modern manufacturing. Today, employment in large-scale manufacturing is about 5 million people, in a country of over a billion. There is little chance of its rising significantly. India's industrialization has been blocked. Indian workers are so well protected from exploitation by industrial bosses that they have no jobs at all. The exact opposite happened in South Korea and Taiwan. Today, the workforce of these countries enjoy wages and conditions Indians can only dream of. The desirable development path goes via rapid growth of output and employment in a profitable modern sector to a tighter overall labour market. This is the path China is on. It is the only desirable path for the country as a whole.

Equal care must be taken over the fashionable crusade for the elimination of child labour. For, once again, contemporary westerners judge the developing countries by the standards they are lucky enough to enjoy. They compare what is happening in a still desperately poor developing country not with the alternatives enjoyed by its residents, but with their own. Approximately 250 million children between the ages of five and fourteen work in developing countries, certainly a far lower proportion of the world's children than ever before in history. Of these, 70 per cent work in agriculture and no more than 10–15 million in export industries, predominantly in south Asia. These children work not because their parents (if they have them) are more wicked than those anywhere else, but because of their poverty. Nothing is better established than the tendency for better-off parents in more prosperous societies to have fewer children and invest more in their education. The decline in birth rates in the developing world has already been dramatic. The population growth rate in middle-income developing countries is forecast at only 0.9 per cent a year between 2000 and 2015. Even in India, it is now forecast at only 1.3 per cent.[18]

The evidence of the impact of rising incomes on child labour is also dramatic. Between 1993 and 1998, the income of the poorest 10 per cent of Vietnamese rose by more than a half, in real terms. This led to a sharp reduction in child labour (mostly on the family farm) and greater investment in their education.[19] Now suppose that western trade sanctions forced child workers out of export-oriented factories instead. If their parents cannot afford to keep them idle (or they have no families to look after them), they will do something else: prostitution, for example, or farm labour. They may work in factories for purely domestic production, most of which will be far worse run than those serving export markets.[20] The conscience of western agitators will have been salved, at the expense of those they allegedly care about. Substantial evidence exists that exactly this happened in Bangladesh in the early 1990s, in response to a campaign against Wal-Mart's purchases of clothing made, in part, by children. Thousands were sacked, many of whom moved on to more dangerous and less well-paid jobs.[21]

It is easy to understand why governments of developing countries view with dismay the campaign for higher labour standards enforced through the World Trade Organization. Does this mean nothing can be done? No, it does not. Encouraging export-led growth from the developing countries would help, since that raises incomes, tightens labour markets and so naturally tends to improve job standards. Aid could be increased to countries that do a reasonable job of policing working conditions, particularly health and safety, but this must apply to all employers, not just to exporters. If the people of high-income countries wish to accelerate the end of child labour, it would help if aid funded the education of poor children, while providing compensation to parents for the incomes they have lost. But imposing export sanctions on countries is a way of penalizing them for their poverty while taking away the best ladder out of it.[22] At best, it is foolish. At worst, it is gross hypocrisy. The test of whether all this talk means anything is whether high-income countries are prepared to put their money where their moralistic mouth is.

Threats to the environment

It is widely accepted among critics of market-driven globalization that it is inherently inimical to protection of the environment. To the extent that it is not inherently inimical, they argue, it is so *de facto*, because of the way the World Trade Organization operates. These propositions, though frequently repeated, suffer from a simple drawback: they are, where not altogether wrong, at least greatly exaggerated. While it is impossible to deal with this complex subject at length, here are some of the most important charges: globalization promotes growth, which is inherently inimical to environmental sustainability; globalization favours transport-intensive and so energy-intensive systems of production and distribution, also inherently inimical to sustainability; globalization encourages an environmental 'race to the bottom'; and the World Trade Organization prevents countries from taking the steps they wish, individually or collectively, to protect themselves from these various environmental harms.[23]

Consider, first, the relationship between globalization and economic growth. On this, Thomas Bode, executive director of Greenpeace International, wrote that 'The modern economy is a fire-breathing vampire of petroleum which is slowly cooking our planet. To claim that a massive increase in global production and consumption will be good for the environment is preposterous.'[24] The objection here, however, is not to trade as such, but to economic growth. One reaction to Bode's view, which is widely shared in the environmental community, is that the chances of persuading the bulk of humanity to forgo economic growth, in order to protect a global environment ravaged by the citizens of the wealthy countries while leaving the latter to enjoy vastly higher living standards, in perpetuity are rightly zero. Yet the chances of persuading the wealthy citizens of high-income countries to reduce their living standards to the global average as a step towards an egalitarian, global, no-growth economy are also zero.[25] Stopping growth is not an option. The challenge is managing it. If this is to be done, one must understand the link between growth and the environment rather better than Bode seems to do.

That link is complex. As people become richer, for example, they insist upon a clean-up of local environmental damage. Alan Krueger and Gene Grossman of Princeton University argued, for example, in 1994 that this happened when a country's GDP per head reached $5,000, roughly where the Czech Republic was then.[26] After about $8,000, they argue, local pollution starts to improve substantially. At the same time, emission of CO_2 increases with levels of GDP per head (though at different rates, since some countries' economies – the US's, for example – are far more CO_2-intensive, at given levels of GDP per head, than others).[27] So the challenge of global warming does increase with GDP. It would be fair, therefore, to conclude that local environmental harms tend to fall after a while, but global harms to rise continuously, as real incomes grow.

In addition, we know from experience that market economies have been far less environmentally damaging than the socialist ones. The former Soviet Union was responsible for some of the world's greatest environmental catastrophes, including the draining of the Aral Sea.[28] China, too, has a poor environmental record. This is so for three reasons: the indifference of dictatorships to political pressure; the indifference of state-owned enterprises to the need to use resources efficiently; and their technological backwardness and desire for self-sufficiency, which led, to take an egregious example, to the use of highly polluting brown coal, instead of petroleum, by the former East Germany.

The fundamental point, however, is this. Economic activities create environmental spillovers. The rational policy to deal with those spillovers is through cost-internalization – policies that confront decision-makers with the costs of what they do. The market must be used to remedy the harms the market would otherwise do. Such internalization needs to be domestic or local, where harms are domestic or local, and global, where harms are global. Whether such policies can be agreed, or implemented, at the global level is, to put it mildly, an open question. But an agreement to global carbon taxes, for example, is certainly less implausible than an agreement to freeze global economic growth. Even before achieving this ambitious goal, it would be a good idea at least to eliminate environmentally harmful subsidies. Among salient examples are subsidies to the use of pesticides and fertilizers in agriculture, to commercial energy production and consumption, and to deep-sea fishing.[29]

Now, second, let us turn to the connection between trade and the environment. Critics argue that, since trade requires transport and transport requires energy, trade must be harmful for the environment.[30] But the significance of this link is enormously exaggerated. Many of the harms to which environmentalists point are not related in any significant way to trade. More energy is used in domestic trade, for example. Deforestation is frequently driven not by exports, but by land-hunger and poverty (since wood is the fuel used by people who cannot afford commercial energy). Similarly, pressure on fragile dryland areas is a result of overpopulation and ineffective property rights. In both cases, trade can be a way of obtaining resources – energy or food, in these cases – more cheaply and in less environmentally damaging ways than locally.

Worse, the absence of trade can be directly harmful to the environment. Highly protected agriculture uses more inputs of fertilizer, pesticide and energy per unit of output than does less protected agriculture. Switzerland, for example, uses ten times as much input of chemicals per unit of land as Argentina or Australia. This point was already noted by Adam Smith, who pointed out that 'by means of glasses, hotbeds and hotwalls, very good grapes can be raised in Scotland, and very good wine too can be made of them at about thirty times the expense for which at least equally good can be bought from foreign countries. Would it be a reasonable law to prohibit the importation of all foreign wines, merely to encourage the making of claret and burgundy in Scotland?'[31] Similarly, BSE (bovine spongiform encephalopathy) was a direct result of intensive feeding of cattle in the UK, a far less suitable environment for cattle rearing than Argentina or Brazil. But the point is a general one. Agriculture supported by high prices is certain to be more intensive in the use of all inputs, including environmentally damaging ones.

Now consider the next argument, that globalization triggers a 'race to the bottom' in environmental regulation. This argument has three elements. The first is that trade encourages the relocation of environmentally damaging processes. The second is that the differences in regulations which promote such relocation are illegitimate. The last is that, as a result, the race to the bottom has in fact occurred. In assessing these arguments, we need to remember that we are dealing with local or national, not global, environmental spillovers.

These dangers are again exaggerated, if not plain wrong. First, there is strong evidence that rich countries are not exporting polluting industry to developing countries. Polluting industries are complex and capital intensive. The benefits from putting such activities in developing countries would be very small, even if regulations were laxer. Moreover, multinational companies would not dare to operate plants in very different ways in different countries. It would save very little, if any, money and could expose them to catastrophically adverse publicity. For all these reasons, developing countries have not increased their share in pollution-intensive exports.[32]

It should be stressed, however, that if industry were to migrate from one country, or part of a country, to another, in response to differences in environmental regulation, that could be entirely appropriate. One of the themes of radical critics of market-led globalization is that it undermines local autonomy.[33] Differences in environmental standards are, however, a natural expression of such autonomy. Differences in incomes, preferences and geography could quite reasonably give different localities, or countries, entirely different environmental standards for local environmental spillovers. If polluting industries were then to migrate from high-standard regions or countries to low-standard regions or countries, the world would be unambiguously better off. The high-standard regions or countries would be able to consume the products of polluting activities without having to host them, and the low-standard regions or countries would have more economic activity, in return for pollution to which they are, relatively speaking, indifferent.

The counter-argument to this position is that industry may use the possibility of such 'regulatory arbitrage' to undermine regulation in the high-standard region or country. Evidently, there is such a risk. But the proper response is also the correct one: regions are not in a zero-sum competition with one another. A region that has a comparative disadvantage in polluting industry, because of local preferences, will generate a comparative advantage in non-polluting activities.

In practice, however, the evidence for such a race to the bottom in environmental regulation is lacking. Research shows that environmental regulations have tended to tighten in developing countries, partly in response to political pressures.[34] It is evident, in fact, that a polluted atmosphere and poisonous water are a rather substantial disadvantage if one wishes to attract multinational companies, since these strongly discourage foreign professionals from living in the country. Evidently, many countries do find it difficult to enforce environmental regulations, because of the weakness, or corruption, of their administrations. But two points are quite clear: first, virtually all the environmental degradation in developing countries has nothing to do with trade – just experience the air pollution from the burning of fuel in Delhi in winter; second, the spread of democracy in the developing world, which has been one of the most attractive features of the despised age of 'neo-liberal' or 'corporate' globalization, as I have noted in Part II above, has greatly strengthened the power of environmental lobbies.

In the high-income countries, too, there is no doubt that environmental standards have been racing to the top, not the bottom, over the last two or three decades. Local air and water quality have improved enormously, in response to tighter regulation. To the extent that they have not done so, it is often as a result of protectionist policies towards agriculture that have promoted heavy use of chemical inputs. In his book *The Sceptical Environmentalist*, Bjorn Lomborg provides a host of examples of the improvement in the local environment in high-income countries over recent decades.[35] Critics may believe that the tightening of standards has not been fast enough. But they cannot doubt the direction of change.

Finally, let us look at the role of the World Trade Organization. Critics argue that it is inherently hostile to environmental regulation. One justification they cite is a series of WTO cases – the 'tuna–dolphin' case between the US and Mexico over the former's banning of imports of tuna caught in nets that killed dolphins; the case between the US, on the one hand, and Venezuela and Brazil, on the other, over the former's standards for cleaner gasoline; and the case between the US, on the one hand, and India, Malaysia, Pakistan and Thailand, on the other, over imports of shrimps caught in nets that endangered turtles. Yet in all these cases the WTO – and the General Agreement on

Tariffs and Trade before it – did not deny the right of the US to protect the environment. But it insisted, rightly, that the US could not discriminate between domestic and foreign production, as it did over cleaner gasoline, and had no right to impose purely unilateral views of how things should be done, particularly when they were unfair. In the case of shrimp, for example, the US banned all imports, including of farmed shrimp, which were no danger to turtles whatsoever.[36]

Three genuine issues arise on the relationship between the WTO and environmental protection. The first is whether countries should have the right to act against process and production methods (PPMs) used elsewhere. Developing countries believe, rightly, that such actions would amount to both a massive infringement of their sovereignty and a severe protectionist barrier. The challenge of identifying where the parts and components that went into a given product came from and proving their compatibility with environmental standards decreed by importing countries would be insuperable. Rules of origin in preferential trade arrangements are bad enough. Rules on PPMs would be an immense barrier to trade. It is intriguing that the critics of globalization who praise local autonomy would deny this absolutely, in this case, even if the standard is freely chosen and the environmental impacts of the methods used in production are also entirely local.

The second issue is the relation between the WTO and Multilateral Environmental Agreements, some of which use trade restrictions as a means of enforcement. Conflicts are conceivable, though none has, as yet, happened. They will arise where members of an MEA apply trade sanctions to a non-member who belongs to the WTO. If, for example, the Kyoto agreement had included trade measures, it would have been amusing to see the consequences of the application of WTO-illegal sanctions against a non-signatory, such as the US.[37] A part of the answer is to limit trade restrictions in such agreements, which are usually inefficient means of achieving an environmental end. An example is the Convention on International Trade in Endangered Species (CITES). It is questionable whether, in the long run, bans on trade in ivory, to take one example, will prove an effective way of preserving elephants. But where trade restrictions are used, some form of accommodation between the MEA and the WTO will need to be achieved.

The third issue concerns the role of scientific evidence. The underlying principle of the WTO on food standards and the environment is that measures should be based on 'sound science'. This, critics allege, conflicts with the precautionary principle, which says, in effect, that anxiety, however ill founded, should be quite enough to justify a ban. This raises a general issue with the WTO, to which I will return below. But the general answer is this. It is entirely possible, within the WTO, to take actions that are outside its reasonable provisions. Trading nations will not agree that their partners can ban imports whenever the whim takes them, since that gives open season to protectionists. But the WTO specifically allows for compensation. Thus if a country decides to impose a ban that cannot be scientifically justified, the sensible answer is compensation.

The conclusion then is that the alleged link between trade liberalization and environmental damage is wholly unsupported by the evidence. What is true, however, is that the management of environmental externalities requires well-targeted measures aimed at making decision-makers aware of the costs. This is also true for global environmental threats, such as global warming. But trade is in no way an obstacle to effective measures against such threats. The obstacle is the unwillingness of countries to impose a high cost upon processes and activities that generate greenhouse gases.[38] Since the biggest malefactors here are the high-income countries, especially the US, it is intolerable to see their environmental lobbies at the forefront of the charge against the WTO. These are environmentalist red herrings; or, to use another metaphor, people busily creating greenhouses should not throw environmentalist stones.

Absurdity of 'localization'

The critics of globalization have what they consider a better alternative. They call it 'localization'. Under localization, the economy would, once again, be under full collective control, as they wish, but at a local level. 'Wherever economic production, labor, and markets can be local, they should be, and rules should help achieve that. International, regional, and sub-regional trade will continue to exist, of course, but should serve as a *final resort* [my emphasis], not as the purpose of the system.'[39] Each country would have an obligation to balance its trade.[40] It would also discriminate in favour of local production, insisting, among other things, that companies would need to locate in the country (or locality) if they wished to sell there.[41] The aim is to end the 'ruthless competition' generated by long-distance trade and the mobility of corporations, except for 'some cash crops and minerals and certain location-specific luxury items like Scotch whisky'.[42] The overriding aim is self-sufficiency, in which each locality, country or region imports only what it 'cannot reasonably produce for itself'.[43]

This attempt to fragment markets – the global into the regional, the regional into the national and the national into the local – raises three questions: the first is why anybody would regard this as a sensible idea; the second is how, in practice, it could be done; and the third is why anybody would consider the consequences for economic security, prosperity, the environment and development to be desirable.

The people who recommend these ideas are, as David Henderson has said, 'new millennium collectivists'.[44] The ideas appeal to activists who wish to bring economic life under political control. Their writings are full of the term 'self-reliance'. But the selves to which they refer are collective selves, not individuals. The active, purposive individual is hardly to be discerned, except as a grass-roots activist or community entrepreneur. Instead, one has a community, in which all hearts beat in sympathy with the aspirations of the activists, while the freedom of individuals to buy what they want, invest where they desire and produce for whatever market they can identify would be eliminated.[45] This is a world for people who wish to spend their lives in meetings, organizing others and being organized by them in turn.

How, then, would such an economy work? There would be barriers to trade, subsidies for local organic agriculture, wind farms and so forth, controls on corporate location, with 'site-here-to-sell' restrictions, and controls on capital flows outside each locality.[46] Competition policy would ensure adequate competition among local companies. But localities would have the right to buy local. Perhaps to disguise the failure of such closed communities, measurement of successful performance would no longer be based on 'traditional economic growth figures like GDP and GNP, but rather on more subjective social and environmental characteristics'. Further, there would be 'a reformed educational system that grasps and can convey the values of this alternative system'.[47] Maybe we should call this new educational department the 'Ministry of Truth'.

The fundamental question, however, is how the controls on trade would work. Apparently, there would be no physical barriers to trade among localities (border posts between Oxford and Reading, for example, or between New York and New Jersey). But there would be barriers at national or regional levels. In practice, therefore, one can assume this would end up as protectionist fortresses at the national or regional (European) level, with the localization honoured largely in the breach.

Now why would the consequences be desirable? Consider four. The first is already indicated in one of the opening quotations to this chapter. The writers assume that 'any nation or community's security would be better enhanced if its own people could grow their own foods'. The emphasis must be on the word 'could'. Subsistence farming is among the riskiest of all human strategies, since starvation is one harvest-failure away. The fact that it would be done on a slightly larger scale does not guarantee its safety. In the 1990s, food accounted for more than 20 per cent of the imports in twenty least developed countries, for more than 30 per cent in more than ten countries and for more than 40 per cent in four countries.[48] The assumption that these countries – many of which are in ecologically fragile, dryland locations – would have greater food security if they were forced to be self-sufficient is absurd. Being able to buy food anywhere in the world is the most secure position one can be in. That is why trade can enhance security. Just ask North Koreans how much more secure they might be if their masters did not practise 'self-sufficiency', but allowed them to export manufactures in return for food, as their neighbours to the south do. But of course one cannot ask them. As is true of all fully closed economies, theirs is a tyranny.

A second consequence is environmental. The proponents believe as a matter of faith, not reason, that these self-sufficient regional, national and local economies would be less harmful to the environment than a global economy. The belief that a 'local' economy is intrinsically less environmentally damaging is completely unjustified, however, as was argued in the previous section. Just think of the example of China's 'Great Leap Forward' of the 1950s and 1960s – a classic localization project, in which every village was encouraged to produce iron. The result was mass starvation, ruined environments and very little usable iron. It was, in fact, a superb demonstration of the fatuity of localization as a means of combining environmental protection with local self-sufficiency. It is true that, if economic activity were reduced to a low enough level, the environment might be helped. At a low enough level, the people would starve to death. But 'impoverish yourselves and save the environment' is not the most saleable of slogans.

A third consequence is that efficiency would cease to be driven upwards, except to the extent that there would be adequate competition in whatever had been defined as the local economy. If price does not matter, as the opening quotation says, then obtaining one's needs at the lowest possible cost does not matter either. UK consumers would still have to suffer from the expensive cars and the electronic equipment that used to break down before Japanese exports arrived in the 1970s. There could not be the intra-industry trade and trade in parts and components that has done so much to raise productivity in almost all countries. With the possible exception of the US, every country would find itself increasingly far from the world's technological frontier. But the frontier would also move more slowly, since there would be a huge diminution in the intensity of competition and so of the pressure to innovate. In addition, if one says that price – and so efficiency – does not matter, one is also saying that it does not matter how inefficiently resources are used. For one of the big efforts made by competitive companies is to reduce resource use. That is, for example, why there have been such large increases in output per unit of energy over the past three decades. That effort, too, would disappear.

The UK does at least have some capacity to generate, use and attract technology for making advanced goods and services. This does not apply to the developing countries. This is the final and most powerful consequence. Development would be hobbled, which is, I fear, what the advocates of localization want. Think, for a moment, of a world in which no country imported what it could not reasonably make. The only things the developing countries could then export would be tropical agricultural commodities (coffee, tea, cocoa, bananas, cotton, but not even sugar) and some minerals (including petroleum, until replaced by wind power). Developing countries are unable to make a single manufactured good that high-countries cannot make. But, by definition, the reverse is not true. There is a huge range of sophisticated products – pharmaceuticals, electronics, advanced machinery, sophisticated aircraft and so forth – that only high-income countries can make.

In this new world in which exports from developing countries have collapsed back into commodity exports, most would have next to no capacity to import any of these high-technology products. Some of the admired leaders of the anti-globalization movement would deprive developing countries even of commodity exports. Bernard Cassen, the chairman of the French anti-globalization Attac movement, has said that 'I'm very surprised by the argument that poor countries, underdeveloped countries, must have more market access to the developed ones. What does that mean, in reality? That means that you expect underdeveloped countries to export. To export what? To export commodities that they need for their own internal market.'[49] As an executed queen of his country might have said, let them eat cocoa. If the policy were pushed to its logical conclusion, developing countries would largely cease to trade among themselves as well, since few are able to make anything others cannot. Indeed, one of the consequences of their attempts at self-sufficiency is that they already trade with one another far too little.

In 2000, developing countries exported $1,060 billion worth of manufactures to the world, which accounted for 71 per cent of their total merchandise exports. They also imported $1,616 billion worth of merchandise of all kinds. If their manufactured exports were eliminated, as advocates of localization apparently recommend, on the ground that they make nothing which cannot be made in the countries where they sell their products, their merchandise imports would need to fall by two-thirds. (This assumes that the balance of trade is to remain the same. Since localizers oppose trade deficits, this is presumably what they expect.) This is, in fact, quite a modest assessment of the reduction in trade that would follow full localization, since temperate agricultural commodities and even many minerals can be supplied within the countries to which they now export, provided they are sufficiently indifferent to the costs of doing so.

This collapse in trade would devastate developing countries, especially exporters of manufactures. The hardest hit would be Bangladesh, China, Taiwan, Israel, South Korea, Malaysia, Mauritius, Mexico, Pakistan, the Philippines and Turkey, in all of which manufactures contribute more than 80 per cent of merchandise exports. Take the example of Mauritius, a small island that, under the localization rules, would have virtually nothing it could sell to the rest of the world (except perhaps tourism). In 1961, a committee headed by James Meade, subsequently to win the Nobel prize for economics, judged the economic future of this tiny sugar-producing island as hopeless. He turned out to be ludicrously wrong. I was privileged as a young economist at the World Bank, on my first mission, in 1971, to see the early stages of the Export Processing Zone that would prove him so. For Mauritius prospered by taking advantage of opportunities for exports of labour-intensive goods, initially clothing. Then it had a population of about 700,000 people living in relative poverty. Today it has a population of a million with a GDP per head of close to $10,000 at PPP. Between 1975 and 2001, Mauritius achieved a 4.7 per cent annual increase in real GDP per head – a cumulative rise of 230 per cent. The life of Mauritians has been transformed. That – and stories like that – would end if these proposals for localization were ever put into full effect.[50]

True, the advocates of localization would presumably argue that a small country such as Mauritius should join a regional arrangement of some kind. But with whom? Its closest neighbours in Africa are also unable to produce the sophisticated products it needs if its people are to sustain what we would nowadays regard as a reasonably civilized life. Without computers or televisions, for example, people would be isolated from the most important tools for learning, communication and interaction with the rest of the planet. The protagonists of localization seem to be aware of at least some of these difficulties. The authors of *Alternatives to Economic Globalization* note that 'some communities are better endowed than others', as indeed they are. Their proposed response is 'redistribution mechanisms'. These are not spelled out. But it seems to have escaped the attention of the authors that redistributive mechanisms entail unbalanced trade, since the means through which transfers are made is an excess of imports over exports. Thus the proposals for balanced trade and those for international redistribution are also mutually inconsistent.

The authors of these books accuse market liberals of arrogant utopianism. Yet it is at least possible to point to democratic countries with open market economies. Where, on the other hand, is one to find an intensely democratic, reasonably prosperous, locally self-sufficient economy? Politically, self-sufficiency has always been the goal of tyrants, for the reason that it increases their control over their subjects. Economically, self-sufficiency has failed to produce prosperity anywhere. The economies that would seem closest to it are North Korea and Cuba, hardly utopias – and not exactly democratic. What the proponents of localization aim for is a dystopia – a world of mutually assured impoverishment, in which the poorest, who most need to trade for what they cannot make, would be the biggest losers. That these people parade themselves as the friends of the poor merely demonstrates how self-deluding people can be. With friends like these, the poor of the world need no enemies.[51]

Concerns about development strategy

Let us turn, at this point, from people who wish to destroy an integrated world economy to more sophisticated analysts who wish to protect developing countries from excessive pressure to move towards free trade. Several scholars argue that the merits of a policy of free trade have been greatly exaggerated and that premature liberalization could significantly damage the prospects of development. Powerful critiques of contemporary orthodoxy on trade and development have been advanced by, among others, Ha-Joon Chang of Cambridge University, Alice Amsden of the Massachusetts Institute of Technology and Dani Rodrik of Harvard University, though other distinguished scholars would argue on similar lines.[52] None of these authors denies the role of trade as 'a handmaiden of growth', in the words of a distinguished economist of an earlier generation, Irving Kravis. On the contrary, all note that successful economies have both increased their integration in the world economy and depended upon it for their success. They are not arguing for a return to the local – or anything like it. Nor are they arguing against use of markets and economic incentives. All recognise that working market institutions are a necessary condition for long-term success. But they resist the idea that across-the-board trade liberalization is a sufficient, or even necessary, condition for rapid economic development. They are right to do so. It is not.

Dr Chang, presumably influenced by the remarkable experience of his own country, South Korea, argues that active 'industrial, trade and technology policies' are 'necessary for socializing the risks involved in the development of infant industries'.[53] He makes this argument on the basis of a historical analysis of the successful economies of today, starting with the first industrializer, the UK. All these economies, notably including the US, Germany, France, Sweden, Belgium and, later on, Japan, South Korea and Taiwan, used a range of active measures to overcome backwardness and promote industrial development. This observation, unquestionably correct, he qualifies in two significant respects: first, this 'does not mean there is only one way of doing it – that is to say, by means of tariff protection'; second, the fact that the use of activist industrial, trade and technology policies 'is necessary does not imply that all countries that use such policies are guaranteed economic success'.[54] What it does mean, however, is that developing countries must be granted the opportunity to use such policies. Otherwise, the incumbent economic powers are 'kicking down the ladder' up which they themselves ascended.

Professor Amsden argues on not dissimilar lines, but from the experience of the developing countries of the post-Second World War period and economic theory. She describes two contemporary strategies for industrial catch-up.

> In one set, embracing China, India, Korea and Taiwan, call them the 'independents' (with the understanding that all latecomers have become more global since World War II), long-term growth was premised on the 'make' technology decision, which was synonymous with the build-up of national capabilities and national firms. In another set, embracing Argentina, Brazil, Chile, Mexico and Turkey, call them the 'integrationists' (with the understanding that no country in 'the rest' has completely relinquished its economic or political autonomy), long-term growth was premised on the 'buy' technology decision, and a reliance on both foreign rules of conduct to discipline business (as provided by membership in NAFTA and the EU), and spillovers from foreign investment and technology transfer to generate wealth.[55]

Moreover, she argues, the interventionism of the first category of countries, to which, in her view, all these latecomers belonged before about 1980, was justified by the simple fact that 'none had sufficient knowledge-based assets to compete in modern industry at world prices. Government intervention arose everywhere in response to the lack of competitiveness rather than to simple cronyism, or the need to "coordinate" investment decisions, or the desire to capture "external economies", or some other typical textbook explanation for government intervention.'[56] In the absence of perfect knowledge, she argues, potentially highly profitable long-term opportunities will never be exploited. It is this obstacle that governments can (and should) help overcome.

Professor Rodrik's position is rather different. In some respects, on the need for investment co-ordination for example, it is close to one Professor Amsden attacks. His central argument is that the benefits of trade liberalization have been greatly exaggerated by its proponents. Policy-makers should instead 'focus on the fundamentals of economic growth – investment, macroeconomic stability, human resources, and good governance – and not let international economic integration dominate their thinking on development'.[57] Rodrik agrees that successful economies become more open, but, he also argues, making an economy more open, by lowering trade barriers, does not guarantee success. On the contrary, his view is that the old highly protectionist import-substitution strategies did rather well. He points to the fact that growth performance for most developing economies was better before 1973 than afterwards.[58] The reason for the subsequent collapse, he suggests, was the failure to sustain macroeconomic stability in response to a series of shocks, particularly the two oil shocks and the debt crisis of the early 1980s.

These are important critiques of liberal trade. Are they also justified? The right response is 'up to a point'.

It is correct that successful economies have intervened to promote industry in a host of different ways, and continue to do so to this day. But one must avoid the fallacy of *post hoc, propter hoc* – because one event preceded another, it also caused it. While some of those interventionist measures have worked, many have not. Even the benefits of import substitution in the nineteenth century are denied.[59] Moreover, of the instruments for industrial promotion, high levels of infant-industry protection, including total bans on competing imports, particularly in the absence of offsetting incentives to export (or export requirements), are extremely inefficient: they create a strong home-market bias in trade policy, thereby taxing competitive exports and limiting the benefits of the support to producers aiming at an uncompetitive and ridiculously small home market. As a result, they have had a well-known and depressing tendency to create perpetual children. As the World Bank has stated, 'typically the long-protected firms have not become efficient and do not in fact survive in the more competitive environment'. The Bank points to the Indian machine-tool industry, long protected with 100 per cent tariffs. When these tariffs were liberalized, Taiwanese producers took a third of the market. Since then, the Indians have fought back, but the successful competitors are new entrants, not the old flabby incumbents.[60]

It is also unquestionably correct that developing countries need to be allowed to use instruments which help them overcome the many obstacles of backwardness and, especially, as Professor Amsden argues, the absence of knowledge of what to do – and how to do it – that is an essential characteristic of that backwardness. They may use them unwisely from time to time. But they have sometimes worked. Sovereign governments should be allowed to take such actions – and, if necessary, learn from their mistakes. But trade measures are, all the same, not the most effective measures to use.

Professor Rodrik's rather different views appear more debatable. But let us first agree with him where agreement is necessary. Trade liberalization, on its own, regardless of the circumstances, will not generate rapid growth. On this, there is no disagreement and never has been, among sensible analysts. No disagreement exists on the need for macroeconomic stability either, nor on the difficulty of achieving it. Nor is there debate on the desirability of 'good government', or higher investment in human and physical resources, other things being equal. For all that, there are good reasons to question both some of Rodrik's propositions and the methods that he – and many other econo-mists – now use to reach their results.[61] Apart from these difficulties, at least two further objections can be made to Rodrik's position.

First, the view that the level of investment *per se* is of overriding importance can be strongly contested. William Easterly, for example, in his masterly analysis of the many failures of development, observes that 'both Nigeria and Hong Kong increased their physical capital stock per worker by over 250 per cent over the 1960 to 1985 time frame. The results of this massive investment were different: Nigeria's output per worker rose by 12 per cent from 1960 to 1985, while Hong Kong's rose by 328 per cent.'[62] Rodrik shows some awareness of this in remarking that if investment were the crux of the matter, 'centrally planned economies would have been the world's best performers over the longer run. Ultimately, the return on investment matters a great deal too.' Indeed, it does. And among its determinants must be how well market institutions operate and distortions in relative prices in the economy. However, these will affect not just the return on investment, but also its level. It is at the least extremely likely that the investment rates in east Asian economies, to which Rodrik (and others) point, are the consequence of the governments' well-known and well-publicised determination to preserve the profitability of exports. Export markets have, it should be stressed, the benefit that for most developing-country producers they are effectively infinite in size. That provides a huge incentive for a profitable exporter to expand capacity.[63]

Second, Rodrik's conclusions on the relative merits of import-substitution strategies are debatable in several respects. One is that his conclusion on the growth performance of economies under import substitution must be qualified by the fact that this is growth at often highly distorted domestic prices, not world prices. Another is that he cannot legitimately assume that the growth performance of the 1960–80 period would have continued if the policies of the import-substitution period had been sustained. The same absurd conclusion on the superiority of Soviet socialism over the market economy could be reached by contrasting the former's growth between 1960 and 1980 with the performance of the Soviet Union and its successor states during the subsequent two decades of admittedly difficult and often mismanaged reforms.

Also, there are, contrary to Rodrik's view, good reasons to believe that an import-substitution strategy will reach natural limits. As imports fall in relation to GDP, it will become increasingly difficult to find even tolerably economic import-substitution projects. In the end, growth will be limited by export and agricultural performance, both stunted by the incentives to import substitution oriented industry.

Finally, the superior ability of east Asian export-oriented economies to adjust to external shocks is not independent of their export-oriented strategy. As a number of economists have observed, the difficulty Latin American countries have found in coping with macroeconomic shocks (whose size in relation to GDP has often been no larger than those confronting the east Asians) is partly a result of the small size of their sectors that produce tradable goods and services. For this reason, a given degree of expenditure switching, in the technical jargon, requires considerably larger changes in real exchange rates in Latin America than have been necessary in east Asia. South Korea has been remarkable for the ease with which it has been able to push out exports in response to domestic recessions and relatively modest changes in the real exchange rate. This is one of the great benefits of an outward-looking strategy and especially one that finds a strong comparative advantage in easily expandable manufactures.

Yet, despite these powerful criticisms, the views of Professor Rodrik need to be taken into account. In particular, he is right to emphasize that much more is involved in successful development than trade policy. It is also unquestionably right, as Chang and Amsden argue, that some of the most successful developing countries – South Korea and Taiwan – did not all follow policies of free trade, though Hong Kong and Singapore remain important exceptions on this score. The creation of indigenous technological capacities has demanded special efforts by developing countries. Now that most developing countries have eliminated the most damaging non-tariff barriers and the highest tariffs, it is reasonable to conclude that further liberalization is no longer among their immediate priorities. It is also reasonable to ask whether WTO rules impose unreasonable constraints on their policy discretion. We will do that in the penultimate section of this chapter.

Traps for commodity exporters[64]

In 2000, export of foodstuffs made up only 9 per cent of developing-country merchandise exports, agricultural raw materials for industry made up 2 per cent and ores and metals made up another 4 per cent. The total of only 15 per cent is down from 24 per cent in 1990. Meanwhile, in 2001, fuels made up 21 per cent of the exports of developing countries and manufactures 61 per cent. It would be easy to conclude from this that exports of primary commodities are no longer important for the developing countries. This would be quite wrong. Many countries are still heavily dependent on these commodities. Examples of countries that earn more than half of their merchandise export revenue – often much more than half – from exports of primary commodities, other than fuels, are: Benin, Burundi, Cameroon, Chile, Côte d'Ivoire, Ethiopia, the Gambia, Ghana, Guatemala, Guinea, Honduras, Kenya, Mozambique, Nicaragua, Niger, Panama, Paraguay, Senegal, Sudan, Tanzania, Uganda, Uruguay and Zimbabwe.[65] In all, more than fifty developing countries depend on three or fewer commodities for more than half their export earnings. In sub-Saharan Africa, seventeen countries obtain three-quarters or more of their export earnings from non-oil commodity exports. Thirty-seven of the countries categorized by the IMF and World Bank as Heavily Indebted Poor Countries (HIPC) obtain more than half of their merchandise export earnings from primary commodities.[66]

Unfortunately, as Figures 10.2 and 10.3 showed, real prices of commodities have fallen far below levels of twenty or thirty years ago.[67] In 2000, for example, tropical beverages were 60 per cent below their 1980 level, in real terms. Foodstuffs were down by a half. Agricultural raw materials and ores and metals were down by around 30 per cent. As Oxfam points out in its report *Rigged Rules and Double Standards*, the prices of eighteen important commodities were 25 per cent lower in real terms in 2000 than in 1980. For eight of these commodities (cocoa, coffee, lead, palm oil, rice, rubber, sugar and tin), the declines exceeded 50 per cent. Not only have prices been weak, but the growth of volumes has been very slow: in the 1990s, trade in primary commodities grew at less than a third of the rate of manufactures. To add insult to all these injuries, prices have been extremely volatile. It is not abnormal for prices to fluctuate from below 50 per cent to above 150 per cent of the average on a year-to-year basis. In 1994–5, when coffee prices were high, Uganda earned $433 million from its coffee exports. In 2000–1, much the same volume gave Uganda just $110 million. No high-income country could begin to cope with such volatility in its export earnings.[68]

Why has this been happening and what can – and should – be done about it? The explanations are straightforward enough. The growth in demand for primary commodities is very slow, but supply is expanding, partly because of new producers and partly because of productivity improvements, and the responsiveness of demand and supply to changes in price (technically, their price elasticity) are very low. To give an example, coffee consumption has been stagnant in the important consuming countries over the past decade, while coffee production is expanding. According to the World Bank, it rose from 96 million bags in 1997–8 to 122.6 million in 2002–3.[69] It takes no genius to foresee the consequences. Relatively small adjustments in supply – a bad harvest in a big producer, for example – generate big shifts in prices. Meanwhile, the demand for raw materials has been adversely affected by the changing pattern of growth and continued innovation. The growth of high technology and services does not demand traditional raw materials and fibre-optic cable has had a devastating impact on the demand for copper, as have plastics on the demand for aluminium.

What can be done about this? To put it bluntly, the only policy that could raise prices, in principle, is supply reduction. The high-income countries could achieve such supply reduction if they wanted to. All of them indulge in large-scale manipulation of supply in their own agricultural policies for just this end. But they do not want to, because it would make them worse off. It is extremely implausible that developing countries could achieve supply reduction on their own. This has been tried before and failed, largely for political reasons: the divergence of interests is substantial and the ability to co-operate limited. The simplest policy would be agreement on a sizeable common export tax, with proceeds remitted to domestic producers. This seems hard to achieve, but agreement on a common supply price seems even less likely. Unfortunately, in the absence of supply management, the growth of privately organized schemes for 'fair trade' in primary commodities will not lead to the higher incomes their proponents desire. They may well raise prices for some producers, but if, as seems plausible, this leads to somewhat higher capacity, as additional investment is made in response to those prices, they will lower returns for everybody else. In practice, the fair-trade movement probably makes virtually no difference: less than 1 per cent of cocoa, tea and coffee sales are carried out on a fair-trade basis. In palm oil and coconut oil, the fair-trade movement is non-existent.[70]

Apart from the fundamental question of supply and demand, three other important policy issues arise in trade in commodities. One is whether it is possible to create more effective schemes for insuring farmers against price volatility. Another is tariff escalation in high-income countries, which discriminates heavily against attempts by developing countries to increase the value added of their products (on which more below). This is a long-standing scandal. It does not become any less so, for that. The last is the extreme concentration of the global commodity trade in the hands of a very small number of large companies. Two companies – Nestlé and Philip Morris – control half the market share for roasted and instant coffee, for example. Oxfam argues that the abolition of marketing boards, however inefficient, removed a certain measure of countervailing power against such oligopsonists. That seems at least plausible. If competition is to be included in the current round of WTO negotiations, this would be a good place to start. In the end, however, commodities seem a bad place for countries to be. Every effort should be made to encourage diversification.

Threats and opportunities of the World Trade Organization[71]

Now let us turn to the next charge – that the World Trade Organization is an anti-democratic organization, run in the interests of transnational corporations, which imposes unwarranted limitations on the legitimate exercise of sovereign discretion, particularly on developing countries. The force and persistence of such complaints demonstrate that the success of the trading system has made it more visible, more intrusive and more potent than ever before. It has, accordingly, far more enemies. When I first became interested in the then GATT, in the 1970s, most people were unaware of its existence. Now the WTO is a hated symbol of globalization. The move from indifference to malevolence is not altogether an improvement.

That the WTO is a very different institution from the GATT of two or three decades ago is clear. First, the WTO now has an increasingly active membership of almost all the countries in the world. Soon it will become universal. Second, with the addition of agriculture, services, trade-related investment (TRIMs) and trade-related intellectual property (TRIPs), in the course of the Uruguay Round, the system covers almost all trade. Third, as liberalization has advanced, the WTO has increasingly come to affect what were thought of as purely domestic regulatory decisions. Examples of such 'deep integration' are the Uruguay Round's agreements on sanitary and phytosanitary standards, which accompanied liberalization of agriculture, and on technical barriers to trade.[72] Fourth, the WTO is also a single undertaking with universal participation in all its disciplines. All members, including developing countries, have found themselves forced to make commitments, including onerous ones.[73] Fifth, the dispute-settlement system has become both more potent and more legalistic than ever before. No longer can a party to a dispute block the adoption of a panel finding. On the contrary, it is unable to halt the inexorable progress of cases.

As argued in Part II above, the WTO is to be regarded as an institutional response to a practical problem: how to sustain a mutually beneficial liberal economy in a world of many sovereign states, of vastly different economic strength and sophistication, all of which are subject to protectionist pressures. Any specific feature is a compromise, open to improvement. But if it is to be improved, one must understand what it is and how it works. This discussion will focus on just thee questions. How does the WTO work? Does the WTO infringe sovereignty? Where does the WTO need to change?

First, then, what does the WTO do? The broad answer is that it helps provide the international public good of open markets.[74] In practice, this good has largely been provided by economies that possess the biggest markets, foremost among them the US and the EU, which provide roughly 40 per cent of the world's total markets for imports (excluding intra-EU trade). Such large players have entered into reciprocal commitments to liberalize trade whose benefits have been spread world-wide through the principle of non-discrimination. As

Douglas Irwin of Dartmouth College argues, 'the WTO is useful because it changes the political economy of trade policy in a way that tends to facilitate trade liberalization as an outcome'.[75] The combination of reciprocity with non-discrimination has created a liberal, law-governed trading system, on the basis of co-operation among sovereign states, each acting in its own perceived self-interest. Economists are right to argue that the calculus underlying the WTO is mercantilist. But they also must agree that this disarmament treaty for mercantilists has worked.

Within these agreements, the sanction against violations is withdrawal of a concession. The aim is to restore the situation before the agreement was disturbed by one of the parties. Thus it is wrong, strictly speaking, to view a trade measure taken in response to a violation as a 'sanction'. It is better to think of such actions as rebalancing the agreement, subsequent to a violation. This system evidently needs a body to determine whether or not a country's rights have been violated. This is the logic of the dispute-settlement system. It is a way for sovereign nations to secure protection from the arbitrary actions of others, by accepting that their freedom to retaliate should be governed by an impartial procedure.

The inequality in the power of nations is not removed by the WTO. It remains the case that countries with big markets are more able to secure market access and deter actions against their exporters than countries with small markets. In practice, dispute-settlement remedies are of little use to small countries, unless the big players voluntarily submit. This reflects the fact that the WTO is not a system of global government, but rather a way of organizing and disciplining the intrinsically unequal capacity for self-help of member states. But to the extent that countries abide by non-discrimination, this capacity for action is effectively at the disposal of all.

For all its merits, the WTO has limits as a tool for liberalizing trade. One is that the WTO is not the only way to liberalize. On the contrary, both high-income and developing countries have liberalized extensively, both unilaterally and in the context of preferential trading arrangements. Another is that international rule-making is not always and necessarily liberalizing. Anti-dumping is an egregious example of bad trade policy that is enshrined in the WTO. The balance-of-payments exemption for import restrictions is another. Yet another limit is that standard reciprocal liberalization does not work in the most contentious sectors, notably agriculture. Again, the WTO's clout has become attractive to those who have no interest in liberalization. The extension of the trading system beyond the explicit goal of trade liberalization began, in the

Uruguay Round, with TRIPs. Nowadays, however, a rich assortment of activists have realized the potential value of the WTO's enforcement mechanisms for their own purposes. Yet a WTO that raises regulatory barriers world-wide and eliminates both valid diversity among regulatory regimes and competition among them could well be worse than no WTO at all.

Now turn to the second big question: does the WTO infringe sovereignty? The broad answer to this question is no. The bedrock of the trading system is enforceable agreements among states, most of them embodied in domestic law. Only governments, with their monopoly of legislation and law-enforcement, can make law. For this reason, the system is unavoidably inter-governmental. The WTO is merely a tiny secretariat (with a budget of about $80 million) servicing a structure of inter-governmental agreements. It is not a government.

It follows that the place for democratic accountability is the legislatures of each of its members. This is where the governments engaged in the trading system need to explain what they are doing and why. It also follows that individual legislatures can no longer determine their own country's trade policy, on a day-to-day basis, even though they continue to set the negotiating authority of their governments and retain the ultimate (and decisive) power of ratification of any results. This limitation on the discretion of legislatures was accepted partly because trade policy cannot be sensibly made, at least by those who refuse to accept unilateral liberalization, without consideration of the trade policies of others.

This self-imposed constraint on the freedom of legislatures does not subvert democracy. It is an expression of it. All modern democracies are constitutional. That is, they recognize that limits can properly be imposed on the discretion of a temporary majority (or plurality) within a legislature. In general, two kinds of interests tend to be over-represented in such legislatures, at the expense of the public at large: concentrated producer interests (producer lobbies); and groups with strong emotional commitments to particular policy goals (notably NGOs). As the late Professor Robert Hudec has noted, reliance on international negotiations to 'circumvent' a legislative process dominated by such groups may be a rational and desirable way to secure a better outcome for the public at large than is likely to emerge from the domestic legislative process.[76]

Those who find their ability to determine domestic legislation reduced resent the international process that has this result. The question, however, is how far the WTO should accommodate their desire to influence the processes of negotiation and dispute settlement more directly, under the general rubric of democracy – or, as Professor Daniel Esty of Yale University puts it, in the interests of the system's 'legitimacy, authoritativeness and a commitment to fairness'. He argues that 'public support cannot be founded on government authority. Individual acceptance is what matters. The organization must therefore demonstrate that it has genuine connections to the citizens of the world and that its decisions reflect the will of the people across the planet. Non-governmental organizations represent an important mechanism by which the WTO can reach out to citizens and build the requisite bridge to global civil society.'[77]

Yet how is the 'will of the people across the planet' to be defined and assessed, other than as expressed by elected governments? There is surely no reason to accept that a collection of NGOs, dominated by the relatively well-resourced institutions of high income countries, represents the 'will of the people across the planet'. The governments of developing countries may reasonably respond that the high income countries' sudden concern for labour standards and environmental protection reflects a hypocritical form of protectionism or, in the case of the environment, a desire to preserve the comforts of its resource-intensive way of life, at the expense of the developing countries' chance of development. It is little wonder that they view the demands for opening the WTO to the NGOs as leaving themselves, grossly underresourced, to face both powerful Northern governments and their NGOs.

In truth, the principles on which a global democracy should be established are not obvious. At present, the WTO works on the basis of a consensus among states with the biggest and most economically significant having, informally, the greatest influence. This seems a reasonable accommodation to the realities of a world in which public goods are provided by a collection of governments. What, after all, is the alternative? One person, one vote would give India and China close to 40 per cent of the votes. This is not the global democracy most radical activists appear to have in mind, though one of them, George Monbiot, has recently recommended just this.[78]

My conclusion then is that demands for popular democracy within the WTO are misplaced. Almost as problematic is the desire to open up the dispute-settlement system to the voices of non-governmental actors. There can be no objection to any wish by panels to obtain the views of qualified experts, including those working for – or funded by – NGOs and private business. But if such voices are to be heard, as of right, a number of important theoretical and practical concerns must be addressed. The non-governmental voices that have a right to be heard must not be limited in some arbitrary way. The other members of the WTO and private corporations, neither of which have this right at present, must also be heard. In addition, some way must be found to fund the involvement of governments and private organizations based in developing countries. A way must also be found to increase funding of the dispute-settlement process, to ensure that it is not utterly overwhelmed. This leaves only the wider issue of transparency to the public at large. Here the way ahead should be relatively uncontroversial. The WTO needs to take forward its programme of symposia and seminars with non-governmental actors. It also needs to improve further the dissemination of documents. The website is an extremely important step in this direction. More of the WTO's activities could also be opened to the press. But, for these things to happen, and particularly for voices from developing countries to be heard, the WTO must be better funded.

Finally, where does the WTO need to change? Here, experience of recent years suggests that the following big issues ought to be (re)considered.

First and most important, the idea of a single undertaking has to be looked at again. Insisting that everybody signs up to everything creates two contradictory pressures – a move to the lowest common denominator and the imposition of what may turn out to be politically intolerable obligations. This would be one way round the impasse now likely to be created by further negotiations on services or by negotiations on investment and competition. Naturally, those who do not participate in such negotiations cannot expect to benefit from the outcome. If the idea of a single undertaking is re-examined, it might also be possible to re-examine consensus. If countries are not bound by everything, they cannot be expected to be consulted over everything.

Second, the dispute-settlement procedure needs to be reconsidered in at least one important respect: where the underlying meaning of the texts is obscure, panels should not try to invent law. They should, instead, encourage parties to return to negotiation. If necessary, they should honestly admit that the law is unclear.[79]

Third, the range of compensation should be broadened, to include financial compensation, since compensation through trade often imposes unfair costs on unrelated parties. It should become quite normal for an impasse between two parties to be settled through financial compensation. The beef hormones case between the US and the European Union seems ripe for such treatment.

Fourth, as discussed above, the question of legitimate infant-industry protection and subsidization needs to be re-examined. In her analysis,

Professor Amsden concludes that 'the liberal bark of the WTO appeared to be worse than its bite'.[80] Nevertheless, without endorsing the wisdom of infant-industry protection as a general idea, the international community needs to consider whether developing countries should have greater freedom to introduce export conditions, export subsidization and other means to promote early stage industrialization.

Fifth, some sort of legal resolution needs to be made of the relationship between the WTO and multilateral environmental agreements.

In all, however, the complaints against the WTO are hugely exaggerated, where not misconceived. It is not a tyranny; on the contrary, it is extremely weak. It is not undemocratic; on the contrary, it is an expression of democratic choices. It can be improved. But, without it, the big powers would do what they want to an ever greater extent than they already do. It would be senseless, if not insane, to prefer that.

Hypocrisy of the rich

Now let us turn to the last – and more than justified – charge, that the rich countries are grossly hypocritical in their treatment of developing countries. They call on developing countries to adjust, liberalize and respond to market forces. But this is not advice that the high-income countries themselves adopt. Instead, high-income countries force the developing countries to take greater account of their own concerns than they themselves do of developing-country concerns. Worse, they handicap the world's poor countries with obstacles to trade far bigger than those they impose on one another. But this is not the only obstacle developing countries confront in taking advantage of global market opportunities. They also need to overcome the hurdles to trade created by one another's barriers.

Average tariffs in the high-income countries are around 3 per cent.[81] But average tariffs on agricultural commodities are almost double those for manufactures. Tariff barriers on labour-intensive products are raised through tariff peaks (tariffs exceeding 15 per cent). Imports at such peaks represent about 5 per cent of total imports of Canada, the European Union, Japan and the US (the 'Quadrilateral' or 'Quad' countries) from developing countries and more than 11 per cent of their imports from the world's poorest countries, the least developed countries. In North America, tariff peaks are commonly found in labour-intensive manufactures, particularly textiles and clothing. In the EU and Japan, they are found, more often, in agriculture, especially processed food. Tariff peaks on imports of footwear are found in all these high-income markets and surpass those on textiles and clothing.

In the US, 6.6 per cent of imports from developing countries are subject to tariffs over 15 per cent. The comparable figure for the EU is 4.9 per cent, for Canada 4.8 per cent and for Japan 2.8 per cent. While average tariffs on all manufactured imports into high-income countries are only 3 per cent, tariffs on labour-intensive manufactured imports from developing countries are 8 per cent and on imports of agricultural commodities from developing countries 14 per cent. Unfortunately, developing countries are also damaged by the protectionism of other developing countries. The average tariff applied by developing countries to their imports from other developing countries is more than three times higher than the average imposed by the high-income countries. The World Bank has calculated that the average tariff faced by the poor (those living on less than two dollars a day, at PPP) in all markets is 14 per cent, against 6 per cent for the rest, as a result of barriers in both high-income countries and other developing countries.

A study by the Progressive Policy Institute in the US gives dramatic indications of these gross inequities. Exports to the US from Bangladesh, with a GDP per head (at market prices) of $370, paid $331 million in tariffs in 2001, or an average rate of 14.1 per cent. This revenue was as big as that levied on exports from France. But French exports were thirteen times as large, so the average rate they paid was only 1.1 per cent. Similarly, exports from Cambodia, with a GDP per head of $260, paid $152 million in tariffs, an average rate of 15.8 per cent, while Singapore's exports paid $96 million, an average rate of only 0.6 per cent. On average, it concluded, the world's least developed countries face tariffs four to five times higher than the richest economies. This is a disgrace.[82]

As has already been mentioned above, tariffs escalate steeply, especially on processed agricultural commodities. This is especially true for the EU and Japan. On average, the tariff on processed commodities is 2.75 times higher than that on unprocessed commodities in the EU. In Japan, the ratio is 3.75. Such escalation makes protection to domestic value added vastly higher than one might realize. To take a simple example: imagine that a given raw product (coffee) faces a tariff of 5 per cent, while the finished product faces one of 14 per cent. Assume also that value added at world prices is divided, half and half, between the production of the raw product and the processing. The 'effective protection' given to the activity of processing then turns out to be 23 per cent.[83]

This is a substantial subsidy. Today, the UK grinds more cocoa than Ghana. Tariff escalation must be a large part of the reason.

Non-tariff barriers also remain significant obstacles for the developing countries. The true level of protection afforded to European industry rises from 5.1 per cent if tariffs alone are included to 9 per cent if non-tariff barriers are taken into account.[84] Among significant obstacles to developing countries are product standards. A World Bank study, cited by Oxfam, showed that implementation of a new EU standard to protect consumers against aflatoxin (a naturally occurring carcinogen) will cost African exporters of nuts, cereals and dried fruits $670 million a year, without generating significant health benefits. Anti-dumping measures are also a severe obstacle to developing-country exporters, particularly to small and inexperienced companies. Between them the US and EU launched 234 anti-dumping cases against developing countries in the five years following the end of the Uruguay Round. Every well-informed economist knows that anti-dumping lacks all economic justification, even in theory, let alone in its still more indefensible practice. Perhaps the most disgraceful episode in a long and shameless history has been the Byrd amendment in the US, which transfers anti-dumping duty revenue directly to the complaining firms. A better way of corrupting the trade-policy system can hardly be imagined, especially since the rules governing the determination of dumping makes a positive finding so absurdly easy.

Preferential trading arrangements have also exploded in number since the 1980s. The most important for the trading system are those between powerful high-income countries and a selected number of favoured developing countries. The European Union was responsible for starting the flood. But the US has become an increasingly active promoter. These discriminatory arrangements create significant difficulties for the less favoured developing countries. They are put at a disadvantage in the markets of the members. Yet some of those excluded from all such arrangements – Bangladesh, for example – are among the world's poorest countries. These arrangements are also potentially an obstacle to further trade liberalization, since beneficiaries will try to defend their preferences. Last but not least, the granting of such discretionary favours gives powerful high-income countries great leverage over weaker trading partners, which they can use, among other things, to ensure support for their positions in the WTO.[85]

In the grand deal of the Uruguay Round, the developing countries agreed, unwillingly, to accept the provisions on trade-related intellectual property, trade-related investment measures and services. The *quid pro quo* was to be liberalization of barriers against exports of textiles and clothing under the multi-fibre arrangement. According to the agreement on textiles and clothing, the high-income countries were to remove quotas from at least 51 per cent of their imports by January 2002. So, ostensibly, they did. But they will in fact have removed quotas from only 12 per cent of the imports that were effectively constrained by quotas. Effectively, the liberalization has been almost entirely back-loaded until 2005. It is now feared that quota restrictions will still apply on more than 80 per cent of developing-country exports in these sectors in 2004. So, instead of a progressive adjustment to the elimination of these restrictions, the cowardly and incompetent authorities of the EU and US have arranged for all the liberalization to occur in a rush in 2005. This undermines the entire idea of phased liberalization – that it compels those affected to adjust in stages. The sudden liberalization at the end of the period is bound to trigger fierce political resistance. That, in turn, is likely to lead to yet more anti-dumping and so-called 'safeguard-protection' actions against surges in exports from developing countries.

Yet perhaps the greatest of all the scandals remains the treatment of agriculture. In this area, one of comparative advantage for many developing countries, they have hardly managed to raise their share of world exports. This is so even though agriculture is, for the high-income countries, of trivial economic importance in terms of GDP, employment and trade. What stops the developing countries is the staggering scale of rich-country subsidies. According to the Organization for Economic Co-operation and Development, total assistance to rich country farmers was $311 billion in 2001, six times as much as all development assistance, indeed more than the GDP of sub-Saharan Africans. In 2000, the EU provided $913 for each cow and $8 to each sub-Saharan African. The Japanese, more generous still, though only to cows, provided $2,700 for each one and just $1.47 to each African. Not to be outdone, the US spent $10.7 million a day on cotton and $3.1 million a day on all aid to sub-Saharan Africa.[86] The priorities shown here are obscene. In order to justify the grotesquerie of its agricultural policy regime, the common agricultural policy, the EU has started to apply the notion of 'multi-functionality'. By this it means that agricultural supports are justified by their ability not only to support farm incomes, but to protect the environment, food security and rural life. The EU is right about the multi-functionality of the CAP, just wrong about the functions its policies serve. The CAP is regressive (since it provides 50 per cent of its benefits to the 17 per cent biggest farmers, who need this help least), wasteful (since it still consumes almost half the EU's budget), environmentally damaging (since it encourages needless intensification of agricultural production) and harmful to developing countries (since it deprives them of markets and undermines the competitiveness of their farmers with its dumping of subsidized surpluses). This is multi-functionality with a vengeance.[87] The picture is little different in the US: only 16 per cent of the support goes to the 80 per cent of the farmers who operate on a relatively small scale.

Unfortunately, while the Uruguay Round brought a little discipline to this sector, it was grossly inadequate. Agricultural support in the EU and US was higher in the late 1990s, as measured by the OECD's Producer Support Estimates, than between 1986 and 1988, the base years for the Uruguay Round agreements. Much of the support is still output related. Moreover, many of the subsidies that are supposed not to affect production do so. Because farm supports are anti-cyclical, they increase the instability of residual world markets, with devastating effects on exporters from developing countries. Moreover, subsidized surpluses are still being dumped on world markets. The US and EU account for around half of all world wheat exports, with prices 46 and 34 per cent respectively below costs of production. In 1998, subsidized exports made up a quarter of global exporters. The EU is the world's largest exporter of skimmed-milk powder, at half the costs of production. It is also the largest exporter of white sugar, at a quarter of the costs of production. Some argue that such dumping can be beneficial to developing countries that are net food importers. With very few exceptions, this is not so. In most developing countries, farmers are not just the majority of the population, but the overwhelming majority of the poor. Thus the dumped products benefit an urban minority at the expense of the rural majority. Often the subsidized food has turned countries into net importers. Without it, they would both be net exporters and possess far healthier rural economies.[88] While the transition to a world of higher international food prices needs to be handled carefully – and food aid needs to be available to help food-importing countries and those vulnerable to harvest failure – it is virtually certain that developing countries would gain hugely from the elimination of current farm policies in the high-income countries. The World Bank has estimated the annual welfare losses to developing countries at $20 billion a year – close to 40 per cent of all development assistance.

This is not, alas, the end of the hypocrisy of the high-income countries. The Uruguay Round also saw the introduction of trade-related intellectual property into what subsequently became the WTO. While patent and similar forms of protection may be appropriate for some of the bigger or more economically advanced developing countries (such as Brazil, China and

India), it is a rent-extraction device for the rest of them, with potentially devastating consequences for their ability to educate their people (because of copyright), adapt designs for their own use (ditto) and deal with severe challenges of public health. The World Bank estimates that transfers from developing countries in the form of licence payments to northern transnational companies, above all those of the US, will rise almost four-fold, from their current level of $15 billion. If so, the sum would fully offset all development assistance. Yet, as was argued in Part II above, there is an obvious inefficiency in restricting the use of knowledge.[89] When it is its use by poor countries that is being restricted, then it is unjust as well. The case of access to medicines is merely the most publicized and egregious example of these costs. It is also remarkable that while the high-income countries have supported their companies in attempts to protect patents abroad, they have no compunction about threatening them at home. The US, for example, threatened Bayer, producer of an effective anti-anthrax medicine, in the aftermath of the anthrax scare in late 2001, unless it reduced its prices. Canada went even further.

Again, while a strong case can be made for liberalization of services, it is noteworthy that the high-income countries have done rather better in securing access for their capital-intensive service providers than in accepting the movement of people as providers of labour intensive services. This is yet another hypocrisy. Nor is this the end of it. Standards on such matters as customs valuation are burdensome for developing countries, as is meeting the standards of high-income countries in such areas as food safety.

Global trade liberalization offers enormous opportunities for developing countries to expand trade and increase their welfare. Work by the World Bank suggests that world income in 2015 would be $355 billion a year more with merchandise-trade liberalization (in 1997 dollars).[90] The developing countries would gain $184 billion annually. Of this, $121 billion would be the benefits from their own liberalization, while the rest would come from liberalization by high-income countries. Nearly 80 per cent of the gains to developing countries would come from liberalization of agriculture. With dynamic benefits added, the Bank estimates developing-country incomes could rise by more than $500 billion a year, with $390 billion of this coming from agriculture and $120 billion from textiles and clothing. To put this in context, the total GDP, in market prices, of the developing countries was $6,300 billion in 2000.

The Bank also adds huge estimates for the gains from liberalization of trade in services. This is obviously, as the Bank says, 'more art than science'. The

barriers in these studies take three forms: a cost penalty reflecting inefficiency; a price mark-up reflecting monopoly; and barriers to cross-border
trade. The Bank concludes that reform by developing countries could
increase their incomes by nearly $900 billion a year, some 4.5 times greater
than their gains from merchandise-trade liberalization – a 9.4 per cent
income gain, compared to base levels. Of this, $670 billion would come from
cheaper trade and transportation.

Finally, the Bank evaluates the consequences of such liberalization. First, it
argues that the unskilled – above all, rural labour – would benefit proportionately most from liberalization that redressed the anti-agriculture bias in most
developing-country trade policy regimes and increased access to world
markets. Wages of the unskilled would rise more than those of the skilled and
returns to capital. Second, there would be substantial displacement of people,
which is one reason why liberalization needs to be credible and carried out
over a lengthy time period. But the benefits would greatly outweigh costs.
Third, under the Bank's baseline scenario world trade would rise to $11,200
billion. With liberalization, this would be $1,900 billion more ($13,100
billion). Developing countries would take the lion's share of this: their exports
would be $1,300 billion higher, $600 billion of which would be increased
exports to high-income countries and $700 billion increased exports to one
another. Developing-country agricultural exports would rise by $200 billion
and textiles and clothing by nearly $180 billion. These figures dwarf any
conceivable increase in foreign aid.

In sum, the treatment of developing countries by the high-income countries
has been a disgrace. Nevertheless, the extent to which the trade route to
prosperity has been blocked must also not be exaggerated. Remember how
successful export-oriented developing countries have been. At the same time,
further liberalization should benefit everybody. The only important proviso is
the one discussed above – that developing countries are able to make the
policy decisions needed to promote their long-term development.

Conclusion

Liberal trade and the world trading system have become a lightning rod
for everything people dislike about our world. But if we look back at the
charges discussed in this chapter, we can see that the criticisms fall into a few
categories. The first contains charges brought by people who believe that the

rise of the developing countries threatens the livelihoods of the privileged citizens of high-income countries. Their complaints are largely, though not entirely, groundless. The second group contains charges brought by people who wish to stop trade everywhere. Their ideas – above all, localization – are both foolish and dangerous, particularly to the people of the developing countries whom they pretend to wish to help. The third group contains charges brought by people who fear that the freedom of action of developing countries is improperly circumscribed, particularly over infant-industry promotion. These arguments are not worthless, though they are exaggerated. It is an issue that needs to be re-examined. The fourth group concerns the WTO as an institution. These complaints are generally wrong and, where not wrong, exaggerated. But the institution is imperfect. It needs to be reformed. The last and much the most persuasive group of charges are complaints about the handicaps now imposed upon the poor, because of the dreadful state of commodity markets and the grotesque hypocrisy of the high-income countries.

In all this, we have omitted one great complaint: the overwhelming power of corporations in running the world economy, governments and global economic institutions, thereby subverting democracy and everything else that is good. That is the topic of the next chapter.

Chapter 11 **Cowed by Corporations**

The struggle between people and corporations will be the defining battle of the twenty-first century. If the corporations win, liberal democracy will come to an end. The great social democratic institutions which have defended the weak against the strong – equality before the law, representative government, democratic accountability and the sovereignty of parliament – will be toppled.

George Monbiot[1]

The astronomical growth in the wealth and cultural influence of multinational companies over the last fifteen years can arguably be traced back to a single, seemingly innocuous idea developed by management theorists in the mid-1980s: that successful corporations must primarily produce brands, as opposed to products.

Naomi Klein[2]

The radical critics of contemporary global economic integration detest corporations. That is probably the one resentment they all share. Armed with brands, to control their consumers, and subservient governments, to curb their workers, corporations run the world, they insist. Corporations exercise unaccountable and irresponsible power. Democracy, freedom, human rights, the planet itself are all at risk. Challenged, the critics note, as if this were almost a decisive point, that of the hundred largest economies in the world, more than half are corporations.

Does any of this make sense? Or are we watching a collective hysteria – a series of paranoid fantasies in which almost everything bad can be attributed to the contemporary transnational corporation? To attempt to address this question, we must, again, try to identify the propositions that critics are making. While on trade and, as we shall subsequently see, finance, a lively discussion continues among professional participants and analysts, the debate about corporations is quite different. Here the criticism comes directly from populists, Marxists or anarchists. For this reason, the criticisms are both more diffuse and more fundamental.

So here are five propositions about the contemporary role of corporations.

First, corporations are more powerful than most countries.

Second, brands give companies control over customers.

Third, foreign direct investment impoverishes recipient countries, particularly poor ones, and their workers. It does so partly by accelerating the race to the bottom in regulation of the environment and workers' rights, already discussed in the previous chapter.

Fourth, foreign direct investment also impoverishes workers in the capital-exporting countries.

Finally, corporations control states, thereby subverting democracy.

Corporations are more powerful than countries[3]

In December 2000, two critics of the power of global corporations, Sarah Anderson and John Cavenaugh of the left-of-centre Institute for Policy Studies in Washington DC, published a short paper in which they argued that fifty-one of the world's hundred biggest economies are corporations.[4] This, the reader was to understand, was not just an intriguing statistic, but an alarming fact about the world. The obvious questions are whether this is true and, if so, whether it matters. When one looks carefully at these questions, the answers turn out to be: no and, again, no.

The two researchers committed what economists would regard as an elementary howler: they confused gross sales with GDP. As Paul de Grauwe of the University of Leuven and Filip Camerman of the Belgian Senate pointed out in a powerful riposte, if their method were applied to GDP one would end up with a vastly bigger number than the correct one. But one would also be double-, triple- or quadruple-counting.[5] Take the example of cars. Bethlehem Steel sells steel wire to Bridgestone tyres; Bridgestone sells tyres to Ford; and Ford sells cars to consumers. If national income statisticians added the sales of Bethlehem Steel, Bridgestone and Ford, the steel would appear three times; it would be triple-counted. What statisticians do, instead, is sum the value added of each company, which is the difference between the value of its sales and the cost of inputs bought from outside the company (and so equals the value attributable to the people and the capital employed by each company). The sale of steel adds to Bethlehem Steel's value added, because making steel is what it does. But the cost of steel is subtracted from Bridgestone's sales, because it is a cost of its business, which is making tyres.

Calculating the value added of companies, rather than the value of their sales, makes a huge difference to the figures. The value added of most companies, notably those in manufacturing, mineral extraction and retail, is a small proportion of their sales. In 2000, for example, the sales of General Motors were $185 billion, but its value added was only $42 billion. Similarly, the sales of Royal Dutch/Shell were $149 trillion, while its value added was just $36 billion. If one computes the size of companies according to their gross sales, fourteen of the fifty largest economies in the world and fifty-one of the largest hundred were companies, in 1999. But, according to de Grauwe and Camerman, measured by value added, only two of the top fifty economies were corporations and thirty-seven of the top hundred.

Even their admittedly rough-and-ready calculations turn out to have been somewhat exaggerated. A subsequent analysis by UNCTAD concluded that, in 2000, just twenty-nine of the world's hundred largest economies were corporations.[6] Again, only two of these were in the top fifty: Exxon Mobil, at forty-fifth, and General Motors, at forty-seventh. The remaining twenty-seven fell in the bottom fifty. There one finds GlaxoSmithKline, at ninety-ninth, nestling just behind Syria; Honda, at ninety-fourth, just behind Slovenia; and mighty GE, at fifty-eighth, just behind Nigeria, Hungary and Bangladesh. For the critics, General Motors is bigger than Denmark and Wal-Mart is bigger than Poland. Properly measured, Denmark is three times as big as General Motors and five times as big as Wal-Mart. Even the biggest company in the world, Exxon Mobil, falls between Chile and Pakistan. Many things can be said about Chile and Pakistan. But who would argue they are great economic powers?

Perhaps more important for those inclined to use such figures as an indication of unbridled corporate power is the disproportion between the economies of big and wealthy countries and even the largest corporations. The US economy is 156 times bigger than the biggest corporation in the world and even the UK's is twenty-three times bigger. Economic activity in powerful countries dwarfs those of the largest corporations. This is not surprising, since it turns out that, in 2000, the top hundred transnational companies generated only 4.3 per cent of global GDP, about as much as the UK alone. The top ten transnationals generated 0.9 per cent of world GDP, about as much as South Korea.

Is it even true that, as Naomi Klein argues, corporations have enjoyed an 'astronomical' increase in wealth? No, is the answer. Between 1990 and 2000, the share of the top hundred corporations in global GDP did rise a little, from 3.5 per cent to 4.3 per cent. But the shares of the top ten, top twenty and top fifty – the world's very biggest companies – have all fallen a little, from 1 per cent to 0.9 per cent, from 1.8 to 1.5 per cent and from 2.9 to 2.8 per cent respectively.[7] What seems to have happened is a slight rise in the share of the bottom fifty against that of the top fifty. But is Klein at least right about corporate profitability? No, again. Overall corporate profits in US GDP rose from a low level in the 1990s, but its average for that decade was no higher than that for the past half-century. It has never since reached the peaks of the 1960s when foreign competition was still a cloud no bigger than a man's hand. In Japan, the world's second largest economy, corporate profitability and shares of corporate profits in GDP were well below levels reached in the booming 1960s.

The claims that companies are bigger and more powerful than countries is not just wrong factually. Far more important, it is misconceived. For lurking behind these claims is a wilful error: a refusal to distinguish power from freedom. Companies differ from countries because they can succeed by obtaining from their customers what they need to pay their suppliers (including their workers and their creditors). Unless they have strong monopoly positions, they cannot force their customers to buy from them. They can only cajole them. The resources they control are the result of free choices made in the marketplace. Countries – or rather governments of countries – are different. They have coercive control over territory. Even the weakest states can force people to do things most of them would very much prefer not to do: pay taxes, for example, or do military service. While a sophisticated modern democracy can rely on much voluntary compliance with its demands, it always has the coercive option available. Companies do not. They are civilian organizations that must win their resources in the marketplace. They rely for survival not on coercion but on competitiveness.

Consider, for a moment, the lesson of Enron's collapse. What was the most important message it sent? Was it that US corporations are occasionally run by crooks? Was it even that corporate accounts are sometimes a fiction? Even if one believes elements of both these propositions (and I do), neither was the most important lesson. What the collapse of Enron demonstrated was that a company can fool its investors, its regulators, its accountants and its suppliers, but it cannot fool the market. Either it manages to earn more money from its customers than it pays out to its suppliers, staff and creditors, or it disappears. It may persuade its creditors to keep it afloat for a while. But it will perish in the end. Enron failed this test and duly disappeared. In Japan, today, the banks are keeping afloat many such dead companies. That is a decision not of the market, however, but of the state. The banks do so only because the Japanese government stands behind them.

Even a tyrant as petty as Robert Mugabe confronts no similar market test. In the long run, when he can no longer steal enough even to pay his army and police, he is likely to lose power. But so long as he possesses effective means of coercion, only even greater force can displace him. Adolf Hitler disappeared because he challenged the world in arms. Saddam Hussein tweaked the feathers of the American eagle too often. But Stalin and Mao killed tens of millions of people and died in power.

The gap between the powers of states and companies is enormous. Does anybody doubt that the US legal system could break up Microsoft if it wished, just as it broke up Standard Oil almost a century ago? Would Microsoft itself not disappear if it failed to make products its customers wished to buy? Just think back to the days of now departed Wang, destroyed by the invention of the personal computer. Corporations even depend on states for the protection of their property. In the 1970s, the world's biggest oil companies watched weak developing-country governments seize their assets. Since their governments chose to do nothing, they were unable to help themselves. Companies were not always so weak. The East India Company had armies and navies with which it was able to conquer a sub-continent. But it could do so only because a state had given it an effective monopoly over an immensely profitable trade.[8] No state would give such power to a company today.

One indication of market power is market concentration. Some critics argue that the wave of mergers-and-acquisitions (M&A) activity has made possible a steep rise in such concentration and so market power. Global M&A activity rose more than five-fold between 1995 and 2000 to a peak of $1,100 billion in 2000, before dropping by some 45 per cent in 2001, as stock markets tumbled. Much of the cross-border activity was concentrated in the service sector (more than half in finance, transport, storage and communications alone). Yet the surge in cross-border M&A activity does not seem to have increased concentration, largely because the proportion of the stock market capitalization of the high-income countries affected was less than 3 per cent, on average, between 1997 and 1999, except in the UK, where it reached 3.5 per cent.[9]

Lawrence White of the Stern School of Business of New York University has concluded that concentration has not increased in the US, since the 1980s, on any measure one might wish to use: employment, payroll or profits. The share of the top fifty companies (as measured by *Forbes* magazine) in the world labour force and in employment among members of the Organization for Economic Co-operation and Development has also fallen slightly since 1994.[10] Shares of these companies in employment are also very modest: a little over 0.2 per cent in the world as a whole and 1.6 per cent among all OECD members. Some critics even complain because large companies offer so few jobs. But one would expect to find large companies dominating the capital intensive areas of the economy, since they have no advantages in labour-intensive businesses. Thus it is not remarkable that the top 500 private companies in the US generate more than half of private sector profits but less than a fifth of employment. That is a reflection of their dominance in capital-intensive sectors. This does not mean that the products, services and innovation they deliver are unimportant. On the contrary, these companies are, as was argued in Part II above, the engines of a dynamic market economy.

The evidence bears out the proposition that companies do not dominate markets, but rather that markets dominate companies. Privatization and international economic integration have made markets more competitive and so companies less powerful within their markets. Think, for a moment, of BT or General Motors, both powerful incumbents two decades or more ago. British Telecom, as a (publicly owned) monopolist, could afford to put customers on long waiting lists for phones – and did. As a company in an increasingly (though still not adequately) competitive market, it cannot. Similarly, General Motors once possessed privileged and profitable access to the world's biggest car market. Ford was its only serious competitor. Now it has to fight it out with Daimler Chrysler, Toyota and Honda as well. If we look at the world as a whole, the effective contestability of markets has increased almost everywhere since the early 1980s. Just think of what has happened to commercial banking and insurance. Concentration measures do not capture this increase in competition well: there may, for example, be only two serious competitors in the supply of civilian aircraft, but there can be little doubt that they compete fiercely. In a global world economy, complacent incumbents are unlikely to last long.

One way of looking at such market pressure is, as de Grauwe and Camerman note, to examine the speed with which the rankings of companies change. They have taken the top ten, twenty and fifty industrial corporations on the *Fortune* list for 1980, respectively, and seen how quickly they drop out. They also looked at the experience of service companies between 1994 and 2000. It turned out that twenty-nine of the top fifty service companies, nine of the top twenty and three of the top ten had dropped out of the relevant category within just six years. Finally, they show that the differences in the relative size of the fifty big companies in the *Fortune* list declined between 1994 and 2000. This suggests that the dominance of the very biggest companies has fallen. In all, the inability of companies to control their destiny is remarkable – and, for believers in the disciplining power of competition, encouraging.

What we see in the view that companies are more powerful than countries are inapposite numbers, mistaken statements of trends and, worst of all, a grossly misleading analytical framework. By comparing the ability of companies to grow by satisfying customers, paying employees and rewarding investors with the ability of governors to exercise coercive power, the critics are guilty of obfuscation, at best, and, at worst, of deliberate misrepresentation. Companies are not comparable with states. Even if they were far larger, they would not be. They are much weaker and, because of their need to survive in markets, vastly better disciplined. If they are not, the solution is more competition. It is only where competition is impossible that regulation should come into play.

Finally, just as critics exaggerate the power of companies, so do they exaggerate the role of power in explaining the relative wealth of countries. They argue that today's high-income countries are rich because they are powerful. This, too, is the wrong way round. They are powerful because they are rich. Denmark, Hong Kong, Sweden, Singapore and Switzerland are rich. Brazil, China, India, Indonesia and Nigeria are poor. It is not power, but internal economic development, that has made the former rich. Similarly, it is not power, but internal economic development, that may make the latter rich. Look today at the three greatest European imperial powers of previous centuries: Great Britain, Spain and Russia. The first is a laggard among Europe's wealthy. The second is further behind. The third is hardly even in the race. Economic success and power are connected, since the former contributes to the latter, other things being equal. But it is a huge mistake to believe that the latter is the route to the former.

'Tyranny' of brands

At this stage, alas, we have to make a brief excursion into the terrain made famous by the Canadian journalist and anti-corporate activist Naomi Klein: the world of brands. Analytically, her book *No Logo* adds nothing to the debate about globalization. Psychologically, however, it is brilliant. Klein succeeded in connecting the sense of personal inadequacy and guilt of the affluent western young to the plight of the world's poor. The thread binding the two together, she argued, is malevolent corporations, which enslave both their customers and their suppliers.

Her starting-point is the power of brands. For me, the revealing moment in Klein's book comes close to the beginning, where she writes:

> I was in Grade 4 when skintight designer jeans were the be-all and end-all, and my friends and I spent a lot of time checking out each other's butt for logos ... At around the same time, Romi, our school's own pint-sized Farrah Fawcett, used to make her rounds up and down the rows of desks turning back the collars on our sweaters and polo shirts. It wasn't enough for her see an alligator or a leaping horseman – it could have been a knockoff. She wanted to see the label behind the logo. We were only eight years old but the reign of logo terror had begun.[11]

In the last century, billions of human beings knew the terror of police states, genocide and government-engineered famines. But, insists Klein, I and people like me have experienced terror, too. We are not just the world's most pampered brats. We know terror too: logo terror'. And I am able to tell you who the terrorists are: corporate 'brandlords'. It is hard to know whether to weep or to laugh over such stuff. But the thought that Klein's book has been a bestseller pushes one into the former camp. For the ideas she advances are not just laughable. They are, as we shall see in the next section, dangerous.

Klein's notion of brand power is not new. It is a modern incarnation of Vance Packard's idea of the power of advertising, which appeared in his classic *The Hidden Persuaders*, published in 1957. Behind this notion stands the equation of the need of corporations to seduce their customers with tyranny. Corporations, goes the argument, do not compete, but control; they are not subservient to customers, but coerce them. This charge – that corporations own customers – is another example of the lie that freedom is slavery. We are free to make choices, however. Insisting upon anything else demeans us. It is because we are free that corporations need to seduce us. Logos exist, therefore, not because corporations are strong, but because they are so weak. As Philippe Legrain argues in the chapter on brands of his book *Open World*, 'it is an old communitarian trick to claim that enlightened individuals . . . know what the people really want, that the views and preferences people express are not what they would think if only they could break free from their social conditioning. The assault on brands is a new, intellectually feeble twist on this old theme.'[12] It is no innocent twist. If freedom is slavery, then slavery can be freedom. Or, as Jean-Jacques Rousseau and his intellectual progeny, a long line of communist tyrants, have argued, people must be forced to be free. Klein's arguments are a pallid modern reincarnation of an ancient evil.

Brands are not just a reflection of corporate weakness, but, as even Klein admits, a source of it. As she remarks, 'brand image, the source of so much corporate wealth, is also, it turns out, the corporate Achilles' heel'.[13] Companies cannot cope with bad publicity. Threatened by the blackmail of protesters, they will do almost anything to satisfy their critics. Occasionally, companies will be right to do so, for what they have done, or condoned, is a scandal. Sometimes, however, they will be wrong to do so, for what they are asked to do may hurt those they are supposed to help. Sacking all the child labour employed in the making of garments in Bangladesh is such a mistake. Forcing production of labour-intensive goods out of developing countries would be even worse.[14] But when corporations are forced to protect the value of their brand in the eyes of their customers, doing what is right does not matter. What matters is pleasing the customer, for, as good businessmen and women, managers know that the customer is always right. They do not control their customers. They are controlled by them. That is why blackmail by activists is successful. What is remarkable, in fact, is not how strong companies are, but how weak. In front of the protests of a small number of Greenpeace activists and some hooligans, principally in Germany, the British government and Shell abandoned a perfectly sensible plan to dump the Brent Spar oil platform at sea in favour of a costlier and less environmentally favourable one of onshore disposal. This is a story not of arrogance but of timidity, not of strength but of vulnerability.

Before leaving brands behind us, it is important to put the issue in context. Klein argues, in the opening quotation, that 'the astronomical growth in the wealth and cultural influence of multinational companies over the last fifteen years' (which, we have seen, is a myth) is due to brands. So let us look more closely at, say, the top fifteen transnational companies in 2000, by value added, according to UNCTAD. These were, in order, Exxon Mobil, General Motors,

Ford, Daimler Chrysler, General Electric, Toyota, Royal Dutch Shell, Siemens, BP, Wal-Mart, IBM, Volkswagen, Hitachi, Total Fina Elf and Verizon Communications. Five of these companies manufacture motor vehicles. All own more than one brand name. General Motors owns many, which has not helped it to be particularly successful. These brands have some value, but the most valuable of the brands owned by companies in this list is probably Mercedes. This brand value simply reflects the quality of the products that carry it. How far that brand can be stretched to products that are not luxury cars is uncertain. Few people buy Toyotas as a statement of glamour or lifestyle (which is why the company decided to invent the Lexus brand for its luxury models); they buy them because of their famous reliability. Yet Toyota has been the world's most successful car manufacturer over the past two decades. Volkswagen won out in Europe for the same reason. Four of these companies are oil companies. How many people pay attention to the name on the pump when they buy petrol? It is not their brands that make these companies successful, but their organizational capacities (though, as we have seen in the case of Shell, their brands do make them vulnerable if consumers detest them). Three – General Electrics, Siemens and Hitachi – are conglomerates rooted in electrical engineering. Brands are not the basis of their success, though the reputation for quality that goes with their names has some value, provided it is maintained. If the Wal-Mart brand, as such, has value it can only be because it tells customers that they can expect bargains. Again, the IBM brand has value, particularly among commercial customers. It speaks of reliability and competence. But if IBM relied on its brand alone, it would, quite swiftly, disappear. Verizon owns licences to supply mobile telephony. These, not its brands, are the most valuable assets it owns.

Consider a few of the other companies that make the list of the top hundred entities by value added. Sony is a valuable brand. However, it tells the buyer not about lifestyle, but about flair, product excellence and production quality. Mitsubishi has no particular brand value. It is another conglomerate. The most valuable assets owned by GlaxoSmithKline are its patents, not its brand. If that were not so, drug companies would not be so worried about competition from generic producers as soon as patents expire. As for Nike, Klein's target, it is an insignificant company: in August 2003, it came 233rd in the list of US companies, by market capitalization. McDonald's is insignificant too. I have succeeded in not drinking any Coca Cola for at least forty years and hope to continue in the same happy state until I die. But people presumably drink it because they like it. It seems an extraordinary notion to me, but less extraordinary than the idea, as arrogant as it is foolish, that millions of people have been successfully brain-washed into drinking something they loathe. What, in sum, is there to say about this fuss over brands? It is much ado about nothing.

Transnational corporations exploit poor countries and workers

Now, let us turn from the ludicrous campaign against brands to something more serious. The most important economic charge, by far, is that trans-national companies make profits by exploiting the poor, particularly poor workers and poor countries. It is important to be quite clear in answering this question. For it has two answers: yes and no.

The 'yes' answer is that the business of any company is to look for opport-unities to turn something cheap into something more expensive. It is, in other words, to add value. The better it is at identifying opportunities and knowing how to add value when it has identified them, the more successful a company will be. One of those opportunities is to use resources (including people) that have, historically, fallen outside the global market economy and are, corres-pondingly, cheap. If it is operating in a competitive economy, however, a company will find it impossible to keep the gains to itself. It will have to share them with its suppliers, its workers and its customers. No doubt it will prefer not to do so. But if it fails to do this, its suppliers, workers and customers will go elsewhere and, in the end, it will go out of business.

The 'no' answer is, however, more important than the 'yes' one. It is not true that most of the opportunities transnationals find to exploit are in poor countries. On the contrary, as we will see, they are finding too few. The diffi-culty facing most poor countries is that they – or, more accurately, the oppor-tunities their poverty would appear to offer – are not being exploited enough. It is also not true that, when opportunities are exploited in poor countries, their citizens are made worse off thereby. Economic life is about beneficial mutual exploitation or, if one wishes to describe it more benignly, about playing positive-sum games. It is right to say that transnational companies exploit their Chinese workers in the hope of making profits. It is equally right to say that Chinese workers are exploiting transnationals in the (almost universally fulfilled) hope of obtaining higher pay, better training and more opportunities than would otherwise be available to them.

Let us try to justify these broad statements by looking at the evidence. It will be helpful, first, to look a bit at the scale of the phenomenon. For there is no question that the growth of foreign direct investment has been a remarkable phenomenon of recent decades, as has been the development of transnational production networks. These are important respects in which today's economic globalization has been different from anything that has gone before. Tables 11.1, 11.2 and 11.3 give relevant background information.[15] Three points stand out: the growth of FDI relative to both world GDP and trade; the fact that, by 2001, the sales of foreign affiliates greatly exceeded world exports; and the fact that foreign affiliates now generate 11 per cent of world GDP. Global output and investment have become increasingly cosmopolitan. This is, beyond question, one of the leading indicators of economic globalization.

It is inevitable that nationalists, anti-capitalists and opponents of big business find such data horrifying. But do they have reason to do so? An alternative view, after all, is that companies go abroad because they have valuable

Table 11.1 Selected indicators of FDI and international production (value at current prices, dollar billions)

	1982	1990	2001
FDI inward stock	$734	$1,874	$6,846
Sales of foreign affiliates	$2,541	$5,479	$18,517
Gross product of foreign affiliates	$594	$1,423	$3,495
Assets of foreign affiliates	$1,959	$5,759	$4,952
Exports of foreign affiliates	$670	$1,169	$2,600
Employment of foreign affiliates (thousands)	17,987	23,858	53,581
World GDP	$10,805	$1,672	$31,900
Gross fixed capital formation	$2,285	$4,841	$6,680*
Royalties and licence-fee receipts	$9	$27	$73**
Exports of goods and non-factor services	$2,081	$4,375	$7,430

Source: UNCTAD, *World Investment Report 2002: Transnational Corporations and Export Competitiveness* (New York and Geneva: United Nations, 2002).

* Data are for 2000.
** Data are for 2000.

Table 11.2 Ratio of FDI to world GDP (at market prices, per cent)

	1982	1990	2001
FDI inward stock	6.8	8.6	21.5
Sales of foreign affiliates	23.5	25.3	58.0
Gross product of foreign affiliates	5.5	6.6	11.0
Assets of foreign affiliates	18.1	26.6	78.2

Source: UNCTAD, *World Investment Report 2002*.

Table 11.3 Activities of foreign affiliates (ratios to world exports of goods and non-factor services, at market prices, per cent)

	1982	1990	2001
Sales of foreign affiliates	122.1	125.2	249.2
Exports of foreign affiliates	32.2	26.7	35.0
Royalties and licence-fee receipts	0.4	0.6	1.0

Source: UNCTAD, World Investment Report 2002.

assets – know-how, organizational capacities and so forth – that can be put to productive and mutually beneficial use in their new locations. Moreover, we know from both theory and experience that inward investment is most likely to be economically harmful when it is enticed by the high barriers to imports that many critics of globalization prefer: in other words, when it is tariff-jumping.[16]

The World Bank has given a splendid recent example of such self-impoverishing incentives to inward investment.[17] In an effort to encourage development of Tierra del Fuego, the southernmost tip of Argentina, the government set up a special production zone for assembling electronic products with generous tariff protection and tax subsidies. Companies were encouraged to assemble electronic goods for resale in the highly protected Argentine markets. Televisions, for example, cost 150–400 per cent more than in international markets. This was so lucrative that companies would bring in finished products, disassemble them and then reassemble them. By 1990, the cost to the bankrupt Argentine Treasury was estimated at 0.5 per cent to 1 per cent of GDP. The producing companies and a few thousand workers gained at the expense of Argentine consumers, taxpayers, victims of the inflationary financing of budget deficits and workers in more competitive industries that were never created. Fortunately, since the early 1980s, most countries have lowered their protectionist barriers, which makes it far more likely that the inward investment has been beneficial. Moreover, this criticism does not, in any case, apply to export-oriented investment.

Critics do not view the increase in FDI in this benign way. On the contrary, they argue that it exploits the poor and vulnerable. The first question to address, therefore, is whether FDI tends to focus on poor vulnerable countries. I have already given a cursory answer to this question – it is no. It is helpful to go a little deeper. In 2001, according to UNCTAD, the total stock of inward direct investment was $6,846 billion. Of this, 66 per cent was located in the developed countries and 32 per cent in the developing countries. The European Union as a whole contained 39 per cent of the world's stock and the

US 19 per cent. Japan, as is well known, is remarkable for its tiny share of global inward investment, at 0.7 per cent. In the developing world, the largest share was Asia's, at 19 per cent. Within Asia, Hong Kong held 6.6 per cent of the world's total, China 5.8 per cent and Singapore 1.5 per cent. Latin America and the Caribbean contained 10 per cent of the world's stock. Sub-Saharan Africa's share was just 1.7 per cent. The least developed countries – the world's poorest countries – contained just 0.6 per cent of the total stock of inward investment. We may conclude then that the EU must be in a dire state, given the damage FDI is supposed to do. The US, too, and Asian developing countries appear to be in trouble, while Africans live happily unexploited. If we forget such absurdities, we reach the conclusion that investors batten on the rich and successful, not on the poor and vulnerable. The evidence suggests, moreover, that this is increasingly the case. If one looks at the cumulative sum of inward flows between 1996 and 2001, the share of the developed countries jumps to 72 per cent. Sub-Saharan Africa's share is just 0.9 per cent and the least developed countries' 0.5 per cent.

This is consistent with the findings of World Bank research, which show that the more advanced the rule of law (after controlling for country size, income, openness, inflation and education), the higher the direct foreign investment.[18] As the Bank notes, 'countries with better investment climates – as indicated by the level of corruption, voice (political openness), rule of law, quality of the regulatory regime, government effectiveness, and political stability – tended to receive an increasing share of total FDI over the 1990s'.[19] The point is obvious. Opportunities for investment do exist in poor countries. But whether they will be exploited by investors will depend on how they judge both the scale of those opportunities (which makes China special) and the likelihood that they will be allowed to exploit them securely (which makes Hong Kong special). The great bulk of direct investment continues to go to countries with high labour costs and strong regulatory regimes, not least on the environment. But these are more than offset, in the eyes of investors, by the benefits of political stability, personal security, excellent institutions, highly skilled workers and large markets. Even among developing countries, investors are most attracted to countries that possess such qualities.[20]

The above discussion looks only at gross, not net, flows. It is evident, however, that net positions are very different from gross, because developing countries are relatively small generators of outward FDI. The net position of the high-income countries was, as one might expect, negative in 2001: their companies had, in aggregate, invested abroad more than had been invested by companies within them. Meanwhile, the net stock inside developing countries was measured at $1,405 billion. This is not an important qualification, however. Those who think FDI harmful must think each individual investment is harmful: the more investment inside a country, the worse off it must be. This damage is not mitigated, on this argument, by the ability of its companies to harm others in their turn. Moreover, the picture on the distribution of the net stocks, among developing countries, is in line with that on gross stocks. Fifty-two per cent of the net stock inside the developing economies was in Asia and 40 per cent in Latin America and the Caribbean in 2001. Twenty-six per cent was in China, the most economically successful developing economy since 1980. Just 8.1 per cent of the net stock of FDI in developing countries was in Africa, 5.3 per cent in sub-Saharan Africa and 2.6 per cent in the least developed countries. Thus data on the distribution of the net stock among developing countries reinforce what we know of the distribution of the gross stock in the world: it goes to relatively successful countries. The world's least developed countries are not exploited by transnationals, but ignored by them, except when they have particularly valuable natural resources.

A second possible qualification is that the analysis ignores size of country. On this argument, the damage depends on the relationship between the magnitude of inward investment and the size of the economy. Relative to GDP, the inward stock of investment in developing countries in 2000 was 30.9 per cent, against 17.1 per cent in the developed countries (though 30.3 per cent in the EU). When one starts to look at individual countries with stocks of inward direct investment that exceed 30 per cent of GDP, the picture that emerges is intriguing. This group of high-inward-investment countries includes a number of high-income countries: Belgium, Denmark, Ireland, the Netherlands, Sweden, the UK, Switzerland and New Zealand. It also includes a number of African countries: Angola, Botswana, Chad, Côte d'Ivoire, Equatorial Guinea, Gambia, Guinea-Bissau, Lesotho, Liberia, Namibia, Nigeria, Seychelles, South Africa, Togo and Zambia. These are mostly resource-rich countries. The list includes Bolivia, Brazil, Chile and Ecuador. It includes a large number of very small Caribbean countries. In Asia, it includes Cambodia, China, Hong Kong, Indonesia, Laos and Malaysia. In central and eastern Europe, it includes the Czech Republic, Estonia, Hungary and Moldova. This list shows that high ratios of inward investment to GDP are compatible with prosperity, but it is also consistent with the opposite. Context is all. Inward investment in the poorest countries is only likely when there are natural resources. Too often a kleptocratic élite then seizes the benefits.

The principal conclusions remain. FDI does not go to the world's poorest and least regulated countries, but to its richest and most regulated. Among developing countries, the largest flows have been to economically dynamic countries, not the poorest and most stagnant ones. The big exception is flows to develop natural resources, which must go where those resources are, however badly governed the countries may be. There is no evidence that FDI impoverishes its recipients, though it can do so in the wrong policy context (or in the context of the natural resource curse, discussed in Chapter 9).

One can add that foreign affiliates often play a beneficial role in generating exports, from both high-income and developing countries. According to UNCTAD, 90 per cent of Ireland's exports, 44 per cent of the exports of the Netherlands and Canada, 39 per cent of Sweden's exports and even 15 per cent of US exports came from foreign affiliates in 1999. In the same year (or 2000), 80 per cent of Hungary's exports, 60 per cent of Estonia's, 56 per cent of Poland's, 50 per cent of the exports of China and Costa Rica, 45 per cent of Malaysia's, 38 per cent of Singapore's and 31 per cent of Mexico's came from foreign affiliates. In Costa Rica, Hungary and Mexico, the top three transnational corporations (TNCs) generated 29 per cent, 26 per cent and 13 per cent of exports respectively. These have all been successful economies. Could they have begun to be this successful without foreign investors?

This brings us to the next charge, which is not that FDI is motivated by a desire to exploit the poor, but that what investment does go to the developing countries operates against the interests of the poor. Again, this proposition is false.

The evidence that transnational companies pay more – and treat their workers better – than local companies do is overwhelming. They can do so because their superior know-how makes them more efficient – that is why these companies have been able to become transnationals in the first place. There is also no question that companies do take advantage of that know-how, as one would expect. If they did not do so, they would have no competitive advantage. Edward Graham, in his excellent book *Fighting the Wrong Enemy*, notes that compensation by US-owned companies in manufacturing was 1.4 times average compensation in high-income countries, 1.8 times in middle-income developing countries, and twice the average in low-income developing countries.[21] Comparable results come from other studies. One showed that wages are higher on the Mexican border, where the investments of US-owned companies are concentrated, than in the rest of Mexico.[22] Similar conclusions have been reached for Venezuela. Indeed, foreign investors tend to pay more even in high-income countries.

An exhaustive study of Indonesian manufacturing, based on analysis of almost 20,000 plants, concluded that the average wage in a foreign-owned plant was 50 per cent higher than in private domestic plants. Total compensation was about 60 per cent higher. More detailed econometric evaluation of the causes of the wage premia, which allows for the education levels of employees, plant size, location, and capital- and energy-intensity, reduces the premium, but does not eliminate it. After controlling for these factors (some of which are themselves related to foreign ownership), the premium is 12 per cent for 'blue-collar' workers and about 22 per cent for 'white-collar' workers. The study finds not only that wages are higher in foreign-owned plants, but that their presence raises wages in domestic plants as well. This must happen because of increased demand in the labour market, technological spillovers, training of workers and managers and so forth.[23] Inward investment thus raises wages. That is exactly what any reasonable person would expect. It is not what wilder critics suggest.

Intriguingly, some critics admit that foreign companies pay better than local ones. Noreena Hertz, for example, author of the *The Silent Takeover*, states that 'It is not only multinational companies that benefit from "open door" policies. Other beneficiaries of such policies are, typically, the host government, corrupt officials and those fortunate enough to gain employment with foreign firms – they tend to pay better and their standards are often higher than those of local firms.'[24] This is puzzling. Hertz probably does not believe that officials are corrupt only because of inward investors. Otherwise, a list which consists of the government and employees looks a desirable one. Even more astounding, the admission that inward investors pay workers more and treat them better follows a diatribe in which it is alleged that there is a race to the bottom on labour regulations, wages and worker rights. It is hard to see how both can be true: foreign companies pay more than local ones (and treat them better), but are also the cause of a race to the bottom on the treatment of labour. It sounds as though they are part of a race to the top. Hertz complains, for example, of the disgraceful treatment of workers in special economic zones in China. Has she considered the dreadful pay and conditions that was the 'iron rice bowl' of the state enterprises?

One can, nevertheless, identify five further criticisms that merit consideration: first, that wages, even if higher than ones provided by domestic competitors, should be still higher; second, that inward investors cause offsetting job losses in the economy; third, that, whatever may be the general situation, these higher wages do not apply in the 'sweatshop industries' –

clothing, footwear, sports goods and toys; fourth, that a race to the bottom is being unleashed in incentives to attract inward investment; and, last but not least, that export processing zones (EPZs) are especially undesirable.

The first argument states, in essence, that if foreign companies are far more productive than domestic ones, they can also afford to pay far more. Otherwise, the pay is unfair. It is unfair to the workers themselves and to the workers in high-income countries with which they are competing. Pay, then, should be set not by general labour market conditions in the company where the investment is made. Rather, one should be rewarded on the basis of the capital intensity and efficiency of the particular plant or company where one works. So a production manager in, say, a clothing factory should be paid a tenth of what his equivalent would be paid in a petroleum refinery. This turns the labour market into a lottery. It would also be absurd, for two reasons. One is that, while it will often make sense for an employer to pay a worker somewhat more than he or she can obtain elsewhere, to improve worker quality, motivate workers and reduce worker turnover, it will not make sense, either for the economy as a whole or for the employer, to pay a huge multiple of that best alternative. The economy's labour market would, as I have noted in the previous chapter, become severely distorted. It would also lose the natural incentive of the cheaper labour (itself caused by the overall poverty) that attracted the investment in the first place. The other element of the answer is that it would be very strange if companies did not, in fact, pay their workers what they saw as their marginal product. In a low-wage country, workers will be hired to perform functions that are mechanized elsewhere. It is perfectly possible, therefore, that marginal product will be far lower than in the country where the direct investment originated, even if the technology employed is not greatly dissimilar.[5]

Some critics argue that the proof of exploitation is the fact that the workers in developing countries are unable to afford the goods they make. This complaint is demented. One works in order to buy not what one makes, but what one needs. An American worker on a Boeing 747 assembly line cannot buy what he makes. Nor can a German worker on a Mercedes Benz production line afford an S Class limousine. A closely related argument points to the small share of the direct labour cost in the final product. Again, so what? The labour cost element in a gallon of petrol is also trivial. The question is whether the companies making the product are earning extraordinary profits. That they have to spend enormous quantities on marketing and distribution is no surprise.

The second question is whether inward investors cause offsetting job losses in the economy. The answer must be that this depends on whether they produce for export or for the domestic market. If one were worried about this effect, one would favour export-oriented investment even more than otherwise. But there is no strong reason to object to such job displacement. The replacement of less efficient by more efficient producers is the foundation of economic advance. It means lower prices, higher real incomes, more choice, better quality and so forth. It is no more reasonable to object to a foreign investor replacing an inefficient domestic company than to object to a more efficient domestic company replacing another. True, the foreign investors repatriate profits. But to the extent that this is the reward on the capital they brought in, some domestic capital must have been released to be used elsewhere.

The third criticism is that, whatever the situation may be in most industries, foreign investors do not benefit their workers in the classic 'sweatshop' industries that one tends to see in export processing zones.[26] These are relatively unimportant industries in themselves: they accounted for less than 10 per cent of world merchandise exports in 1997 and well under 7 per cent of the stock of US direct investment abroad in 1998, according to Edward Graham.[27] But they are extremely important for developing countries, since they have so often proved to be the first step on the development ladder. Fortunately, it seems clear that here, too, workers are better off than if these jobs did not exist, which is exactly what one would expect: otherwise, the companies would have no workers. Theodore Moran points out that:

> surveys by the International Labor Organization, for example, have regularly found that the pay for workers in EPZs, while extremely low by the standards of developed countries, is higher than what would be available in the villages from which the workers come. Similarly, the U.S. Department of Labor reports that firms producing footwear and apparel generally pay more than the minimum wage and offer conditions substantially better than those that prevail in agriculture. Other surveys have found that, on average, jobs in foreign-owned, export-oriented factories offer higher pay and better working conditions than comparable jobs in domestic companies.[28]

One of the most significant, and little noted, benefits of employment in these industries is that so many of the workers are women. Yes, unquestionably, by the standards of high-income countries, they have poor jobs with dreadfully low wages. But they are jobs. That is itself revolutionary in many countries.

Consider Bangladesh, for example. Before there was a clothing industry, local traditions forbade women from working in factories. Now 95 per cent of the 1.4 million workers in clothing manufacture are women, while 70 per cent of all the women in formal sector employment work in this industry. Bangladeshi women, as is true of other female workers in Asia and Latin America, indicate that factory work offers a measure of autonomy, status and self-respect. As female participation and female incomes rise, a higher proportion of family incomes tends to be spent on education, health and nutrition. Working in factories postpones marriage and increases the resources future wives bring into marriage.[29] All these are enormous gains. For a western visitor such jobs may seem unimaginably bad. But some of the alternatives – total dependency as housewife or despised daughter, prostitution, agricultural labour or begging – are worse. No case can be made for depriving these people of this opportunity, unless one can offer a credible alternative. This is, of course, not to justify physical abuse, bullying and blatant exploitation of vulnerable workers. Nor does it justify failing to remedy obvious safety hazards. But the deeper challenge is how to improve conditions for workers in the entire economy, not just those who work for export, still less those who produce branded goods. This is particularly important since conditions in domestically oriented factories (let alone the informal sector) tend to be worse than in export-oriented plants. Attacking the latter is mere tokenism. To be upset over poverty is entirely justifiable; to block a route out of it, in response, is not.

Now let us look at the fourth of these criticisms: that a race to the bottom is being unleashed in incentives to attract inward investment. Here the evidence is rather different: there is not much, if any, race to the bottom on environmental or labour regulations, as was argued in the previous chapter. While there is much rhetoric about the race to the bottom on labour regulations, evidence of this is lacking. Limits on trade union activity are common, but that has been true in many developing countries for a long while (as it was in today's high-income countries at comparable stages of development). It is also true that in a number of cases export processing zones provided for greater flexibility (over hours, for example) than in the domestic economy. How important this is must be a matter of judgement. One might well argue that allowing people to vary working hours is a desirable way of improving the labour market. Against this, Moran recounts a number of specific examples in which foreign investors, particularly those engaged in more sophisticated operations, encourage or even organize *improvement* in the treatment of labour. This is partly to head off labour unrest and partly to improve the functioning of their own operations. The reason this makes sense is evident. It is not in the interests of a rational employer to employ embittered people.[30] More broadly, an exhaustive study by the Organization for Economic Co-operation and Development of labour regulations in seventy-five countries that generate almost all trade and foreign investment concluded that workers' rights had not worsened significantly in any. In seventeen – including Brazil, South Korea and Turkey – they had greatly improved.[31]

Instead of a race to the bottom on regulations, what one sees is a race to the top on incentives. In an earlier study, Moran estimated that 116 countries offer incentives to foreign investors.[32] These incentives fall into three categories: fiscal, financial and others. High-income countries tend to offer financial incentives – outright bribes, in other words. Developing countries tend to provide fiscal incentives – tax reductions, tax holidays, accelerated depreciation, investment allowances, duty drawbacks and so forth. The effectiveness of such incentives is doubtful, as is their economic desirability. This is particularly true of selective or, worst of all, firm-specific, tailor-made incentives. General across-the-board improvements in the business climate are far more likely to make sense. There is, in fact, good reason to believe that the competition across the globe in offering such incentives is wasteful and foolish. The World Bank suggests that there is scope for international agreement to curb this competition. That would be one good reason to support an international agreement on investment. This should also interest developing countries since, sometimes at least, they find themselves in competition with the treasuries of the high-income countries. What is clear, however, is that the underlying folly here is not that of investors, but that of governments. They need to find a way to bind their hands.[33]

One final criticism about the race to the bottom must be rejected. This is the complaint that investors are prepared to move to cheaper-labour countries too easily. Whether that is feasible depends on the technology. But the underlying process in which, as countries become richer and their labour costs rise, the activities that use unskilled labour most intensively move to still poorer and cheaper countries is not a drawback, but a benefit. The Japanese have described this pattern as 'wild geese flying'. Thus the production of apparel moved from Japan, to Hong Kong, to Korea and Taiwan, to Mauritius and Bangladesh, and then on to China, where it is likely to stay for a long time. As old opportunities migrate, new ones emerge. Moran makes clear, in the cases of the Dominican Republic, the Philippines and Costa Rica, that this shift to activities that used physical and human capital more intensively is highly desirable. In fact, it is how 'sweatshops' disappear.[34]

Finally, let us look at the complaints directed specifically at EPZs. According to the World Bank, the number of these rose from 175 in fifty-three countries in 1987 to 500 in seventy-three countries by 1995. In response, Naomi Klein argues that:

> The current mania for the EPZ (export processing zone) model is based on the success of the so-called Asian Tiger economies, in particular the economies of South Korea and Taiwan. When only a few countries had the zones, including South Korea and Taiwan, wages rose steadily, technology transfers occurred and taxes were gradually introduced. But as critics of EPZs are quick to point out, the global economy has become much more competitive since those countries made the transition from low-wage industries to higher-skill ones. Today, with seventy countries competing for the export-processing-zone dollar, the incentives to lure investors are increasing and the wages and standards are being held hostage to the threat of departure. The upshot is that entire countries are being turned into industrial slums and low-wage ghettos, with no end in sight.[35]

So are EPZs a good way of attracting inward investment in labour-intensive, export-oriented industry? This is a complex question. A part of the answer is that they have proved a helpful instrument of development for many countries – Klein could, for example, have added Mauritius to her list.[36] But they are indeed problematic. This is, to some extent, because they have been used as a way round the obstacles created by highly protected, excessively regulated domestic economies. Yet all the evidence suggests that EPZs work best when they are integrated with the rest of the domestic economy. Even without that, they can still provide some jobs and exports, which is better than nothing. But it is best if they can obtain the full range of backward linkages into the economy. To advance, they need access to good infrastructure, educated labour and an ability to obtain competitively priced local inputs. For these reasons, putting EPZs in remote areas, in the hope of generating rapid employment growth, normally fails. The important point about South Korea and Taiwan is not that they had EPZs, but that, in important respects, they *were* EPZs. In some cases, however, Mexico being an example, the practices of an EPZ have spread throughout the economy.

Klein raises another issue, however, which is whether these zones can work when so many countries are trying to attract the same companies to produce much the same thing. This question can be raised more broadly about the benefits for developing countries of attempting to export manufactures today, as compared with three decades ago. The answer is complex. One element is that competition is indeed greater now, as is the pool of labour to be absorbed into the industrial economy. It is likely that wages will rise more slowly than they did in the earlier, more limited cases of export-led growth. Another element is that the high savings and investment rates of many developing countries could still generate rapid growth alongside increased exports. Yet another is that the more developing countries liberalize their own barriers to trade, the greater the opportunities they should find to trade with one another. Yet another element is that 'industrial slums and low-wage ghettos' may be bad, but being entirely without them, as much of sub-Saharan Africa is today, is worse. And perhaps the most powerful answer is that exactly the same argument was made by a number of analysts in the early 1980s. Yet the world then saw the rapid rise of the economy of its biggest country, at least partly on the basis of labour-intensive exports. The narrow EPZ strategy is flawed. But an intelligent strategy of integration into the world economy is not.

What, then, are the conclusions? Foreign direct investment is not directed at exploiting the poor. On the contrary, it goes largely to the rich and successful. When it does go to poor countries, there is unambiguous evidence that it benefits workers who are paid more and treated better by foreign employers. The fact that wages paid by investors are lower in developing countries than in rich ones is a perfectly reasonable response to local conditions. Again, workers in highly labour-intensive industries – the 'sweatshop industries' – also benefit from foreign direct investment. There is evidence not so much of a race to the bottom on regulation as of a race to the top on incentives. Finally, EPZs are imperfect mechanisms, but they are potentially useful.

Corporate investment abroad impoverishes workers

Labour representatives in high-income countries, notably the US, have also made much of the argument that the export of capital harms them, by forcing them to accept lower wages or lose their jobs. To this Edward Graham responds that most investment goes to other high-income countries, many of which have wages close to – or even higher than – those in the US. Eighty per cent of the stock of US investment abroad in 1997 was located in other high-income countries. Most investment abroad is not particularly labour-intensive, for precisely this reason. It is true that investment in developing countries is relatively labour intensive. But that still does not mean jobs are lost. This is partly because, as a matter of logic, there is no connection between these microeconomic changes and overall employment. But it is also the case that US direct investment and exports tend to be complementary – the more there is of the former, the more there is of the latter. Thus, as one might expect, investment abroad simultaneously destroys and creates jobs. Graham concludes that 'this analysis provides no reason to believe that outward FDI either creates or destroys domestic jobs on a net basis. On the other hand, there seems little question that FDI can contribute to a redistribution of jobs among activities. But generally, this redistribution is from the lower-paying to higher paid jobs. That, of course, is good news for US workers as a group.'[5] To all this should be added the significant fact that, in 2001, the stock of inward investment in the US was valued at $1,321 billion, virtually identical to the stock of outward investment, at $1,381 billion. Thus the US has had no signif- icant net outflow. It has, instead, benefited from an exchange of capital, predominantly with other high-income countries.

A different question is whether the threat of outward investment has reduced union bargaining power. Trade unions were able to share in the monopoly rents enjoyed by certain protected industries. In the US, steel and automobiles are the most important examples. In 1980, for instance, steel workers received wages that were 157 per cent of the average wages of US production workers in manufacturing, while automobile workers received 143 per cent. But these industries have since become subject to global competition. As profitability has declined, relative wages have fallen. By 2000, wages in the steel industry were down to 135 per cent of the US manufacturing average, while those in automobiles were down to 134 per cent. But these losses have only been in small part due to direct investment abroad, which has affected automobiles but not steel. The big change has been increased competition from trade and inward direct investors. The position of a labour aristocracy within the US has been eroded by increased global competition in the era of globalization, in which the possibility of outward investment has played a modest part.

Nevertheless, the opportunity for foreign direct investment has changed the relationship between companies and their workers in three important respects. The first is that the 'national coalition' between companies and workers is broken. Today, companies with foreign plants do not share a protectionist interest with their work-force. For those of us who wish to see opportunities to trade sustained, indeed extended, that is a desirable change. But it is a change all the same. The interests of a transnational company are not the same as those of the country from which it originates or of the workers it has historically employed. It has become, to coin a phrase, a 'rootless cosmopolitan'. It is impossible to read the literature of the critics, particularly those who identify with the trades unions, without realizing that this rootlessness is the thing they most detest. They want their companies under national, or local, political control and identifying with their national, or local, labour forces, not employing people abroad. They want them to remain part of a cosy community and ignore the interests of outsiders.

The second is a more specific aspect of this general point. Companies have an additional opportunity of exit. This is a threat they can use in bargaining. How credible that threat is, in any particular case, must vary a great deal. But it is a threat that makes it impossible for the labour force to impose costs on its employers that go beyond some sticking point. If one identifies with the interests of these workers, against others, including workers abroad, then this is a loss. The third change, equally obvious, is that the possibility of outward investment, as is also true of trade, 'turbocharges' the market economy, to use the idiom coined by Edward Luttwak.[38] That is to say, it tends to increase the pace of economic change. Economic change always imposes losses, as well as gains. In a properly run market economy, gains outweigh losses. But the net gains from any individual market-driven change are usually small in relation to the gross gains and losses. The closure of a plant, to be replaced by one in another country, is a particularly visible symbol of such rapid change.

Corporations dominate politics

As the quotation at the beginning of this chapter from the British writer and activist George Monbiot shows, for many critics, the opposition to corporations is not merely to their economic roles, narrowly defined, but even more to their role in politics, both domestic and international. Monbiot sees the corporation as a bastion of unaccountable power that dominates the political process and subverts democracy. It is anti-democratic, just as aristocracy was. Moreover, 'If the corporations win, liberal democracy will come to an end.' I look at a world in which democracy has never before been so widespread. Monbiot – and others in the 'movement' – looks at the world and sees democracy's end. Who is right?

One possible answer is: both. The reason is that what are involved are, as I noted in Chapter 5 above, different definitions of democracy. Many of the critics think of a democracy as a system allowing an active body of homogeneous citizens to reach collective decisions on all the matters that concern them, through deliberation and, ultimately, voting. This is the democracy of the Greek *polis* or the town meeting. It has powerful attractions. It is also evident that massive wealth, including giant corporations, makes a mockery of such a notion of democracy. It threatens the replacement of democracy with what Aristotle called oligarchy or, in its malign form, plutocracy. Yet we must ask whether this is a plausible view of democracy in the modern era. The decisions governments take are technically complex and often have repercussions across the world. The economy is regulated, specialized and technologically advanced. Governments themselves are larger, more complex, more intrusive and more internationally engaged than ever before. It is impossible for the citizenry to reach sensible decisions on most of the matters that come before governments. In practice, therefore, the government by engaged citizens the critics desire would come down to government by single-issue, activist organizations. Yet government by Greenpeace or trades unions is no more inherently democratic than government by Shell or the Confederation of British Industry. Greenpeace has its own organizational imperatives: it must attract attention and mobilize support. If this means exaggeration, misrepresentation or downright deceit, as over the Brent Spar platform, so be it. In practice, therefore, the recommended shift would be from plutocracy to demagogy, another malign Aristotelian category.

What we now live in are pluralist democracies. For reasons explained best by Mancur Olson, when obtaining influence is costly, organizations with the largest interests and the greatest ability to eliminate free riders dominate. Critics are right to argue that corporations are among those interests. But corporations are not alone. Other groups have shown ability to organize: trades unions, farmers (at least in high-income countries) and campaigning groups. Instead of informed debate among the wider citizenry, we have ended up with periodic elections (with declining turnouts) that punctuate the engagement between an interventionist, regulatory state on the one hand and a plethora of well-organized special interests on the other. Is it a pretty picture? No. Is it easily remediable? No.

Christ may have managed to eliminate the money changers from the Temple. But nobody will eliminate special interests from contemporary democratic politics. Ironically, the more activists are successful in imposing environmental and other regulations, the more the economic special interests, including corporations, will become engaged in lobbying. All the same, Monbiot's position is at the extreme end of the hysterical. Corporations have influence. But the view that they run contemporary states is nonsense.

Competition policy, in both the US and the EU, has constantly curtailed the ambitions of powerful companies. Consider, for example, the EU's decision to prevent General Electric from purchasing Honeywell in 2001. Then look at regulation. Contrary to what critics allege, the raft of regulatory measures in both the US and the EU has constantly risen, not least over the environment, health and safety. One of the most striking examples has been rising labour market regulation under Tony Blair's government in the UK, because it runs counter to the constant allegation that the government is the stooge of big business. The CBI has opposed the government again and again – and lost. Finally, look at the anti-corporate activities of the legal system, especially in the US, but now increasingly in the UK as well.[39] Many think the trial lawyers are a blight, but that they operate against the interests and desires of the corporations is evident.

Some critics may grant this, grudgingly. But they will insist that it was corporations that drove the 'neo-liberal' agenda of the 1980s and 1990s. Actually, no. Many entrenched corporate monopolists were opposed to greater competition, above all from abroad. European car manufactures, for example, opposed the opening of their markets to the Japanese. Steel and textile producers have tended to be strongly protectionist. Many corporations were opposed to privatization. I remember a lunch with the late Arnold Weinstock just before the privatization of British Telecom. His company, GEC, was the supplier of equipment to the UK's monopoly supplier of telecoms services. It was a cosy, cost-plus monopoly. He knew that privatization and liberalization would put an end to this position. He inveighed against the idea of privatization as impractical and theoretical. He was wrong on its impracticality, but right on its consequences for GEC. When, more than a decade later, this failed telecoms equipment supplier tried to rejuvenate itself, as Marconi, it imploded. Liberal economies are competitive, dynamic and unforgiving, precisely what most incumbents loathe. Corporations would be happier with monopolies and cartels. It was not corporations that pushed liberalization and privatization, but governments (and, behind them, intellectuals) convinced this was in the interests of their countries. Companies adapt, however. They have to do so.

Is it not true, then, that corporations have used their influence over the international agenda of their countries, including the WTO, to undermine regulations everywhere? Again, the answer is no. One of the ironies of this view is that the historic explanation for the GATT and then WTO was that it allowed governments to go round protectionist corporate lobbies to achieve liberalization in the interests of their citizens – the precise opposite of what critics now allege. It is true, however, that governments and export-oriented corporations shared the view that their foreign counterparts should not be allowed to undermine agreed liberalization with a raft of non-tariff barriers, disguized as health, safety or environmental regulations. In this sense, then, an assault on regulations was part of the negotiating process. It is also true that some industries did come to realize the potential value of the WTO as a way of imposing their regulatory agenda. This was true of the industries seeking protection of intellectual property during the Uruguay Round. Yet even here there is an irony. The US government needed the support of the intellectual property coalition to achieve greater trade liberalization, which it believed (rightly) was in the interests of the US and the wider world. It needed that support to counter the opposition of enemies of liberal trade. If the left had retained its historic understanding of the value of liberal trade, the intellectual property coalition would have been unnecessary.

The bottom line is that corporations have influence, but not decisive power. Moreover, many other forces have influence in contemporary democracies. Nor is there any simple means of excluding corporate interests from democratic politics. It is right, however, to consider how far the role of corporations in setting policy agendas, notably over trade, should be promoted or curtailed. As the distinguished American international economist Alan Deardorff remarks, it is right to be attuned 'to the role that special interests, including but not limited to corporations, play in the setting of international economic policies and in the writing of the international rules under which such policies are conducted'.[40] This far then I agree with Monbiot. He is not wrong to be concerned. But his fear that democracy will founder under the assault of corporate interests is wildly exaggerated.

Conclusion

Perhaps the core faith of globalization's critics is the power and the malevolence of the corporation. This is their Satan. When one looks closely one finds that corporations are not more powerful than countries and do not dominate the world through their brands. It is clear also that inward investment benefits recipient countries, given the right policies, and, above all, the workers the corporations employ. Many of those who protest at the conditions of workers in developing countries do so in comparison to their own happy state, not in comparison to the often awful alternatives confronting the world's poor.

Difficult though it may be for some to believe, there are worse places to work than those we call 'sweatshops'. There is also little, if any, evidence of a race to the bottom on regulation, though there is certainly an undesirable race to the top on subsidies. It would be good to reach global agreement on how to curtail this.

Finally, the role of corporations in democracy does make one uncomfortable, but it cannot be eliminated. Above all, it must not be exaggerated. The notion that the liberal economic policies of the past two decades or more, or the structure and rules of the contemporary WTO, are the result of a single-minded plot by corporate interests is plain wrong. Ideas mattered far more than interests. The essentially Marxist idea that we live in pseudo-democracies because of the power of money was wrong then and it is wrong now. It is right to be on guard against the power of all special interests. It is wrong to assume that any one group dominates. At this stage, however, having touched on the role of the corporation in politics, we need to look more broadly at the impact of globalization on the state. That is the topic of the next chapter.

Chapter 12 **Sad about the State**

> *Sovereign states are waging a war of competitive deregulation, forced on them by the global free market. A mechanism of downward harmonization of market economies is already in operation. Every type of currently existing capitalism is thrown into the melting pot. In this contest the socially dislocated American free market possesses powerful advantages. . . .*
>
> *All the familiar models of market institutions are mutating as global competition is played out through the structures of sovereign states. It is a basic error to think that this is a contest that any of the existing models can win. All are being eroded and replaced by new and more volatile types of capitalism. The chief result of this new competition is to make the social market economies of the post-war period unviable while transforming the free-market economies that are its nominal winners. . . .*
>
> *Global mobility of capital and production in a world of open economies have made the central policies of European social democracy unworkable. By so doing they have made today's mass unemployment a problem without a simple solution.*
>
> John Gray[1]

A spectre haunts the world's governments. That spectre is globalization. Critics of globalization argue that predatory market forces are making it impossible for beneficent governments to shield their peoples from the beasts of prey that lurk beyond their borders. On the free-market side of the debate, proponents counter that beneficent market forces are preventing predatory governments from fleecing their peoples. While the two sides disagree on the benefits of globalization, both agree that impotent politicians must now bow before omnipotent markets.[2]

This has become one of the clichés of our age. But it is (almost) total nonsense. The notion that unbridled market forces are making governments either impotent or irrelevant is wrong. In the last chapter, I discussed a narrow version of this thesis: the idea that the visible hand of the corporation has government firmly in its grip. In this chapter, I move on to a somewhat more abstract position: that the invisible hand of market forces is rending the fabric of civilized government. No man has done a better job of articulating this viewpoint than the British philosopher John Gray. For this reason, I open with quotations from his book *False Dawn.*³

To be fair to Gray, he is merely repeating, in his doom-laden way, what politicians say all the time. They insist they have no choice: globalization makes slashing taxes, cutting spending, reducing regulations and so on inescapable. But this is a dishonest excuse for pursuing the right policies. Worse, it is a dangerous one. There are good reasons to adopt these policies, but the pressures of globalization are not foremost among them. Politicians are not alone in this. Many pundits have encouraged the world to believe not just that globalization is inescapable, but even that every country must adopt much the same policies in response. Thomas Friedman, the *New York Times* columnist, author of *The Lexus and the Olive Tree*, is a leading example.⁴ He agrees with Gray that every country in the world will have to become like the US or perish, at least economically. At its extremes, the view that governments must embrace globalization or perish mutates into the proposition that, in our highly liberalized, high-technology, borderless world, governments are altogether passé. This view is still more absurd than the idea that governments are impotent.

Before articulating these arguments at greater length, I need to narrow down the criticisms levied against the implications of globalization for the state. I can identify three.

First, international economic integration is undermining the capacity of sovereign states to choose their tax and regulatory structures. In particular, it is destroying the high-tax, high-regulation European economic model. More specifically, it has made the redistributive policies of the welfare state impossible. As such, it represents an assault on democracy.⁵

Second, the integration of capital markets has destroyed the capacity of governments to run the fiscal and monetary policies they need to pursue full employment.

To these I will add another proposition, from the opposing side, that globalization renders the state not just impotent but unnecessary.

Globalization as choice

As I have argued above, notably in Part III, governments have chosen to liberalize their policies in recent decades. If integration is chosen, rather than imposed, it is impossible to argue that it renders states impotent. Their potency is displayed in the choices they make. The question, rather, concerns the trade-offs they confront. Given the technology, how far will governments find themselves constrained, once they have chosen openness? And if they are constrained, should their citizens care? Might they find the constraints on the state desirable, rather than the opposite?

Before considering these questions further, it is necessary to begin with three preliminary points.

First, states open up their economies to trade and the movement of capital and (to some extent) labour because this is in their interests and in the interests of their citizens. Experience has greatly strengthened the credibility of the view that the opening up of trade and of most capital flows is in the interests of most citizens in the short run, and virtually all citizens in the long run.[6] This is why the high-income countries chose to open their economies, initially to trade and then to capital flows. Moreover, because integration increases economic opportunities and wealth, it also strengthens the legitimacy and so stability of states. Not coincidentally, the world's most stable countries are the prosperous, market-oriented democracies. In contrast, the governments that tried hardest and longest to imprison their peoples, in the belief (or pretence) that they were protecting them from the cruel winds of competition, have foundered, as their prisoners came to look with great longing on what was going on outside and with growing disdain on their jailers. This destroyed the former Soviet empire. Today, only North Korea remains quite this closed.

Second, technology dictates which sectors are most affected by opening. It has its biggest impact on activities involving dematerialized information: telecommunications, portfolio capital, financial services, entertainment and the media. In these activities technology generates more integration than ever before and makes it far more difficult for the state to regulate and control activities. Global communications are a Trojan horse: when the Internet is present in a country, it is more difficult to control what citizens do with it. However, modern technology is a two-edged sword: it also makes it easier to regulate and monitor the movement of physical objects, both goods and people. Finally, there remain many activities to which opening is more or less irrelevant: domestic services are one example; most health care is another; education is, for the moment, yet another. These, moreover, are not just large, but growing, parts of high-income economies. In most high-income countries, relatively non-tradable services amount to two-thirds of GDP, or more.

Third, as I have already noted in Chapter 6, the choice between opening and closure is never all or nothing. It is more difficult to regulate capital flows when goods and services flow freely, but it is not impossible. Many European countries did this until the early 1990s. Similarly, it is possible for foreign direct investment to flow freely, while preserving barriers to trade in goods (and vice versa).

Taxation and regulation

If a state cannot raise taxes, it must wither away. Thus critics of globalization are right to focus on the ability of states to raise the revenue they need to finance their promises. If, as Gray states, social democracy is doomed, then this is where the ruin will begin. The high-tax social democratic states will find their revenue collapsing or their economies imploding (or both), as capital and at least relatively skilled labour flood out. Moreover, all the other regulations they impose – on the environmental impact of business, on health and safety, on the treatment of labour and so forth – can be seen as further aspects of the ability to tax. A minimum wage, or an environmental regulation, can best be viewed in this way, since the desired outcome could also be achieved by an explicit tax, combined with a subsidy. A minimum wage is equivalent to a (variable) tax on cheap labour, whose proceeds are directly remitted to the workers. If a government can raise taxes, it can, in general, impose regulations as well. And if it cannot raise taxes, because the tax base will disappear, it will be unable to impose regulations either.

Evidence on taxation

What then is the evidence on the ability of the governments of the high-income countries to impose taxes or regulations? Let us start with Table 12.1, which shows the growth of government in the course of the twentieth century. Four points shine out from these figures. The first is the enormous – and unrepeatable – growth of the functions of the state over the course of the twentieth century. The second is the variations among the high-income countries. The ratio of total public spending in the highest-spending country

Table 12.1 General government expenditure (as share of GDP, per cent)

Country	1913	1937	1960	1980	1996
Australia	16.5	14.8	21.2	34.1	35.9
Austria	17.0	20.6	35.7	48.1	51.6
Canada	n.a.	25.0	28.6	38.8	44.7
France	17.0	29.0	34.6	46.1	55.0
Germany	14.8	34.1	32.4	47.9	49.1
Italy	17.1	31.1	30.1	42.1	52.7
Ireland	n.a.	25.5	28.0	48.9	42.0
Japan	8.3	25.4	17.5	32.0	35.9
Norway	9.3	11.8	29.9	43.8	49.2
Sweden	10.4	16.5	31.0	60.1	64.2
Switzerland	14.0	24.1	17.2	32.8	39.4
UK	12.7	30.0	32.2	43.0	43.0
US	7.5	19.7	27.0	31.4	32.4
Simple average	13.1	23.8	28.0	41.9	45.0

Source: Vito Tanzi and Ludger Schuknecht, *Public Spending in the 20th Century: A Global Perspective* (Cambridge: Cambridge University Press, 2000).

(Sweden) to the lowest (the US), in 1996, was two to one. In general, the highest ratios of public spending to GDP are now to be found in northern continental Europe (a category that includes France). Lower ratios are found in Japan, the US and the other 'Anglo Saxon' countries. The third is that there is not the slightest sign of a reversal of the trend towards bigger government in the most recent period. Of the countries in the list, only Ireland had a lower ratio of public spending in GDP in 1996 than in 1980, while the UK's, notwithstanding all Mrs Thatcher's efforts, was the same. The last point is that to describe the period after 1980 as a return to *laissez faire*, or as marking the collapse of the state and the end of social democracy, borders on the unhinged. Never before have states been so omnipresent. It is possible to argue that the growth of the state has slowed. So, indeed, it has. But it could hardly have done otherwise. By 1980, average public spending was 41.9 per cent of GDP. In Sweden, it was 60 per cent. If the same proportionate rise in the share of spending in GDP had occurred between 1980 and 1996 as between 1960 and 1980, the whole OECD region would now look like Sweden and Sweden's public spending would exceed GDP.[7] By 1980, further growth at the rate seen in previous decades was impossible. That may have been a shock to many politicians, but it was an inescapable one.

These are, to put it at its mildest, a very long way from being 'nightwatchmen' or minimum states. Not only is government spending enormous, but a decidedly modest proportion goes on defence, justice, infrastructure and the other classic functions of the liberal state. According to an important book on the long-run growth in the role of government in high-income countries, by Vito Tanzi (then at the International Monetary Fund) and Ludger Schuknecht (of the staff of the European Central Bank), by 1995 government spending on subsidies and transfers varied between 13.1 per cent of GDP in the US and 35.9 per cent in the Netherlands.[8] In the high-spending countries, subsidies and transfers made up more than half of total spending. For example, Sweden's spending on transfers and subsidies, education and health exceeded 50 per cent of GDP and made up close to 80 per cent of total government spending. While extreme in its generosity, Sweden's pattern of spending is representative of the northern continental European welfare states.

Again, as the Belgian economist Paul de Grauwe has observed, between 1980 and 1995 social spending continued to rise in virtually all the significant high-income countries, globalization notwithstanding.[9] The data from Tanzi and Schuknecht strongly support this. Between 1980 and 1995, the share of public spending on subsidies and transfers in GDP rose, on average, from 21.4 per cent to 23.2 per cent of GDP in a group of seventeen high-income countries. The share stayed the same or, much more frequently, rose in every country, except Belgium (a modest fall from 30.0 per cent to 28.8 per cent of GDP), Ireland (a fall from 26.9 to 24.8 per cent), the Netherlands (from an almost unbelievable 38.5 to 35.9 per cent) and New Zealand (from 20.8 to 12.9 per cent). What has happened to taxation has also happened to regulation. As Legrain puts it: 'Environmental laws are generally much tougher than they were twenty years ago: petrol taxes are higher, cars are required to emit less pollution, companies have had to reduce their emissions of noxious chemicals into the air and water: many now have to recycle a lot of their waste too.'[10] Clive Crook of *The Economist* has argued, with excellent reasons, that 'big government, far from being dead, has flourished mightily'.[11]

Return now to that growth in government spending. Since fiscal deficits have not been exploding (but have rather grown smaller), taxes must have been rising as well.[12] So indeed they have. Table 12.2 shows the ratio of tax revenue to GDP for 1965, 1980, 1990 and 2000. It will be seen that over the period 1960 to 2000 the share of tax revenue in GDP has risen in every one of the countries listed. But the size of the increase has varied from 4.9 per cent of GDP in the US to 19.2 per cent in Sweden. None of these countries had a lower share of tax revenue in GDP in 2000 than in 1980, and only one

Table 12.2 General government tax revenue (as share of GDP, per cent)

Country	1965	1980	1990	2000	Increase 1965–2000
US	24.7	27.0	26.7	29.6	4.9
Japan	18.3	25.1	30.1	27.1	8.8
Germany*	31.6	37.5	35.7	37.9	6.3
France	34.5	40.6	43.0	45.3	10.8
Italy	25.5	30.4	38.9	42.0	16.5
UK	30.1	35.2	36.8	37.4	7.0
Canada	25.6	30.7	35.9	35.8	10.2
Denmark	29.9	43.9	47.1	48.8	18.9
Sweden	35.0	47.5	53.6	54.2	19.2
Australia	21.9	27.4	29.3	31.5	9.6
EU 15 (unweighted average)	27.9	36.0	39.5	41.6	13.7
Unweighted average of OECD countries	25.8	32.1	35.1	37.4	11.6

Source: OECD, Revenue Statistics 1965–2001 (Paris: Organization for Economic Co-operation and Development, 2002).

* United Germany from 1991.

(Canada) had a lower share in 2000 than in 1990, but that decline was a mere 0.1 per cent of GDP. The broad picture is of continuous increases in the overall incidence of taxation.

One might expect, however, that the taxation of relatively mobile capital and personal income would have fallen. This, too, seems to be untrue. Taxation of corporate income, as a share of GDP, is shown in Table 12.3. Over the OECD area as a whole, it rose from 2.2 per cent of GDP in 1965 to 2.4 per cent in 1980, 2.7 per cent in 1990 and 3.6 per cent in 2000.[13] In most of the countries listed in the tables, the ratio of corporate tax revenue to GDP rose substantially, Australia, the UK, Sweden, France and Germany being significant examples. In the European Union, as a whole, the ratio rose from an unweighted average of 1.9 per cent of GDP in 1965 to one of 3.8 per cent in 2000.

Many who argue that international economic integration has undermined the ability to tax capital point to the lowering of corporate tax rates. But the combination of lower marginal tax rates with higher average rates, as a result of reduced allowances and exemptions, is both efficient and desirable. Finally, the most important feature of the table is, again, the variety. In 2000, the share of corporation tax in GDP varied from 1.8 per cent of GDP in Germany, which appeared to have an exceptionally inefficient corporation tax regime, to 6.5 per cent in Australia.

Table 12.3 Tax on corporate income (as share of GDP, per cent)

Country	1965	1980	1990	2000	Increase 1965–2000
US	4.0	2.9	2.1	2.5	−1.5
Japan	4.1	5.5	6.5	3.6	−0.6
Germany*	2.5	2.0	1.7	1.8	−0.7
France	1.8	2.1	2.3	3.2	1.4
Italy	1.8	2.4	3.9	3.2	1.4
UK	1.3	2.9	4.1	3.7	2.4
Canada	3.8	3.6	2.5	4.0	0.2
Denmark	1.4	1.4	1.5	2.4	1.0
Sweden	2.1	1.2	1.7	4.1	2.0
Australia	3.6	3.3	4.1	6.5	2.9
EU 15 (unweighted average)	1.9	2.1	2.6	3.8	1.9
Unweighted average of OECD countries	2.2	2.4	2.7	3.6	1.4

Source: OECD, Revenue Statistics 1965–2001.

* United Germany from 1991.

Tax on personal income is also revealing. Most of this is paid by relatively high earners who are, one would assume, the most mobile part of a high-income country's labour force. These are also the people in whom is invested the country's human capital. Thus a decline in the ability to tax income might indicate that personal mobility had become a significant constraint on countries' ability to raise taxes. Again, the statistics from the Organization for Economic Co-operation and Development do not support this proposition. The simple average of the taxation of personal income in the European Union of fifteen members rose from 7.2 per cent of GDP in 1965 to 10.9 per cent in 2000 (see Table 12.4). In the OECD, as a whole, the average rose from 7.0 per cent of GDP in 1965 to 10.5 per cent in 1980 and 10.7 per cent in 1990 before falling slightly, to 10.0 per cent, in 2000. It rose quite sharply in the US. The rise in Canada was even more striking. But the biggest increase was Denmark's, from 12.4 per cent of GDP in 1965, to 25.7 per cent in 2000. In 2000, the ratio of income tax to GDP varied from 5.6 per cent in Japan to 25.7 per cent in Denmark. These variations are explained by differences in the structure of tax revenue, which varies a great deal across countries, as well as by differences in the tax revenue required to finance public spending.[14]

The conclusion is straightforward. There is no sign of an inability to sustain tax revenue among the high-income countries. This is true even though average tax rates are twice as high in some countries as they are in others. But this raises

Table 12.4 Tax on personal income (as share of GDP, per cent)

Country	1965	1980	1990	2000	Increase 1965–2000
US	7.8	10.5	10.1	12.6	4.8
Japan	4.0	6.1	8.1	5.6	1.6
Germany*	8.2	11.1	9.8	9.6	1.4
France	3.7	4.7	5.1	8.2	4.5
Italy	2.8	7.0	10.2	10.8	8.0
UK	10.1	10.3	10.0	10.9	0.8
Canada	5.8	10.5	14.7	13.2	7.4
Denmark	12.4	22.9	24.8	25.7	13.3
Sweden	17.1	19.5	20.6	19.3	2.2
Australia	7.5	12.0	12.6	11.6	4.1
EU 15 (unweighted average)	7.2	11.1	11.1	10.9	3.7
Unweighted average of OECD countries	7.0	10.5	10.7	10.0	3.0

Source: OECD, Revenue Statistics 1965–2001.

* United Germany from 1991.

another question. Are there any signs that the higher-tax countries are, in some sense, uncompetitive? In his paper, de Grauwe takes as his indicator of competitiveness the rankings from the yearly *World Competitiveness Report*, published by the International Institute for Management Development (IMD) in Lausanne, and relates these to ratios of social security spending in GDP. He finds a modest positive correlation: the higher the social security spending, the more competitive the country. It is not difficult to understand why this positive correlation might exist: a generous social security system increases people's sense of security and so may make them more willing to embrace change.

The objection to de Grauwe's procedure is that the IMD indices are arbitrary. Can we obtain some more direct indicators of competitiveness? The answer is yes. If there is anything to the notion of competitiveness to which Gray and others who think like him appeal, they must mean something different from overall economic performance, by which we mean growth, productivity, employment and so forth. Poor economic performance can, after all, happen to closed economies just as easily as to open ones (more easily, as a matter of fact). The notion that a dire fate is now, and only now, in this age of globalization coming to the social democratic states of western Europe must follow from international economic integration: low protection against imports and high mobility of capital and people. A sign of the feared lack of competitiveness (caused by excessive taxation and regulation) might be weak trade performance or might, still more, be an outflow of capital and skilled people, which would amount to the disappearance of the tax base. So one question is whether the highly taxed and regulated European economies suffer from these ailments. The answer is no.

Let us start with trade. It turns out that, in 2002, the US ran a trade deficit of $480 billion and the UK one of $52 billion. But all the highly taxed EU economies – France, Germany, Italy, Austria, Belgium, Denmark, Finland, the Netherlands and Sweden – ran trade surpluses. The eurozone as a whole ran trade surpluses in every single year between 1992 and 2002. Another possible way of looking at trade performance is in terms of the export performance relative to a country's markets. If we look at the performance of a number of significant EU member states between 1993 and 2002, we find that the exports of goods from highly taxed Austria, Belgium, the Netherlands, Finland and Sweden all grew faster than their markets.[15] Japan (a very low-tax country) performed very badly indeed, with export volumes falling at a compound annual rate of 5.6 per cent a year, relative to its markets. The US also performed poorly, with export volumes falling at 1.4 per cent a year, relative to its markets. The US did worse not just than the list of high-tax small countries, but also than France (whose relative export volumes fell at 0.2 per cent a year), Germany (with declines of 1.1 per cent a year) and Italy (with declines of 1.0 per cent a year). If we look at shares in world exports, we find that between 1992 and 2002 France's fell from 6.4 per cent to 5.0 per cent and Germany's from 11.9 per cent to 9.9 per cent. Meanwhile, the US share fell from 11.7 per cent to 10.6 per cent and Japan's from 9.5 per cent to 6.6 per cent. There is no sign of an exceptional deterioration in the trade performance of the highly taxed and regulated continental European economies. That these countries' export shares have been falling is not surprising. They are unavoidably slow-growing, after all, since they have close to stagnant populations. Even if their productivity growth were as fast as that of the US, they would grow more slowly, just for this reason.

A slightly less economically illiterate way of assessing 'competitiveness' is in terms of flows of capital and labour. A highly taxed 'uncompetitive' economy might find itself bleeding capital, for example, particularly corporate capital. This might be shown by the inverse of one of the trade tests discussed above: the current account. A net capital exporter – that is, a country which is exporting some of its capital stock abroad – must have a current account surplus (which is, by definition, equal to the capital account deficit – the net outflow of capital in a given period). If we look at the eurozone as a whole, we do find it ran a small surplus of 0.2 per cent of GDP in 2001. Over the entire 1993–2002 period the average current account surplus of the eurozone was a mere 0.7 per cent of GDP. If we look at a cross-section of high-tax countries in 2001, we find that Finland ran a current account surplus of 7.1 per cent of GDP, Belgium one of 4.0 per cent of GDP and Sweden one of 3.9 per cent of GDP. But the big continental countries had small current account deficits: France one of 1.6 per cent of GDP, Germany one of 0.2 per cent of GDP and Italy none at all. One of the best ways to put the net capital outflow in proportion is to relate it to gross national savings. What we are asking then is what proportion of the savings in a given country was exported (net) abroad in a given year. In 2001, Finland exported 25.4 per cent of its gross national savings in this way, Sweden exported 17.5 per cent, Belgium exported 16.1 per cent and Denmark exported 13.2 per cent. In France the figure was just 7.5 per cent, in Germany 1.0 per cent and in Italy zero.

To put these figures into some sort of perspective, we must remember that the national savings rates of these highly taxed continental European countries are higher than in the US or UK. In 2001, for example, the gross national savings rate of the US was just 16.1 per cent of GDP, while it was only 15.4 per cent in the UK. These countries needed to import capital. Among the big continental countries, France's gross national savings rate was 21.4 per cent of GDP, Germany's 19.8 per cent and Italy's 20 per cent. Thus the highly taxed continental countries are, by comparison with the Anglo-Saxon countries, naturally capital surplus. Because they save more, they are in a position to help satisfy the capital-craving of the US and UK. But, even after their export of capital, they invested domestically as much as, or more than, the US, as a share of GDP. There is, in other words, no sign of de-capitalization or capital flight from highly taxed continental European countries. If anything, the opposite is the case. Since the highly taxed continental European countries have slower growth of population than the US, their domestic availability of physical capital is not falling, relative to the US, but rising.

This examination of the capital outflow is, however, at an aggregate level. Uncompetitiveness might show, in the form of large net outflows of foreign direct investment. The UNCTAD *World Investment Report* allows us to analyse this possibility. Yet again, the positions vary substantially across these countries. Belgium and Austria had surpluses in the stock of inward investment over outward investment in 2000 (of 19.9 per cent, 2.9 per cent and 0.2 per cent of GDP respectively). They were, in other words, net recipients. Finland, the Netherlands, Sweden and France were in the opposite position: they had net stocks abroad (of 23 per cent, 17.9 per cent, 17.7 per cent and 13.5 per cent of GDP respectively). Denmark was almost perfectly in balance. So were Germany and Italy (with net stocks abroad of 1.1 per cent and 6.3 per cent of GDP respectively). None of these countries had a net stock abroad as big as the UK's 32.7 per cent, however. What seems to be happening is that small countries with large transnational companies hold large net stocks of capital abroad. This explains the positions of Finland, the Netherlands and Sweden. Apart from this, what is striking is the variety of national positions. There is no sign that highly taxed countries, in general, suffer from a huge, unrequited outflow of corporate capital. While the big continental countries are in reasonable balance, it is the UK that has the largest net stock abroad.

The conclusion is that lack of competitiveness is nowhere to be found in these highly taxed countries. Particularly important is the finding that they are not suffering a haemorrhage of capital or of skilled people. Being rich and stable, with superb social services, they are net importers of people. While immigrants are, on balance, less skilled than the local population, their number includes a sizeable proportion of highly educated people. While skilled continentals do emigrate, temporarily or even permanently, to gain education or to work in the UK and US, the net outflow of such people is small in relation to the (constantly growing) supply.

Abiding relevance of comparative advantage

How is this possible? How can some countries have much higher tax and regulatory burdens than others and yet show none of the signs of a lack of international competitiveness? Are we not told by Professor Gray that 'American free markets work to undercut both European and Asian social market economies. Both are threatened by the American model because each business bears social obligations that in the United States it has shed'? Again, he insists, 'tax competition among advanced states works to drain public finances and make a welfare state unaffordable'. Yet again, 'the effect of competition from countries in which a regime of deregulation, low taxes and a shrinking welfare state has been imposed is to force downwards harmonization of policies on states which retain social market economies'. And then again, 'capital will migrate to the countries in which goods can be made for the world's consumers in rich countries at lowest labour costs'.[16]

Since OECD countries are, in aggregate, large net importers of capital, not exporters (because the importers, principally the US, import far more than the others export), one might conclude that Gray does not know what he is talking about. One would be right to do so. He does not. But to understand why he is wrong, one must move from the damning facts, laid out above, to the underlying theory.[17] Gray is convinced that the theory of comparative advantage cannot apply when capital is, to any significant extent, mobile. He is wrong. But it is important to spell out precisely why he is wrong and whether he could, under any circumstances, be right. In other words, we must define, as precisely as possible, what competition among countries does, and does not, mean in a world in which financial (or physical) capital is mobile. In so doing, we will be able to understand why it is perfectly possible for countries to have, as we have shown, high taxes and regulatory standards, but no loss of international competitiveness. In so doing, we will take the analysis of comparative advantage further than was possible in the brief discussion in Part II above.

That Gray does not understand the theory of comparative advantage is shown elsewhere in his book where he writes of Britain's ending of free trade in the 1930s that 'it was abandoned only when the loss of Britain's comparative advantage in international trade became intolerable'.[18] This is nonsense. A country cannot lose its comparative advantage. Its comparative advantage can change. It is even possible that this change is, in some relevant sense, undesirable. But a country has to have a comparative advantage in something.

If, under self-sufficiency, the relative prices of different goods and services (and so, under competition, their marginal costs) differ from their relative prices in world trade, the country will gain from trade. It will do so by expanding the production of goods that are more expensive in world trade (and so more rewarding) than at home, while allowing shrinkage of those that are less expensive. Moreover, this logic would apply even if a given factor of production (such as capital) were perfectly mobile, provided the distribution of some other factors of production (natural resources, social and human capital or knowledge) varied across countries and so generated sources of comparative advantage. For reasons that have been a principal theme of this book – and are taken for granted by the people who would happily throw the idea of comparative advantage onto the intellectual scrapheap – these differences among countries today are bigger than they have ever been in history, assisted by the wealth of some countries and the poverty of others. Far from being less relevant than before, comparative advantage has never been more relevant.

Differences in natural resources are evident enough. But much the most significant differences are in what is also the most important source of wealth and poverty: the historically engendered stock of behaviour, values and explicit and implicit knowledge embodied in a population – a country's social and human capital, in other words. To the extent that the reward to labour exceeds that available to unskilled workers in poor countries, it can only be because rich-country workers have more capital at their disposal. A huge proportion of this capital is embodied within them. It is who they are. One can go much further than this. The contributions of physical and human capital cannot be separately identified, since even the ability to make profitable use of physical capital is embodied in populations. That is why, after the Second World War, West Germany's economy was able to rebound so dramatically (in the right market-oriented policy environment). Profitable physical investment is driven by the know-how embodied in a country's people. If the population of Iran were, overnight, to replace Germany's, how long would one expect it to remain among the richest countries in the world? Some poor countries possess within them a stock of values, behaviours and institutions that are better adapted to running a modern economy than others. It is not surprising to find that China, until just a few centuries ago the world's most advanced economy, is among them, as was Japan in an earlier generation.[19] In the right policy environment, such countries are likely to grow rapidly and accumulate physical and human capital more quickly than others. Even so, development does not make jumps. Among the processes that take most time is creating a population adapted to – and adept at – running a sophisticated, high-technology economy.

Not only is development – or its absence – embodied in populations, but fine-grained differences among them will determine patterns of relative excellence. The differences in the economic structures of Germany and the UK, for example, both prosperous high-income countries, reflect these countries' histories and contemporary cultures. They also determine the two countries' patterns of comparative advantage. These are not superficially rooted, but embedded in long-term historical processes. However, trade allows the rest of the world to exploit German engineering or the British ability to provide a global financial centre.

(Im)mobility of resources

Human populations are, in normal circumstances, geographically fixed. But not only is the human population anchored; so, notwithstanding all the hyperbole about globalization, is the vast bulk of its capital. By and large, people will invest their savings where they believe they will be safest. People who live in stable, prosperous countries believe their investments are safest at home. (Latin American rich people, in contrast, seem to believe everywhere is safer than home.) Their next favourite destination is other rich countries, with similar behaviour, values and institutions to their own. Then they are prepared to put money in those relatively poor countries that offer the most attractive relationship between risk and reward. Since virtually all developing countries are (rightly) seen as relatively risky places for foreigners to put their money and since only a few have the ability to compensate for that riskiness with credible offers of exceptional reward, the quantity of capital that flows to developing countries is, as I have already pointed out, quite small. One of the principal reasons for this unfavourable relationship between risk and reward is, yet again, the characteristics of the populations in the countries concerned – their education, values, behaviour and so forth. In fact, if we look at developing countries that have succeeded in accumulating physical capital quickly, we find that this has always been overwhelmingly internally generated. Today, for example, China is investing close to 40 per cent of GDP. All of this is being financed domestically. The inflow of foreign direct investment matters rather as a way of accelerating the transfer of know-how and so speeding up the pace of development.

Even the mobility of corporations is exaggerated. There are few, if any, true transnational corporations. They are anchored, instead, in one, or at most a few, specific countries. While these companies are exceptionally well placed to manage the risks of global investment and intra-company trade, they cannot easily divorce themselves from their homes. Most corporations obtain location-specific benefits that are of importance to them. This is obviously true of land-intensive activities (such as mining). However, it is also true of activities that take advantage of human skill, or cultural assets: German or Swiss engineering is an obvious example. While corporations may diversify the location of their activities, at the margin, they are normally unwilling to abandon their homes altogether.

Let us take this analysis of resource immobility a little further. Imagine a world in which there were no legal restrictions on mobility of people or capital. But imagine also that there are many goods, including public goods, *that one can only consume where one lives.* This is the world of local governments. In a classic article, Charles Tiebout argued that governments would compete by providing location-specific public goods.[20] Owners of mobile factors of production would move to the jurisdiction that gives them the combination of taxes and services they prefer. There is no reason to suppose that this location would be the one with the lowest taxes. Even capital, the most mobile of all factors of production, will flee from a jurisdiction so under-taxed that it fails to provide decent and reliable justice. Capital will also be attracted by a jurisdiction with a highly educated labour force or any other complementary asset which raises its prospective return. Self-evidently, the attraction of location-specific public goods will be still greater for workers, who will want to live in places that are safe, have pleasant amenities, offer good public services and enjoy high overall incomes. The question is not where the tax is lowest, but rather where the welfare derived from the bundle of local amenities, income-earning opportunities and taxes is the highest. After all, tax revenue does not go up in smoke. It is spent on things. Parents in high-income countries mostly wish their children to share in their own culture, something that can be fully achieved only if they grow up at home. Moreover, because culture, education and tastes vary profoundly, what might seem shockingly expensive to, say, an American will seem quite appropriate to a Dane, a Swede or a Frenchman. In all, if one takes all the determinants of a prosperous, pleasant and diverting existence, it is not at all obvious why many of the latter should prefer the US.

This local government model can be extended in another direction: towards the economics of geography. Assume that economic development generates location-specific beneficial spillovers. As a region develops, infrastructure and skills accumulate that are of benefit in other contexts. Silicon Valley has been a good example of a region that has gained from such location-specific spillovers. As development proceeds, a region will build the foundations for its next successes. And, because these foundations are location-specific, they can, within reason, be taxed. The high-income countries of today are the beneficiaries of such a positive feedback process over up to two centuries.

What, then, am I saying? The answer is that the bulk of the resources that make the difference between wealth and poverty are immobile. This is not just because there are legal restrictions on the mobility of people, but because the people of high-income countries do not, for the most part, want to move even if taxes at home are higher, because they are satisfied with the bundle of amenities they are able to consume. Because resources, particularly people, are immobile, patterns of comparative advantage, which are, in the contemporary world, dictated by differences in relative supplies of human and social capital, are also deeply rooted. Moreover, because the most significant income-earning resources are quite immobile, taxes can vary dramatically, as they do. Moreover, the incidence of taxation depends on how mobile particular activities or factors of production are. It is easiest therefore to tax immobile land and labour and less easy to tax mobile labour and capital. Corporate capital falls in between.

On the (ir)relevance of competitiveness

Armed with this analysis, we can begin to understand why Gray's warnings about the uncompetitiveness of a highly taxed and regulated economy are nonsense. He assumes, as all such pundits do, that real wages (and the costs of other relatively immobile factors of production) are given from outside. That is what businessmen assume, quite naturally, because it is true for them. A businessman must obtain capital, labour – indeed everything – in competitive markets. If he does not provide these resources with the return given by the market as a whole, his business will disappear. But the vast bulk of Swedes are not in the same labour market as Americans. They are in a national labour market. If taxes rise, real disposable incomes, after tax, will fall in the market as a whole. The high social security charges in Germany, France or Italy will not make these economies uncompetitive. They will instead reduce the disposable incomes, after tax, of German, French or Italian workers. Of course, the total welfare of Germans, Frenchmen and Italians need not fall, provided they value what the state provides. Gray has committed an elementary howler: he is applying what economists would call 'partial equilibrium' reasoning to a 'general equilibrium' question.

Exactly the same logic applies to environmental regulations. Gray writes: 'consider environmental costs. If, in one country, environmental costs are "internalised" by a tax regime that forces them to be reflected in the costs of enterprises, but those enterprises are forced to compete in a global market with enterprises in other countries that do not carry such environmental costs, *the countries* that require businesses to be environmentally accountable will be at a systematic disadvantage [my emphasis].' This, too, is nonsense. Imagine that all companies in a given country have to pay a tax on polluting activities. If one assumes, only for simplicity, that the return to capital is given internationally and the prices of all outputs are given in world markets, then these companies will need to pay lower wages, with the biggest proportionate reductions in the most polluting industries. But remember that wages for people of a given skill must be roughly the same across the economy. So, as the economy adjusts to the new taxes, three things will happen: overall real wages in that particular economy will fall, compensated by the pleasure of a better environment, industry will move to less polluting technologies and the output of pollution-intensive industries will shrink, as such output goes partly abroad. In practice, however, for reasons already discussed, the latter effect seems to be very small. Above all, none of this has anything to do with the competitiveness of countries. On the contrary, the tax (or regulation) will achieve exactly what it is intended to do. It will reduce pollution, partly by changing the industry mix and partly by changing technologies, thereby increasing the welfare of the population. As an offset to this increase in welfare, real wages will fall in terms of goods and services (other than pollution).

The question, then, is whether the notion of competitiveness of countries, under globalization, has any relevance. The answer is that it does, but in very different ways from those popularly supposed. Two legitimate meanings can be identified: changes in the terms of trade – the relation between the prices of exports and imports (already discussed briefly in Chapter 10); and overall economic performance. Neither is what those worried about competitiveness mean.

To understand the way the terms of trade affect a country's welfare is simple enough. Assume that people export in order to import. There is, as Adam Smith pointed out long ago, no other good reason for doing so. Exports, in other words, are the cost of acquiring imports. The terms of trade indicate the exports needed to acquire a given quantity of imports. The more favourable the prices, the smaller the volume of exports needed to obtain a given quantity of imports. Thus an improvement in the terms of trade means a country is becoming more competitive – its exports are becoming more valuable, in other words. A deterioration in the terms of trade means it is becoming less competitive – it has to work harder to obtain a given quantity of imports. The paradox of the popular debate is that improvements in competitiveness, thus defined, are generally seen as a deterioration instead. The availability of cheaper imports, which improves the terms of trade, is seen as a *reduction* in competitiveness. The reason for this is that, as usual, people are confusing the fate of the particular import-competing sectors with that of the economy as a whole. The true danger is not this, but is that a new competitor emerges in a country's export markets (or pushes up the prices of its imports). That does make a country worse off, or less competitive, if one wishes to use this language.

Two examples will illuminate these possibilities. Conceive of the high-income countries as just one country, the North. The North imports labour-intensive manufactures from a composite of developing countries, the South, and exports capital-intensive goods in return. Both the North and the South have balanced trade. That is to say, they spend what they earn (which is the same thing as buying that they export in order to import). This assumption of balanced trade is important. Many of those who think of the North as becoming uncompetitive, without limit, as low-wage countries start to export seem to imagine that the latter will be willing to export without spending the income they earn on something else that they want (more than the products they export). It should be evident that this is absurd.

Now imagine that, in line with our discussion above of comparative advantage, China enters as a new and still cheaper exporter of labour-intensive manufactures than the old South. Assume that China, too, spends what it earns. What happens then? The relative prices of labour-intensive manufactures fall in world trade. This represents an improvement in the terms of trade for the North and a worsening of the terms of trade for the South. The North becomes unambiguously richer, while the South becomes, on these assumptions, equally unambiguously poorer. But this improvement in its terms of trade also shifts the internal distribution of incomes in the North away from unskilled labour and towards owners of capital (physical and human). The rise in the aggregate real incomes of the North and the worsening of the relative incomes of unskilled labour are two sides of the same coin.[21]

Under these assumptions, the competitiveness of the North improves: it is able to obtain more for less. This has been the experience of high-income countries. Of the group of seven leading high-income countries, all but Canada and Germany enjoyed terms-of-trade improvements in the 1990s. According to the World Bank, Japan's terms of trade improved by 40 per cent (which is, presumably, why its volume performance was so poor). Now imagine a different world, one in which the South exports primary commodities and the North undifferentiated manufactures. Suppose China enters world markets as a competitor for Northern manufactures in the markets of the South. Under these circumstances, the terms of the trade of the North worsen. It becomes worse off. But protecting its own markets would be no help. The challenge it faces is China's ability to sell manufacture to the South on more favourable terms than had been previously available from the North. China is now a genuine competitor of the North on world markets. The question, however, is how big the North's losses might be. As I have indicated in Chapter 10, they are likely to be very modest. Thus, while this sense of competitiveness of countries has meaning, its practical significance is small.

As I mentioned above, many of those who think of competitiveness mean overall performance. They are referring to productivity, employment and overall growth. These are perfectly legitimate objectives of policy. There is no question that the level of taxation and regulations, as well as the quality of public services, have an impact on economic performance. But this impact does not come via anything that can be called competitiveness. Policies matter to the extent that they adversely affect performance. The notion of competitiveness is irrelevant.

Fiscal termites

I have argued that there is no evidence, so far, of any collapse in the ability of highly taxed countries to proceed with business as usual. This is so for much the same reason that comparative advantage remains powerful: resources, above all human beings, are much less mobile than many suppose. Moreover, because the idea of a country as a pool of largely immobile resources (including its people) remains relevant, the notion of the competitiveness of countries, on the model of the competitiveness of companies, is nonsense.

Some professional analysts argue, however, that the ability to raise taxes will erode in future. Tanzi, for example, notes that 'in most countries in recent years, the tax level has stopped growing'.[22] But that is more because of electoral resistance than because of any insuperable difficulty in collecting taxes. Tanzi believes this is about to change. Indeed, he provides a list of 'fiscal termites' gnawing at the foundations of fiscal regimes. These insects include: more cross-border shopping; increased mobility of skilled labour; growth of electronic commerce; the expansion of tax havens; the development of new financial instruments and intermediaries; growing trade within multinational companies; and the possible replacement of bank accounts with electronic money embedded in smart cards. In effect, he argues that there will be not just greater mobility than at present, but also less traceability of transactions.

The list is impressive. That governments take it seriously is demonstrated by the attention being devoted, within the OECD and the European Union, to 'harmful tax competition', exchange of information and the implications of electronic commerce.[23] In other words, governments are, like any other industry, forming a cartel to halt what they see as 'ruinous competition over taxation'. Yet the threat governments face must not be exaggerated. To appreciate this, it is helpful to analyse fiscal developments under three heads: developments in factor mobility; collection of information on income and spending; and the impact of the Internet on both mobility and collection of information.

Enhanced mobility of capital flows and spending is a result of globalization. Greater difficulty in obtaining information about their citizens is another. As the impact of mobility works through, jurisdictions may find it increasingly difficult to know what their residents own. Yet, again, it is vital not to exaggerate the difficulties. People are inherently physical. Most of what they consume is also physical. It is, in consequence, difficult to disguise their location or their consumption and, in consequence, the income that finances it.

Again, let us consider taxation of spending. Where there are no border controls, tax rates on spending will tend to converge for items in which transport costs are a relatively small part of the cost. Transport costs may be low, either because distances are short or items are valuable in relation to their costs. Nobody would travel from London to France to buy one packet of cigarettes, for example, but they will find it profitable to do so for thousands. However, where there continue to be controls at the border, this problem will be less significant.

A paper by Stéphane Buydens of the OECD argues, plausibly, that the impact of the Internet will be felt in four main areas: taxes on spending; tax treaties; internal pricing of multinational companies; and tax administration.[24] Pure Internet transactions – betting, downloading of films or music – may be hard to tax, though the means of payment should be traceable. But where the Internet is used to buy goods, this should be less of a problem. It will then be necessary for the fiscal authorities to obtain the co-operation of suppliers. If these are large public companies, that may not be hard. Such companies have to co-operate with the authorities of the jurisdictions in which they raise capital and employ people. The Internet also creates a problem in identifying the location of a server. If one cannot do so, how is tax to be levied and tax treaties applied? But none of this should be exaggerated. A persuasive analysis by Turner for the UK suggest that at most 1 per cent of overall government revenue (about 0.4 per cent of GDP) might be affected.[25] Problems may also arise with taxing multinational companies, since it is becoming more difficult to locate their activities. But ways can always be found: through taxation of a portion of world-wide income, for example.

What are the conclusions for the future of taxation? The first is that the combination of economic liberalization with advances in technology poses some challenges. Taxes on spending may have to be recast and taxation of corporate profits redesigned. Second, the ability of governments to impose taxes that bear no relation to the benefits provided to the payers may be more constrained than hitherto. But people will still be willing to pay for desired, location-specific amenities. Third, the implications of all these changes is often exaggerated. Taxation of corporate income is, for example, rarely more than 10 per cent of fiscal revenue. Taxes on labour income and spending are the universal pillars of the fiscal system. Yet even lofty Scandinavian taxes are not forcing skilled people to leave in droves. Finally, governments will use exchange of information and other forms of co-operation to sustain revenue, if necessary, and may even consider international agreements on minimum taxes. They will certainly force the publicly quoted companies that continue to dominate transactions in the world economy, both online and offline, to co-operate with fiscal authorities. If tax authorities are able and willing to collect and share information on transactions within their area of jurisdiction, worries about the consequences of open borders for evasion would be diminished. But competition among governments will not be eliminated.

One further controversy on taxation is worth considering: what is known as 'harmful tax competition'. Within the European Union, attention is being paid, in this context, to taxation of corporate and portfolio capital. The issue has also been discussed at some length within the OECD.[26] The focus here is, quite rightly, not on the broad structure of taxation policy, but on specific discriminatory or distorting practices. The view taken is that 'location decisions should be driven by economic considerations and not primarily by tax factors'. The principle seems sensible, but the borderline between economic and tax considerations is not clear cut. It is relatively clear what is happening if the tax rate on foreign capital is below that on domestic capital in a particular jurisdiction. However, if a country chooses to provide a lower level of amenities and taxes, this is an economic choice that has fiscal consequences.

The right overall conclusion is that cross-border tax competition has some effect on the structure of taxation. The broad effect of mobility is to increase the tendency towards erosion of the tax base, through evasion and avoidance, which arises whenever marginal tax rates are penal. Indeed, this is a general proposition: internationalization of an economy augments the impact of policies, but does not change the nature of that impact. Minimum wages normally reduce employment. Where a country is open to imports of labour-intensive products, the reduction will be bigger. High marginal taxes lead to reduced supply of the taxed factors and goods. But when an economy is open to the world, this reduction is likely to be faster and the costs to government correspondingly more visible. This has been one reason for the reduction in high marginal rates of income taxation throughout the world over the past two decades. However, there were sound domestic incentive reasons for this change, in any case. The bottom line is that the opening of economies and the new technologies are reinforcing constraints that have already developed within domestic economies and politics.

Governments of countries are becoming just a little more like local governments. The result will not be minimal government. But, like every other institution, governments will be forced, by greater openness, to provide value for money to those who pay for their services. They will have to relate the taxes they charge a little bit more closely to the amenities they provide. This is bad news only for predatory states, or the interests that want them to be predatory.

Income redistribution

It follows from the above discussion that use of the fiscal system for income redistribution is constrained by international economic integration, but only to a modest degree. It is possible for governments to continue to redistribute income to the extent that those responsible for the more highly taxed activities or factors of production cannot – or do not wish to – evade or avoid that taxation. They may, in fact, be quite willing to pay the taxes, because they regard income redistribution as a location specific benefit. That may be because they identify with the beneficiaries, or fear that they could themselves become beneficiaries, or treasure the greater personal security that comes from living among people who are not in a desperate plight. Alternatively, they may merely be unable to evade or avoid those taxes without relocating physically outside the jurisdiction, which they are loath to do. For all these reasons, as experience of the northern European welfare states shows, it is possible to sustain a high measure of redistributive taxation and, in particular, of social insurance. Indeed, Professor Dani Rodrik has argued that small open economies have higher ratios of public spending in GDP, to insure citizens against the risks inherent in exposure to the international economy.[27] In big countries, by contrast, the diversification of the economy itself tends to provide a form of implicit insurance. What is certain, in any case, is that income redistribution is possible, provided the case is made and then accepted by the electorate.

While it is perfectly possible to operate redistributive policies and particularly social insurance in an open economy, this fact may not be enough to convince all groups that such openness is in their interests. If, in particular, capital and mobile labour have the option of 'exit', in addition to 'voice', and if opening to trade adversely affects the income-earning possibilities of unskilled labour – as many argue is true within high-income countries – then these workers may find themselves worse off as a result of opening. This possibility exists, but the evidence does not provide much support for it.

Regulation

As mentioned above, the principles that apply to taxation apply also to regulation. Some regulations are deemed to be in the interests of the regulated. Being monitored by the Securities and Exchange Commission of the US, for example, is a signal of quality. Other regulations ensure the provision of location-specific goods: clean-air standards are a good example of this. In neither case should the opening of an economy undermine the regulation. If people want to live where the air is clean, they will choose jurisdictions that ensure this, even if the price is regulation. More broadly, regulations should be seen as a tax and, like any tax, mobile factors of production will be better able to avoid paying it. If, for example, an environmental standard were imposed on an activity that could be relocated somewhere else, the cost will be shifted on to an immobile factor of production – workers, for example. Alternatively, the activity will relocate. Either outcome would be politically unpopular. But this does not mean that the consequences are undesirable. In particular, if the aim is to reduce a locally polluting activity, this reduction will be still quicker if it is relocated altogether.

Deficit financing

Professor Gray also argues, as do many others, that globalization has ended not just the ability to tax and regulate, but also the ability of governments to pursue full employment through fiscal mechanisms. 'During the 1980s,' he writes,

> the largest sovereign nation state, the United States, was able to deploy Keynesian-style expansionist policies when it engaged in a large arms build up; but it is doubtful if anything similar could be attempted by the United States in present circumstances. President Clinton's experience early in his first administration, when bond markets inflicted high interest rates as a deterrent against potential fiscal laxity, taught him that even the world's

'borrower of last resort' is vulnerable to the judgement of the global market in government bonds.[28]

This also is almost total nonsense. Even the prediction has turned out to be wrong. Between 2000 and 2003, according to the OECD, the US fiscal position will have swung by 6 per cent of GDP, from a surplus of 1.4 per cent to a deficit of 4.6 per cent. This is the biggest US fiscal boost in peacetime. It came at a time when the US is heavily dependent on borrowing from abroad. But it has so far not brought much of a peep from the bond market. If it were sustained, however, it would bring much more than a peep and for very good reasons. Such deficits cannot be continued in the long run. They spell inflation.

It is doubly wrong, in fact, to argue that globalization has put an end to the ability of benign and well-intentioned governments to manage demand through monetary and fiscal means. First, governments are far from benign. Most of the governments of the high-income countries created a massive inflation, culminating in the 1970s, which destroyed the wealth of all those who had been foolish enough to trust in their promises. By the late 1970s, the British government, for example, had eliminated close to 99 per cent of the real value of its historic irredeemable debt. Second, macroeconomic policy was already vulnerable to the hostile reaction of the private sector to such malfeasance irrespective of globalization. Even in a closed economy, long-term nominal rates of interest will rise if a government pursues a consistently inflationary policy, partly to compensate for inflation and partly to insure against the inflation risk. Similarly, if a government relies on the printing press to finance activity, there will be flight from money into goods, services and assets.

In the purely domestic context, however, these reactions may be slow, at least initially. A government may be able to pursue an inflationary policy over a long period, with attractive consequences for real economic activity, before market chickens come home to roost. If a capital market is open, the most important change is that the reaction of a government's creditors can be quicker and more brutal, because the holders of government debt and money have a larger menu of alternatives. This will show itself in a collapsing exchange rate. Is that a bad thing? Hardly. It forces governments to finance their spending openly and honestly, rather than deceitfully through the inflation tax. Nor does it prevent governments from creating a policy regime that is capable of stabilizing the economy. A reasonably competent inflation-targeting central bank will achieve that automatically, except in extreme circumstances, when monetary policy ceases to be effective. The only exception to this proposition arises if there exists a long-run trade-off between inflation and unemployment, a proposition for which there is next to no support.

Yet the most puzzling feature of the argument employed by Professor Gray and those who support this position is the view that there is something inherently progressive about deficit finance. One would have thought it evident that those who believe in the virtues of an active government, under democratic control, would wish its actions to be as open and transparent as possible. The inflation tax is the most covert and obscure form of taxation. It is a breech of trust. It is inconsistent with the fundamental democratic principle that taxes should be voted in parliament. It redistributes money arbitrarily from creditors to borrowers, the old to the young, the financially ignorant to the adept and those who trust government to those suspicious of it. It destroys trust and destabilizes society. It is nothing short of grotesque to believe that good government, still more social democratic government, depends on it.

Constraints on developing countries

This discussion, unlike those in the previous three chapters, has focused on the position of the high-income countries. This is largely because critics have concentrated on the constraints on their ability to sustain high taxes and regulatory standards in a globalizing world. But the position of developing countries is somewhat different. Part of this difference derives from their greater vulnerability to financial instability, which will be the subject of the next chapter. But part comes from elsewhere. Developing countries generally have low average tax rates, compared with high-income countries. Similarly, regulation is relatively ineffective in developing countries. These phenomena arise partly because income generated by farmers and small businesses, particularly in the informal sector, is hard to tax, partly because incomes are low and partly because administrations are ineffective, ill-organized, underpaid and often corrupt as well. The failures of administration and governance are, in turn, both cause and consequence of the pervasive mistrust of government that is a striking feature of most developing countries.

In these circumstances, the constraints imposed by international economic integration are double-edged. To the extent that governments know they are constrained by the ability of their people to take their money elsewhere, or leave altogether, and their people know they know this, greater confidence should, slowly, grow up between citizens and the state. That, in turn, is a basis for any successful high-income society and economy. While such constraints may prove painful, from time to time, they should also be seen as a long-term advantage. It is easier to collect taxes in a country whose people trust government to provide services and believe those taxes are fair and fairly administered than in a country whose government is corrupt, predatory or brutal. At the same time, governments may occasionally wish to intervene in a sensible manner, but find their intentions thwarted by private sector suspicion.

Yet, once again, it is a grave mistake to assume that constraints are imposed by the acceptance of international economic integration alone. Capital flight from countries with notional exchange controls is universal. Similarly, no country can prevent the flight of skilled people if it fails to provide them with adequate opportunities – and security – at home. As the collapse of the Soviet Union and the transformation of Maoist China shows, regulatory competition among countries will affect the closed as much as the open. This is not because of international economic integration itself. It is more because differences in economic performance become a focus of dissatisfaction, leading ultimately to collapse of regimes.

Desirability of constraints

The implication of all this is that a country which chooses international economic integration accepts constraints on its action. Nevertheless, the hypothesis that these constraints mean the withering away of the state's capacity to tax, regulate or intervene is completely wrong. It would be more accurate to say that the impact of international economic integration is to accelerate the market's response to policy, by increasing the range of alternative options available to those affected.

Yet the question must not just be what impact international economic integration has on the options enjoyed by governments, but whether such constraints are desirable. There are two powerful reasons for believing they are.

The first and most important is that the assumption of a benevolent welfare-maximizing government is naive and implausible. International economic integration increases competition among governments – something that exists even when countries fiercely resist the integration, as the fate of the Soviet Unions shows. This competition constrains the ability of governments to act in a predatory manner. However, that constraint is normally desirable, particularly for its own citizens.

The second is that a benevolent government needs to find ways to bind itself, in order to increase the credibility of its commitments to the private sector, both domestic and foreign. One of the best ways of doing so is to make commitments to other governments, as in the WTO, or to powerful outside private parties. Even China has come to recognize the benefits it can gain from being able to make international commitments of this kind. Indeed, WTO membership is an effective way of importing the rule of law.

Does globalization make states impotent? No, it constrains them in valuable ways and so makes them better able to serve the properly defined long-run interests of their citizens. The severity of constraints should also not be exaggerated. As long as a government provides services that residents wish to enjoy, it can continue to tax, regulate and intervene. International integration merely tends to make policy more transparent and government more predictable, both of which are desirable.

Globalization does not make states unnecessary

The proposition that globalization makes states unnecessary is even less credible than that it makes states impotent. If anything, the exact opposite is true, for at least three reasons.

First, the ability of a society to take advantage of the opportunities offered by international economic integration depends on the quality of public goods, such as protection of property rights, personal security, a non-corrupt civil service and education. Without the legal arrangements, in particular, the potential web of rewarding contracts is vastly reduced. This may seem a trivial point, but a very large proportion of the world's economies have failed to achieve these essential preconditions of success.

Second, the state normally defines the identity of human beings. A sense of belonging is a part of people's sense of security. It is perhaps not surprising that some of the most successfully internationally integrated economies are small, homogeneous countries with a strong sense of collective identity.

Third, all forms of international governance rest on the ability of individual states to provide and guarantee order. The WTO, for example, is not a body of self-executing rules. On the contrary, they can be exercised only by sovereign states. The bedrock of international order is the territorial state, with a monopoly of coercive power within its jurisdiction. Cyberspace does not fundamentally change this, since economies are ultimately concerned with – and run for – human beings, who have physical presence and, in consequence, physical location. Since states are territorial jurisdictions, they are the bedrock of global order.

The implication is that, just as globalization does not make states impotent, it does not make them unnecessary either. On the contrary, for people to be successful in exploiting the opportunities afforded by international integration, they need states, at both ends of their transactions. This is why failed states, disorderly states, weak states and corrupt states are shunned states – they are the black holes of the global economic system.

Globalization as opportunity and challenge

To return to the propositions with which this chapter began, we can state that there is no evidence of the disappearance of a well-managed state's ability to tax and spend at levels it chooses. Nor is there any good reason to expect it. The notion that countries compete directly with one another, as companies do, is nonsense. It is nonsense because the most important source of both wealth and comparative advantage, namely people, is highly immobile.

Integration is a choice, with consequences. But if it is harder to run inflationary policies, that is all to the good. Similarly, if predatory taxation is more difficult to impose, that also is beneficial. Provided a state does not abuse its powers, it will continue to have a great deal of freedom of manoeuvre. What is must do, however, is convince its people that it is providing them with services they wish to possess. It must serve its people rather than behave as if it owns them.

Nor is the state in any way less necessary than before. The ability of people to take advantage of economic opportunities depends heavily on the quality of their state. True, as the world economy integrates and spillovers across borders become more important, global governance is likely to become still more essential. But that need come not at the expense of the state, but rather as an expression of the interests the state embodies. As the focus of identity, source of order and basis of governance, the state remains as essential in an era of globalization as it has ever been.

Chapter 13 **Fearful of Finance**

The extent of the control over all life that economic control confers is nowhere better illustrated than in the field of foreign exchanges. Nothing would at first seem to affect private life less than a state control of the dealings in foreign exchange, and most people will regard its introduction with complete indifference. Yet the experience of most continental countries has taught thoughtful people to regard this step as the decisive advance on the path to totalitarianism and the suppression of individual liberty. It is in fact the complete delivery of the individual to the tyranny of the state, the final suppression of all means of escape – not just for the rich but for everybody. Once the individual is no longer free to travel, no longer free to buy foreign books or journals, once all the means of foreign contact can be restricted to those of whom official opinion approves or for whom it is regarded as necessary, effective control of opinion is much greater than that ever exercised by any of the absolutist governments of the seventeenth and eighteenth centuries.

Friedrich A. Hayek[1]

Any sudden event which creates a great demand for actual cash may cause, and will tend to cause, a panic in a country where cash is much economized, and where debts payable on demand are large.

Walter Bagehot[2]

Markets do show a tendency towards equilibrium when they deal with known quantities, but financial markets are different. They discount the future, but the future they discount is contingent on how the financial markets discount it at present. Instead of a predictable outcome, the future is genuinely uncertain and is unlikely to correspond to expectations. The bias inherent in market expectations is one of the factors that shape the course of events. There is a two-way interaction between expectations and outcomes that I call 'reflexivity'.

George Soros, *George Soros on Globalization*[3]

In the late-1990s, five hitherto successful Asian emerging-market economies suffered an astounding swing, from feast to famine, in the availability of foreign finance. The crisis that ensued swept across the world. It also changed our understanding of the risks of financial openness and stimulated a controversy that has not ended to this day.

In 1996, Indonesia, Malaysia, the Philippines, South Korea and Thailand ran an aggregate current account deficit of just under 5 per cent of their combined GDP. This was the amount by which their access to foreign finance allowed them to spend *more* than their aggregate national incomes. Just two years later, in 1998, this deficit had turned into an aggregate surplus of 10.6 per cent of GDP. That was the amount by which they were then spending *less* than national incomes, in order to reduce their net indebtedness to the rest of the world. In just two years, therefore, these countries had been forced to reduce spending in relation to national incomes by an amount equal to 15.5 per cent of their combined GDP. This is an extraordinarily large adjustment. It would be the equivalent of a shift in the US current account from a deficit of $500 billion to a surplus of over $1,000 billion in two years. Moreover, the crisis-hit countries achieved this adjustment in spending relative to output when they were also suffering recessions. In aggregate, the GDP of the five crisis-hit countries shrank by 8.1 per cent in 1998.

What is astonishing is not that these countries fell into a severe crisis during this period of adjustment, but that they coped at all. In fact, they managed astonishingly well. Not only did the balance of payments adjust quickly, but GDP rose by 7 per cent in 1999 and 7.3 per cent in 2000. By 2001, the aggregate GDP of the five countries was already 13 per cent higher than it had been in 1996. The GDP of the star performer, South Korea, was up 22 per cent.[4] But Indonesia, the worst hit, had failed to return to 1996 GDP levels even by 2001.

Financial crises have hardly been rare events during the decades of globalization. The World Bank has estimated that there were 112 systemic banking crises in ninety-three countries between the late 1970s and the end of the twentieth century.[5] Another study counted ninety-five crises in emerging market economies and another forty-four in high-income countries between 1973 and 1997. Seventeen of the crises in emerging market economies were banking crises, fifty-seven were currency crises and twenty-one were 'twin crises' (both banking and currency), the most damaging of all. Nine of the crises in the high-income countries were banking crises, twenty-nine were currency crises and six were twin crises. Altogether, therefore, there were twenty-six pure banking crises, eighty-six currency crises, and twenty-seven twin crises. The authors of the latter study – Barry Eichengreen of the University of California at Berkeley and Michael Bordo of Rutgers – argue that 'relative to the pre-1914 era of financial globalization, crises are twice as prevalent today'. But they also conclude that they are not, in general, more severe.[6] This is not altogether encouraging.

What makes it still more discouraging is the contrast between the early post-Second World War decades and the more recent few decades. Between 1945 and 1971, in what might be called the 'age of financial repression', there had been only thirty-eight crises in all, with just seven twin crises. Emerging market economies experienced no banking crises, sixteen currency crises and just one twin crisis in this period. Then, between 1973 and 1997, there were 139 crises. The age of financial liberalization has, in short, been an age of financial crises.

Yet the financial crises of 1997 and 1998 were pivotal events, for three reasons. First, the crises were almost entirely unforeseen. The east Asian developing countries had been the world's star performers for decades. Virtually nobody expected so many of them to succumb to such severe financial crises so quickly. Second, they were very costly, not only in terms of GDP forgone and human misery, but also because of the fiscal costs of rescuing the banking systems. In Indonesia, for example, the increase in the stock of public debt in the year of the crisis was 50 per cent of GDP. In South Korea and Thailand, it was between 30 and 40 per cent of GDP.[7] Third, they spread not just throughout the region, but throughout the world, to embrace Russia, Brazil and even a giant US hedge fund, Long-Term Capital Management.[8]

It is against this background that we need to consider the critics of financial globalization. For it is far easier here to understand the force of the complaints. Indeed, they are echoed by many distinguished economists, above all Joseph Stiglitz, Nobel-laureate and chief economist of the World Bank at the time of the Asian crisis.[9] In my own writings for the *Financial Times*, I have shared many of the complaints. In this area, there are also important criticisms from the free-market side of the debate, which need to be addressed as well. Indeed, one of the striking features of this debate is that the right and the left often agree in attacking the middle. This is particularly true where the target is the IMF, probably the most hated of all the world's multilateral economic institutions (though the WTO is a close rival). Here, then, are three propositions about finance, to be addressed below.

First, the liberalization of controls on capital flows and consequent integration into the global capital markets is a catastrophic blunder for emerging market economies. It brings massive risks and modest, if any, rewards.

Second, the IMF, as an institution, is myopic, hidebound, arrogant, demanding and incompetent. It has, as a result, done considerable damage to developing countries over the decades during which it has concentrated its malign attentions upon them.

Third, if there is to be capital-market integration by developing countries, there have to be substantial institutional reforms, at the core, not just on the periphery, of the world economy. These should include significant changes in the regulation of financial markets and their central institutions. One possibility is a tax on speculative transactions in foreign exchange markets, originally recommended by another Nobel-laureate, the late James Tobin. Moreover, if there is to be no global lender of last resort, there must be some way of imposing standstills on capital outflows These would then be a part of a bankruptcy procedure for countries.

Alleged folly of capital account opening

In 1990, net private capital flows to emerging market economies were just $40 billion. By 1996, they had reached $329 billion. Then, just two years later, the net flow was down to $144 billion. Emerging-market economies had responded to the cornucopia of foreign finance prudently. In 1990, they ran an aggregate current account deficit of $16 billion. By 1996, this had risen to $96 billion. While a sizeable increase, this was still much less than the increase in the private capital inflow. In 1996, increases in foreign currency reserves by emerging market economies amounted to $86 billion. The previous year they had been $96 billion. Thus, these countries were squirrelling away a great deal of the fresh money for the inevitable rainy day. But it was not to be enough. When the inflow collapsed, so, too, did the current account deficits. By 1998, the aggregate current account deficit of the emerging market economies was

$8 billion. In 1999, they ran an aggregate *surplus* of $30 billion.[10] In other words, instead of being able to spend more than their incomes they were suddenly being forced to cut spending. Reductions in spending are always painful. But when retrenchment is so swift it is far more painful.

This was not the first time in recent decades that the world witnessed a move from famine to feast, and back again, in the provision of finance to emerging-market economies. The first time was the age of the 'recycling' of petro-dollars, following the two oil-price shocks of the 1970s. Private net flows to emerging-market economies then rose from $4 billion in 1978 to $71 billion in 1981, before collapsing, after the Mexican debt crisis of 1982, to $5 billion in 1986. The current account deficits of emerging-market economies rose from $28 billion in 1978 to a peak of $69 billion in 1981, before collapsing to $8 billion in 1984. During that cycle, the aggregate current account deficit of Latin America, the most affected region, rose from 2.3 per cent of GDP in 1978 to 5 per cent in 1982, before being forced into a surplus of 0.8 per cent of GDP in 1984. This was not dissimilar to what happened to the Asia-Pacific region in the 1990s. There the current account deficit rose to an aggregate deficit of 2.2 per cent of GDP in 1996, before shifting to a surplus of 5 per cent of GDP in 1998.

For emerging-market finance to experience one huge financial crisis in a generation may be a misfortune. To experience two looks very much like carelessness. Moreover, it looks as though much the same people committed the carelessness: the bankers. In the 1990s, net credit from commercial banks to emerging market economies rose from $9 billion in 1990 to $124 billion in 1996, before collapsing to *minus* $52 billion in 1998 and 1999. Commercial banks continued to extract money from emerging market economies in 2000, 2001 and 2002. The swing of $175 billion in commercial-bank net lending between 1996 and 1998 accounted for virtually all of the overall reduction of $184 billion in private finance of emerging markets between those two years. The picture in the earlier crisis was identical. Between 1981 and 1986, private net flows to emerging markets fell by $66 billion, from $71 billion to $5 billion. Over the same five years, the net flows from commercial banks went from $56 billion to minus $9 billion, a swing of $65 billion. Commercial bankers were the proximate cause of both crises. No other source of finance has been as unstable. Foreign direct investment has been particularly stable. Direct investment in emerging-market economies rose from $14 billion in 1990 to $92 billion in 1996, but then kept rising to $149 billion in 1999. It then stayed at $136 billion in 2000 and $134 billion in 2001 before falling modestly to $107 billion in 2002.

A simple conclusion would be that, given the instability of the flows and the costs imposed by the need to adjust to the shifts in the fancies of the world's financial markets, particularly its commercial bankers, the sensible thing to do is to fence them out. The gadarene rush of the banking swine is to be avoided at all costs. They trample you down on the way in and then again on the way out. 'It has', argues Professor Stiglitz, 'become increasingly clear that all too often capital account liberalization represents risk without a reward. Even when countries have strong banks, a mature stock market, and other institutions that many of the Asian countries did not have, it can impose enormous risks.'[11]

Astonishingly, a paper from the IMF itself appears to support this view. The authors, one of whom was the IMF's chief economist at the time the paper was released, notes that there are powerful reasons for believing international financial integration would benefit the economy.[12] These include: augmenting domestic savings; reducing the cost of capital through better allocation of risk; transferring technological and managerial know-how; stimulating domestic financial development; making a highly specialized economy less risky; enforcing commitment to better economic policies; and a way of signalling greater friendliness to foreign investors. Unfortunately, the evidence does not indicate that these effects are as potent as one might hope. It is true that more financially integrated economies grow faster than less integrated ones over the last three decades. But it is perfectly possible (indeed likely) that the causation goes the other way, from faster growth to integration, not the other way round. From a careful review of the existing empirical literature, the authors reach the conclusion that there is no strong evidence of a positive association between financial integration and economic growth. There is, however, some evidence that foreign direct investment does have a strongly positive impact on growth, as does portfolio equity. The same is not true of debt-creating flows.[13]

Why, then, is there such little evidence on the positive impact of capital account liberalization on economic growth? One answer is that access to capital is not, in fact, the decisive constraint on economic growth. It is social and human capital, as well as the overall policy regime, that matter. This then connects to a second answer, which is the correlation between poorly executed liberalization and subsequent crises. A crucial aggravating factor is the pro-cyclical behaviour of international finance and, at its worst, 'sudden stops' in the provision of capital, which inevitably generate crises, as was so spectacularly the case for Latin America in the 1980s and East Asia in the 1990s.[14]

The overall conclusion is that finance is different from trade. While openness to trade is normally beneficial and requires relatively few complementary policy changes, the same is not true of finance. Given the deep-seated difficulties inherent in any financial system, discussed in Part II of this book, liberalization is bound to be a far trickier matter. Too often it has created opportunities for blunders matched by equally spectacular malfeasance, by both suppliers and recipients of capital. It is not surprising that FDI has worked relatively well, since the risks are borne by those directly responsible for managing the assets. The same is not true where debt is concerned. It appears, therefore, that the activists who protest against direct investment above everything have got things almost exactly the wrong way round.

Yet this cannot be the end of the matter. It is not difficult to see why full convertibility of the currency might be desirable, after all. One good reason is given by Hayek. If we regard choices as valuable in their own right, then there are few choices more important to people than those to travel and, if necessary, to escape from oppressive, exploitative or predatory regimes. This is self-evidently true in big ways. It is also true in smaller ones. In the 1960s, it was forbidden for British citizens to take more than tiny amounts out of the country. This was worse than humiliating and unpleasant. The policy was designed to allow the government to avoid the exchange rate effects of a policy of inflation designed to maintain full employment in the presence of trade union pressures. This was a predatory policy. It ended up by wiping out the savings of a sizeable portion of the British middle classes. If money could have been taken out of the country, these dangerous and ultimately unsustainable policies would have been halted far sooner. This is the sense in which, as discussed in the previous chapter, the possibility of capital mobility desirably constrains the state. That is one reason for welcoming capital account liberalization, notwithstanding all the difficulties.

Now consider a second reason for convertibility. It is clear that a well-run and regulated financial system is a tremendous economic asset. Its functions are central to the good performance of the economy and to the ability of the population to live their lives in a tolerable manner. The purpose of the financial system is to mobilize savings, allocate capital, monitor management and transform risk. This is not just for the élite. Think, for example, of poor farmers. Consider the benefit they can obtain from the ability to put money by safely, to obtain adequate insurance of their harvests, to sell their crops in advance in liquid and competitive markets, or to buy useful assets before they have saved up the money they need. By performing these functions, the financial system can transform the effectiveness of the economy. A great deal of empirical work, much of it summarized in a comprehensive evaluation published by the World Bank in 2001, has demonstrated that the size of the financial sector alone, regardless of its sophistication, has a strong causal effect on economic performance.[15] As the study notes, 'there is now a solid body of research strongly suggesting that improvements in financial arrangements precede and contribute to economic performance'.[16] In terms of its impact on growth, the most important effect seems to be on productivity, not on the accumulation of capital.

Yet how are developing countries with what are, in general, tiny financial markets to obtain the first class financial sectors that they need? Among the developing countries, only China and Brazil have financial sectors with assets that amount to even 1 per cent of the global total. In about a third of all countries the total assets of the banking system are less than $1 billion, smaller than those of an insignificant local bank in the US. Another third have assets of less than $10 billion.[17] Yet, in 2000, the world's fiftieth largest bank, KeyCorp of the US, had assets of $83 billion.[18] It is impossible for such tiny markets to support competition among self-standing national players with realistic aspirations to world-class performance. Unless one believes the world's poor deserve only low-quality financial services, the answer has to include substantial inward foreign direct investment in the sector. Outsiders bring five benefits. The first is superior know-how and efficiency. The second is the ability to exploit the economies of scale generated in world markets. The third is the ability to piggy-back on the skills and experience of the home-country regulator of the new entrant into the financial market. The fourth is a desirable disruption of domestic insider connections that allow the monopolization of the financial system by groups of powerful people, at the expense of the taxpayer and small customers, as both providers and would-be users of funds. Last, countries with a higher proportion of foreign-owned banks and a smaller proportion of state-owned banks are also less prone to financial crises, perhaps because the foreign banks are better regulated, better managed or merely more immune to pressures for imprudent lending.[19]

Moreover, many of the fears about the presence of foreign banks have proved misplaced. There is no hard evidence, notes the World Bank,

> that the local presence of foreign banks has destabilized the flow of credit or restricted access to small firms. Instead, the entry of these banks has been associated with significant improvements in the quality of regulation and disclosure. The very threat of entry has often been enough to galvanize the

domestic banks into overhauling their cost structure and the range and quality of their services, with the result that foreign entry has often proved not to be as profitable for the entrants as they may have anticipated.[20]

While it unnecessary to have completely free flows of finance in order to attract inward investment into the sector, some liberalization is essential and more is desirable. Inward direct investment must be liberalized. Investors must also believe that they will be able to repatriate their capital and remit earnings (which requires convertibility on the current account). To function well, not least in managing their risks, foreign financial companies will also need access to global financial markets. Indeed, their ability to exploit these markets successfully is one of the reasons for encouraging their presence. For all these reasons, a symbiosis exists between both current and capital account liberalization and the contribution made by the presence of foreign financial enterprises in the economy. This is a second reason for aspiring to capital account liberalization.

A third reason is that, in the right environment and properly done, the potential benefits ought, in principle, to be realizable, at manageable cost. Massive financial crises are not inevitable. Professors Dobson and Hufbauer argue that the gains from capital flows already match those from more liberal trade.[21] Peter Henry of Stanford University has argued, on similar, albeit more restricted, lines that when emerging-market stock exchanges are opened to foreign investors, dividend yields fall, the capital stock grows faster and the growth rate of output per worker rises. All this calls into question 'the increasingly popular view that capital account liberalization brings no real benefits'.[22]

Whether or not that is already the case, it is easy to see that the gains should be substantial if the propensity to crisis could be reduced and, as we shall see, there are good reasons to believe it can be. Moreover, as Dobson and Hufbauer also point out, international capital flows have not caused all crises.[23] In many cases, they suggest, domestic malfeasance and incompetence did the damage unaided. Even when foreign capital was involved, domestic blunders were always a contributory cause. Not infrequently, the role of the foreign capital was to reveal the rottenness of the financial system. Finally, the aftermath of the crisis has usually brought with it huge improvements, including to the regulatory regime. For all these reasons, the net benefits of liberalization ought to outweigh the costs, particularly if one takes a sufficiently long-run view. Most informed Koreans would, for example, now agree that the 1997 crisis, however humiliating and painful at the time, was a necessary part of the maturation of their economy. Indeed, it is hard to think of any financial system that has not advanced through the fires of repeated crises. Mexico is another example of a country that seems on the way to gaining a far better financial system than it has ever had before. Similarly, after its crisis in the early 1980s, Chile ended up with a superior system to those of other Latin American countries. Some analysts believe this is one of the most important reasons for its improved economic performance over the 1980s and 1990s.[24]

A fourth reason for believing that financial liberalization is desirable is that controls are themselves both costly and increasingly ineffective. Controls on the movement of foreign exchange are a prime source of corruption and law-breaking by otherwise honest people. The former subverts the quality of the administration. The latter undermines the rule of law. In national emergencies, such controls can be sustained without serious damage. But in the long run they are corrosive. Not only are such controls directly corrupting, but, by separating the domestic financial system from that of the rest of the world, they make far easier its capture and corruption by domestic vested interests. Moreover, as a country becomes more integrated in trade, it is increasingly difficult to make blanket controls effective. It is possible for businesses to export capital through the under-invoicing of exports and the over-invoicing of imports, for example, or through offsetting agreements made with foreign business partners. The scale of capital flight from countries with controls can be enormous. It is evident, for example, from the relationship between published figures on the current account, capital inflows and the accumulation of foreign exchange reserves that illegal exports of capital from China have been in excess of $100 billion. Worse, when illegal capital flight has occurred, the persistence of controls has merely encouraged the investors to keep their money outside the country.[25]

A fifth reason for believing the elimination of controls is desirable is that it should force review and reform of the financial sector. By now, everybody should know that the combination of blanket guarantees to the banking system (including a pegged exchange rate) with weak regulation and capital account liberalization is lethal. Thus the decision to liberalize should itself force a reconsideration of the explicit and implicit guarantees given by the state. Similarly, a decision to liberalize ought to force the government to look at the connections between financial institutions and borrowers and the other conflicts of interest that are likely to prove even more damaging in such circumstances. Again, a financial system requires an effective bankruptcy regime. If the capital account is to be liberalized, this becomes still more important. Foreign capital is inevitably unstable if it has no confidence in the protection of its property rights.

A final reason for accepting the ultimate desirability of the elimination of controls is that it is what the high-income countries have now done. All countries that aspire to that status will ultimately wish to follow suit. They should at least prepare themselves for that stage in development.

For all these reasons, therefore, the elimination of controls on capital movement is a desirable objective. But it is one that also carries substantial risks. The right answer is not to avoid liberalizing for ever, but to carry it through in a carefully thought out and disciplined manner. In that way, it may be possible to achieve the objectives of integration without the crises that have, so often, punctuated movement in that direction.

Follies of the IMF[26]

If capital account liberalization is controversial, the IMF is even more so. It would take a book to address all the complaints made against it. For many outsiders, the debate about the role of the Fund may seem too technical to be worthwhile. But it is also too central to the debate about financial liberalization to avoid. For this reason, we need to look at the most obvious criticisms: the IMF applies a one-size-fits-all policy of austerity to all countries; it failed to foresee the risks of capital account liberalization; its policy recommendations for dealing with the Asian crisis, in particular, amounted to screaming 'fire' in a burning building, thereby turning a problem of illiquidity into one of insolvency; it has created moral hazard by lending too much and bailing out the imprudent lenders who are its true masters, at the expense of innocent people in crisis-hit countries; and it is too subservient to the interests of the Group of Seven leading high-income countries and especially the US. There are many other complaints. But these will surely do.

First, the charge of a one-size-fits-all approach to policy. Professor Stiglitz has made this complaint, along with many others, in his book on globalization, writing that:

> it's unlikely that an IMF mission, on a three-week trip to Addis Ababa, Ethiopia's capital, or any other developing country, could really develop policies appropriate for that country. ... Outsiders can play a role, in sharing the experiences of other countries, and in offering alternative interpretations of the economic forces at play. But the IMF did not want to take

on the mere role of an adviser, competing with others who might be offering their ideas. It wanted a more central role in shaping policy. And it could do this, because its position was based on an ideology – market fundamentalism – that required little if any consideration of a country's particular circumstances and immediate problems. . . . Suffering and pain became part of the process of redemption, evidence that a country was on the right track. . . .

The IMF has done a good job of persuading many that its ideologically driven policies were necessary if countries are to succeed in the long run. . . . But IMF programmes go well beyond simply ensuring that countries live within their means.[27]

These are sweeping charges. How far would I go along with them? The answer is that Professor Siglitz is right only up to a point. The IMF has been a secretive and arrogant organization, though both charges are far less applicable today than they were a few years ago. Its technical approach to both monetary and fiscal policies has often been questionable. It has also frequently made debatable assumptions about the availability of finance, particularly of aid, in the long run. It has interfered too heavily in the details of revenue and spending decisions, quite apart from a vast range of microeconomic policies. Its conditionality has, consequently, been too complex and intrusive. It has lent again and again to the same incompetent countries. It has, in effect, assumed responsibility for running many developing countries, particularly small and poor ones, as though it were proconsular agent for the finance ministries of the G7. This has created many difficulties, but the most important by far is confusion of political responsibility. Policies mandated by a mixture of adverse circumstances and incompetence are too frequently blamed on the IMF instead. While that may be politically convenient for the government, and especially for the finance ministry, which often needs all the excuses (and backing) it can obtain, such use of the IMF as the scapegoat conceals from the population both the responsibility for a crisis and the inevitability of the means of escaping from it.

As even Stiglitz grudgingly admits, countries must live within their means. The joke goes that the letters IMF stand for 'it's mostly fiscal'. Unfortunately, it mostly is. The correct criticism of the Fund is that it is a hedgehog – that is, someone who knows just one big trick – pretending to be a fox – that is, a flexible master of many tricks. But what it knows as a hedgehog is almost always relevant. It *is* mostly fiscal. Countries with solid fiscal positions rarely enter into a serious economic crisis. As we were reminded in Asia in 1997 and

1998, countries with apparently sound public finances can have a mountain of more or less explicit off-balance-sheet liabilities. A bankrupt banking system is an oft-repeated example. More frequently, however, the fiscal unsustainability of a country's position is evident. The IMF is then the doctor, brought in usually too late, and, as bearer of the bad news, blamed for the pain. And when a country is in the midst of a fiscal crisis, the IMF reduces the severity of the adjustment, since it provides funds that would otherwise be unavailable. Thus the notion that the IMF generally imposes more austerity than is necessary in the circumstances is implausible. Beggars, as they say, cannot be choosers. Countries that have to turn to the IMF *are* beggars. They cannot choose but adjust. The only question is how.

In short, the 'one-size-fits-all' charge has force. But the force is not overwhelming, since, unfortunately, a vast range of countries manages to fall into exactly the same predicament: they spend beyond their means and run out of the credit, at home or abroad, needed to continue in this happy state of affairs. By and large, the solution is also always the same: governments must reduce their spending in relation to revenue. The IMF is there to rescue countries, by making the adjustment that little bit less painful than it would otherwise be. But it has no more responsibility for the calamity than an ambulance crew at the scene of a car crash.

Now turn to the second charge: that the IMF failed to foresee – and warn against – the risks of premature, ill-planned and worse-implemented capital account liberalization. The IMF is guilty. It is in good company, that of the US Treasury, to name but one guilty party. But, as the institution charged with responsibility for global macroeconomic instability, it bears heavy blame for failing to warn of the dangers and, indeed, for failing to establish the necessary in-house expertise to evaluate them. In its assessment of the IMF's handling of the Indonesian, South Korean and Brazilian crises of 1997, 1998 and 1999, the newly established Independent Evaluation Office concluded that 'IMF surveillance was more successful in identifying macroeconomic vulnerabilities than in recognizing and analyzing in depth the risks arising from financial sector and corporate balance sheet weaknesses and the governance-related problems that contributed to those weaknesses.'[28] This is bureaucratic phraseology for 'The Fund blew it.' Unquestionably, it did.

Then consider the third charge: fund policy recommendations for dealing with the Asian crisis amounted to screaming 'fire' in a burning building, thereby turning a problem of illiquidity into one of insolvency.[29] The charge comes from Professor Stiglitz, the fiercest of all the professional critics of the

IMF's performance during the crisis.[30] A similar attack was made by Jeffrey Sachs, then at Harvard University but now at Columbia.[31] This is not the place for a detailed evaluation of the way the IMF handled the Asian crisis. It is also easy, in hindsight, to recognize mistakes made under the pressure of events. Nevertheless, it is important to identify where it went wrong, including the points on which its fiercest critics were right at the time. Nobody would now doubt, for example, that the Fund failed to warn adequately of the dangers of liberalization. Equally, it is more evident today than it was to observers at the time that a number of these countries had mishandled not just the liberalization of their financial systems and controls on foreign exchange, but also elementary features of exchange rate management and macroeconomic policy. The Fund is perhaps to blame for not having discovered this sooner. But it was not to blame for the absurd decisions with which policy-makers persisted to well beyond the bitter end. Several countries, for example, actively encouraged short-term foreign currency borrowing. South Korea, astoundingly, permitted *only* such short-term borrowing, principally via the banking system. This was in keeping with its traditional (and now abandoned) emphasis on keeping out foreign direct investment and promoting development through active manipulation of the banking system, which was, in effect, an arm of the developmental state (and its liabilities, correspondingly, covert public debt).

Again, both Thailand and South Korea allowed the defence of their exchange rate pegs to continue to the point at which their foreign currency reserves were exhausted, while concealing this salient fact from the IMF, the markets and, it goes without saying, their populations. Equally, the short-term foreign currency liabilities of the banking systems and corporate sector of Indonesia, Thailand and South Korea came as an unpleasant surprise only after the crisis broke. Again, the long Asian boom had concealed the increasingly unsound state and indeed corruption of sizeable parts of the financial system. In the case of Indonesia, for example, the Suharto family and its associates had behaved far worse than most outsiders had realized.[32] For none of this was the IMF responsible and, by the time it was called in, it was equally far too late to achieve the painless remedies sought by Stiglitz.

Turn to the remedies the Fund imposed. It is universally accepted that the initial requirement that fiscal policy be tightened was an inappropriate throwback to standard IMF remedies. It was a blunder. To be fair, this requirement was abandoned quite swiftly. Equally, it is now widely agreed that the Christmas tree of loan conditions imposed by the IMF – some at the behest of the US Treasury, some even at the urging of economic reformers in the afflicted countries – was a mistake. In general and rightly, the IMF has decided to prune the range and intrusiveness of its conditionality.

Some – the *Wall Street Journal*, for example – criticize the IMF for allowing currencies to depreciate. But this seems a nonsensical complaint. How, exactly, countries with no foreign currency reserves and huge net liabilities in foreign currency, much of it short term, were to avoid devaluation is, to put it at its mildest, not obvious. Far more legitimately controversial were linked decisions to provide large 'bail out' packages (though not as large as they seemed, since much of the money supposedly available from bilateral donors was a mirage) and raise short-term interest rates to minimize the fall in currencies.

Stiglitz protests against the packages because they allowed many of the most irresponsible lenders, particularly the commercial banks, to escape more or less unscathed, at the expense of the people of the indebted countries who then had to repay the loans. As he remarks, 'the money . . . enabled the countries to provide dollars to the firms that had borrowed from Western bankers to repay the loans. It was thus, in part, a bailout to the international banks as much as it was a bailout to the country; the lenders did not have to face the full consequences of having made bad loans.'[33] Ironically, not dissimilar complaints were made by those Stiglitz would call 'free market fundamentalists' to the effect that the big bail-outs were creating serious moral hazard. Indeed, the Asian crisis, some would argue, was a direct consequence of the Mexican rescue of less than three years before.

Similarly, Stiglitz and Sachs, and a host of others, also protested against the decision to raise interest rates to slow the currency collapses. Given the highly indebted state of the corporate sector, high interest rates were, they correctly argued, bound to increase the rate of bankruptcy and so the extent of the economic depression. Against this, the IMF could, and did, argue that accelerated declines in the value of the currencies would, given the foreign currency indebtedness of the banks and the corporate sectors, also accelerate the rate of bankruptcy and so the slide into recession. To this the critics responded that, in an environment of financial fragility, high domestic interest rates were more likely to undermine confidence in the currency than increase it, thereby achieving the opposite of what the IMF intended. They also added that there was at least some justice in the bankruptcy of those who had borrowed heavily in foreign currency, but far less so in the forced insolvency of those who had relied more heavily on domestic currency borrowing. Finally, they noted, if the aim were to prevent a run across the exchanges, it would have been far better to impose a standstill on withdrawals of funds and, if necessary, temporary controls on capital outflows.

To these points, in turn, the IMF and its defenders have replied that the high interest rates were in effect quite briefly and that rates were lowered as soon as currencies stabilized. Furthermore, it was impossible to separate the deserving from the undeserving in a crisis that, one way or another, was bound to affect everyone. Finally, the IMF did not have the ability to impose a standstill on withdrawals. In the case of South Korea, the G7 governments did indeed do this at the very end of 1997, but were able to do so only because of the concentration of lending in the international commercial banks. At the same time, all the governments of the crisis-hit countries were desperate to avoid a default. Outside advisers might have a very different view. But this was, beyond question, a sovereign decision. It was not, on the evidence of what default normally means for a country, an irrational one.

So who is right? I would now argue that the IMF cannot be found 'not guilty' of the charge of blundering its way through the crisis. The case is, in the Scottish legal terminology, 'not proven'. This ignorance is partly because we are unable to run controlled experiments in economics. Moreover (and fortunately), crises on this scale do not happen that often. When a crisis of confidence of this magnitude occurs, especially one that destroys domestic confidence, as was the case in Indonesia, there are no painless escapes. The big mistakes were made by almost everybody involved before the crisis hit. After the crisis started, all options were difficult.

In particular, whether or not the IMF was right on interest rate policy is a matter of fine judgement. The report of the Independent Evaluation Office of the IMF concludes that high interest rates were not the cause of the Indonesian output collapse, for the simple reason that they were not implemented. Real interest rates were increasingly negative during the early months of the programme. On South Korea, too, it concludes that high interest rates could not have been the chief cause of the recession. The more important cause was contraction of credit flows from what had become an insolvent banking system. On the fundamental decision not to declare a default, if that could be avoided, I believe the decision of the government of South Korea proved correct, in the aftermath. But it is equally easy to envisage situations in which, by avoiding a default, governments and the IMF have together imposed a heavy burden on the taxpayers of the indebted countries. Whether they are then worse off than they would have been if their countries had defaulted is uncertain.

Have the IMF bail-out packages created serious moral hazard, which was our fourth charge? Both the assumption that the answer must be a resounding 'yes' and the view that the right response is to stop providing support in crises are unwarranted.[34] It must be stressed, in the first place, that the fact of moral hazard is insufficient to rule out a policy. We do not close down fire brigades because they encourage householders to take risks with fire. Normally, we would combine whatever causes the moral hazard with some sort of regulation. Houses are subject to fire regulations, for example. In the second place, it is far from clear that the moral hazard has been as important as many critics argue. Those who think it has been tend to start from the assumption that markets are incapable of making mistakes. But we know that they can make big ones. It is important also to remember that a sizeable part of the flow to Asian crisis countries took the form of portfolio equity and bonds whose holders suffered large losses. In addition, prior to the crisis, spreads on bonds to what turned out to be the crisis-hit countries fell to low levels, only to explode upwards once the crisis hit. This strongly suggests that the investors had underestimated the risks. If they had been confident of being bailed out, spreads need not have risen. Similarly, if commercial banks had been confident of being bailed out, they need not have taken their money out. In which case there might have been no crisis.[35] Finally, whatever may have been the case for lenders, the governments of the crisis-hit countries cannot have been under any illusions about what such a crisis would mean for them and their countries. IMF bail-outs have never spared countries considerable pain. All the governments in power at the time the crisis hit fell, with the exception of Malaysia's.

This is not to argue that moral hazard played no part in the crises, merely that international lending was not its prime source. Government guarantees to banking systems in capital-importing and capital-exporting countries have been of decisive importance in one financial crisis after the other. However, these guarantees were given not by the IMF, but by governments, including by the governments of the G7 countries. If the effects of moral hazard on the financial system are to be eliminated, this is where one would have to start.[36]

The final charge against the IMF is that it is a tool of the G7, particularly of the US and, more particularly still, of Wall Street. The answer to this charge is obvious: guilty. The institution responds to the realities of power and the self-defined interests of its dominant player. If Japan had, for example, been willing to take on the US Treasury and set up its suggested Asian Monetary Fund, the position of the IMF would have been very different. It is intriguing that

Stiglitz, who strongly supports this idea, is also against the bail-outs that such a fund would surely have made possible. It is quite possible to imagine changing the IMF's governance arrangements to give greater voting weights to countries likely to borrow from it. But it is equally clear what would then follow. The creditors would use some other instrument for dealing with debtors, quite possibly bilateral ones. The trick of making multilateral institutions work is to recognize the realities of power, without succumbing entirely to them. The question is whether the IMF has gone as far as it can towards achieving the practical degree of independence from the pressures of the powerful. It was too subservient to the US during the 1990s. This was made possible by the relatively informal way in which decisions were, in practice, taken. Improved transparency and openness and greater willingness by other G7 countries to take on the US, where it is wrong, would be a help.

Where, then, do I come out? In the uncomfortable middle. Do I believe the IMF did a wonderful job in the 1990s? The answer is an unambiguous no. Do I believe the world would be better off with no IMF? The answer is an equally unambiguous no. If the IMF did not exist, countries would not be left alone to sink or swim. They would be subject to even more confused outside pressures. If crises hit, they would have to deal directly with the US Treasury. That would be no improvement. Can we create an all-wise, self-disciplined, transparent and democratic IMF? The answer is again is an unambiguous no. But we can do better. We have to.

Better policies at the core and the periphery

Suppose that we accept that capital account liberalization is not only likely to proceed, but that, on balance, it is desirable that it should. What policy changes are then needed to make financial liberalization work without the repeated crises of the last two to three decades?

Some of what is needed is, by now, uncontroversial. One requirement is improved transparency and far higher regulatory standards. The financial and economic position of countries needs to be known. If, for example, a central bank has pledged its reserves in the forward market, it would be better if creditors knew the fact before it was too late. Indeed, if the central bank knew the creditors would know, it would be far less likely to make such a blunder, as Thailand's central bank did in 1997. Supporting these changes in transparency have been a number of international efforts at raising standards. Among these are the IMF's Codes of Good Practices on Transparency in Monetary and Financial Policies and on Fiscal Standards; the Basel Committee's Core Principles for Effective Banking Supervision, and standards for security regulation, insurance supervision and payments systems. These are all assessed as part of the Financial Sector Assessment Program, a joint effort of the IMF and World Bank and national supervisory agencies. Meanwhile, the World Bank takes the lead in assessing standards in four other areas: corporate governance (a standard developed by the OECD); accounting; auditing; and insolvency and creditor rights. Improved transparency is also required of activities of the IMF. Much progress has been made: increasingly, staff assessments of individual economies – the 'Article IV reports' – and Letters of Intent, describing IMF-supported programmes, are published. Stanley Fischer, former first deputy managing director of the IMF, describes the changes as a 'revolution in transparency and a revolution within the Fund'.[37]

Another, almost equally uncontroversial requirement is changes in exchange rate regimes. Most, though not all, economists would now agree that the combination of more or less managed floating exchange rates with some form of inflation-targeting central bank is the best policy for relatively large countries that are also relatively closed to trade or trade heavily with more than one currency bloc. Small open countries, particularly those with flexible economies or with a dominant trading partner, probably do best either to adopt that currency as their own or to set up a strict currency board. Adjustable-peg exchange rate regimes in which countries try to reconcile monetary autonomy with freedom for capital flows are unviable in the long run. This is a matter no longer just of theory, but of all too painful experience. It must be noted, however, that a number of economists still hope for a return, in one form or another, to the gold standard, namely, a world of credibly fixed exchange rates with an anchor that is itself of credible long-term value. The argument for a global money is easy enough to understand. But the difficulties in the way of achieving it in a world with hundreds of sovereigns and an equally well-entrenched tradition of state-created money are, for the moment, insuperable.

Yet there also lie in the way of creating the smoothly operating and integrated capital markets that we seek two deep and interconnected difficulties: fragility and sovereignty. Financial markets are, for reasons that are now well known, marked by the inherent difficulties of uncertainty, asymmetric information, adverse selection and inability of principals to control their agents. This can all be put in a still broader way. It is in finance that we are invited to make long-term, irrevocable commitments. But we do not wish to do so. We may not wish to do so because we do not know when we need to be liquid again, which is why we put money in short-term deposits in banks and let them take the long positions. We do not wish to do so because it is too easy for those with whom we place our money to cheat us, in one way or the other. This is why we place our money with people or institutions we feel we have reason to trust: our own government; well-known business organizations; or organizations regulated within our own jurisdiction or by some other jurisdictions in whose probity and competence we have faith. The dominant theme of financial transactions is not, on the whole, risk-taking but caution, or, as often, an oscillation between greed and fear.[38]

In most countries and in relatively less developed countries, in particular, banks are overwhelmingly the most important financial institutions, for precisely these reasons. Their names are well known. They give the appearance of solidity: bank managers go to great trouble to make them seem so. They are often 'too big to fail'. The money placed within them is generally available on a short-term basis and so readily available in the event of need. They provide invaluable services, of which the most important is a mechanism for effecting payment simply, safely and quickly. But it makes no sense for all the money placed in banks to be invested in assets that are as safe, low-yielding and short term as their liabilities. So banks lend long to risky projects and are, as such, subject to maturity, credit and interest rate risks. To make a good return on capital, they economize on it. This makes them still riskier. Governments respond by insuring them against runs (through the lender-of-last-resort function) and even, to a greater or less extent, against large-scale insolvency of their debtors (through deposit insurance or even wider guarantees). In countries where governments have taken an active role in promoting development, banks have always been the favoured instruments. Apparently fiscally prudent governments can, as a result, have off-balance-sheet implicit liabilities that amount to a sizeable fraction of GDP. As the World Bank shows, it is normal for banking crises to cost the government well over 10 per cent of GDP.[39]

Banks have one other salient characteristic: their loans are debt, payable at par. Often the debt is fairly short term, at least in relation to the investments it has financed. This means that, in a crisis, adjustment occurs not through prices, but through quantities. The debtor must find the money or be declared bankrupt. But in a generalized crisis, in which almost all debtors seek to do the same thing, they cannot succeed. All they can do in scrambling to pay their debts is generate a deep recession, as Walter Bagehot suggested in the quotation at the head of this chapter. This is what a great American economist, Irving Fisher, called 'debt-deflation'. Other forms of debt can have much the same effect. But bank debt, usually being shorter term and, in most countries, also being larger than other debt, has always been the most important source of debt deflation. If one seeks a contemporary example, look at Japan.

Banks are the epicentres of financial fragility.[40] The central role of banks in generating the financial feast and famine of the past three decades, particularly in relation to emerging market finance, is entirely predictable. If we are to manage a financially integrated world better than we have done so far, banks must be more effectively caged in the countries at the core of the financial system and those at the periphery. There are many good ideas for improving the safety of financial systems. But the best ones must go with the grain of the market. Deposit insurance must be precisely and narrowly defined, with banks paying more for their insurance the smaller their capital in relation to their assets and the bigger the risks they appear to be running. Capital adequacy should be checked on a 'mark-to-market' basis – that is, on the basis of the market value of assets. Where loans cannot be so valued, regulators should make sure they understand the history and prospects of the bank's debtors. Provisioning must be adequate. Supervisors must be more than adequately paid and shielded against pressures from powerful banks and their clients. Given all the difficulties in regulating banks, especially in emerging-market economies, one of the best ideas is that banks should be required to have, in addition to normal capital, a substantial amount of relatively low-yielding, uninsured subordinated debt. This serves not only as a cushion for losses, but as a signal to regulators. There needs also to be pressure on bank management which has too great an incentive to exaggerate the performance of the institution it runs. The management of any systemically important bank that has to be rescued by the state should be disbarred, as a matter of course, from further work in the financial industry. A substantial fine should also be levied. Remember the fundamental point. Big banks have consistently operated in the knowledge that their profits are private and losses, if large enough, public. In other words, the institutions they run are underpinned by the state. Managers are, in an important sense, public servants. If they abuse that trust, they should be treated accordingly.

It is important to appreciate the reality that the fragility of banking systems, in particular, is not restricted to emerging-market economies. There the problems are merely more visible. Exactly the same fragilities exist in the banking systems of the core countries. Moreover, being vastly larger, these banks have the capacity to do vastly greater damage, as well. The fads and fancies of foolish bankers in the core countries have lain behind most of the financial crises of the past three decades. When elephants stampede, they trample down everything in the way. That is what happened to Latin America in the 1970s and 1980s and then east Asia in the 1990s. For this reason Dobson and Hubauer have rightly argued that making the world safer requires changes at both the core and the periphery. They argue that not only the behaviour of the banks but even that of hedge funds is directly related to the frailty of banking. Their recommendations include strengthening the new Basel capital accord, increasing the accountability of supervisors, tightening up on deposit insurance and reviewing the behaviour of large portfolio investors.[41]

Now turn to the second feature of our financial world: multiple sovereignties of very different quality and perceived trustworthiness. Historically, capital flows have predominantly gone to countries in whose governments the providers have trust. This is generally either because their political culture is similar or because they are part of formal or informal empires. Trust is hard to create – and easy to lose. The domestic assets of governments cannot be seized. The decision by a government to service debt is also always as much political as economic. Governments always have the option to default, openly or through inflation. The state is a more or less explicit party to a transaction that engages its citizens, any aspect of which is executable within its jurisdiction, since it creates the laws and judicial and administrative systems that determine how foreigners can expect to be treated in the event of difficulties. A bank in New York may believe it is lending to a business in São Paolo. But whether it has recourse against the assets of that business depends on the federal, state and local jurisdictions.

Certain things follow. Lending occurs in very few currencies. This is partly because few currencies are trusted. It is also because contracts in those currencies are written outside the borrowing country. International lending creates currency risk, since most emerging-market economies can borrow from foreigners only in a foreign currency. But their central banks cannot be lenders of last resort in a foreign currency, as the Asian crisis demonstrated. In the event of exchange rate shocks, the government, the financial system and much of the corporate sector can fall into difficulties simultaneously. Because of the suspicion of foreign jurisdictions, lenders are prone to flee. On longer-term loans, the risk premia in interest rates can be so high that default becomes almost inevitable. When serious difficulties do arise, one confronts, at once, the question of how a sovereign insolvency (or illiquidity) is to be managed.

The additional element of multiple sovereignties engaged in all international financial transactions creates deep challenges. At the regulatory level, it is important for governments to minimize currency mismatches within their financial systems. Again, the best way will be via market signals: floating exchange rates should make the need to watch such mismatches more carefully evident to bankers and non-financial corporations. The extent of sovereign borrowing in foreign currencies should be limited, certainly to levels well below those that seem reasonable in domestic currency. This is particularly important before a country has achieved a high credit rating. Remember the normal rule that no borrower can have a higher credit rating than its government. In addition, domestic laws should give adequate protection to all creditors. The absence of effective domestic bankruptcy procedures is one reason for panics by foreign lenders.

At this point, we must confront the most difficult of all questions: what is to be done when a sovereign falls into financial difficulties, because of its own foreign currency borrowing, borrowing by the banking system, or borrowing by a large and politically influential component of the corporate sector? The question is now sometimes referred to as 'private sector involvement', by which is meant the need for private lenders to bear some of the pain in the event of a crisis. This is the biggest of all the challenges, because a sovereign default, or risk of one, is not so much a rare event as a very special one. It is a special event because there exists no superior body, juridically, to which appeal can be made. To put the point another way, a sovereign cannot be made bankrupt and put into some form of administration, as can any other entity. If it could be, it would not be a sovereign.[42] More than two decades ago, a distinguished American commercial banker, Walter Wriston, said that countries do not go bust. He was right. Countries do not go bust. Their bankers do – and have done so repeatedly throughout history. Sovereigns, even if they do not go bust, do, however, fall into difficulties. The question is what should then be done.

Why is private sector involvement not just appropriate but inevitable? One reason is that the IMF does not now have – and will never be given – enough money to let lenders escape unscathed from all conceivable crises. The other is that it is not undesirable that the IMF should have enough money to achieve this, since that is bound to create a significant degree of moral hazard without any likelihood of adequate offsetting regulation. It is also unclear why foreign lenders should always escape unscathed, at the expense of a burden on the taxpayers of the borrowing country. Yet even if we accept that private sector involvement of some kind is both desirable and inevitable, how is it to be managed in practice? There are risks. If lenders knew they would always lose in a panic, the panic will come still sooner, though that may be offset by a reduced willingness to take risks in the first place.

The current policy, agreed in Prague in September 2000, distinguishes four cases: those where policy adjustment and official financing should allow the member to regain full market access swiftly; those where official adjustment and policy action need to be combined with a voluntary agreement among creditors to avoid the collectively ruinous rush to the door; those where early restoration of full market access is unrealistic and comprehensive debt restructuring may be required; and, finally, those where members may have to resort to a temporary payments suspension or standstill, while the Fund would be prepared to lend into arrears to private creditors, provided the country is making an effort to work co-operatively with its creditors and is meeting other programme requirements.[43] If one were to apply the ideas of illiquidity and insolvency (always difficult to do in the case of sovereigns), the first two fall under the former and the last under the latter, with the third unclear.

This framework, observes Mr Fischer, runs into four possible difficulties: a voluntary agreement to rollover debt is reached, but subsequent slippage by the country undermines the ability of the official sector to insist upon its continuation; regulators may be unwilling to encourage rollovers by banks under their jurisdiction, because they may believe in some case that doing so is inconsistent with their supervisory responsibilities; the emphasis on purely voluntary debt restructurings makes sense only where illiquidity is the difficulty; the last and, as Fischer states, most profound difficulty occurs where a temporary standstill or suspension is required, since *there is no accepted framework in which a country in extremis can impose a payments suspension or standstill pending agreement with its creditors to support the restoration of viability – and that accordingly any country contemplating a standstill faces enormous uncertainties about what will happen to the economy if it does so* [emphasis in original]. Furthermore, adds Fischer, *those uncertainties are compounded by the absence of an accepted legal framework in which the debtor and its creditors can work to seek to restore viability*.[44]

Many economists now accept that such a mechanism is essential. The idea is an old one. It was taken up by Professor Sachs in 1995 and has subsequently been developed by Anne Krueger, first deputy managing director of the IMF, through her proposal for a Sovereign Debt Restructuring Mechanism.[45] Yet the idea remains controversial, for understandable reasons.

It is possible to argue that the ability to impose a standstill in the case of a run on a country is, in fact, in everybody's interests. Indeed, in the absence of a true lender of last resort or some informal way of co-ordinating creditor behaviour, there is no other obvious way of dealing with the kind of panic that hit South Korea in December 1997, short of accepting a messy default. Yet this is not how it is likely to appear to creditors. They will see their rights impaired and, correspondingly, the pain suffered by the debtor reduced. This will, in turn, make their loans less safe, since, in dealing with a sovereign debtor, pain is the only penalty for bad behaviour. Consequently, it can be argued that the net result of these proposals will be to raise the cost of funds to emerging market borrowers, perhaps even endangering the entire sovereign debt market.[46] It is for this reason that emerging-market borrowers themselves have almost universally opposed any suggestions that appear to make a standstill or outright default easier.

These objections are answerable. In particular, the principal sanction on a sovereign standstill or default would remain: its loss of reputation. I have no difficulties with the provision of sufficient money to a country in South Korea's December 1997 situation to allow it to pay off its creditors. The only condition would be that the country will be able to repay the money to the official sector, as Korea could and indeed did. But if such funds are not to be made available, it must be better to impose an orderly standstill than watch on the sidelines as a country fully able to meet its obligations in reasonable time slides into messy and unnecessary default. Where a default is inevitable, the need for an official mechanism is less overwhelming. Negotiations are then inescapable and, as inescapably, messy. But none of these possibilities undermines the most important lesson of both theory and experience, which is that borrowing in foreign currencies must be undertaken prudently. Governments must be concerned about both their own liabilities and those of the country as a whole, and especially of the financial system. Regulations and taxes should be designed to ensure that decision-makers are aware of the collective risks. For all these reasons, it is sensible to do exactly the opposite of what many critics of globalization desire, namely, to encourage equity investment and, in particular, inward direct investment.

Two further issues need to be addressed. One is very close to the question of sovereign bankruptcies. It is 'odious debt', the debt bequeathed by illegitimate regimes. Together with the heavy official debts now borne by some of the world's poorest countries, these debts do more to undermine the legitimacy of sovereign borrowing than anything else. Why, people quite reasonably ask, should innocent people have to repay debt incurred by the tyrants who persecuted them when in office? Michael Kremer and Seema Jayachandran of Harvard have put forward the clever idea that an institution should be set up to declare, in advance, whether a regime is odious and its borrowing correspondingly illegitimate. If such loans were unenforceable in the courts of the originating country, the effect would be to starve the odious regime of funds, without undermining the successor's ability to borrow. This would be the smartest of all smart sanctions. Such a regime would work so long as the institution could only make its judgements prospectively. The authors suggest a clever addition: the international financial institutions – the IMF and World Bank – might publicly declare that a given country's policies are not, in their view, consistent with subsequent repayment. Should the country fall into subsequent difficulties, they will not lend to it in order to help rescue any foolish creditors. Such lending would not be deemed illegitimate, merely risky.[47]

The final, and very different, reform proposal is the so-called Tobin tax. Some critics of globalization favour the tax because they expect it to raise revenue for the finance of development assistance. That is a very different question. The late Nobel-laureate economist James Tobin proposed the tax, however, to reduce currency speculation – throw sand in the wheels, as he put it. The more successful it is at that, the less revenue it will raise. Professor Tobin's suggestion was of a very low tax on each individual currency transaction. This, he believed, would make it easier for governments to pursue their own monetary and fiscal policies, without undue concern about the exchange rate. The idea raises three questions: would it stabilize currency markets? Would it be desirable to stabilize those markets in that way? Is it feasible? The answer to all these questions is probably no. On the first, any very low tax would not prevent big jumps in exchange rates and might make the day-to-day course more, not less, volatile, since it would reduce hedging activity. For the same reason, it is far from evident that the tax would be desirable. People are mesmerized by the trillions of dollars in trading, but the vast majority of this is hedging activity and unlikely to have any significant net effect on the market. Finally, while some people believe it might be possible to collect the tax at the point of settlement among the big commercial banks, the feasibility of the idea is open to question. The clever people in financial markets would probably be able to discover ways of making the same trades in other markets.

Conclusion

As Professor Eichengreen has remarked, 'the crisis problem is back'.[48] Nobody can be satisfied with what has happened as emerging-market economies have tried to integrate into world capital markets. The gains have been questionable and the costs of crises enormous. It would be easy to conclude that the simple lesson is: do not liberalise. But, for a host of reasons, emerging-market economies should ultimately plan to integrate into the global capital markets, with emphasis on the words 'ultimately' and 'plan'. What has happened so far has been a series of blunders on both sides. Equally, the record of the IMF, though not as dismal as many of its critics believe, is far from a proud one. Surely its biggest mistake was failing to warn countries adequately of the dangers that confronted them. While countries may have had to learn from painful experience, one would have hoped that the organization charged with advising them could have done a better job of doing so.

The challenge now is to help emerging-market economies engage with world capital markets more successfully. It can be done. But changes are needed. They will have to rethink domestic regulation, laws and behaviour in such areas as the role of banks, the place of foreign financial institutions, deposit insurance and other guarantees, bankruptcy regimes and exchange rate policies. They will also have to be careful about exposing their countries to large-scale foreign currency borrowing. Equity is safer, with foreign direct investment best of all. Factories do not walk. Changes will also be needed at the global level, not least in sorting out how the private sector is to be treated during financial crises. The world cannot afford another series of comparable crises. It must act now to prevent them.

Part V   **How to Make the World Better**

Chapter 14   Today's Threats, Tomorrow's Promises

The natural effort of every individual to better his own condition, when suffered to exert itself with freedom and security, is so powerful a principle, that it is alone, and without any assistance, not only capable of carrying on the society to wealth and prosperity, but of surmounting a hundred impertinent obstructions with which the folly of human laws too often incumbers its operations; though the effect of these obstructions is always more or less either to encroach upon its freedom, or to diminish its security. In Great Britain industry is perfectly secure; and though it is far from perfectly free, it is free or freer than in any other part of Europe.

Adam Smith[1]

This year, 2002, over 100 million Europeans went to the polls. Where were the extreme protesters and their agendas? Why didn't they set out their ideas directly in the democratic marketplace? Because they would not get public support. Many even disdain the parliamentary system, saying it is unrepresentative and corrupt, claiming that only they maintain the pure and uncontaminated truth. These extremists, who lay claim to follow the heritage of Gandhi and Martin Luther King, are really the descendants of strictly reactionary and even more utopian early fascists and Marxists. The last time the far left and far right held hands in the streets of Europe was to fight against decadent democracies in the 1930s.

Mike Moore, former director general of the World Trade Organization[2]

The 1980s and 1990s witnessed the collapse of the Soviet communist tyranny, an unprecedentedly rapid spread of democracy and nigh on universal economic liberalization. East and south Asia, home to 55 per cent of humanity, enjoyed a leap towards prosperity. Yet critics of globalization talk of this period of hope and achievement as if it were a catastrophe. Some do so out of a genuine and understandable dismay over the extent of poverty and misery in a world of plenty, but then reach the wrong conclusions on the causes and cures. Others do so because they lament the death of the revolutionary tradition that held sway over the imaginations of so many over two centuries. Most of these critics compare the imperfect world in which we live with a perfect one of their imagining. It is in their way of viewing what has happened in the world, rather than the details of their critique, that those hostile to global economic integration are most in error.

What we must do is build upon what has been achieved, not, as so many critics wish, throw it all away. In the era after 11 September 2001, that co-operative task has certainly become far more difficult. For peoples to sustain openness to one another is far harder at a time of fear than at a time of confidence. But the task has also become more urgent. A collapse of economic integration would be a calamity. Not only would it deprive much of humanity of hope for a better life. It would also, inevitably, exacerbate friction among the countries of the world.

This final chapter addresses this challenge. It does not do so by advancing an elaborate blueprint for a new world order. That would almost certainly be futile and quite certainly be beyond its scope. It focuses instead on four big issues. First, it analyses whether another collapse of global economic integration, similar to that of the 1914–45 period, is likely. Second, it emphasizes the core dilemma of our world – the one that arises in trying to reconcile commitments to national sovereignty and democracy with the desire for universal prosperity and the provision of global public goods. Third, it considers how far the anti-globalization critique helps us deal with those dilemmas. Finally, it suggests some possible routes forward.

Threats to globalization

The international economic integration of the late nineteenth century went into reverse. Is the present move towards integration likely to suffer the same fate? To answer this question, one needs to take account of the differences and similarities between these two epochs considered in Part III. The breakdown last time was the consequence of the combined force of international rivalry, instability, interests and ideas. How likely are the same four horsemen of the apocalypse to return?

International rivalry

The first cause of the breakdown in the 1930s was the collapse of harmonious international relations, as rivalries among the great powers and the rise of communism and fascism fragmented the globe. Today, however, the situation is different, in four fundamental respects.

First, there is a single undisputed hegemon, the US, and little chance of a war among great powers in the near future, except just conceivably between the US and China over Taiwan. Yet China is not, at present, powerful enough to be a rival of the US. True, a unilateralist US may, in time, create a balancing coalition against it. Even so, a move to open hostilities seems quite improbable.

Second, all the great powers have abandoned the atavistic notion that prosperity derives from territorial gains and plunder rather than internal economic development and peaceful exchange. One of the striking features of today's war against terrorism is that all the world's great powers are on the same side.

Third, all the great powers share a commitment to market-led economic development and international economic and political integration.

Fourth, global institutions and habits of close co-operation reinforce the commitment to co-operation.

All these are powerful differences between the world of nearly a century ago and today's world. Against this, we must note one obvious parallel. The breakdown of the early twentieth century occurred, in part, because of the pressures to accommodate rising powers in the global economic and political order. The rise of China will, in time, create comparable pressures. If the US remains wedded to notions of global primacy rather than of a shared global order, conflict with a rising China would seem inevitable. In addition, China's rise will force uncomfortable economic adjustment on the rest of the world. These are already creating protectionist pressures, notably so in the US. It is not, alas, impossible to envisage a spiral of mutual hostility that undermines the commitment to a liberal international economic order.

Today, however, instead of such a breakdown in relations among the world's most important powers, we confront an alternative threat: mega-terrorism. Some fear that terrorist outrages on the scale of the attacks on New York and Washington of 11 September 2001 – or even bigger ones – will end the commitment to open borders. It is not difficult to envisage the devastating impact on confidence in open borders of a nuclear device smuggled into a country on a container ship. Closely related fears concern the weapons of mass destruction being developed by regimes hostile to the liberal world order, in general, and the US, in particular. At worst, such regimes might collaborate with terrorists to inflict vast, and virtually untraceable, damage on civilized states.

Fear of what might come across borders must act as a tax on globalization. If countries had to be sure of the safety of every shipment and person that crossed their borders, much of today's globalization would become impossible. Yet that would also hand the victory to the terrorists and their sponsors. At present, it does not appear that the world's response to 11 September will be to close borders. That would only exacerbate desperation in the world's less economically successful countries. Global co-operation to control terrorists and improved security measures seem a more appropriate and effective route. But the danger is a genuine one. It cannot be ignored.

Instability

The decisive event in the collapse of the integrated economy of the late nineteenth and early twentieth century was the Great Depression in the US and the financial and exchange rate crises that rolled across the world in the 1930s.[3] In developing countries, as was noted in Part IV, financial and exchange rate crises have come with depressing frequency over the past two decades. Substantial financial and exchange rate crises also erupted among the other advanced economies in the 1980s and early 1990s. Japan is still struggling with the aftermath of its 'bubble economy', while the US has also suffered a huge stock-market bubble, which reached its maximum extent in 2000.[4]

All these are signs of significant financial instability. Yet it is almost impossible to believe that the outcome will be another 1930s. The move to floating rates has, as Max Corden foresaw, significantly reduced the risk of such crises.[5] The woes inflicted upon Argentina by the collapse of its currency board at the end of 2001 should, therefore, be viewed as the end of an era rather than as the beginning of a new one. Its crisis has also had remarkably little effect on other emerging-market economies. The flood of what the nineteenth-century British economic commentator Walter Bagehot once called 'silly money' into the emerging markets, which followed the end of the Cold War, has become a trickle. Much of the transfer is now taking place in the longer-term and more sustainable form of foreign direct investment. For all these reasons, the likelihood of massive waves of financial crises in emerging-market economies has declined. It is also striking that, despite these crises, no significant country has reversed the commitment to liberal trade or even to freedom from exchange controls. That even includes Argentina. Today, such policies are seen as a dead end – the quickest way to join Castro's Cuba or Kim Jong Il's North Korea in far from splendid isolation.

Interests

The third force underlying the disintegration of the earlier form of global-ization was protectionist interests. Yet these, too, have been significantly modified and ameliorated by contemporary economic developments.

The rise of the internationally integrated transnational company has reduced the ability (and willingness) of producers to wrap themselves in national flags. It is no accident that protectionist interests are strongest in predominantly nationally owned and operated industries – such as steel and agriculture. In most modern industries – including services – the largest companies are not national. Is a Toyota factory in the US less or more American than a General Motors factory in China? Is Goldman Sachs in Frankfurt less or more American than HSBC in New York? The answer to such questions is: who knows? Modern companies have global interests. The same is true of many of their most valued employees. Nationalists find the cosmopolitan attitudes of companies and many top-level employees particularly objectionable. A significant consequence, however, is the breakdown in the ability and willingness of companies to collab-orate with trades unions in the demand for protection. Developing countries have been affected by the same trends. Inward FDI and intra-industry trade diffuse traditional protectionist interests. The concept of a purely national business sector has become increasingly irrelevant and, just as in industrial countries, this diffuses protectionist lobbying.

The increase in service sector employment and the decline in employment in manufacturing has, along with the rise in the portion of the population in retirement, reduced the share of the voters whose jobs are directly vulnerable to import competition. Consumers have also become accustomed to foreign products. They may complain, as workers, about imports. But they still like the products foreign companies provide. Many in high-income countries express concern about the decline in relative wages and employment opportunities of the unskilled. But the political power of this group of people has, with the general decline of the industrial working class, diminished. Moreover, the consensus of economists, disputed by only a minority of politicians, is that this decline in opportunities has reflected changes in technology, not in trade.

In addition, the existence of multilateral institutions and a web of strong international commitments makes it far more difficult for protectionist interests to capture legislatures, as they once did. There is too much at stake for countries to reverse the commitments they have made. Even the administration of George W. Bush, wedded though it is to unilateralism, never said that it should ignore its obligations under the WTO, even though it is the most binding multilateral economic commitment of the US.

Ideas

The final element in the twentieth-century collapse of the liberal international order began at home with the rise of anti-liberal ideas. There are parallels today, particularly in what the former chief economist of the OECD, David Henderson, has called 'new millennium collectivists' – the groups who unite to protest against global capitalism.[6] But this group of protesters is very different – and much less intellectually coherent – from the opponents of liberalism of a century ago. Then the antagonists of liberalism converged around two ideas: radical socialism and racially defined nationalism. Both groups called for control of the state over the economy and primacy of the collective over the self-seeking individual. Both sought, and knew what they wanted to do with, power. That made them extraordinarily dangerous.

The intellectual origins of today's anti-liberal movement are, as I noted in Part I of this book, far more diverse. They include environmentalists, development lobbies, populists, socialists, communists and anarchists. In a review of Mike Moore's book on his time at the WTO, Rosemary Righter of the London *Times* argues, correctly, that 'the anti-globalization brigade is a hotchpotch of contradictions, linking Left and Right, Poujadists, protectionists and environmentalists, nationalists and anarchists, stolid religious charities and, depressingly, veterans of the heady days of radical chic when Western activists brandished Mao Zedong's Little Red Book while millions were being murdered in the Cultural Revolution'.[7]

These groups are united only in what they oppose. They are rooted in no cohesive social force, such as the organized working class. They largely reject party politics. They offer no alternative way of running an economy. They are split in their objectives: some want greater national sovereignty, while others want global government, some want development in poor countries, while others want to halt it; some are against international integration, while accepting some forms of the market economy; some want to return to an environmentally pure past; some are against the corporation; some are against oppressive states; and some are against any and all economic change. Part of what some protesters say – notably on the hypocrisy of the advanced countries and the plight of the poor – is valid. But a political movement cannot beat something with nothing. A movement that offers only protest is unlikely to triumph.

Second time as farce

Yet even though history is unlikely to repeat itself, the danger to our open world economy is not small. The combination of fears of terrorism, economic instability, protectionist reactions to economic change and the rise of new competitors, particularly China, and protesters against economic integration could yet do grave damage.

The great dilemma

It seems plausible, therefore, that global economic integration will not collapse, as it did in the early twentieth century. But that does not mean it will advance in ways that provide the greatest possible opportunities for the largest possible proportion of humanity. Let us step back, for a moment, and consider the biggest obstacle to a more even spread of global prosperity and the provision of essential global public goods. That obstacle is neither global economic integration nor transnational companies, as the critics allege, but the multiplicity of independent sovereigns. It is not just the failure of states but their existence that creates many of the problems we now confront.[8] This is not an argument for world government, which would, even if feasible, bring many problems of its own. But it is a demand for recognition of the inevitable consequences of a world divided into many sovereign states of vastly different competence.

Think, first of all, of global inequality. Inequality among individuals has exploded over much of the past two centuries, not because of increased inequality within countries, but because of the divergent growth of different societies. Then, over the past two decades, the accelerated growth of a number of very large, poor countries, above all China and India, appears to have reduced global inter-personal inequality. But a huge number of countries containing some 1.5 billion people lag ever further behind. The overwhelming probability is that some, though not all, of these countries will continue to do so in decades to come. If so, not only absolute difference in standards of living but even relative gaps in living standards will continue to grow between the richest and the poorest countries in the world. Today, that ratio is some seventy-five to one. A century ago, it was about ten to one. In half a century, it could all too easily be 150 to one.

What lies behind such massive divergences in performance? A large part of the answer is cumulative historical forces that go back centuries. As some countries have grown richer, they have become better able to afford high standards of education, health and public services. As their citizens have become better informed and more prosperous, they have insisted on higher standards in public life. At a certain point, economic growth has become a routine. A positive cycle of reinforcement has then gone from the economy to polity and society, and back again. Meanwhile, at the opposite end of the spectrum of success, some societies have become stuck in a powerful vicious cycle. Very low standards of living have meant correspondingly limited ability to provide any of the necessary public goods that underpin economic growth. Education remains inadequate and illiteracy rife. Economic activity remains extremely unsophisticated. Ambitious people view politics as a way to extract the wealth unavailable in normal economic activity. The result is corruption or, at worst, civil war. Among large states, the United States may be seen as an exemplar of the first kind of society and Nigeria as an exemplar of the second. Among small states, one might contrast Finland with Sierra Leone.

The forces at work do not, fortunately, only cause divergence. There are also forces for convergence. The accumulated know-how and markets of the high-income countries offer opportunities for economic catch-up. But the evidence suggests that some societies are far better able to catch up than others. Natural-resource abundance has proved a handicap for many, for a host of reasons, not least the opportunities it gives for rent-seeking by politicians. In contrast, labour abundance seems to work well, though only in the right policy environment, not least because it creates a direct connection between effort and reward. In an economy whose wealth is based on the efforts of its citizens, rather than on riches that come out of the ground, a government's ability to extract resources while failing to provide valuable services in return is limited. The mutual dependence of the citizens and state forms the basis of a functioning social contract. If the state breaks that contract, by extortion, the economy fails to grow or even retrogresses. None of these constraints works as effectively in resource-rich countries

It we ask further what would be the most powerful mechanism for ensuring that the forces of economic convergence overwhelm those of divergence, the answer has to be jurisdictional integration. The European Union is a regional system of jurisdictional integration. It imposes an obligation on all its members to accept freedom to trade, migrate and move capital. Such integration is not just an obligation, it is a credible commitment. These commitments have made the EU an extraordinarily successful machine for generating economic catch-up among previously poorer members, from Italy in the 1950s and 1960s to Ireland in the 1990s. Now the same forces are to be unleashed in the ten new members from central and eastern Europe which joined in 2004. If similarly credible obligations could be spread globally, there can be little doubt that convergence would tend to accelerate. At present, as I have noted, capital flows to developing countries are modest. But if the commitments to protecting property and allowing capital to move freely were credible everywhere, the movement of capital to poor countries would greatly increase. Again, if people could move freely from poor and failing countries to richer ones, global inequality and extreme poverty would certainly both fall substantially.

We can go even further. Imagine jurisdictional integration not just in the sense of the contemporary EU, but in the sense of a contemporary federal state, say, the United States. Imagine that the US was not one of the world's countries, but had become a global federation offering equal voting rights for all. Far greater resources would then flow to the poorer regions of this imaginary world-including US, to finance infrastructure, education, health and the machinery of law and order. This should not be surprising. We know very well that money is spent by a country on those with a political voice. In 2001, total official assistance from rich countries to all developing countries amounted to $52 billion. This was substantially less than the sums spent by the British government on the education of that country's young people and roughly a seventh of what the rich countries spend on direct and indirect assistance to their farmers. Provided such a world-country avoided imposing unnecessarily high costs on labour in the poorer regions, as Germany did mistakenly after unification in the early 1990s, convergence should be accelerated still further.

These thought experiments illuminate what is far and away the most important source of inequality and persistent poverty: the fact that humanity is locked into almost 200 distinct countries, some of which are prosperous, well governed and civilized, while many others are poor, malgoverned and apparently incapable of providing the basis of a tolerable existence. Since the success of the economy depends on the quality of the state, this inequality in the quality of states guarantees persistent inequality among individuals.

The multiplicity of countries, their divergent historical experiences and the differences in the quality of the regimes they live under do not merely help perpetuate mass poverty and global inequality. They also make it difficult to ensure the provision of global public goods. The underlying constraint is free-riding. While everybody should be better off if countries combined to provide global public goods, it is usually in the interests of individual countries to let others bear the cost. This, however, is not the only difficulty. Some public goods may be of far greater importance to some countries than to others. Elimination of AIDS from southern Africa is an obvious example: it is of overriding importance to the countries concerned, but of much less moment to those far away. But the resources needed to tackle such a disease may be unavailable in the countries most directly affected. Similarly, those likely to be most damaged by global warming may well not be those that have done most to cause it. Indeed, that is certainly the case.

These obstacles to creating a better world are created by deep-seated conflicts among the values the contemporary world holds dear. We believe in self-governing sovereign states, democracy and, if not in greater global equality, at the least in alleviation of global poverty. But rich sovereign democracies will always use the bulk of their resources to tackle the problems of their own citizens and protect themselves against disruption from abroad. They will control immigration tightly and be strongly inclined towards protecting their citizens from the impact of imports from the rest of the world. Similarly, an impoverished sovereign state must rely largely on its own resources. At worst, an incompetent, plundering, even murderous regime may assail its people without hindrance. At best, it will struggle to create the conditions for greater prosperity.

This is, to repeat, not an argument for world government. Even if it were achievable, such a leviathan would almost certainly crush the enterprise and competition that generates economic advance. Nor could such a world-state be meaningfully democratic. Even in the EU, differences in culture, language and sense of identity make it hard to generate anything approximating to a European politics. Elections without a shared political space are barren. At best, they generate remote technocracies. At worst, they can end up with the tyranny not so much of the majority as of enraged and self-interested minorities. But the globe's political fragmentation is, none the less, a big obstacle to the achievement of many of the objectives the critics of globalization hold dear. Only a few lunatics – the localizers – believe that the prosperity of the citizens of existing countries would be enhanced by fragmenting the integrated markets of contemporary national economies into self-sufficient village or manorial economies. But the world economy is fragmented, notwithstanding the progress made towards exploiting at least some of the potential gains from economic integration in recent decades. For that, the principal explanation is the world's political fragmentation.

Learning from the critique

How are we to reconcile the reality of a world divided into unequal sovereignties with exploitation of the opportunities offered by international economic integration? That is the challenge we confront. How far, in turn, do the critics of market-led globalization help us to answer this question? The answer is: hardly at all, partly because of the divergence of opinions they offer and partly because many live in a fantasy world. Anarchists, for example, believe in the possibility of a society without government and coercion. But without a state, power rests with gangsters: Sierra Leone is hardly a model on which the world can – or should – be expected to build. Those in favour of economic localization apparently believe the power of corporations would be smaller if they were freed from the pressures of global competition. Again, deep greens want to halt economic advance, whatever the wishes of humanity. Protest may be fun. But it is a basis for neither effective policy nor mature politics.

Many of the critics argue that more sovereign discretion should be granted to countries than at present, particularly in relation to the World Bank and International Monetary Fund, but also in relation to the rules of the World Trade Organization. Yet many – sometimes even the same people – argue that such discretion should be limited in order to ensure environmental protection.

The argument then is not about the principle of sovereign autonomy, but rather about what countries should be required to do and not to do. Yet others argue in favour of autonomy for developing countries to pursue the strategies they desire, while expecting high-income countries to maintain open borders and provide more development assistance. Others, in turn, argue that high-income countries should be free to protect their workers from unfair competition from developing countries, while forcing developing countries to accept minimum environmental and labour standards. This is a cacophony, with loud disagreements over whether countries should be free to do as they wish, over which countries should enjoy such freedom, and over what areas of policy they should be allowed to choose.

A narrower set of questions is how far the specific criticisms analysed in Part IV should inform our ideas about the appropriate direction for reform. The analysis suggests that at least some of the points that critics have made do need to be taken into account. Among the most important are:

- the case for permitting infant industry promotion (though not necessarily protection) in developing countries;
- the arguments for high-income countries to open their markets in favour of exports from developing countries;
- the need to be aware of the risks of mismanaged liberalization of capital controls;
- the risk that institutions might be captured by special interests, as was the case for the agreement on trade-related intellectual property in the Uruguay Round;
- the case for international regimes that deal with global environmental challenges;
- the need to set the argument for international economic integration together with those for sound public finances, macroeconomic stability, financial stability, adequate investment in education, health and infrastructure, encouragement for innovation and, above all, the rule of law.

These are legitimate, albeit limited, concerns. But the more hysterical complaints of the critics of international economic integration are nonsense. Transnational companies do not rule the world. Neither the WTO nor the IMF can force countries to do what they would prefer not to do. Crises do not afflict sound financial systems. Global economic integration does not render states helpless. Nor has it created unprecedented poverty and inequality. The critics represent the latest – and least intellectually impressive – of a long series of assaults on the market economy. Yet, however unimpressive their arguments, these critics are dangerous, because they can give protectionist interests legitimacy. The critique allows protectionists to claim that they benefit the poor of the world as they deprive them of the opportunity to earn their living on world markets.

Global challenge

What sort of world should people who understand the power of market forces for human betterment now support? What role should international institutions play? And what are the proper limits of national sovereignty? None of these are simple questions. Difficult choices arise. There is no one set of right answers. My suggestions come in 'ten commandments of globalization'.

First, the market economy is the only arrangement capable of generating sustained increases in prosperity, providing the underpinnings of stable liberal democracies and giving individual human beings the opportunity to seek what they desire in life.

Second, individual states remain the locus of political debate and legitimacy. Supranational institutions gain their legitimacy and authority from the states that belong to them.

Third, it is in the interest of both states and their citizens to participate in international treaty-based regimes and institutions that deliver global public goods, including open markets, environmental protection, health and international security.

Fourth, such regimes need to be specific, focused and enforceable.

Fifth, the WTO, though enormously successful, has already strayed too far from its primary function of promoting trade liberalization. The arguments for a single undertaking that binds all members need to be reconsidered, since that brings into the negotiations a large number of small countries with negligible impact on world trade and gives them disproportionate power.

Sixth, the case for regimes covering investment and global competition is strong. But it would be best to create regimes that include fewer countries, but contain higher standards.

Seventh, it is in the long-run interest of countries to integrate into global financial markets. But they should do so carefully, in full understanding of the risks.

Eighth, in the absence of a global lender of last resort, it is necessary to accept standstills and renegotiation of sovereign debt.

Ninth, official development assistance is far from a guarantee of successful development. But the sums now provided are so small, just over a fifth of a per cent of the gross domestic product of the donor countries, that more would help if given to countries with reasonably sound policy regimes. But aid should never be so large that it frees a government from the need to raise most of its money from its own people.

Tenth, countries should learn from their own mistakes. But the global community also needs the capacity and will to intervene where states have failed altogether.

All these commandments matter. But the first two are the most important. The view that states and markets are in opposition to one another is the obverse of the truth. The world needs more globalization, not less. But we will only have more and better globalization if we have better states. Above all, we must recognize that inequality and persistent poverty are the consequence not of the still limited integration of the world's economy but of its political fragmentation. If we wish to make our world a better place, we must look not at the failures of the market economy, but at the hypocrisy, greed and stupidity that so often mar our politics, in both developing and developed countries.

The sight of the affluent young of the west wishing to protect the poor of the world from the processes that delivered their own remarkable prosperity is depressing. So, too, is the return of all the old anti-capitalist clichés is as if the collapse of Soviet communism had never happened. We must, and can, make the world a better place to live in. But we will do so only by ignoring these siren voices. The open society has, as always, its enemies both within and without. Our time is no exception. We owe it to posterity to ensure that they do not triumph.

Notes

Preface

1 'On Mitford's History of Greece', *Knight's Quarterly Magazine*, November 1824.
2 The world 'liberal' has become almost unusable nowadays. Broadly speaking, contemporary liberals can be divided into those who emphasize freedoms from the state and those who rely on a benevolent state to provide welfare and other interventions in the interest, in particular, of the disadvantaged. The former tend to emphasize economic freedoms. The latter tend to emphasize social freedoms. The former generally call themselves classical liberals in the United Kingdom and libertarians or, in some guises, conservatives in the United States, while their opponents condemn them as 'neo-liberals' or 'ultra-liberals'. At the turn of the nineteenth and twentieth centuries, the latter were known as 'new liberals' in the United Kingdom. In the United States, they have long been called 'liberals'. An alternative name, suggested by the political sociologist Ralph Dahrendorf, would be 'social liberals', though it would be clearer if such social liberals could be called 'social democrats'. That would leave the word liberal largely in its original or classical sense. In this book, the liberalism is essentially that of John Stuart Mill and embraces economic, personal and civic freedoms. Its basic creed is contained in the classic statement in Mill's *On Liberty* of 1859 – 'The sole end for which mankind are warranted, individually or collectively, in interfering with the liberty of any of their number is self-protection. ... His own good, either physical or moral, is not a sufficient warrant.' There is an excellent discussion of these distinctions in Samuel Brittan, *Towards a Human Individualism* (London: John Stuart Mill Institute, 1998). There, Sir Samuel Brittan embraces the term 'redistributive market liberal', suggested by Adair Turner, former director general of the Confederation of British Industry, to describe classical liberals who accept the desirability of redistribution of incomes in favour of the poor.
3 W. M. Corden, *The Theory of Protection* (Oxford: Clarendon Press, 1971). Corden's teaching of that time also subsequently appeared in his characteristically lucid *Trade Policy and Economic Welfare* (Oxford: Clarendon Press, 1974), whose second edition appeared in 1997.
4 Ian Little, Tibor Scitovsky and Maurice Scott, *Industry and Trade in Some Developing Countries: A Comparative Study* (London: Oxford University Press, for the Organization for Economic Co-operation and Development, 1970). This overview drew on country studies of Brazil, Mexico, India. Pakistan, Taiwan and

the Philippines. Of these both the best and the most important for me, since I subsequently worked on India for the World Bank, was Jagdish N. Bhagwati and Padma Desai, *India: Planning for Industrialization* (London: Oxford University Press, for the Organization for Economic Co-operation and Development, 1970).

5　Martin Wolf, *India's Exports* (New York: Oxford University Press, for the World Bank, 1982).

6　Bela Balassa, *Development Strategies in Semi-industrial Economies* (Baltimore: Johns Hopkins University Press, for the World Bank, 1982).

7　Jagdish N. Bhagwati, *Anatomy and Consequences of Exchange Control Regimes: Foreign Trade Regimes and Economic Development*, Vol. XI (New York: Ballinger Publishing, for the National Bureau for Economic Research, 1978); Anne O. Krueger, *Liberalization Attempts and Consequences: Foreign Trade Regimes and Economic Development*, Vol. X (New York: Ballinger Publishing, for the National Bureau for Economic Research, 1978).

8　The best account I have read of why the Bank failed as a development institution is by Bill Easterly, formerly of the World Bank Staff. See William Easterly, *The Elusive Quest for Growth: Economists' Adventures and Misadventures in the Tropics* (Cambridge, Massachusetts: MIT Press, 2001), especially chapter 2.

9　See, for example, his *Dissent on Development: Studies and Debates in Development Economics* (Cambridge, Massachusetts: Harvard University Press, 1972).

10　Donald B. Keesing and Martin Wolf, *Textile Quotas against Developing Countries*, Thames Essay No. 23 (London: Trade Policy Research Centre, 1980).

11　Robert E. Hudec, *Developing Countries in the GATT Legal System*, Thames Essay No. 50 (Aldershot: Gower, for the Trade Policy Research Centre, 1987).

12　This thesis is advanced with passion by Brink Lindsey of the Washington-based Cato Institute in *Against the Dead Hand: The Uncertain Struggle for Global Capitalism* (Washington DC: John Wiley, 2002). An excellent study of the rebirth of market liberalism is Daniel Yergin and Joseph Stanislaw, *The Commanding Heights: The Battle between Government and the Marketplace that is Remaking the Modern World* (New York: Simon & Schuster, 1998).

Chapter 1:　Enter the 'New Millennium Collectivists'

1　This happy label for the protesters against globalization was coined by David Henderson, formerly head of economics at the Organization for Economic Co-operation and Development. See his *Anti-Liberalism 2000: The Rise of New Millennium Collectivism* (London: Institute of Economic Affairs, 2001).

2　*Financial Times*, 31 December 1993. It is worth remembering that Balladur was a prime minister of the French right.

3　See 'Global Integration: Currents and Counter-Currents', Walter Gordon Lecture, Massey College, University of Toronto, 23 May 2001.

4　John Lloyd provides an excellent analysis from a left-of-centre perspective in *The Protest Ethic: How the Anti-Globalization Movement Challenges Social Democracy* (London: Demos, 2001).

5 Mancur Olson, *The Rise and Decline of Nations: Economic Growth, Stagflation, and Social Rigidities* (New Haven, Connecticut: Yale University Press, 1982).

6 Jagdish Bhagwati, *Free Trade Today* (Princeton: Princeton University Press, 2002), p. 48.

7 Susan Aaronson provides a fascinating account of the politics of street protest in the United States in her *Taking Trade to the Streets: the Lost History of Public Efforts to Shape Globalization* (Ann Arbor, Michigan: Michigan University Press, 2001). A scholarly study of the new ideological lobbies is I. M. Destler and Peter J. Balint, *The New Politics of American Trade: Trade, Labor, and the Environment* (Washington DC: Institute for International Economics, 1999). A hymn to the joys of high-minded protest is a central element of Naomi Klein's bible for the protesters, *No Logo* (London: Flamingo, 2000). I provide a jaundiced view in 'what the world needs from the multilateral trading system', in Gary P. Sampson (ed.), *The Role of the World Trade Organization in Global Governance* (Tokyo: United Nations University Press, 2001), pp. 187–91.

8 Vincent Cable, in his outstanding short analysis of globalization, lists five categories of anti-globalizers: nationalists, mercantilists, regionalists, dependency theorists and deep greens. The first four categories on this list have similar attitudes to those of the anti-liberal movements of a century ago, though Cable adds the special twist of what he calls 'fair traders' (a peculiarly American variety of nationalist). Mercantilists are nationalists in economic dress. Regionalists are also nationalists, but with a larger perspective. This is evidently true of those Europeans who favour a fortress Europe, because they consider the old nation states too small to achieve the needed degree of self-sufficiency and political autonomy. The difference between Jean-Marie Le Pen and many members of the French élite is that the former prefers being narrowly French to exercising world power through Europe, while the latter prefer exercising world power through Europe to being narrowly French. Again, dependency theorists take the Leninist view of imperialism as their starting-point. For them, any international capitalist order is exploitative *ex hypothesi*. Deep greens are new, however, since they oppose all economic development. But, useful though it is, Cable's list excludes many contemporary currents of opinion, such as human rights activists, labour rights activists, women's rights activists, development lobbies, health lobbies, consumer groups, cultural anti-globalizers and so forth. See Vincent Cable, *Globalization and Global Governance*, Chatham House Papers (London: Royal Institute of International Affairs, 1999), pp. 121–3. Given the extraordinary range of protesting groups, this discussion focuses on what they are all against – the liberal global economy – and on their arguments.

9 Henderson, *Innocence and Design: The Influence of Economic Ideas on Policy* (Oxford: Basil Blackwell, 1986).

10 Lloyd, *The Protest Ethic*, p. 21.

11 See Joseph E. Stiglitz, *Globalization and its Discontents* (London: Allen Lane, Penguin Press, 2002).

12 See, for example, George Soros, *The Crisis of Global Capitalism* (New York: Little Brown, 1999) and *Open Society: Reforming Global Capitalism* (New York: Public Affairs, 2000).

13 See, among many other writings, Dani Rodrik, *Has Globalization Gone Too Far?* (Washington DC: Institute for International Economics, 1997).

14 See Viviane Forrester, *The Economic Horror* (Cambridge: Polity Press, 1999) and John Gray, *False Dawn: The Delusions of Global Capitalism* (London: Granta, 1998).

15 See Larry Elliott and Dan Atkinson, *The Age of Insecurity* (London: Verso, 1998), Willam Greider, *One World, Ready or Not: The Manic Logic of Global Capitalism* (New York: Simon Schuster, 1997), Noreena Hertz, *The Silent Takeover: Global Capitalism and the Death of Democracy* (London: William Heinemann, 2001), Klein, *No Logo*, Edward Luttwak, *Turbo Capitalism: Winners and Losers in the Global Economy* (London: Weidenfeld & Nicolson, 1998) and George Monbiot, *Captive State: The Corporate Takeover of Britain* (Basingstoke: Macmillan, 2000).

16 Patrick J. Buchanan, *The Great Betrayal: How American Sovereignty and Social Justice are being Sacrificed to the Gods of the Global Economy* (Boston: Little Brown, 1998).

17 Resistance to cultural globalization is too often presented as benign. It is worth remembering that one of the values to which these fanatics objected was the equality of women visible to them in the US armed forces in Saudi Arabia. Extreme suppression of women was, after all, one of the most prominent features of the culture of the Taliban in Afghanistan. This is not the only respect in which 'anti-globalization' forces are also 'deeply reactionary'. But one of the ironies of the anti-globalization movement is that it contains feminists and proponents of equal rights for homosexuals, even though the spread of western culture is disseminating those ideas world-wide.

18 See Stephen Roach, 'Back to Borders', *Financial Times*, 28 September 2001.

19 John Gray, *New Statesman*, 24 September 2001. I dealt with his arguments and those of Mr Roach in my column, 'How Trade can Help the World', *Financial Times* 3 October 2001.

20 Thus, in *Jihad vs McWorld: Terrorism's Challenge to Democracy* (New York: Ballantine Books, 1995 and 2001), p. xv, Benjamin R. Barber of Rutgers University argues that terrorism, or Jihad, as he calls it, is a response to McWorld, which is his label for 'the aggressive neoliberal ideology' that has promoted 'a global market society more conducive to profits for some than justice for all.' In his eyes, therefore, the terrorists, however abhorrent their actions, are extreme opponents of 'neoliberal globalization' and, as such, should be ranked alongside its other opponents. Incidentally, as a good liberal, in the American sense, Professor Barber believes that the right response is more democracy everywhere. But the evidence that Islamic terrorists are interested in democracy is, to put it mildly, slight.

21 Among the books in support of the global market economy that I have particularly enjoyed are Johan Norberg's *In Defence of Global Capitalism* (Stockholm: Timbro, 2001) and Philippe Legrain's *Open World: the Truth about Globalization* (London: Abacus, 2002). I have also benefited from John Micklethwait and Adrian Wooldridge, *A Future Perfect: The Challenge and Hidden Promise of Globalization* (New York: Random House, 2000). Important official contributions are *Globalization, Growth & Poverty: Building an Inclusive World Economy* (Washington DC: World Bank,

2002) and *Eliminating World Poverty: Making Globalization Work for the Poor*, White Paper on International Development, Secretary of State for International Development, December 2000, www.globalisation.gov.uk. The book that comes closest to the present one in its theme, though it takes a more thoroughgoing libertarian line, is Brink Lindsey, *Against the Dead Hand: The Uncertain Struggle for Global Capitalism* (New York: John Wiley, 2002). I much admire the verve and imagination of Thomas Friedman's *The Lexus and the Olive Tree* (London: HarperCollins, 2000), though I believe Friedman is occasionally carried away with the exuberance of his own verbosity. On trade, I have benefited most from Jagdish Bhagwati, *Free Trade Today* (Princeton: Princeton University Press, 2002) and Douglas A. Irwin, *Free Trade under Fire* (Princeton: Princeton University Press, 2002).

22 John McMillan of Stanford University's Graduate School of Business provides a fascinating and largely convincing analysis of what makes markets work in *Reinventing the Bazaar: a Natural History of Markets* (New York: W.W. Norton, 2002).

Chapter 2: What Liberal Globalization Means

1 Mario Vargas Llosa, 'Liberalism in the New Millennium', in Ian Vásquez (ed.), *Global Fortune: The Stumble and Rise of World Capitalism* (Washington DC: Cato Institute, 2000), chapter 1.

2 Wolfgang Reinicke, now at the World Bank, notes that 'a search of the ABI Inform Database, which covers 800 professional publications, academic journals and trade magazines on economic and business affairs, produced no book or article title from 1971 with the word global or globalization; a similar search for 1995 found almost 1,200 entries. See Wolfgang H. Reinicke, *Global Public Policy: Governing without Government* (Washington DC: Brookings Institution, 1998), p. 234, n. 20. Vincent Cable, writing in 1999, suggests that the term was first used in *The Economist* '40 years ago'. See Vincent Cable, *Globalization and Global Governance*, Chatham House Papers (London: Royal Institute of International Affairs, 1999), p. 1.

3 Paul Hirst and Grahame Thompson, *Globalization in Question: The International Economy and the Possibilities of Governance*, second edition (Cambridge: Polity Press, 1999), p. xiii.

4 See, for example, Anthony Giddens, *The Third Way: The Renewal of Social Democracy* (Malden, Massachusetts: Polity Press, 1999).

5 Hirst and Thompson, *Globalization*, p. xiii.

6 Anne O. Krueger, 'Trading Phobias: Governments, NGOs and the Multilateral System', John Bonython Lecture, 10 October 2000 (www.cis.org.au/JBL/JBL00.htm), p. 2.

7 David Henderson, *The MAI Affair: A Story and its Lessons* (London: Royal Institute of International Affairs, 1999).

8 Lindsey, *Against the Dead Hand*, p. 275, n. 1. It is peculiar that this crucial definition is placed in a footnote, even if it is the first one.

9 Thomas Friedman, *The Lexus and the Olive Tree* (London: HarperCollins, 2000).

10 *Ibid.*, pp. 76–7.
11 Clive Crook, 'Globalization and its Critics', *The Economist*, 29 September 2001.
12 See Peter L. Berger, 'Four Faces of Global Culture', *National Interest*, 49 (1997), pp. 23–9 and Berger and Samuel P. Huntingdon (eds), *Many Globalizations: Cultural Diversity in the Contemporary World* (Oxford: Oxford University Press, 2002). The notion of Davos Man, named after the location of the annual meeting of the World Economic Forum, was advanced by Harvard's Professor Huntingdon in his influential book *The Clash of Civilizations and the Remaking of World Order* (New York: Simon & Schuster, 1996). Benjamin Barber of Rutgers University has labelled the modern consumer capitalism creating mass popular culture 'McWorld'. See Benjamin R. Barber, *Jihad vs. McWorld: Terrorism's Challenge to Democracy* (New York: Ballantine Books, 1995 and 2001).
13 Berger, 'Introduction', in Berger and Huntingdon, *Many Globalizations*, p. 16.

Chapter 3: Markets, Democracy and Peace

1 János Kornai, the distinguished Hungarian economist, wrote this in 'What the Change of System from Socialism to Capitalism Does and Does Not Mean', *Journal of Economic Perspectives*, Winter 2000, p. 36.
2 Yet in a fascinating account of the role of evangelical religion in Chile, Arturo Fontaine Talavera argues that this form of religion changes behaviour in ways conducive to greater material success. Thus 'the relation between a Christian life and economic success is central to the evangelical experience'. See Arturo Fontaine Talavera, 'Trends towards Globalization in Chile', in Peter L. Berger and Samuel P. Huntingdon (eds), *Many Globalizations: Cultural Diversity in the Contemporary World* (Oxford: Oxford University Press, 2002), p. 273.
3 In an important review of institutional economics, Oliver Williamson of the University of California, Berkeley, divided the analysis into four levels: first, customs, traditions, norms and religions, which change very slowly and are not directly governed by economics; second, the institutional rules of the game – property rights and the working of the political system, the judiciary and the bureaucracy; third, the play of the game, or the governance of institutions; and, finally, resource allocation. The discussion here concerns the first level, but the greater part of this chapter is concerned largely with the wider implications of the second level. The third and fourth are considered in the next chapter. See Oliver Williamson, 'The New Institutional Economics: Taking Stock, Looking Ahead', *Journal of Economic Literature*, September 2000, pp. 595–613.
4 The classical liberal trinity consisted of life, liberty and property, which Thomas Jefferson, in the Declaration of Independence, turned into life, liberty and the pursuit of happiness. Among the best accounts of the basic features of a free society and, in particular, the role of law is in Friedrich A. Hayek, *The Constitution of Liberty* (Chicago: University of Chicago Press, 1960).
5 This point is made by David Landes in *The Wealth and Poverty of Nations* (London: Little Brown, 1998), particularly in his discussion of the contrast between the

seventeenth- and eighteenth-century progress of the Netherlands and Great Britain and the stagnation of Portugal and Spain.

6 See Peter L. Bernstein, *Against the Gods: The Remarkable Story of Risk* (New York: John Wiley, 1996) for the development of the theory of risk and its links to the development of financial markets in particular.

7 Olson, *Power and Prosperity: Outgrowing Communist and Capitalist Dictatorships* (New York: Basic Books, 2000), p. 25.

8 John McMillan insists, rightly, that 'a market works well only if people can trust each other'. See his *Reinventing the Bazaar: A Natural History of Markets* (New York: W. W. Norton, 2002), p. 11.

9 Joel Mokyr, *The Lever of Riches: Technological Creativity and Economic Progress* (Oxford: Oxford University Press, 1990), p. 302. Professor Mokyr also writes that 'what made the West successful was neither capitalism, nor science, nor an historical accident such as a favorable geography'. This is a surprising statement. It is hard to accept that persistent technological improvement had nothing to do with market forces, if that is what one means by capitalism.

10 Charles Calomiris, *A Globalist Manifesto for Public Policy*. The Tenth Annual IEA Hayek Memorial Lecture. Occasional Paper 124 (London: Institute of Economic Affairs, 2000), p. 30. A seminal text on the value of the political division of Europe into enduring states is the masterpiece of Eric L. Jones, *The European Miracle: Environments, Economies, and Geopolitics in the History of Europe and Asia* (Cambridge: Cambridge University Press, 1981, second edition 1988). In his book, *Unintended Consequences: the Impact of Factor Endowments, Culture and Politics on Long-Run Economic Performance* (Cambridge, Massachusetts: MIT Press, 1990), Deepak Lal argues in addition that the legal basis of western property rights was provided by the Roman Catholic Church, in order to ensure bequests in its favour and extend its political power. The two revolutionaries who brought this about were Pope Gregory the Great in the sixth century and Pope Gregory VII in the eleventh century. The Church also provided a home for philosophical and scientific inquiry throughout the middle ages.

11 In a brilliant short account of the flourishing of the Chinese market economy after 1000, most notably under the Sung dynasty (960–1279), the American historian William McNeill argues that the decisive fact in bringing the market to heel was the continued power of the state. 'Capitalists in China were never free for long to reinvest their profits at will. Anyone who accumulated a fortune attracted official attention. Officials might seek to share privately in an individual's good fortune by accepting bribes; they might instead adjust taxes and prices so as to allow the state to tap the new wealth; or they might prefer preemption, and simply turn the business in question into a state monopoly.' William H. McNeill, *The Pursuit of Power: Technology, Armed Force and Society since A.D. 1000* (Chicago: University of Chicago Press, 1982), p. 49. In 1078, China produced 125,000 tons of iron. In 1788, production in England and Wales was still only 76,000 tons. *Ibid.*, p. 27.

12 Douglass C. North, 'Institutions, Transaction Costs, and the Rise of Merchant Empires', in James D. Tracy (ed.), *The Political Economy of Merchant Empires: State*

Power and World Trade 1350–1750 (Cambridge: Cambridge University Press, 1991), p. 33.

13 *Ibid.*

14 Rafael La Porta, Florencio Lopez-de-Silanes, Cristian Pop-Eleches and Andrei Shleifer, 'The Guarantees of Freedom', National Bureau of Economic Research Working Paper 8759, www.nber.org, February 2002, p. 1.

15 *Ibid.*

16 A striking example of the self-defeating nature of populism is Argentina. In 1950, Argentina's real gross domestic product per head in 1990 international dollars was $4,987. By 1998, after decades of populism, it was $9,219. By way of contrast, Italy, from which many Argentinians had come, had a GDP per head of $3,502 in 1950 and $17,759 in 1998. See Angus Maddison, *The World Economy: A Millennial Perspective* (Paris: The Development Centre of the Organization for Economic Co-operation and Development, 2001).

17 Amy Chua, *World on Fire: How Exporting Free Market Democracy Breeds Ethnic Hatred and Global Instability* (New York: Doubleday, 2003).

18 Olson, *Power and Prosperity*, p.41.

19 *Ibid.*, p. 42.

20 La Porta et al., 'The Guarantees of Freedom', p. 7.

21 Consider the remarkable and encouraging moves to democracy in South Korea and Taiwan.

22 I have taken some of these points from my Orwell Lecture, given at Birkbeck College, London University in 2001. See Wolf, 'Nation, State and Globalization', mimeo.

23 Jane Jacobs, *Systems of Survival: A Dialogue on the Moral Foundations of Commerce and Politics* (New York: Vintage Books, 1992).

24 Francis Fukuyama, *The End of History and the Last Man* (London: Hamish Hamilton, 1992).

25 The literature on the different types of capitalist economy is large. See, for example, Michel Albert, *Capitalism against Capitalism* (London: Whurr Publishers, 1993) or, more recently, Ronald Dore, *Stock Market Capitalism: Welfare Capitalism – Japan and Germany versus the Anglo-Saxons* (Oxford: Oxford University Press, 2000). The differences are important, particularly in relation to corporate governance and the role of the stock market. But they can be and – I will argue – often are exaggerated.

26 Some would argue that Singapore suggests the possibility of combining freedom of enterprise with traditional Asian hierarchical political values. It would be quite surprising if the country's paternalism long survived the passing of the generation of the founders of its prosperity. South Korea, Taiwan and Japan are increasingly 'western' in their political values.

27 The *Human Development Report 2002* lists countries by political freedom, rule of law and government effectiveness and lack of corruption. The advanced liberal democracies are at the top on all these characteristics. See *Human Development Report 2002: Deepening Democracy in a Fragmented World* (New York: Oxford

University Press, for the United Nations Development Programme, 2002), Table A1.1.

28 Richard E. Baldwin and Philippe Martin, 'Two Waves of Globalization: Superficial Similarities, Fundamental Differences', National Bureau of Economic Research Working Paper 6904, www.nber.org, January 1999, p. 3.

29 These data are from World Bank, *World Development Indicators 2002* (Washington DC: World Bank, 2002), Table 1.1.

30 See John Oneal and Bruce Russett, 'The Classical Liberals were Right: Democracy, Interdependence, and Conflict, 1950–1985' *International Studies Quarterly*, 11 (June 1997), pp. 267–94.

31 Thomas Friedman, *The Lexus and the Olive Tree* (London: HarperCollins, 2000), p. 253.

32 David Held and Anthony McGrew, David Goldblatt and Jonathan Perraton, *Global Transformations: Politics, Economics and Culture* (Cambridge: Polity Press, 1999), p. 57. Although far from elegantly written, this book is a superbly researched source of information on globalization.

33 *Ibid.*, p. 53.

34 *Ibid.*

35 Ernest Gellner, *Nations and Nationalism* (Oxford: Basil Blackwell, 1983).

36 This point is well put in Brink Lindsey, 'The Invisible Hand vs. the Dead Hand', in Ian Vásquez (ed.), *Global Fortune: The Stumble and Rise of World Capitalism* (Washington DC: Cato Institute, 2000), pp. 43–54.

37 See D. Potter, D. Goldblatt, M. Kiloh and P. Lewis (eds), *Democratization* (Cambridge: Polity Press, 1997), p. 9.

Chapter 4: The 'Magic' of the Market

1 Vaclav Havel, *Summer Meditations* (New York: Alfred A. Knopf, 1992), p. 62.

2 William H. McNeill, *The Pursuit of Power: Technology, Armed Force and Society since A.D. 1000* (Chicago: University of Chicago Press, 1982), p. 22.

3 *Ibid.*, p. 21.

4 Jared Diamond, *Guns, Germs and Steel: The Fates of Human Societies* (New York and London: W. W. Norton, 1997) and Douglass C. North, *Structure and Change in Economic History* (New York: W. W. Norton, 1981) present interesting complementary accounts of the agrarian revolution. The former emphasizes the unique ecology of the areas where this revolution began, particularly the variety of domesticable plants and animals. The latter points to the economic incentives to shift from the hunter-gatherer to the tiller-hunter-gatherer and, finally, the tiller stage, as population grew. Intriguingly, warrior-rulers of agrarian societies viewed hunting as a mark of their superior status. It would be consistent with contemporary evolutionary psychology for the loss of hunting to have been felt as emasculating.

5 Stationary and roving bandits were the late Mancur Olson's felicitous description of the human parasites to whom peasants were vulnerable. Stationary bandits protected the peasantry from the bandits of the roving kind in return for taxation.

They were monopolists of coercion. As such, they had an interest in promoting the productivity of their peasants, since they would also benefit from it. For the peasant, therefore, the shift from roving to stationary bandit was normally beneficial. Both sides would benefit, though the stationary bandit would benefit most. Sooner or later stationary bandits cemented their position by calling themselves emperor or king and claiming some form of divine claim to power. See Mancur Olson, *Power and Prosperity: Outgrowing Communist and Capitalist Dictatorships* (New York: Basic Books, 2000), chapter 1.

6 Jared Diamond suggests that the agrarian revolution came late to the Americas because of the North-South axis of the twin continents, the limited number of domesticable crops and animals and the difficulty of domesticating those that there were (maize, for example). The geographical axis made it harder to transfer crops bred for different latitudes. In the event, the late emergence of civilization in the Americas and their isolation from the decisive continent in human history, Eurasia, doomed the societies of the Americas to destruction by European greed and European diseases. See Diamond, *Guns, Germs and Steel*.

7 On this at least, the classic anti-liberal tract by Karl Polanyi is correct, though he certainly understates the significance of barter and exchange in human history. See Polanyi, *The Great Transformation: The Political and Economic Origins of our Time* (Boston: Beacon Press, 1957 (first published 1944)), chapter 5.

8 On the historic status of merchants, see K. N. Chaudhuri, 'Reflections on the Organizing Principle of Premodern Trade', in James D. Tracy (ed.), *The Political Economy of Merchant Empires: State Power and World Trade 1350–1750* (Cambridge: Cambridge University Press, 1991), especially pp. 426–7.

9 See David Landes, *The Unbound Prometheus: Technological Change and Industrial Development in Western Europe from 1750 to the Present* (Cambridge: Cambridge University Press, 1969), and Deepak Lal and H. Myint, *The Political Economy of Poverty, Equity and Growth* (Oxford: Clarendon Press, 1996).

10 See David Landes, *The Wealth and Poverty of Nations: Why Some are So Rich and Some So Poor* (London: Little Brown, 1998), p. 513.

11 In the literature on technology, the innovator is the person who makes an invention economically profitable. He or she brings inventions within the purview of the market.

12 Joel Mokyr, *The Lever of Riches: Technological Creativity and Economic Progress* (Oxford: Oxford University Press, 1990), pp.11–12.

13 Angus Maddison, *The World Economy: A Millennial Perspective* (Paris: Development Centre of the Organization for Economic Co-operation and Development, 2001), p. 28.

14 Maddison, *The World Economy*, pp. 46 and 42.

15 There has been much debate about why a Promethean take-off did not occur in the Islamic world. A large part of the reason must be environmental. Much of the Islamic world is in a desert zone, which limited agricultural productivity. There was virtually no possibility of using running water to power machinery. Water power was the precursor of steam in western Europe. Coal and iron were

unavailable, while oil was discovered and exploited only in the twentieth century. The puzzle about the Islamic world is not that it lagged behind Europe up to the mid-twentieth century, but why it fell far behind east Asia in the second half of the twentieth century.

16 This point has often been noted. See, for example, the important article 'Divergence, Big Time', by the World Bank economist Lant Pritchett in the *Journal of Economic Perspectives*, Vol. 11, No. 3 (Summer 1997), pp. 4–6.

17 Economists loathe cultural explanations for economic success. Yet it is striking how limited the group of successful economics are from the cultural point of view. It is easy to understand that a literate agrarian civilization, with a tradition of large-scale commerce and rational bureaucracy, will find it easier to jump into modern economic growth than hunter-gatherers or a culture with no comparable traditions. Even so, this leaves the puzzle of the dire performance of almost all of the Islamic world and the mediocre performance of Latin America. The former was, not so long ago, among the world's most advanced civilizations and the latter was a European offshoot. India, long a laggard, now seems to be beginning its take off into sustained growth in real incomes per head.

18 The last ratio is from the World Bank's, *World Development Indicators 2002* (Washington DC: World Bank, 2002).

19 Pritchett, 'Divergence, Big Time', p. 14.

20 The food hysterias of recent years, particularly in Europe, belie this fact. But it is worth remembering that, to take just one example, cow's milk was an extremely dangerous drink before pasteurization. Tuberculosis was just one of the deadly threats it provided.

21 John McMillan, *Reinventing the Bazaar: A Natural History of Markets* (New York: W. W. Norton, 2002), p. 5.

22 Much of the best work on the informal sector is by the Peruvian Hernando De Soto. See *The Other Path: The Invisible Revolution in the Third World* (New York: Harper & Row, 1989).

23 McMillan, *Reinventing the Bazaar*, p. 135.

24 See James Q. Wilson, 'The Morality of Capitalism', John Bonython Lecture, 15 October 1997 (www.cis.org.au/JBL/JBL97.htm), p. 3.

25 On the economic meaning of ownership, see Oliver Williamson, *The Economic Institutions of Capitalism* (New York: Free Press, 1985) and Oliver Hart, *Firms, Contracts and Financial Structure* (Oxford: Clarendon Press, 1995).

26 The classic article is Ronald Coase, 'The Problem of Social Cost', *Journal of Law and Economics*, Vol. 3 (October 1960), pp. 1–44.

27 See on this Olson, *Power and Prosperity*, chapters 3 and 4.

28 This discussion is partly based on two columns written for the *Financial Times*: 'A Manager's Real Responsibility', 30 January, 2002 and 'A Rescue Plan for Capitalism', 3 July 2002.

29 Kenneth Arrow, *Essays in the Theory of Risk-Bearing* (Chicago: Markham, 1971), p. 224.

30 The Dutch and British East Indies Companies were early examples of such hybrid institutions.

31 Alfred Chandler, *The Visible Hand* (Cambridge, Massachusetts: Harvard University Press, 1977).

32 McMillan, *Reinventing the Bazaar*, p. 169.

33 The classic article on the transaction-cost theory of the firm is Ronald Coase, 'The Nature of the Firm', *Economica*, Vol. 4, No. 6 (1937), pp. 386–405. A survey of contemporary developments is in Oliver Williamson, 'The New Institutional Economics: Taking Stock, Looking Ahead', *Journal of Economic Literature*, September 2000, pp. 595–613. The economic analysis of institutions in terms of transaction costs is among the most impressive developments in economics of the past few decades. Companies may emerge because of economies of scale and scope. But the reason why economies of scale dictate the creation of hierarchies is that a large investment in fixed capital demands a large, flexible and complex labour force, a steady stream of inputs and an equally steady revenue from sales. Hierarchy, then, works much better than a series of spot markets. One cannot hire the labour force on a daily basis. Nor can one write down a contract that specifies all the requirements of employment.

34 McMillan, *Reinventing the Bazaar*, p. 175.

35 This assumes that ownership rights vest with shareholders. The argument for such shareholder control is that the shareholders are the people who bear the residual risk in the company, because they are the least protected by contracts. If it were possible to specify all contracts, shareholders would not be needed. But under these assumptions there would be no companies. As Professor McMillan remarks, 'ownership is society's way of handling the unexpected'. See *Reinventing the Bazaar*, p. 91. In countries that do not offer shareholders effective ownership rights, ownership of shares is likely to be more limited and returns are likely to be lower. But companies then need to be financed in some other way, because shareholders are at extreme risk of being expropriated, as has been the case in Japan.

36 The classic study of the logic of collective action, which argued that concentrated interests will be better served than widely shared ones because collective action has public good properties – that is, free-riders cannot be prevented from sharing in the benefits – is by Mancur Olson. See *The Logic of Collective Action* (Cambridge, Massachusetts: Harvard University Press, 1965).

37 This discussion is drawn from a column in the *Financial Times*: 'The Capitalist Growth Machine', 5 June, 2002.

38 William J. Baumol, *The Free-Market Innovation Machine: Analyzing the Growth Miracle of Capitalism* (Princeton: Princeton University Press, 2002).

39 See *Human Development Report 2001: Making New Technologies Work for Human Development* (New York: Oxford University Press, for the United Nations Development Program, 2001), pp. 103–4.

40 *Finance for Growth: Policy Choices in a Volatile World* (Washington DC: World Bank, 2001), p. 5.

41 A shorter version of this section was published as Martin Wolf, 'The Morality of the Market', *Foreign Policy*, September/October 2003, pp. 46–50.

42 Media moguls, such as Rupert Murdoch, are more powerful, though even their influence has its limits.

43 Wilson, 'The Morality of Capitalism', p. 2.

44 *Ibid.*, p. 5.

45 Naomi Klein, *No Logo* (London: Flamingo, 2000), p. 187.

46 Michael Hardt and Antonio Negri, *Empire* (Cambridge, Massachusetts: Harvard University Press, 2000), p. 413.

Chapter 5: Physician, Heal Thyself

1 George Orwell, 'The Lion and the Unicorn' (1940) in Sonia Orwell and Ian Angus (eds), *George Orwell: The Collected Essays, Journalism and Letters*, Vol. 4 (London: Penguin Books, 1970).

2 See, on one part of this – the over-emphasis on physical investment and later on investment in human capital – William Easterly, *The Elusive Quest for Growth: Economists' Adventures and Misadventures in the Tropics* (Cambridge, Massachusetts: MIT Press, 2001), chapters 2 and 4. See also, on planning, Part I of Ian M. D. Little, *Economic Development: Theory, Policy and International Relations* (New York: Basic Books, 1982) and Deepak Lal, *The Poverty of 'Development Economics'*, Hobart Paper No. 16 (London: Institute of Economic Affairs, second edition, 1997). Peter Bauer was the first intellectually significant critic of such ideas. See his *Dissent on Development: Studies and Debates in Development Economics* (Cambridge, Massachusetts: Harvard University Press, 1972).

3 Brink Lindsey, *Against the Dead Hand: The Uncertain Struggle for Global Capitalism* (Washington DC: John Wiley, 2002), chapter 2.

4 John McMillan, *Reinventing the Bazaar: A Natural History of Markets* (New York: W. W. Norton, 2002), p. 151.

5 The planner's arrogance towards the desires of ordinary people runs like a black thread through Naomi Klein's assault on brands. See Klein, *No Logo* (London: Flamingo, 2000).

6 McMillan, *Reinventing the Bazaar*, p. 150.

7 Rafael La Porta, Florencio Lopez-de-Silanes, Cristian Pop-Eleches and Andrei Shleifer, 'The Guarantees of Freedom', National Bureau of Economic Research Working Paper 8759, www.nber.org, February 2002.

8 Amartya Sen, 'What is the Role of Legal and Judicial Reform in the Development Process?', Keynote Address at the Comprehensive Legal and Judicial Development Conference, 5–7 June 2000, World Bank, Washington DC, p. 13.

9 The above points are taken from Daniel Kaufmann, 'Misrule of Law: Does the Evidence Challenge Conventions in Judiciary and Legal Reforms?', July 2001, World Bank, draft.

10 See William H. McNeill, *The Pursuit of Power: Technology, Armed Force and Society since A.D. 1000* (Chicago: University of Chicago Press, 1982), pp. 106–11.

11 See on the implications of British financial superiority Paul Kennedy, *The Rise and fall of the Great Powers: Economic Change and Military Conflict from 1500 to 2000* (New York: Vintage, 1989).

12 In their important book, Vito Tanzi and Ludger Schuknecht conclude that much of the increase in public spending in the high-income democracies since 1960 has

failed to raise welfare. Much redistributive spending is simply churning, for example, with taxes being raised from – and then spent on – the same people. Similarly, much spending on government consumption is wasted. See Tanzi and Schuknecht, *Public Spending in the 20th Century: A Global Perspective* (Cambridge: Cambridge University Press, 2000) especially chapter VII.

13 See McMillan, *Reinventing the Bazaar*, pp. 182–7.

14 Harold Demsetz, 'Information and Efficiency: Another Viewpoint', *Journal of Law and Economics*, Vol. XII, No. 1 (1969), p. 1.

15 Benjamin R. Barber, *Jihad vs. McWorld: Terrorism's Challenge to Democracy* (New York: Ballantine Books, 1995 and 2001); p. 243. Noreena Hertz's book on the takeover of politics by corporations is based on a still more egregiously naive view of the democratic political process. See Hertz, *The Silent Takeover: Global Capitalism and the Death of Democracy* (London: William Heinemann, 2001). A far more sophisticated, though still critical, view of the relationship between markets and democracy is contained in Mark H. Moore, 'The Market versus the Forum', in John D. Donahue and Joseph S. Nye Jr (eds), *Governance amid Bigger, Better Markets* (Washington DC: Brookings Institution, 2001), chapter 13. I return to this issue in the fourth part of the book, which deals with the criticisms of a global market economy.

16 Mancur Olson, *Power and Prosperity: Outgrowing Communist and Capitalist Dictatorships* (New York: Basic Books, 2000), pp. 93–4.

17 As a columnist on the *Financial Times*, I understand that my influence on policy is several orders of magnitude greater than that of most ordinary citizens. Democratic politics are extremely inegalitarian in such ways. Everyone may have an equal vote, but not everyone has an equal voice.

18 This is the most important conclusion of Tanzi and Schuknecht. *Public Spending in the 20th Century*.

19 On corruption, see McMillan, *Reinventing the Bazaar*, chapter 11, and Tanzi and Schuknecht, *Public Spending in the 20th Century*, pp. 167–70. On the remarkable and horrifying story of Mobutu, see the wonderful book by my former colleague Michaela Wrong, *In the Footsteps of Mr Kurtz: Living on the Brink of Disaster in the Congo* (London: Fourth Estate, 2000).

20 See Easterly, *The Elusive Quest for Growth*, p. 222.

21 Easterly, *The Elusive Quest for Growth*, pp. 223–6.

22 *Ibid.*, p. 232.

23 *Human Development Report 2002: Deepening Democracy in a Fragmented World* (New York: Oxford University Press, for the United Nations Development Programme, 2002).

24 Hernando DeSoto, *The Other Path: The Invisible Revolution in the Third World* (New York: Harper & Row, 1989).

25 *Human Development Report 2002*, Table A1.1. The index does not cover all countries.

26 Easterly, *The Elusive Quest for Growth*, p. 246.

27 This is the perspective of Kaufmann, 'Misrule of Law'.

28 *Washington Post*, cited in *ibid.*, p. 1.

29 See Jagdish N. Bhagwati, *Free Trade Today* (Princeton: Princeton University Press, 2002), pp. 36–41. There will be more on this in the next chapter.
30 One of the most disappointing features of Joseph Stiglitz's book, *Globalization and its Discontents* (London: Allen Lane, Penguin Press, 2002) is that the distinguished author seems to assume that the governmental monopoly of power will almost always be exercised benevolently. Neither theory nor experience is consistent with this assumption.

Chapter 6: The Market Crosses Borders

1 Adam Smith, *An Inquiry into the Nature and Causes of the Wealth of Nations* (Oxford: Clarendon Press, 1976), p. 457.
2 The tension between the forces creating global markets and political fragmentation were the central theme of a classic book by Richard Cooper of Harvard University: *The Economics of Interdependence: Economic Policy in the Atlantic Community* (New York: McGraw-Hill, 1968). Since Professor Cooper wrote this seminal work, the problem of the Atlantic community has become a global one.
3 An interesting analysis of alternative views of the foundations for the governance of the world economy is contained in Robert Gilpin, *Global Political Economy: Understanding the International Economic Order* (Princeton: Princeton University Press, 2001), chapter 15. Professor Gilpin discusses 'the new medievalism' and 'transgovernmentalism', but concludes that states remain the foundation of any global economic order, particularly the major states.
4 Excellent recent discussions of the underlying arguments for liberal trade are contained in Jagdish N. Bhagwati, *Free Trade Today* (Princeton: Princeton University Press, 2002). Professor Bhagwati is the world's leading trade economist. Also excellent are Douglas A. Irwin, *Free Trade under Fire* (Princeton: Princeton University Press, 2002) and *Against the Tide: An Intellectual History of Free Trade* (Princeton: Princeton University Press, 1996). Much of the discussion below draws on these sources. Also helpful is W. Max Corden, *Trade Policy and Economic Welfare* (Oxford: Clarendon Press, 1974, second edition 1997).
5 Irwin, *Free Trade under Fire*, pp. 29–48
6 Retold in Irwin, *Free Trade under Fire*, p. 25, note 5.
7 As will be seen in Part IV below, among the distinguished authors whose analysis of the consequences of globalization is vitiated by this error is John Gray in his *False Dawn: The Delusions of Global Capitalism* (London: Granta, 1998).
8 The economist who has argued most powerfully that countries do not compete like companies is Paul Krugman. See 'Competitiveness: A Dangerous Obsession', *Foreign Affairs* 73 (March–April 1994), pp. 28–44 and 'Ricardo's Difficult Idea: Why Intellectuals Don't Understand Comparative Advantage', in Gary Cook (ed.), *The Economics and Politics of International Trade*, Volume 2 of *Freedom and Trade* (London: Routledge, 1998).
9 Irwin, *Free Trade under Fire*, p. 30
10 Peter H. Lindert and Jeffrey G. Williamson, 'Does Globalization Make the World More Unequal?', paper presented at the National Bureau of Economic Research

conference on Globalization in Historical Perspective Santa Barbara, California, 3–6 May 2001, p. 25.

11 Guchuran Das, *India Unbound* (New York: Alfred A. Knopf, 2001), p. 175.

12 Even Jagdish Bhagwati, a staunch free-trader, has taken this position. See Jagdish N. Bhagwati, 'The Capital Myth', *Foreign Affairs*, Vol. 77 (May–June, 1998), pp. 7–12.

13 A discussion of many of the issues is contained in Forrest Capie, *Capital Controls: A 'Cure' Worse than the Problem* (London: Institute of Economic Affairs, 2002).

14 Ronald W. Jones, *Globalization and the Theory of Input Trade* (Cambridge, Massachusetts: MIT Press, 2000), pp. 135–6.

15 On crises, see *Finance for Growth: Policy Choices in a Volatile World* (Washington DC: World Bank, 2001), chapter 2.

16 Data are from *Global Development Finance: Financing the Poorest Countries, Analysis and Summary Tables 2002* (Washington DC: World Bank, 2002).

17 Robert E. Lucas, 'Why doesn't Capital Flow from Rich to Poor Countries?' *American Economic Review*, 80 (May 1990), pp. 92–6.

18 See Edward M. Graham, *Fighting the Wrong Enemy: Antiglobal Activists and Multinational Enterprises* (Washington DC: Institute for International Economics, 2000), p. 172.

19 The positive impact of inward foreign direct investment on British manufacturing is one of the themes of Geoffrey Owen's book, *From Empire to Europe: the Decline and Revival of British Industry since the Second World War* (London HarperCollins, 1999).

20 See Lucas, 'Why doesn't Capital Flow?', and Wendy Dobson and Gary Clyde Hufbauer, *World Capital Markets: Challenge to the G-10* (Washington DC: Institute for International Economics, 2001), chapter 1.

21 An interesting analysis of the Asian financial crisis of 1997–8 that stresses moral hazard created by government guarantees is contained in Giancarlo Corsetti, Paolo Pesenti and Nouriel Roubini, 'Paper Tigers? A Model of the Asian Crisis', National Bureau of Economic Research, Working Paper 6783, www.nber.org, November 1998.

22 World Bank, *World Development Report 1995: Workers in an Integrating World* (Oxford: Oxford University Press, for the World Bank, 1995), pp. 10–14.

23 The increasing-return story is well told by William Easterly in *The Elusive Quest for Growth: Economists' Adventures and Misadventures in the Tropics* (Cambridge, Massachusetts: MIT Press, 2001), chapter 8.

24 This is the core of the late Mancur Olson's theory of why economies diverge to such a large extent. See his article 'Big Bills Left on the Sidewalk: Why Some Countries are Rich and Others Poor', *Journal of Economic Perspectives*, Vol. 10 (Spring 1996), pp. 3–24.

25 Daron Acemoglu, Simon Johnson and James A. Robinson, in 'Reversal of Fortune: Geography and Institutions in the Making of the Modern World Income Distribution', National Bureau of Economic Research Working Paper 8460, 2001, and *Quarterly Journal of Economics*, Vol. 117, argue that the rich places of today were poor in 1500 and vice versa, because European colonizers

imposed extractive institutions on the rich places they seized (such as India and Mexico) and wealth-generating institutions on the poor ones (such as North America). The theory is neat. But many of the rich countries of 1500 already had efficient wealth-extracting institutions imposed by already established élites. All the colonizers needed to do was take them over. That was certainly true in India. The difference may be that in rich agrarian societies extractive systems were well in place and have survived in the hands of local politicians to this day. But in sparsely settled places, institutions that generated wealth had to be created. It is probably no accident that all those institutions were introduced by the British.

26 See Bhagwati, *Free Trade Today*, especially p. 29.
27 The examples of failed infants are without end. My personal favourite is of the Morris Oxford, a not particularly successful car designed in the 1950s, which was still being manufactured and sold as the Ambassador in India in the 1990s. The Indian car industry finally started to grow up only with investment by foreign multinational businesses. Producers of failed infants are, alas, an important obstacle to trade liberalization.
28 This section draws in part on Martin Wolf, 'Richard Cobden and the Democratic Peace', in Gary Cook (ed.), *The Economics and Politics of International Trade: Freedom and Trade*, Volume II (London and New York: Routledge, 1998), chapter 13.
29 Graham, *Fighting the Wrong Enemy*, p. 174.

Chapter 7: Globalization in the Long Run

1 Charles Darwin, *The Descent of Man and Selection in Relation to Sex*, Second Edition (London: John Murray, 1882), p. 122.
2 Robert Wright, *Nonzero: The Logic of Human Destiny* (New York: Pantheon Books, 2000).
3 *Ibid.*, p. 196.
4 *Ibid.*, p. 209.
5 *Ibid.*, p. 211.
6 See on the struggle of the mercantilist state against universalism (the Church) and localism (lords and cities), Eli Heckscher, *Mercantilism* (London: Allen & Unwin, 1955).
7 Wright, *NonZero*, p. 198.
8 I recognize that the idea that some civilizations are more 'advanced' than others is now an unacceptable statement. I mean by this something relatively straightforward: to reach the political, social, technological, economic and cultural sophistication of twelfth-century China, it was necessary to pass through prior stages of political organization and economic development. Most of humanity had not done so. Whether the more 'advanced' is better is another matter. But hunter-gatherer bands do not evolve out of empires (unless the latter collapse); empires evolve out of hunter-gatherer bands (in the right circumstances and over a long period). See, on the long-term ecological advantages of Eurasia, Jared Diamond,

Guns, Germs and Steel: The Fates of Human Societies (New York and London: W. W. Norton, 1997).

9 Ronald Findlay, 'Globalization and the European Economy: Medieval Origins to the Industrial Revolution', in Henryk Kierzkowski (ed.), *Europe and Globalization* (Basingstoke: Palgrave Macmillan, 2002), p. 44.

10 William H. McNeill, *Plagues and People* (New York: Doubleday Anchor Books, 1977).

11 Findlay, 'Globalization and the European Economy', p. 46.

12 The American historian William H. McNeill discusses the growth of the Chinese navy and its subsequent abandonment during the fifteenth century in his book *The Pursuit of Power: Technology, Armed Force and Society Since A.D. 1000* (Chicago: University of Chicago Press, 1982), pp. 42–8. From 1371 to 1567, private voyages to foreign lands were forbidden by the imperial court. In 1436, the court 'issued a decree forbidding the construction of new seagoing ships' (*ibid.*, p. 45).

13 Findlay, 'Globalization and the European Economy', p. 45.

14 On the clock, see David Landes, *The Wealth and Poverty of Nations: Why Some are So Rich and Some So Poor* (London: Little Brown, 1998), p. 55. On what Europe obtained from China, see *ibid.*, chapter 4.

15 Findlay, 'Globalization and the European Economy', pp. 40–3.

16 Eric L. Jones, *The European Miracle: Environments, Economies, and Geopolitics in the History of Europe and Asia* (Cambridge: Cambridge University Press, 1981, second edition, 1988), p. 84.

17 Eric Williams, *Capitalism and Slavery* (Chapel Hill: University of North Carolina Press, 1944).

18 Stanley L. Engerman, 'The Slave Trade and British Capital Formation in the Eighteenth Century: A Comment on the Williams Thesis', *Business History Review*, Vol. 46 (1972), pp. 430–43.

19 Findlay, 'Globalization and the European Economy', p. 60.

Chapter 8: Rise, Fall and Rise of a Liberal Global Economy

1 Friedrich A. Hayek, *The Road to Serfdom* (Chicago: University of Chicago Press, 1972 (first published 1944)), pp. 21–2.

2 Much of this chapter is taken from Martin Wolf, 'Is Globalization in Danger?', *The World Economy*, Festschrift in honour of Max Corden, Vol. 26, No. 4 (April 2003), pp. 393–411.

3 Kevin H. O'Rourke, 'Europe and the Causes of Globalization, 1790 to 2000', in Henryk Kierzkowski (ed.), *Europe and Globalization* (Basingstoke: Palgrave Macmillan, 2002), p. 65. This fascinating article brings together the results of important scholarly work on the history of globalization, including work done by Professor O'Rourke together with Harvard's Jeffrey Williamson.

4 *Ibid.*, pp. 65–70.

5 *Ibid.*, pp. 65–8.

6 *Ibid.*, p. 68.

7 Angus Maddison, *Monitoring the World Economy 1820–1992* (Paris: Organization for Economic Co-operation and Development, 1995 and 1998).

8 Richard Baldwin and Philippe Martin, 'Two Waves of Globalization: Superficial Similarities, Fundamental Differences', National Bureau of Economic Research Working Paper 6904, www.nber.org, January 1999, p. 11.

9 *Ibid.*, p. 15.

10 See on this Robert Feenstra, 'Integration of Trade and Disintegration of Production in the Global Economy', *Journal of Economic Perspectives*, Vol. 12 (1998) pp. 31–50.

11 Michael D. Bordo, Barry Eichengreen and Douglas A. Irwin, 'Is Globalization Today Really Different than Globalization a Hundred Years Ago?', National Bureau of Economic Research Working Paper 7195, www.nber.org, June 1999, Figure 2.

12 *Ibid.*, pp. 10–11.

13 *Globalization, Growth & Poverty: Building an Inclusive World Economy* (Washington DC: 2002), p. 32.

14 O'Rourke, 'Europe and the Causes of Globalization, 1790 to 2000', p. 70.

15 Maurice Obstfeld and Alan M. Taylor, 'Globalization and Capital Markets', National Bureau of Economic Research Working Paper 8846, www.nber.org, March 2002.

16 Baldwin and Martin, 'Two Waves of Globalization: Superficial Similarities, Fundamental Differences', p. 8.

17 Michael Bordo, Barry Eichengreen and Jongwoo Kim, 'Was There Really an Earlier Period of International Financial Integration Comparable to Today's?', National Bureau of Economic Research Working Paper 6730, www.nber.org, September 1998, p. 4. On British net assets, see Forrest Capie, *Capital Controls: A 'Cure' Worse than the Problem* (London: Institute of Economic Affairs, 2002), p. 33.

18 Baldwin and Martin, 'Two Waves of Globalization: Superficial Similarities, Fundamental Differences', p. 8.

19 *Ibid.*, p. 10.

20 Obstfeld and Taylor, 'Globalization and Capital Markets', pp. 56–60, especially Figure 9.

21 Data are from *World Economic Outlook April 2002: Recessions and Recoveries* (Washington DC: International Monetary Fund, 2002).

22 These data are derived from *World Development Indicators 2002* (Washington DC: World Bank, 2002).

23 The important observation that domestic investment was highly correlated with domestic savings was made in a classic article by Martin Feldstein and C. Horioka, 'Domestic Savings and International Capital Flows', *Economic Journal*, Vol. 90 (June 1980), pp. 314–29.

24 Obstfeld and Taylor, 'Globalization and Capital Markets', p. 59.

25 *Ibid.*, p. 58.

26 *Ibid.*, Figure 10 and pp. 59–60.

27 Michael Twomey, *A Century of Foreign Investment in the Third World* (London: Routledge, 2000), cited in O'Rourke, 'Europe and the Causes of Globalization,

1790 to 2000', p. 72. A similar picture is given by Maddison for all foreign capital in contemporary developing countries. The ratio to GDP was 21.7 per cent in 1998, against 10.9 cent in 1973 and 4.4 per cent 1950. In 1914, however, it was 32.4 per cent, up from 8.6 per cent in 1870. See Maddison, *The World Economy: A Millennial Perspective* (Paris: Development Centre of the Organization for Economic Co-operation and Development, 2001), Table 3–3.

28 Edward M. Graham, *Fighting the Wrong Enemy: Antiglobal Activists and Multinational Enterprises* (Washington DC: Institute for International Economics, 2002), pp. 110–13.

29 These data are from United Nations Conference in Trade and Development, *World Investment Report 2000: Cross-border Mergers and Acquisitions and Development* (New York, United Nations 2000), Annex Table B.1.

30 Bordo, Eichengreen and Kim, 'Was There Really an Earlier Period of International Financial Integration Comparable to Today's?', pp. 16–18.

31 Barry Eichengreen and Michael D. Bordo, 'Crises Now and Then: What Lessons from the Last Era of Financial Globalization?', National Bureau of Economic Research Working Paper 8716, www.nber.org, January 2002, pp. 9–10.

32 Peter H. Lindert and Jeffrey G. Williamson, 'Globalization and Inequality: A Long History', April 2001, paper prepared for the World Bank Annual Conference on Development Economics – Europe, Barcelona, 25–27 June 2001.

33 Paul Hirst and Grahame Thompson, *Globalization in Question: The International Economy and the Possibilities of Governance*, second edition (Cambridge: Polity Press, 1999), p. 23.

34 Baldwin and Martin, 'Two Waves of Globalization: Superficial Similarities, Fundamental Differences', p. 19.

35 O'Rourke, 'Europe and the Causes of Globalization, 1790 to 2000', p. 73.

36 Lindert and Williamson, 'Globalization and Inequality', Table 1.

37 O'Rourke, 'Europe and the Causes of Globalization, 1790 to 2000', pp. 74–6.

38 C. Harley, 'Transportation, the World Wheat Trade and the Kuznets cycle, 1850–1913', *Explorations in Economic History*, Vol. 17 (1980), pp. 218–50.

39 O'Rourke, 'Europe and the Causes of Globalization, 1790 to 2000', p. 76.

40 *Ibid.*, pp. 74–5.

41 World Bank, *World Development Report 1995* (Washington DC: Oxford University Press, for the World Bank, 1995).

42 Bordo, Eichengreen and Irwin, 'Is Globalization Today Really Different than Globalization a Hundred Years Ago?', p. 17.

43 France Cairncross, *The Death of Distance* (London: Orion, 1997).

44 Bordo, Eichengreen and Irwin, 'Is Globalization Today Really Different than Globalization a Hundred Years Ago?', p. 17.

45 David Hummels, 'Time as a Barrier', mimeo, Purdue University, cited in O'Rourke, 'Europe and the Causes of Globalization, 1790 to 2000', p. 75.

46 Adair Turner, *Just Capital: The Liberal Economy* (London: Macmillan, 2001).

47 On the background to the expansion of the world economy in the nineteenth century, see O'Rourke, 'Europe and the Causes of Globalization, 1790 to 2000', pp. 76–8.

48 A powerful discussion of the assault on liberalism that led to the First World War and the breakdown of the global economic order is contained in Brink Lindsey, *Against the Dead Hand: The Uncertain Struggle for Global Capitalism* (New York: John Wiley, 2002), chapter 4.

49 Ernest Gellner has best expressed the view that nationalism was an economically useful product of industrialization in his classic book *Nations and Nationalism* (Oxford: Basil Blackwell, 1983).

50 The link between social security and the first globalization is made by Sir Anthony Atkinson in 'Globalization and the European Welfare State at the Opening and Closing of the Twentieth Century', in Henryk Kierzkowski (ed.), *Europe and Globalization* (Basingstoke: Palgrave Macmillan, 2002), chapter 12. See especially his Figure 12.1, which shows the introduction of welfare state programmes by twenty-four European states from 1880 onwards.

51 See Kevin H. O'Rourke and Jeffrey G Williamson, on the rise of wages in relation to the rent on land in the nineteenth century, in 'From Malthus to Ohlin: Trade, Growth and Distribution since 1500', National Bureau of Economic Research Working Paper 8955, www.nber.org, May 2002, especially Figure 3.

52 O'Rourke, 'Europe and the Causes of Globalization, 1790 to 2000', pp. 78–9.

53 Harold James, *The End of Globalization: Lessons from the Great Depression* (Cambridge, Massachusetts: Harvard University Press, 2001), chapter 3.

54 Lindsey, *Against the Dead Hand*, p. 67.

55 Cited in *ibid.*, p. 73.

56 *Ibid.*, p. 76.

57 Eichengreen and Bordo, 'Crises Now and Then',

58 Vladimir I. Lenin, 'The Impending Catastrophe and How to Combat it (1917)', in *Lenin's Economic Writings*, ed. Meghnad Desai (Atlantic Highlands, New Jersey: Humanities Press International, 1989 [1917]), p. 212.

59 Lindsey, *Against the Dead Hand*, pp. 76–7.

60 Vito Tanzi and Ludger Schuknecht, *Public Spending in the 20th Century: A Global Perspective* (Cambridge: Cambridge University Press, 2000), Table 1.1.

61 Baldwin and Martin, 'Two Waves of Globalization', pp. 26–7.

62 Rudi Dornbusch, 'A Century of Unrivaled Prosperity', in Ian Vásquez (ed.), *Global Fortune: The Stumble and Rise of World Capitalism* (Washington DC: Cato Institute, 2000), chapter 5, p. 14.

63 *Ibid.*, pp. 9–10.

64 Joseph Schumpeter, *Capitalism, Socialism and Democracy* (New York: Harper & Row, 1976 (first published 1942)).

65 See Lindsey, *Against the Dead Hand*, especially chapter 5.

66 See chapter 10, below. See also *Rigged Rules and Double Standards: Trade, Globalization and the Fight against Poverty* (Oxfam International, 2002), www.maketradefair.com and World Bank, *Globalization, Growth & Poverty: Building an Inclusive World Economy* (Washington DC: World Bank, 2002), chapter 2, especially pp. 55–61.

67 *Ibid.*, pp. 96–105.

68 The most important texts were: Ian Little, Tibor Scitovsky and Maurice Scott,

Industry and Trade in Some Developing Countries: A Comparative Study (London: Oxford University Press, for the Organization for Economic Co-operation and Development, 1970); Jagdish N. Bhagwati, *Anatomy and Consequences of Exchange Control Regimes: Foreign Trade Regimes and Economic Development*, Vol. XI (New York: Ballinger Publishing, for the National Bureau for Economic Research, 1978); Anne O. Krueger, *Liberalization Attempts and Consequences: Foreign Trade Regimes and Economic Development*, Vol. X (New York: Ballinger Publishing, for the National Bureau for Economic Research, 1978); Bela Balassa, *Development Strategies in Semi-industrial Economies* (Baltimore: Johns Hopkins University Press, for the World Bank, 1982).

69 See Peter Bauer, *Dissent on Development* (Cambridge, Massachusetts: Harvard University Press (1972).

70 The macroeconomic side of the new consensus was explored and explained in Ian M. D. Little, Richard N. Cooper, W. Max Corden and Sarath Rajapatirana, *Boom, Crisis and Adjustment: The Macroeconomic Experience of Developing Countries* (Oxford and New York: Oxford University Press, for the World Bank, 1993).

71 Barry Eichengreen, *Towards a New International Financial Architecture: A Practical Post-Asia Agenda* (Washington DC: Institute for International Economics, 1999), p. 108.

72 See on the rebirth of liberalism, David Henderson, *The Changing Fortunes of Economic Liberalism: Yesterday, Today and Tomorrow* (London: Institute of Economic Affairs, 1998), Part 3.

Chapter 9: Incensed about Inequality

1 'Labor's New Internationalism', *Foreign Affairs*, Vol. 79, January–February 2000.

2 Ignacio Ramonet, *Le Monde Diplomatique*, May 1998. Cited in Xavier Sala-I-Martin, 'The Myth of Exploding Income Inequality in Europe and the World', in Henryk Kierzkowski (ed.), *Europe and Globalization* (Basingstoke: Palgrave Macmillan, 2002), p. 11.

3 Paul Ehrlich, *The Population Bomb* (New York: Ballantine Books, 1968).

4 World Bank, *Globalization, Growth & Poverty: Building an Inclusive World Economy* (Washington DC: 2002), Table 1.1, p. 34.

5 *Ibid.*, p. 36.

6 These data are from World Bank, *World Development Indicators 2002* (Washington DC: World Bank, 2002).

7 World Trade Organization, *International Trade Statistics 2002* (Geneva: WTO, 2002), and T. N. Srinivasan, *Eight Lectures on India's Economic Reforms* (New York: Oxford University Press, 2000), p. 73, for the data on China in the 1970s and a comparison between China and India.

8 United Nations Conference on Trade and Development, *World Investment Report 2002: Transnational Corporations and Export Competitiveness* (New York: United Nations, 2002).

9 World Economic Forum, *The Global Competitiveness Report 2001–02* (New York: Oxford University Press, 2002).

10 See, on the role of government, particularly chapter 5, above.

11 See, on this, Johan Norberg's splendid tract, *In Defence of Global Capitalism* (Timbro, 2001), pp. 102 and, more generally, 98–113.

12 See, for example, Xavier Sala-I-Martin and Arvind Subramanian, 'Addressing the Natural Resource Curse: An Illustration from Nigeria', May 2003, mimeo.

13 See World Bank, *Globalization, Growth & Poverty*, pp. 38–40.

14 See, on this debate, Daron Acemoglu, Simon Johnson and James A. Robinson, 'Reversal of Fortune: Geography and Institutions in the Making of the Modern World Income Distribution', National Bureau of Economic Research Working Paper 8460, 2001, and *Quarterly Journal of Economics*, Vol. 117; William Easterly and Ross Levine, 'Tropics, Germs and Crops: How Endowments Influence Economic Development', National Bureau of Economic Research Working Paper 9106, August 2002; and Jeffrey D. Sachs, 'Institutions Don't Rule: Direct Effects of Geography on Per Capita Income', National Bureau of Economic Research Working Paper 9490, February 2003. The first of these papers emphasizes the role of colonial history in explaining the poverty of previously wealthy tropical countries. The second argues that location affects development only through institutions. The third argues against the second the case of malaria, a tropical disease with a directly negative impact on development.

15 A study that brought out the benefits of trade by focusing on natural barriers of distance is: Jeffrey Frankel and David Romer, 'Does Trade Cause Growth?', *American Economic Review*, June 1999.

16 See, on the resource curse, specifically, Alan Gelb and associates, *Oil Windfalls: Blessing or Curse?* (New York: Oxford University Press, for the World Bank, 1989), Jeffrey Sachs and Andrew Warner, 'Natural Resource Abundance and Economic Growth' Harvard Institute for International Development (November 1997), Ricardo Hausmann and Roberto Rigobon, 'An Alternative Interpretation of the "Resource Curse": Theory and Policy Implications', National Bureau of Economic Research Working Paper 9424, December 2002, and Sala I-Martin and Subramanian, 'Addressing the Natural Resource Curse'. On the argument that natural resources generate civil wars, see Paul Collier and A. Höffler, 'Greed and Grievance in African Civil Wars', *Quarterly Journal of Economics* (forthcoming).

17 See, on the role of resources in development, World Bank, *World Development Report 2003: Sustainable Development in a Dynamic World: Transforming Institutions, Growth and Quality of Life* (New York: Oxford University Press, for the World Bank, 2003), pp. 148–56.

18 The great critic of foreign aid was, of course, the late Peter (Lord) Bauer. See, for example, 'Foreign Aid: Abiding Issues', in *From Subsistence to Exchange and Other Essays* (Princeton: Princeton University Press, for the Cato Institute, 2000), chapter V.

19 See World Bank, *Globalization, Growth & Poverty*, pp. 32–3.

20 GDP at purchasing power parity is so important a concept for comparisons of standards of living across countries that it needs some explanation. The underlying aim is to compare standards of living across countries with very different relative

prices. In particular, in poor countries, with low productivity and real wages, non-tradable services are far cheaper than they are in rich countries if one converts at official exchange rates. Thus, converted in this way, the standards of living of people in poor countries are severely underestimated and inequality in incomes correspondingly exaggerated.

One can think of this in the following simplified way. Imagine two countries, the US and China, both of which produce one traded manufactured good and one non-tradable service. An American produces one unit of the manufactured good in an hour and one unit of the service (think of it as a single haircut). A Chinese produces only a tenth of a unit of the manufactured good in an hour, but also produces one unit of the service. If one assumes away protection, the prices of traded goods must be the same in the two countries. Now assume the dollar is worth ten Chinese Renminbi at the official exchange rate. Then the Chinese worker must earn just one Renminbi an hour ($0.1), while the American earns a dollar an hour. The price of a haircut is a dollar in the US, but one Renminbi in China. The exchange rate then underestimates the standard of living of the Chinese, because each haircut cost a tenth as much as it does in the US, at the official exchange rate, even though a haircut is a haircut is a haircut (more or less).

How then is one to make comparisons of standards of living that correct for these differences in relative prices? The method designed in an important research project three decades ago was to value consumption around the world at common international prices. Those prices were a weighted average of world prices, with the weights being global consumption of the products and services in question. To take our simple example, if half the haircuts in the world are consumed by Americans and half by Chinese, then the weighted cost of a haircut is $0.55. Then these values are normalized, to make the GDP of the US (the benchmark country) at PPP and actual dollars the same. When these international prices are applied to developing countries, GDP is increased hugely. For China, for example, according to the World Bank, gross national income per head at PPP is almost five times as high at PPP as at the official exchange rate ($4,951 in 2000, against $1,063). The underlying reason is that the value of non-tradables is increased substantially at international prices.

This is the only way of comparing standards of living across countries. But it has inevitable drawbacks. Among the most important are the difficulty of comparing quality of goods and, above all, services across countries. In addition, the prices at which standards of living are compared do not correspond to those confronted by anybody when making their spending decisions. Note also that, at PPP, a developing country contains a bigger service-producing sector than at market prices.

One final implication is worth noting. When countries grow, productivity in the production of tradable goods normally rises more rapidly than in the production of non-tradables. The cost of the latter then rises, at market prices. In the example, when Chinese productivity equals that of the US, a unit of manufactures will continue to cost a dollar (ten Renminbi), but a haircut will also cost a dollar. A regular American visitor to China finds that the cost of the haircut has risen, in dollars. He is worse off. The Chinese are better off, because of the increase in productivity, but the relative price of services has risen in relation to goods. This phenomenon is known as an appreciation of the real exchange rate. Under the assumption of a fixed exchange rate, it should show up as higher inflation in China than in the US, entirely in the prices of services, in dollars. When China's productivity in tradables is the same as that of the US, the market and PPP exchange rates should also become (virtually) the same.

21 The measure used is the 'gini coefficient', a measure that falls between zero for absolute equality and unity for extreme inequality. The coefficient is calculated as follows. Draw a curve showing cumulative shares in incomes against cumulative shares in the population, with the two axes of the same length. Draw also the line showing perfect equality, which would be a 45 degree line. Then the ratio of the area between the 45 degree line and the curve showing cumulative shares in incomes, to the total area under the 45 degree line is the gini coefficient. If all income belonged to one person, the curve drawn would follow the axes, in which case the coefficient would be unity. If all incomes were evenly shared, the curve would be the 45 degree line, in which case the coefficient must be zero. Gini coefficients for the countries of the world vary between close to 0.25 for egalitarian high-income countries, such as Denmark and Japan, and close to 0.6 for Brazil, the world's most inegalitarian country. In 1997, the US index was 0.41 and the UK's 0.37. See World Bank, *World Development Indicators 2002*, Table 2.8.

22 Data come from Angus Maddison, *Monitoring the World Economy, 1820–1992* (Paris: Development Centre of the Organization for Economic Co-operation and Development, 1995 and 1998) and the International Monetary Fund's *World Economic Outlook*. See Andrea Boltho and Gianni Toniolo, 'The Assessment: The Twentieth Century – Achievements, Failures, Lessons', *Oxford Review of Economic Policy*, Vol. 15, No. 4 (Winter 1999), pp. 1–17, Table 4.

23 François Bourguignon and Christian Morrison, 'Inequality among World Citizens', *American Economic Review*, Vol. 92, No. 4 (September 2002), pp. 727–44. The data of GDP per head, at PPP, and population size are, again, from Maddison, *Monitoring the World Economy*. Data were assembled for thirty-three countries or groups of countries, with each country or group of countries comprising 1 per cent of world population or GDP in 1950. Data on income distribution are taken from a number of different sources. For details, see Bourguignon and Morrison, 'Inequality among World Citizens', pp. 729–80. Evidently, taking this analysis back to 1820 required making heroic assumptions.

24 The measure of inequality used in the chart is the mean logarithmic deviation. This has the advantage of being additive: the sum of inequality within countries and between countries equals total inequality. The measure of inequality can be thought of as the proportional difference between the median of the distribution and its mean. The more skewed the distribution to the right (higher incomes), the bigger the proportional gap between median (the middle person in the distribution) and mean (the average person). If, for example, mean world income were $5,000 per head and median world income were $1,000 per head, the median person would have 80 per cent less than the mean. This would amount to a mean logarithmic deviation of 0.8.

25 Bourguignon and Morrison, 'Inequality among World Citizens', p. 733.

26 See Ximena Clark, David Dollar and Aart Kraay, 'Decomposing Global Inequality, 1960–99', World Bank, Washington DC, 2001, mimeo, reported in *Globalization, Growth & Poverty*, World Bank, 2002, Surjit S. Bhalla, *Imagine There's No Country: Poverty, Inequality and Growth in the Era of Globalization* (Washington DC: Institute for International Economics, 2002) and Xavier Sala-I-Martin, 'The Disturbing "Rise" of Global Income Inequality', April 2002, mimeo and 'The World Distribution of Income (Estimated from Individual Country Distributions)', May 2002, mimeo.

Clark, Dollar and Kraay use GDP data at PPP to construct estimates of inequality among households in the high-income countries, the developing countries and the world as a whole for 1960 to 1995.

Bhalla uses data on GDP at PPP from the World Bank's *World Development Indicators* (including the CD-ROM) and Angus Maddison, *Monitoring the World Economy* and *The World Economy: A Millennial Perspective* (Paris: Development Centre of the Organization for Economic Co-operation and Development, 2001). He also uses data from Robert Summers and Alan Heston, 'A New Set of International Comparisons of Real Product and Price Levels for 130 Countries, 1950–85', *Review of Income and Wealth*, Vol. 30, pp. 1–25. His data on income distribution are from Klaus Deininger and Lyn Squire, 'A New Data Set Measuring Income Inequality', *World Bank Economic Review*, Vol. 10, No. 3 (September 1996), pp. 565–92, and the *World Income Inequality Database* from the United Nations University's World Institute for Development Economics Research, at www.wider.unu.edu/wiid. He also uses data collected by the Asian Development Bank. Bhalla covers 149 countries for 1950–2000.

In both the papers cited above, Sala-I-Martin uses GDP data from Alan Heston, Robert Summers and B. Aten, Penn World Table Version 6.0, Center for International Comparisons at the University of Pennsylvania (CICUP), December 2001. His data on distribution of income are also from Deininger and Squire, 'A New Data Set Measuring Income Inequality'. Sala-I-Martin's analyses cover 128 countries from 1970 to 1998.

27 Branko Milanovic, 'True World Income Distribution, 1988 and 1993: First Calculation Based on Household Surveys Alone', October 1999, mimeo. Milanovic uses household surveys for data on spending in national currencies, but converts these into dollars with PPP exchange rates, just as do the studies using national account for average spending and income. These surveys cover 86 per cent of the world's population in 1988 and 91 per cent in 1993. They cover about 95 per cent of the world's current dollar GDP.

28 Milanovic, 'True World Income Distribution', Abstract.

29 *Ibid.*, p. 51.

30 Robert Wade, 'Winners and Losers', *The Economist*, 26 April 2001. Professor Wade also cites another World Bank study, using the same data sets: Yuri Dikhanov and Michael Ward, 'Measuring the Distribution of Global Income', World Bank, 2000, mimeo.

31 I discussed some of these points in a debate with Robert Wade of the London

School of Economics. See 'Are Global Poverty and Inequality Getting Worse?', *Prospect*, March 2002, pp. 16–21.

32 Shaohua Chen and Martin Ravallion, 'How did the World's Poorest Fare in the 1990s?', World Bank, Washington DC, 2000, mimeo. This discrepancy between surveys and national accounts is discussed at length by Bhalla, *Imagine There's No Country*, pp. 78–87 and chapter 7.

33 See United Nations Development Programme, *Human Development Report 2003: Millennium Development Goals: A Compact among Nations to End Human Poverty* (New York: Oxford University Press, for the United Nations Development Programme, 2003), p. 40.

34 Bourguignon and Morrison, 'Inequality among World Citizens', Table 1.

35 Cynics might suppose this is the Bank's nightmare. Fortunately for the Bank, though not for the world, poverty seems most unlikely to be eliminated in the near future, particularly since richer societies tend to define their poverty lines upwards, more or less *pari passu*.

36 Poverty lines are defined as $1.08 a day at 1993 PPP.

37 Professor Sala-I-Martin discusses those discrepancies in section 3D of his paper, 'The World Distribution of Income'.

38 See on this debate, Bhalla, *Imagine There's No Country*, chapter 7, World Bank, *Global Economic Prospects*, pp. 32–3, and Martin Ravallion, 'The Debate on Globalization, Poverty and Inequality: Why Measurement Matters', World Bank, no date, www.worldbank.org.

39 See Thomas W. Pogge and Sanjay G. Reddy, 'Unknown: The Extent, Distribution and Trend of Global Income Poverty', 16 July 2003, mimeo, pp. 1–2.

40 *Ibid.*, p.12.

41 Where not otherwise indicated, data in this section come from World Bank, *World Development Indicators 2002* (Washington DC: World Bank, 2002).

42 Indur M. Goklany, 'The Globalization of Human Well-Being', Policy Analysis No. 447, Cato Institute, Washington DC, 22 August 2002.

43 Maddison, *The World Economy*.

44 It is worth noting that if drugs are to prove a remedy for the AIDS catastrophe in Africa, it will only be because the wealth and technology of the high-income countries allowed them to invent the treatments activists argue should be provided to Africans at very low cost. As Goklany remarks, 'a certain level of global inequality may even benefit the poor as rich countries develop and invest in more expensive medicines and technologies that then become affordable to the poor'. See Goklany, 'The Globalization of Human Well-Being', p. 1.

45 The data from the FAO are cited in *ibid.*, p. 7.

46 World Bank, *Globalization, Growth and Poverty*, p. 48.

47 David Dollar and Aart Kraay, 'Growth is Good for the Poor', Policy Research Working Paper No. 2587 (Washington DC: World Bank, 2001).

48 Bhalla, *Imagine There's No Country*, pp. 36–46. Bhalla argues that the conclusion of Dollar and Kraay is biased by the inclusion of central and eastern Europe (including the former Soviet Union), where a huge widening in inequality coincided with a fall

in incomes. This tends to make the elasticity of the incomes of the poor with respect to rising average incomes, in the sample as a whole, closer to unity (i.e. the falling shares in income of the eastern European poor as income falls is interpreted in the pooled cross-section regression as a rising share as income rises).

49 World Bank, *Globalization, Growth & Poverty*, pp. 49–50.

50 This is true in China, too. Labour has benefited. The difference is that spatially uneven growth offsets this. South Korea and Taiwan were too small to have comparable regional effects.

51 The impact of trade liberalization on internal inequality in developing countries is discussed, with further references to a large literature, in Peter H. Lindert and Jeffrey G. Williamson, 'Does Globalization Make the World More Unequal?', paper presented at the National Bureau of Economic Research conference on Globalization in Historical Perspective, Santa Barbara, California, 3–6 May 2001.

52 *Ibid.*, p. 31.

53 See Jean-Marc Burniaux, Thai-Thanh Dang, Douglas Fore, Michael Förster, Mario Mira d'Ercole and Howard Oxley, 'Income Distribution and Poverty in Selected OECD Countries', OECD Economics Department Working Paper 189, Paris, OECD, March 1998, www.oecd.org.

54 Wolfgang Stolper and Paul A. Samuelson, 'Protection and Real Wages', *Review of Economic Studies*, Vol. 9 (1941), pp. 58–73.

55 See Jagdish N. Bhagwati, 'Play It Again Sam: A New Look at Trade and Wages', in *The Wind of the Hundred Days: How Washington Mismanaged Globalization* (Cambridge, Massachusetts: MIT Press, 2000), chapter 11, and, on the relative price of labour-intensive imports into the US, Robert Z. Lawrence and Matthew J. Slaughter, 'International Trade and American Wages in the 1980s: Giant Sucking Sound or Small Hiccup?' *Brookings Papers on Economic Activity*, No. 2 (1993), pp. 161–211. The strongest voice on the other side has been Adrian Wood. See his *North–South Trade, Employment and Inequality* (Oxford: Clarendon Press, 1994), and 'Globalization and the Rise in Labour Market Inequalities', *Economic Journal*, Vol. 108 (September 1998), pp. 1463–82. For a recent assessment of the literature, see Douglas A. Irwin, *Free Trade under Fire* (Princeton: Princeton University Press, 2002), pp. 95–9.

56 This is reinforced by the fact that the increase in wage inequality has varied substantially across the high-income countries. Since all were exposed roughly equally to imports of labour-intensive products, one might have expected all these countries to experience roughly equal increases in inequality. Alternative explanations are that most continental European countries (and Japan) had smaller immigration rates than the US (or UK), that they had a bigger relative increase in the supply of highly skilled worker (so ameliorating the impact of skill-biased technical change) and that they had a smaller increase in the skill-bias itself. These possibilities are discussed in Daron Acemoglu, 'Cross-Country Inequality Trends', National Bureau of Economic Research Working Paper 8832, March 2002.

57 Lindert and Williamson, 'Does Globalization Make the World More Unequal?', p. 33.

Chapter 10: Traumatized by Trade

1 John Cavenaugh and others, *Alternatives to Economic Globalization: A Better World is Possible,* Report of the International Forum on Globalization (San Francisco: Berrett-Koehler, 2002), p. 120.

2 World Bank, *World Development Indicators 2002* (Washington DC: World Bank, 2002).

3 If one relates the cost of labour to that of value added per worker for a mixed sample of twenty high-income and developing countries, one obtains an R2 of 0.94 and an elasticity of the cost of labour with respect to value added per worker of 0.92 (see equation on Figure 10.1).

4 Stephen S. Golub, *Labor Costs and International Trade* (Washington DC: American Enterprize Institute for Public Policy Research, 1999), cited in Edward M. Graham, *Fighting the Wrong Enemy: Antiglobal Activists and Multinational Enterprises* (Washington DC: Institute for International Economics, 2000), pp. 90–1.

5 This would be considerably higher using a standard PPP conversion, as much as 25 per cent of US levels. But equipment used in manufacturing is unlikely to be much cheaper in China than in the US, though construction will be. On balance, however, conversions at market exchange rates probably give a better picture of investment per person than PPP conversions.

6 More precisely, the marginal product of labour will rise over time as total factor productivity and the capital stock per worker rises. In a competitive labour market, employers cannot avoid paying the marginal product, whether they wish to or not.

7 Technically, factor substitution will offset higher total factor productivity, to keep labour-intensity and the marginal product of labour low.

8 First, there is growth on the extensive margin, with use of the additional capital to add new workers to the active labour force of the modern sector and, second, there is growth on the intensive margin, with rising capital per worker and so wages.

9 Philippe Legrain, *Open World: The Truth about Globalization* (London: Abacus, 2002), pp. 38–9.

10 Gary Burtless, Robert Z. Lawrence, Robert E. Litan and Robert J. Shapiro present a lucid analysis of the link between demand, trade, productivity and employment in manufacturing in *Globaphobia: Confronting Fears about Open Trade* (Washington DC: Brookings Institution, 1998), chapter 3, especially pp. 48–56. The book traces the actual share of manufacturing in total US employment between 1964 and 1992 and a hypothetical share, with no trade deficit. The two lines diverge very little. See *ibid.,* Figures 3–7.

11 William Greider, *One World, Ready or Not: The Manic Logic of Global Capitalism* (New York: Touchstone, 1998), p. 321.

12 Underconsumption theories of depression have been around for over a century. But the difficulty, if it exists, arises only because of the failure to co-ordinate decisions to save and invest, as J. M. Keynes argued in the 1930s. Consider that, today, the world economy absorbs at least seven times the real quantity of goods

and services that it did in the 1930s, when the widespread assumption was that it suffered from an unmanageable surplus of potential output.

13 These data are from World Bank, *Global Economic Prospects and the Developing Countries 2003: Investing to Unlock Global Opportunities* (Washington DC: World Bank, 2003), Table 1.10.

14 Legrain, *Open World*, p. 64.

15 Helen Rahman of Shoishab, an Oxfam-funded organization in Bangladesh, cited by Johan Norberg, *In Defence of Global Capitalism* (Stockholm: Timbro, 2001), p. 43.

16 The International Labour Organization's core labour standards are: the right to set up a free trade union, including the right to strike and bargain collectively; abolition of forced labour; a ban on the worst forms of child labour; and the elimination of discrimination in employment and occupation. There can be no disagreement over abolition of forced labour, although even here a difficulty arises over whether prisoners should be allowed to do paid labour and, if so, under what conditions. All the others are highly debatable. Does the right to strike include protection against dismissal for failing to do one's job when striking? Do employers have a right to lock workers out? Can closed shops be outlawed? And how does one define and implement anti-discrimination legislation? These apparently benign standards are an opportunity for mischief. They could easily be used to attack reasonable practices in virtually any developing country (and at least a number of developed ones). Just how difficult it is to define standards in a satisfactory manner is made clear in a superb discussion by Theodore Moran, in *Beyond Sweatshops: Foreign Direct Investment and Globalization in Developing Countries* (Washington DC: Brookings Institution, 2002), chapter 4. He notes, among other things, that the US would seem likely to fall foul of these standards, on some plausible definitions. It has certainly not ratified a number of them. Among the examples of the difficulties is the elimination of discrimination: is 'affirmative action', as practised in the US or Malaysia, discriminatory or anti-discriminatory? This remains a highly contentious issue within US politics and jurisprudence. It is little wonder that the number of countries which has signed up to these ILO standards greatly exceeds the number prepared to enforce them. On these points, see also Jagdish N. Bhagwati, 'Trade Liberalization and "Fair Trade" Demands: Addressing the Environmental and Labour Standards Issues', in *A Stream of Windows: Unsettling Reflections on Trade, Immigration and Democracy* (Cambridge, Massachusetts: MIT Press, 1998), especially pp. 258–66.

17 These points are made in Graham, *Fighting the Wrong Enemy*, pp. 96–9.

18 World Bank, *World Development Indicators 2002* (Washington DC: World Bank, 2002).

19 World Bank, *Globalization, Growth & Poverty: Building an Inclusive World Economy* (Washington DC: World Bank, 2002), pp. 118–19.

20 See Graham, *Fighting the Wrong Enemy*, p. 101.

21 Norberg, *In Defence of Global Capitalism*, pp. 186–7.

22 In principle, it might be possible to target sanctions against a particular plant or

company, in the same way as anti-dumping duties. In practice, however, it seems inconceivable that this would be feasible for the classic 'sweatshop' products – clothing, shoes, toy-making and sporting goods. Companies in these sectors are easily closed down and recreated and their products cannot easily be identified.

23 Legrain notes that the impact of trade liberalization on the environment is the product of five distinct effects: relocation of global production in line with comparative advantage; a more rapid spread of advanced technologies; a boost to economic growth; increased spending on cleaning up the environment by people as they become richer; and, possibly, a regulatory arbitrage as producers threaten to locate to countries or regions with lower environmental standards. The balance between these is inherently unknowable in advance. See *Open World*, pp. 243–4.

24 Letter to *The Economist*, 10 December 1999, cited in *ibid.*, p. 237.

25 In 2000, the global average national income, at PPP, was $7,410, while the average in high-income countries was $27,770. Thus the average living standard of the citizens of the rich countries would need to fall by almost three-quarters.

26 Gene Grossman and Alan Krueger, 'Economic Growth and the Environment', National Bureau of Economic Research Working Paper 4634, February 1994.

27 CO_2 emissions per head in the US are roughly double those of the European Union and Japan.

28 What happened to the Aral Sea is discussed in World Bank, *World Development Report 2003: Sustainable Development in a Dynamic World: Transforming Institutions, Growth and Quality of Life* (New York: Oxford University Press, for the World Bank, 2003), p. 21.

29 See, on the so-called 'win–win' issues, Gary P. Sampson, *Trade, Environment, and the WTO: The Post-Seattle Agenda* (Baltimore: Johns Hopkins University Press, for the Overseas Development Council, 2000), chapter 4, and Legrain, *Open World*, pp. 241–3.

30 See, for example, Cavenaugh and others, *Alternatives to Economic Globalization*, p. 28.

31 Adam Smith, *An Inquiry into the Nature and Causes of the Wealth of Nations*, Oxford: Clarendon Press, 1976.

32 See M. Mani and D. Wheeler, 'In Search of Pollution Havens? Dirty Industry in the World Economy 1960–1995', *Journal of Environment and Development*, Vol. 7, No. 3 (1998), pp. 215–47, cited in World Bank, *Globalization, Growth & Poverty*, p. 132.

33 See, for example, Cavenaugh and others, *Alternatives to Economic Globalization*, chapter 4, 'The Case for Subsidiarity: Bias Away from the Global Towards the Local'. Intriguingly, this chapter, though it makes much of the case for local autonomy, does not seem even to recognize the possibility that different localities would choose entirely different environmental standards. Nor does it appear to recognize that, by insisting on 'site-here-to-sell' policies, such localities cannot use these standards to reduce local pollution, by insisting that the more polluting activities be located in localities that care less about their consequences.

34 D. Wheeler, 'Racing to the Bottom? Foreign Investment and Air Pollution in Developing Countries', Policy Research Working Paper No. 2524, Development Research

Group, World Bank, Washington DC, 2001. Wheeler shows that air quality has improved in the industrial heartlands of Brazil, China and Mexico.

35 Bjorn Lomborg, *The Sceptical Environmentalist: Measuring the Real State of the World* (Cambridge: Cambridge University Press, 2001).

36 Legrain, *Open World*, pp. 280–1, and, for a more technical discussion, Sampson, *Trade, Environment and the WTO*, especially pp. 144–51.

37 This issue is well discussed in Duncan Brack, 'Environmental Treaties and Trade: Multilateral Environmental Agreements and the Multilateral Trading System', chapter 11 in Gary P. Sampson and W. Bradnee Chambers (eds), *Trade, Environment and the Millennium* (Tokyo: United Nations University, 1999). See also Martin Wolf, 'What the World Needs from the Multilateral Trading System', in Gary P. Sampson (ed.), *The Role of the World Trade Organization in Global Governance* (Tokyo: United Nations University Press, 2001), p. 203.

38 If the world decided it had to deal effectively with the emission of greenhouse gases, the only fair and effective mechanism would be to set aggregate global emission targets (on a declining trend), allocated to each country on an equal basis per head and then traded. This would automatically generate huge payments for atmospheric services from the high-income countries to the rest. Naturally, this is not going to happen (or, indeed, anything like it).

39 Cavenaugh and others, *Alternatives to Economic Globalization*, p. 107.

40 *Ibid.*, p. 213.

41 *Ibid.*, p. 143, and Colin Hines, *Localization: A Global Manifesto* (London: Earthscan Publications, 2000), p. 32.

42 Hines, *Localization: A Global Manifesto*, pp. 242 and 244.

43 Cavenaugh and others, *Alternatives to Economic Globalization*, p. 213.

44 David Henderson, *Anti-Liberalism 2000: The Rise of New Millennium Collectivism* (London: Institute of Economic Affairs, 2001).

45 Hines, *Localization: A Global Manifesto*, p. 33.

46 Cavenaugh and others, *Alternatives to Economic Globalization*, pp. 110–13.

47 *Ibid.*, pp. 112–13.

48 United Nations Development Programme, *Making Global Trade Work for People* (London: Earthscan Publications, 2003), pp. 128–9.

49 Bernard Cassen, 'Who are the Winners and Who are the Losers of Globalization?', speech at the Amis UK conference Globalization in Whose Interest?, Conway Hall, London, 17 June 2000, cited in Norberg, *In Defence of Global Capitalism*, p. 112.

50 The story of Mauritius is well explained by Dani Rodrik, *The New Global Economy: Making Openness Work*, Policy Essay No. 24 (Baltimore: Johns Hopkins University Press, for the Overseas Development Council, 1998), pp. 44–8.

51 To my astonishment, these points are made, if anything even more forcefully, by George Monbiot, a well-known campaigner against 'corporate globalization', in *The Age of Consent: A Manifesto for a New World Order* (London: HarperCollins, 2003), pp. 51–5.

52 See Ha-Joon Chang, *Kicking Away the Ladder: Development Strategy in Historical Perspective* (London: Anthem Press, 2002), Alice Amsden, *The Rise of 'The Rest':*

Challenges to the West from Late-Industrializing Economies (Oxford: Oxford University Press, 2001), and Rodrik, *The New Global Economy.*

53 Chang, *Kicking Away the Ladder*, p. 126.
54 *Ibid.*, pp. 126–7.
55 Amsden, *The Rise of 'The Rest'*, p. 281
56 *Ibid.*, pp. 282–3.
57 Rodrik, *The New Global Economy*, p. 1.
58 *Ibid.*, chapter 4.
59 See, for example, Douglas A. Irwin, 'Did Import Substitution Promote Growth in the Late Nineteenth Century?', National Bureau of Economic Research Working Paper 8751, February 2002.
60 World Bank, *Globalization, Growth & Poverty*, pp. 100–1.
61 Economists have become increasingly dependent on the abilities of computers to analyse huge databases to justify their hypotheses. But such analyses confront enormous conceptual and practical difficulties. Many of the explanatory variables cannot be measured with any degree of precision or, where they can, do not mean what their users say they do. In the case of the debate over openness, for example, this is as true of the proponents of liberalization as it is of the critics. The classic analysis consists of data for a hundred countries or more, of vastly different size and significance, in which a mass of data over many years is pooled, on the assumption that it all comes, in some relevant sense, from the same sample. Economic growth or some other outcome is then related to a host of more or less well-specified and measured variables. In the case of regressions for the importance of trade, for example, measures used have tended to include openness to trade (trade ratios to GDP), gravitational measures (distance from markets and transport costs), black-market premia for foreign exchange, average ratios of tariff revenue to GDP and coverage of trade by non-tariff barriers. All of these are highly defective: trade ratios are as much the consequence of development as of policy, gravitational measures evidently exclude policy, black-market premia are a measure of macro-economic disequilibrium, tariff ratios ignore the impact of high tariffs on volumes of imports (and so underestimate protective effect), and coverage measures not only suffer from this defect (outright prohibitions cover no imports) but provide no measure of the protective effect. Thus, standard empirical estimates of the impact of trade policy on growth are close to worthless. Similar points to these are made by T. N. Srinivasan of Yale University and Jagdish Bhagwati in 'Outward-Orientation and Development: Are Revisionists Right?', 17 September 1999, mimeo. Professors Srinivasan and Bhagwati conclude that the superiority of policies that do not bias trade excessively against exports is best supported by the series of detailed country studies carried out in the late 1960s and 1970s.
62 William Easterly, *The Elusive Quest for Growth: Economists' Adventures and Misadventures in the Tropics* (Cambridge, Massachusetts: MIT Press, 2001), p. 67.
63 It is puzzling that, in emphasizing investment, Professor Rodrik does not also emphasize the savings that finance it. By and large, the Asian economies have been high-saving economies. The conventional view on this is that it reflects the absence

64 This section draws heavily on Oxfam, *Rigged Rules and Double Standards: Trade, Globalization and the Fight against Poverty* (Oxford: Oxfam International, 2002), www.maketradefair.com. While there are points to disagree with in this report, it makes an extremely valuable contribution to the discussion of trade policy issues as they affect developing countries.

65 These data are from World Bank, *World Development Indicators 2002*.

66 Oxfam, *Rigged Rules and Double Standards*, pp. 150–1.

67 The deflator used for calculating real prices is dollar unit value index of exports from the five leading high-income exporters of manufactures: US, Germany, Japan, France and the UK.

68 Oxfam, *Rigged Rules and Double Standards*, pp. 150–3.

69 World Bank, *Global Economic Prospects 2003*, pp. 181–2.

70 On the fair trade movement, see Oxfam, *Rigged Rules and Double Standards*, pp. 166–7.

71 The literature on the world trading system, the GATT and the WTO is enormous. This discussion draws directly from Wolf, 'What the World Needs from the Multilateral Trading System' in Gary P. Sampson (ed.), *The Role of the World Trade Organization in Global Governance* (Tokyo: United Nations University Press, 2001), chapter 9, and John H. Jackson, 'The WTO "Constitution" and Proposed Reforms': Seven "Mantras" Revisited', *Journal of International Economic Law*, 2001, pp. 67–78. A good general discussion of how the WTO works is contained in World Trade Organization, *WTO Policy Issues for Parliamentarians* (Geneva: WTO, 2001). See also the discussion in Part II, above.

72 The idea of deep integration is discussed at length by Nancy Birdsall and Robert Z. Lawrence in 'Deep Integration and Trade Agreements: Good for Developing Countries?', in Inge Kaul, Isabelle Grunberg and Marc A. Stern (eds), *Global Public Goods: International Cooperation in the 21st Century* (New York: Oxford University Press, for the United Nations Development Programme, 1999), pp. 128–51.

73 On the costly consequences of parts of the WTO for developing countries, see J. Michael Finger, 'The WTO's Special Burden on Less Developed Countries', in *Cato Journal*, Vol. 19, No. 3, (Winter 2000), pp. 425–37.

74 A pure public good has two characteristics: first, nobody can be prevented from consuming it; second, it can be consumed without being depleted. The first quality makes the good 'non-excludable'; the second makes it 'non-rival'. Such goods cannot normally be provided adequately by the market. A global compact to liberalize trade has strong public-good elements. Many of these take the form of network effects. Thus every member country (and often non-members as well) gains from a trade agreement between the US and EU on the basis of non-discrimination.

75 Douglas A. Irwin, 'Do We Need the WTO?', *Cato Journal*, Vol. 19, No. 3, (Winter 2000), p. 353.

76 Robert E. Hudec, ' "Circumventing Democracy": The Political Morality of Trade Negotiations', *New York University Journal of International Law and Politics* (1993), pp. 311–22, reprinted in Hudec, *Essays on the Nature of International Trade Law* (London: Cameron May, 1999), chapter 7.

77 Daniel Esty, 'Environmental Governance at the WTO: Outreach to Civil Society', in Sampson and Chambers, *Trade, Environment and the Millennium*, pp. 97–8.

78 Monbiot, *The Age of Consent: A Manifesto for a New World Order.*

79 The idea that dispute settlement should become less legalistic and more diplomatic is advanced by Claude E. Barfield in *Free Trade, Sovereignty, Democracy: The Future of the World Trade Organization* (Washington DC: American Enterprise Institute, 2001).

80 Amsden, *The Rise of 'The Rest'*, pp. 268–71. Careful examination of the WTO suggests that developing countries still have plenty of opportunities for (often unjustified) protection.

81 Except where indicated otherwise, the information below on barriers to market access and their cost comes from either World Bank, *Global Economic Prospects and the Developing Countries 2002: Making Trade Work for the World's Poor* (Washington DC: 2002), chapter 2, or Oxfam, *Rigged Rules and Double Standards*, chapter 4.

82 Progressive Policy Institute, 'America's Hidden Tax on the Poor: The Case for Reforming US Tariff Policy', Washington DC, March 2002, pp. 10–12.

83 If the raw material costs a dollar, without protection, the finished product would cost $2, giving a value added in processing of exactly a dollar. If you were to import the unprocessed commodity, you would pay $1.05. If you were to import the finished product, you would pay $2.28. Thus a processor in the importing country can generate a domestic value added of $1.23, in domestic prices, out of a value added, at world prices, of only a dollar. This means an effective protection of 23 per cent. Effective protection was the theme of W. Max Corden's *The Theory of Protection* (Oxford: Clarendon Press, 1971).

84 Patrick Messerlin, *Measuring the Costs of Protection in Europe: European Commercial Policy in the 2000s* (Washington DC: Institute for International Economics, 2001).

85 The most passionate academic opponent of free-trade arrangements has been Jagdish N. Bhagwati. See, among other things, his 'The FTAA is Not Free Trade', in *The Wind of the Hundred Days: How Washington Mismanaged Globalization* (Cambridge, Massachusetts: MIT Press, 2000), chapter 27, and *Free Trade Today* (Princeton: Princeton University Press, 2002).

86 These remarkable data are taken from the United Nations Development Programme, *Human Development Report 2003: Millennium Development Goals: A Compact among Nations to End Human Poverty* (New York: Oxford University Press, for the United Nations Development Programme, 2003), pp. 155–6.

87 That France is the chief obstacle to the liberalization of the CAP merely demonstrates the extraordinary cynicism of its expressed concern for developing countries.

88 See United Nations Development Programme, *Human Development Report 2003*, Box 8.8 on this topic.

89 It should be noted that the current development of patents in many areas is profoundly disturbing. Trivial inventions and fundamental life forms are being patented. The justifications for some of this are far from evident.

90 These estimates are from World Bank, *Global Economic Prospects and the Developing Countries 2002*, pp. 166–76.

Chapter 11: Cowed by Corporations

1   George Monbiot, *Captive State: The Corporate Takeover of Britain* (Basingstoke: Macmillan, 2000), p. 17.

2   Naomi Klein, *No Logo* (London: Flamingo, 2000), p. 3.

3   This section draws, in part, from my column 'Countries Still Rule the World', *Financial Times*, 6 February 2002.

4   Sarah Anderson and John Cavenaugh, 'Top 200: The Rise of Corporate Global Power', Institute for Policy Studies, Washington DC, December 2000. Anderson and Cavenaugh are co-authors of John Cavenaugh and others, *Alternatives to Economic Globalization: A Better World is Possible*, Report of the International Forum on Globalization (San Francisco: Berrett-Koehler, 2002), cited in the previous chapter.

5   Paul de Grauwe and Filip Camerman, 'How Big are the Big Multinational Companies?', www.econ.kuleuven.ac.be/ew/academic/intecon/Degrauwe, 2003.

6   United Nations Conference on Trade and Development, 'Are Transnationals Bigger than Countries?', TAD/INF/PR/47, 12 August 2002, www.unctad.org.

7   *Ibid.*

8   On the history of corporate power and its contemporary forms, see Daniel Litvin, *Empires of Profit: Commerce, Conquest and Corporate Responsibility* (London: Texere, 2003).

9   The data in this section come from World Bank, *Global Economic Prospects and the Developing Countries 2003: Investing to Unlock Global Opportunities* (Washington DC: World Bank, 2003), p. 52.

10 Cited in World Bank, *Global Economic Prospects 2003*, pp. 52–3.

11 Klein, *No Logo*, p. 27.

12 Philippe Legrain, *Open World: The Truth about Globalization* (London: Abacus, 2002), p. 127.

13 Klein, *No Logo*, p. 343.

14 David Henderson, former chief economist of the OECD, has argued powerfully against some of the ideas of corporate social responsibility with which companies have responded to their critics. See his *Misguided Virtue: False Notions of Corporate Responsibility* (London: Institute of Economic Affairs, 2002).

15 Except where otherwise indicated, data in this section come from United Nations Conference on Trade and Development, *World Investment Report 2002: Transnational Corporations and Export Competitiveness* (New York and Geneva: United Nations, 2002).

16 See on this Edward M. Graham, *Fighting the Wrong Enemy: Antiglobal Activists and Multinational Enterprises* (Washington DC: Institute for International Economics, 2000), pp. 84–5.

17 World Bank, *Global Economic Prospects 2003*, p. 91.

18 *Ibid.*, p. 68.

19 *Ibid.*

20 FDI consists of purchases of equity, reinvested earnings and intra-company loans. It may be argued that data on the second and third will bias the data in the direction of countries that are already hosts to large amounts of FDI. Edward Graham has shown, however, that the share of high-income countries in new equity flows from the US remained close to 80 per cent in the early 1990s, which is more than in the early 1980s. See Graham, *Fighting the Wrong Enemy*, pp. 111–12. Critics may also argue that data are biased by the inclusion of mergers and acquisitions on the ground that it is greenfield investment that is most exploitative. It is not at all obvious why this should be so. One might argue, instead, that the worst characteristics of ruthless capitalism are shown in M&A activity.

21 Graham, *Fighting the Wrong Enemy*, pp. 93–4.

22 *Ibid.*, p. 94.

23 Robert E. Lipsey and Fredrik Sjöholm, 'Foreign Direct Investment and Wages in Indonesian Manufacturing', National Bureau of Economic Research Working Paper 8299, May 2001.

24 Noreena Hertz, *The Silent Takeover: Global Capitalism and the Death of Democracy* (London: William Heinemann, 2001), p. 42.

25 It is conceivable that, in highly capital-intensive industries, the marginal product of labour moves almost instantaneously from very high to close to zero. In that case, there may be many different wages consistent with payment of the marginal product of labour. But while such an employer might be able to pay more without changing his operations in any way, it is most unlikely to be an important issue in terms of competitiveness, or the wage bill, since such plants are likely to employ very few people and their wage bill is likely to be a very small part of their total cost. On the broader issues raised here, see Graham, *Fighting the Wrong Enemy*, pp. 96–8.

26 While needlessly dreadful working conditions exist in developing countries, use of the term 'sweatshop' is rhetoric, not analysis.

27 *Ibid.*, p. 101.

28 Theodore H. Moran, *Beyond Sweatshops: Foreign Direct Investment and Globalization in Developing Countries* (Washington DC: Brookings Institution, 2002), p. 13. Philippe Legrain provides an excellent antidote to the view that all such facilities are sweatshops in a discussion of a visit to a Nike subcontractor in Vietnam. See his *Open World*, pp. 54–61.

29 Moran, *Beyond Sweatshops*, pp. 15–16.

30 *Ibid.*, chapter 3.

31 Organization for Economic Co-operation and Development, *Trade, Employment and Labour Standards* (Paris: OECD, 1996).

32 Theodore Moran, *Foreign Direct Investment and Development: The New Policy Agenda for Developing Countries and Economies in Transition* (Washington DC: Institute for International Economics, 1998).

33 On these incentives and the competition among countries that has ensued, see World Bank, *Global Economic Prospects 2003*, pp. 82–4.

34 Moran, *Beyond Sweatshops*, chapter 3.
35 Klein, *No Logo*, p. 208.
36 Moran, *Beyond Sweatshops*, pp. 19–21.
37 Graham, *Fighting the Wrong Enemy*, p. 122. The entire argument is in pp. 106–25.
38 Edward Luttwak, *Turbo Capitalism: Winners and Losers in the Global Economy* (London: Weidenfeld & Nicolson, 1998).
39 This subject is well discussed by Legrain, *Open World*, pp. 147–50.
40 Alan V. Deardorff, 'What Might Globalization's Critics Believe?', *The World Economy*, Vol. 26, No. 5 (May 2003), pp. 657–8.

Chapter 12: Sad about the State

1 John Gray, *False Dawn: The Delusions of Global Capitalism* (London: Granta, 1998), pp. 78, 79, 89.
2 The discussion in this chapter draws heavily on Martin Wolf, 'Will the Nation State Survive Globalization?', *Foreign Affairs*, Vol. 80 (January/February 2001), pp. 178–90. That was itself based on 'The Nation State in a Global World', presented at the Harry Oppenheimer Colloquium on Globalization, funded by the Ernest Oppenheimer Memorial Trust, in Stellenbosch, South Africa, in February 2000. A further discussion of some aspects of this appeared in the winter 2001 issue of the *Cato Journal*.
3 The opposing view is splendidly presented by Adair Turner in *Just Capital: The Liberal Economy* (London: Macmillan, 2001), especially chapter 8. Turner, in turn, relies on the celebrated demolition by Paul Krugman of the notion of competition among nations. These appear in 'Competitiveness: A Dangerous Obsession', *Foreign Affairs*, Vol. 73 (March–April 1994), pp. 28–44 and *Pop Internationalism* (Cambridge, Massachusetts, and London: MIT Press, 1997). Also good is the discussion in Philippe Legrain, *Open World: The Truth about Globalization* (London: Abacus, 2002) chapter 6.
4 Thomas Friedman, *The Lexus and the Olive Tree* (London: HarperCollins, 2000).
5 That is the principal thesis of Noreena Hertz, *The Silent Takeover: Global Capitalism and the Death of Democracy* (London: William Heinemann: 2001).
6 The sole exception among capital flows is short-term capital. It would be quite widely accepted nowadays that taxation of inflows of short-term capital may increase stability in emerging market economies, particularly during a transition to full integration of the financial system.
7 These figures on public spending include government consumption and investment, and transfers. While government consumption and investment cannot exceed GDP, by definition, transfers can. In theory, the government could take all income away in tax and then give it back in a series of rounds whose total tax incidence summed to more than 100 per cent. In practice, in the OECD region as a whole, about half of government spending was on transfers and half on consumption and investment (a little under a quarter of GDP in each case). See Vito Tanzi and Ludger Schuknecht, *Public Spending in the 20th Century: A Global Perspective* (Cambridge: Cambridge University Press, 2000), p. 31.

8 *Ibid.*
9 Paul de Grauwe, 'Globalisation and Social Spending', CESifo Working Paper 885, www.econ.kuleuven.ac.be/ew/academic/intecon/Degrauwe, 2003.
10 Legrain, *Open World*, p. 167.
11 Clive Crook, 'The World Economy: The Future of the State'. *The Economist*, 20 September 1997.
12 It is important to note that, as inflation falls, the inflation-compensating element in the interest rate diminishes. So, with lower inflation, nominal deficits must be smaller if real deficits are to be held constant. To put this another way, the inflation tax diminishes and must be replaced with other, more specific taxes.
13 An important qualification is that these figures do not indicate the incidence of taxation. It may well be that corporation tax is largely shifted on to workers and consumers. If so, the figures on the ostensible burden of corporation tax would not indicate this. But, short of a fully specified general equilibrium model, it is impossible to know who pays tax. What matters most, in fact, is that high-tax countries are able to raise the taxes they seek.
14 Denmark, for example, raises virtually no revenue from separate social security taxes. But in 2000 France raised 16.4 per cent of GDP from social security taxes and only 8.2 per cent of GDP from personal income tax.
15 Organization for Economic Co-operation and Development, *Economic Outlook 2003/1*, No. 73 (Paris: OECD, June 2003).
16 Gray, *False Dawn*, pp. 79 and 87–8.
17 In 'Ricardo's Difficult Idea: Why Intellectuals Don't Understand Comparative Advantage', Gary Cook (ed.), *The Economics and Politics of International Trade*, Vol. 2 of *Freedom and Trade* (London: Routledge, 1998), chapter 3, Krugman asks why literary intellectuals not only fail to understand the theory of comparative advantage, but do not seem to be feel ashamed of their failure.
18 *Ibid.*, p. 15.
19 The historical status of China's economy, in many ways a rival to western Europe until 1800, is the theme of Kenneth Pomeranz's book, *The Great Divergence: China, Europe and the Making of the Modern Economy* (Princeton and Oxford: Princeton University Press, 2000).
20 See Charles Tiebout, 'A Pure Theory of Local Expenditures', *Journal of Political Economy*, Chicago, Vol. 64 (1956), pp. 416–24.
21 Intriguingly, Professor Gray seems to believe in this theorem, even though the assumptions under which it holds are highly restrictive, while he rejects comparative advantage, even though it holds quite generally, for reasons already explained. See, for his views on factor-price equalization, Gray, *False Dawn*, p. 85, and on comparative advantage, *ibid.*, pp. 81–3.
22 Tanzi, 'Globalization and the Future of Social Protection', IMF Working Paper, WP/00/12, January 2000, www.imf.org.
23 See *Harmful Tax Competition: An Emerging Global Issue* (Paris: OECD, 1998) and *Electronic Commerce: Taxation Framework Conditions* (Paris: OECD, October 1998).

24 Stéphane Buydens, *Electronic Commerce: Answering the Emerging Taxation Challenges* (Paris: OECD, 2000), http://www.oecd.org/daf/fa/e_com/e_com.htm.
25 Turner, *Just Capital*, pp. 259–60.
26 OECD, *Harmful Tax Competition.*
27 Dani Rodrik, *Has Globalization Gone Too Far?* (Washington DC: Institute for International Economics, 1997).
28 Gray, *False Dawn*, p. 91.

Chapter 13: Fearful of Finance

1 Friedrich A. Hayek, *The Road to Serfdom* (London: Routledge & Kegan Paul, 1944), p. 69, cited in Forrest Capie, *Capital Controls: A 'Cure' Worse than the Problem?* (London: Institute of Economic Affairs, 2002), p. 15.
2 Walter Bagehot, *Lombard Street: A Description of the Money Market* (London: John Murray, 1873).
3 George Soros, *George Soros on Globalization* (New York: Public Affairs, 2002), pp. 109–10.
4 Data in this paragraph come from the Washington-based Institute for International Finance and the report of the Independent Evaluation Office of the IMF on the capital-account crises in Indonesia, South Korea and Brazil.
5 World Bank, *Finance for Growth: Policy Choices in a Volatile World* (Washington DC: World Bank, 2001), p. 75.
6 Barry Eichengreen and Michael D. Bordo, 'Crises Now and Then: What Lessons from the Last Era of Financial Globalization', National Bureau of Economic Research Working Paper 8716, www.nber.org, January 2002.
7 World Bank, *Finance for Growth*, Figure 2.1.
8 Paul Blustein has provided a splendid account in *The Chastening: Inside the Crisis that Rocked the Global Financial System and Humbled the IMF* (New York: Public Affairs, 2001).
9 See, above all, his *Globalization and its Discontents* (London: Allen Lane, Penguin Press, 2002) and also Ha-Joon Chang (ed.), *Joseph Stiglitz and the World Bank: The Rebel Within* (London: Anthem Press, 2001).
10 Except where otherwise stated, all data are from the Institute for International Finance.
11 Stiglitz, *Globalization and its Discontents*, p. 99.
12 Ewar Prasad, Kenneth Rogoff, Shang-Jin Wei and M. Ayhan Kose, 'Effects of Financial Globalization on Developing Countries: Some Empirical Evidence', 17 March 2003, www.imf.org, pp. 23–6.
13 *Ibid.*, pp. 31–3.
14 The tendency of capital flows to dry up at certain times is stressed by Guillermo Calvo and Carmen M. Reinhardt, in 'Capital Flow Reversals, the Exchange Rate Debate and Dollarization', *Finance and Development*, Vol. 36 (September 1999), pp. 13–15 and in 'When Capital Inflows Come to a Sudden Stop: Consequences and Policy Options', in Peter Kenen and Alexander Swoboda (eds), *Reforming the International Monetary and Financial System* (Washington DC: International

Monetary Fund, 2000), pp. 175–201.

15 World Bank, *Finance for Growth*, chapter 2. See also Wendy Dobson and Gary Clyde Hufbauer: *World Capital Markets: Challenge to the G-10* (Washington DC: Institute for International Economics, 2001), chapter 1.

16 World Bank, *Finance for Growth*, p. 5.

17 *Ibid.*, p. 19.

18 Dobson and Hufbauer, *World Capital Markets*, Table 2.1.

19 World Bank, *Finance for Growth*, p. 21.

20 *Ibid.*, pp. 20–1.

21 Dobson and Hufbauer, *World Capital Markets*, p. 67.

22 Peter Blair Henry, 'Capital Account Liberalization: The Cost of Capital, and Economic Growth', National Bureau of Economic Research Working Paper 9488, February 2003.

23 *Ibid.*, p. 69.

24 *Ibid.*, p. 39.

25 A good simple account of the costs of controls is in Capie, *Capital Controls*.

26 I have drawn heavily in this section on the work of Kenneth Rogoff of Harvard University, erstwhile Economic Counsellor and Director, Research Department, IMF. See 'An Open Letter by Kenneth Rogoff to Joseph Stiglitz', www.imf.org, 2 July 2002, 'An Institution that Eases Financial Pain', *Financial Times*, 27 September 2002 and 'The IMF Strikes Back', *Foreign Policy*, January/February 2003. All of these articles are available at www.imf.org.

27 Stiglitz, *Globalization and its Discontents*, pp. 36–7.

28 Independent Evaluation Office of the International Monetary Fund, report on capital-account crises in Brazil, Indonesia and South Korea, www.imf.org, August 2003, p. 15.

29 Stiglitz, *Globalization and its Discontents*, p. 97.

30 See *ibid.*, chapter 4.

31 See Steven Radelet and Jeffrey Sachs, 'The East Asian Financial Crisis: Diagnosis, Remedies, Prospects', *Brookings Papers on Economic Activity*, No 1 (1998), pp. 1–90. For a relatively neutral account of the Asian crisis see Barry Eichengreen, *Capital Flows and Crises* (Cambridge, Massachusetts and London: MIT Press, 2003); chapter 9. Stanley Fischer, first deputy managing director of the IMF at the time, provided his side of the story in 'The International Financial System: Crises and Reform', The Robbins Lectures at the London School of Economics, delivered in October 2001. See also Fischer, 'Financial Crises and Reform of the International Financial System', National Bureau of Economic Research Working Paper 9297, October 2002.

32 See Figure 1.11 of World Bank, *Finance for Growth*, for an astonishing demonstration of the tentacles of the Suharto family. The wider problem was the pyramid structures that allowed control over companies by families and individuals with small equity stakes. This has also tended to mean high ratios of debt to equity. Prior to the Asian crisis much of this debt was in foreign currency, since its interest rates were (apparently) very low.

33 Stiglitz, *Globalization and its Discontents*, p. 95.

34 This assumption lay behind the recommendations of the so-called Meltzer Commissions, after Allan Meltzer, its chairman. More precisely, this was the report of the International Financial Institution Advisory Commission (IFIAC) (Washington DC: United States Congress, 2000).

35 On the question of moral hazard, see Thomas D. Willett, Aida Budiman, Arthur Denzau, Gab-Je Jo, Cesar Ramos and John Thomas, 'The Falsification of Four Popular Hypotheses about the Asian Currency Crisis', *The World Economy*, Vol. 27 (January 2004), pp. 25–44. See also Kenneth Rogoff 'Moral Hazard in IMF Loans: How Big a Concern?', *Finance and Development*, Vol. 39 (September 2002).

36 A nuanced discussion of moral hazard in international financial crises is in Dobson and Hufbauer, *World Capital Markets*, pp. 130–3.

37 Fischer, 'Financial Crises and Reform of the International Financial System', p. 22.

38 The caution that characterizes financial markets is the theme of an interesting book by Daniel Ben-Ami, *Cowardly Capitalism: The Myth of the Global Financial Casino* (Chichester: John Wiley, 2001).

39 World Bank, *Finance for Growth*, Table 2.1.

40 This is a central theme of an excellent survey of global finance by Clive Crook of *The Economist*. See Clive Crook, 'Global Finance: A Cruel Sea of Capital', *The Economist*, 3 May 2003.

41 Dobson and Hufbauer, *World Capital Markets*, chapter 3.

42 It is an intriguing question whether members of the eurozone are still sovereign in this sense. My guess is that when the first member defaults, it will be put under some form of administration. That may prove a decisive further step on the way towards a true federal state.

43 Fischer, 'Financial Crises and Reform of the International Financial System', pp. 31–2.

44 *Ibid.*, p. 35.

45 See Kenneth Rogoff and Jeromin Zettelmeyer, 'Bankruptcy Procedures for Sovereigns: A History of Ideas, 1976–2001', *IMF Staff Papers*, Vol. 49, No. 3, 2002, pp. 470–507 and Jeffrey Sachs, 'Do We Need an International Lender of Last Resort?' The Frank D. Graham Memorial Lecture presented at Princeton University, 1995, mimeo. See also www.imf.org for a number of papers on the SDRM.

46 Andrei Shleifer makes exactly this argument in 'Will the Sovereign Debt Market Survive?' National Bureau of Economic Research Working Paper 9493, February 2003.

47 Michael Kremer and Seema Jayachandran, 'Odious Debt', National Bureau of Economic Research Working Paper 8953, May 2002.

48 Eichengreen, *Capital Flows and Crises*, p. 46.

Chapter 14: Today's Threats, Tomorrow's Promises

1 Adam Smith, *An Inquiry into the Nature and Causes of the Wealth of Nations* (Oxford: Clarendon Press, 1976), book IV, chapter 5.

2 Mike Moore, *A World Without Walls: Freedom, Development, Free Trade and Global Governance* (Cambridge: Cambridge University Press, 2003), p. 187.

3 See Harold James, *The End of Globalization: Lessons from the Great Depression* (Cambridge, Massachusetts: Harvard University Press), chapter 2.

4 On the recurrent bouts of financial instability, see Edward Chancellor, *Devil Take the Hindmost: A History of Financial Speculation* (Basingstoke and Oxford: Macmillan, 1999). On the Wall Street bubble, see, among other publications, Andrew Smithers and Stephen Wright, *Valuing Wall Street: Protecting Wealth in Turbulent Markets* (New York: McGrawHill, 2000).

5 See W. Max Corden, *Economic Policy, Exchange Rates, and the International System* (Oxford: Oxford University Press, and Chicago: University of Chicago Press, 1994).

6 See David Henderson, *Anti-Liberalism 2000: The Rise of New Millennium Collectivism* (London: Institute of Economic Affairs, 2001).

7 Rosemary Righter, 'Free for All', *Times Literary Supplement*, 26 September 2003, p. 6.

8 A good discussion of the problem of supplying global public goods is contained in Inge Kaul, Isabelle Grunberg and Marc A. Stern (eds), *Global Public Goods: International Co-operation in the 21st Century* (New York and Oxford: Oxford University Press, for the United Nations Development Program, 1999).

References

Aaronson, Susan Ariel. *Taking Trade to the Streets: The Lost History of Public Efforts to Shape Globalization*. Ann Arbor, Michigan: Michigan University Press, 2001.

Acemoglu, Daron. 'Cross-Country Inequality Trends', National Bureau of Economic Research Working Paper 8832, March 2002.

Acemoglu, Daron, Simon Johnson and James A. Robinson. 'Reversal of Fortune: Geography and Institutions in the Making of the Modern World Income Distribution'. National Bureau of Economic Research Working Paper 8460, 2001, and *Quarterly Journal of Economics*, Vol. 117.

Albert, Michel. *Capitalism against Capitalism*. London: Whurr Publishers, 1993.

Amsden, Alice. *The Rise of 'The Rest': Challenges to the West from Late-Industrializing Economies*. Oxford: Oxford University Press, 2001.

Anderson, Sarah and John Cavenaugh. 'Top 200: The Rise of Corporate Global Power'. Institute for Policy Studies, Washington DC, December 2000.

Arrow, Kenneth. *Essays in the Theory of Risk-Bearing*. Chicago: Markham, 1971.

Atkinson, Anthony. 'Globalization and the European Welfare State at the Opening and Closing of the Twentieth Century'. In Henryk Kierzkowski (ed.), *Europe and Globalization*. Basingstoke: Palgrave Macmillan, 2002, chapter 12.

Bagehot, Walter. *Lombard Street: A Description of the Money Market*. London: John Murray, 1873.

Balassa, Bela. *Development Strategies in Semi-industrial Economies*. Baltimore: Johns Hopkins University Press, for the World Bank. 1982.

Baldwin, Richard E. and Philippe Martin. 'Two Waves of Globalization: Superficial Similarities, Fundamental Differences'. National Bureau of Economic Research Working Paper 6904, www.nber.org, January 1999.

Barber, Benjamin R. *Jihad vs. McWorld: Terrorism's Challenge to Democracy*. New York: Ballantine Books, 1995 and 2001.

Barfield Claude E. *Free Trade, Sovereignty, Democracy: The Future of the World Trade Organization*. Washington DC: American Enterprise Institute, 2001.

Bauer, Peter T. *Dissent on Development: Studies and Debates in Development Economics*. Cambridge, Massachusetts: Harvard University Press, 1972.

Bauer, Peter T. 'Foreign Aid: Abiding Issues'. In *From Subsistence to Exchange and Other Essays*, chapter 5. Princeton: Princeton University Press, for the Cato Institute, 2000.

Baumol, William J. *The Free-Market Innovation Machine: Analyzing the Growth Miracle of Capitalism.* Princeton: Princeton University Press, 2002.

Ben-Ami, Daniel. *Cowardly Capitalism: The Myth of the Global Financial Casino.* Chichester: John Wiley, 2001.

Berger, Peter L. 'Four Faces of Global Culture'. *National Interest,* 49 (1997), pp. 23–9.

Berger, Peter L. and Samuel P. Huntingdon (eds). *Many Globalizations: Cultural Diversity in the Contemporary World.* Oxford: Oxford University Press, 2002.

Bernstein, Peter L. *Against the Gods: The Remarkable Story of Risk.* New York: John Wiley, 1996.

Bhagwati, Jagdish N. *Anatomy and Consequences of Exchange Control Regimes: Foreign Trade Regimes and Economic Development,* Vol. XI. New York: Ballinger Publishing Company, for the National Bureau for Economic Research, 1978

Bhagwati, Jagdish N. 'Trade Liberalization and "Fair Trade" Demands: Addressing the Environmental and Labour Standards Issues'. In *A Stream of Windows: Unsettling Reflections on Trade, Immigration and Democracy.* Cambridge, Massachusetts: MIT Press, 1998.

Bhagwati, Jagdish N. 'The Capital Myth'. *Foreign Affairs,* Vol. 77 (May–June 1998), pp. 7–12.

Bhagwati, Jagdish N. *The Wind of the Hundred Days: How Washington Mismanaged Globalization.* Cambridge, Massachusetts: MIT Press, 2000.

Bhagwati, Jagdish N. *Free Trade Today.* Princeton: Princeton University Press, 2002.

Bhagwati, Jagdish N. and Padma Desai. *India: Planning for Industrialization.* London: Oxford University Press, for the Organization for Economic Co-operation and Development, 1970.

Bhalla, Surjit S. *Imagine There's No Country: Poverty, Inequality and Growth in the Era of Globalization.* Washington DC: Institute for International Economics, 2002.

Birdsall, Nancy and Robert Z. Lawrence. 'Deep Integration and Trade Agreements: Good for Developing Countries?' In Inge Kaul, Isabelle Grunberg and Marc A. Stern (eds), *Global Public Goods: International Cooperation in the 21st Century.* New York: Oxford University Press, for the United Nations Development Programme, 1999, pp. 128–51.

Blustein, Paul. *The Chastening: Inside the Crisis that Rocked the Global Financial System and Humbled the IMF.* New York: Public Affairs, 2001.

Boltho, Andrea and Gianni Toniolo. 'The Assessment: The Twentieth Century – Achievements, Failures, Lessons'. *Oxford Review of Economic Policy,* Vol. 15, No. 4 (Winter 1999), pp. 1–17.

Bordo, Michael D., Barry Eichengreen and Douglas A. Irwin. 'Is Globalization Today Really Different than Globalization a Hundred Years Ago?' National Bureau of Economic Research Working Paper 7195, www.nber.org, June 1999.

Bordo, Michael D., Barry Eichengreen and Jongwoo Kim. 'Was There Really an Earlier Period of International Financial Integration Comparable to Today's?' National Bureau of Economic Research Working Paper 6738, www.nber.org, September 1998.

Bourguignon, François and Christian Morrison. 'Inequality among World Citizens'. *American Economic Review,* Vol. 92, No. 4 (September 2002), pp. 727–44.

Brack, Duncan. 'Environmental Treaties and Trade: Multilateral Environmental Agreements and the Multilateral Trading System'. Chapter 11 in Gary P. Sampson and W. Bradnee Chambers (eds), *Trade, Environment and the Millennium*. Tokyo: United Nations University, 1999.

Brittan, Samuel. *Towards a Human Individualism*. London: John Stuart Mill Institute, 1998.

Buchanan, Patrick J. *The Great Betrayal: How American Sovereignty and Social Justice are being Sacrificed to the Gods of the Global Economy*. Boston: Little Brown, 1998.

Burniaux, Jean-Marc, Thai-Thanh Dang, Douglas Fore, Michael Förster, Marco Mira d'Ercole and Howard Oxley. 'Income Distribution and Poverty in Selected OECD Countries'. OECD Economics Department Working Paper 189. Paris: OECD, March 1998, www.oecd.org/eco/ecowp.

Burtless, Gary, Robert Z. Lawrence, Robert E. Litan and Robert J. Shapiro. *Globaphobia: Confronting Fears about Open Trade*. Washington DC: Brookings Institution, 1998.

Buydens, Stéphane. *Electronic Commerce: Answering the Emerging Taxation Challenges*. Paris: OECD, 2000, http://www.oecd.org/daf/fa/e_com/e_com.htm.

Cable, Vincent. *Globalization and Global Governance*. Chatham House Papers. London: Royal Institute of International Affairs, 1999.

Cairncross, Frances. *The Death of Distance*. London: Orion, 1997.

Calomiris, Charles. *A Globalist Manifesto for Public Policy*. The Tenth Annual IEA Hayek Memorial Lecture. Occasional Paper 124. London, Institute of Economic Affairs, 2002.

Calvo, Guillermo and Carmen M. Reinhardt. 'Capital Flow Reversals, the Exchange Rate Debate and Dollarization'. *Finance and Development*, Vol. 36 (September 1999), pp. 13–15.

Calvo, Guillermo and Carmen M. Reinhardt. 'When Capital Inflows Come to a Sudden Stop: Consequences and Policy Options'. In Peter Kenen and Alexander Swoboda (eds), *Reforming the International Monetary and Financial System*. Washington DC: International Monetary Fund, 2000, pp. 175–201.

Capie, Forrest. *Capital Controls: A 'Cure' Worse than the Problem?* London: Institute of Economic Affairs, 2002.

Cavenaugh, John and others. *Alternatives to Economic Globalization: A Better World is Possible*. Report of the International Forum on Globalization. San Francisco: Berrett-Koehler, 2002.

Chancellor, Edward. *Devil Take the Hindmost: A History of Financial Speculation*. Basingstoke and Oxford: Macmillan, 1999.

Chandler, Alfred. *The Visible Hand*. Cambridge, Massachusetts: Harvard University Press, 1977.

Chang, Ha-Joon (ed.). *Joseph Stiglitz and the World Bank: The Rebel Within*. London: Anthem Press, 2001.

Chang, Ha-Joon. *Kicking Away the Ladder: Development Strategy in Historical Perspective*. London: Anthem Press, 2002.

Chaudhuri, K.N. 'Reflections on the Organizing Principle of Premodern Trade'. In James D. Tracy (ed.), *The Political Economy of Merchant Empires: State Power and World Trade 1350–1750*. Cambridge: Cambridge University Press, 1991.

Chen, Shaohua and Martin Ravallion. 'How did the World's Poorest Fare in the 1990s?' World Bank, Washington DC, 2000, mimeo.

Clark, Ximena, David Dollar and Aart Kray. 'Decomposing Global Inequality, 1960–99'. World Bank, Washington DC, 2001, mimeo.

Coase, Ronald. 'The Nature of the Firm'. *Economica*, Vol. 4, No. 6 (1937), pp. 386–405.

Coase, Ronald. 'The Problem of Social Cost'. *Journal of Law and Economics*, Vol. 3 (October 1960), pp. 1–44.

Collier, Paul and A. Hoffler. 'Greed and Grievance in African Civil Wars'. *Quarterly Journal of Economics* (forthcoming).

Cooper, Richard. *The Economics of Interdependence: Economic Policy in the Atlantic Community*. New York: McGraw-Hill, 1968.

Corden, W. Max. *The Theory of Protection*. Oxford: Clarendon Press, 1971.

Corden, W. Max. *Trade Policy and Economic Welfare*. Oxford: Clarendon Press, 1974, second edition 1997.

Corsetti, Giancarlo, Paolo Pesenti and Nouriel Roubini. 'Paper Tigers? A Model of the Asian Crisis'. Working Paper 6783, National Bureau of Economic Research, www.nber.org, November 1998.

Coyle, Diana. *Paradoxes of Prosperity: Why the New Capitalism Benefits All*. New York: Texere, 2002.

Crafts, Nicholas. *Globalization and Growth in the Twentieth Century*. IMF Working Paper WP/00/44. Washington DC: International Monetary Fund, 2000.

Crook, Clive. 'Globalization and its Critics'. *The Economist*, 29 September 2001.

Corden, W. Max. *Economic Policy, Exchange Rates, and the International System* (Oxford: Oxford University Press, and Chicago: University of Chicago Press, 1994).

Crook, Clive. 'Global Finance: A Cruel Sea of Capital'. *The Economist*, 3 May 2003.

Darwin, Charles. *The Descent of Man and Selection in Relation to Sex*. Second edition. London: John Murray, 1882.

Das, Guchuran. *India Unbound*. New York: Alfred A. Knopf, 2001.

De Grauwe, Paul and Magdalena Polan. 'Globalisation and Social Spending', CESifo Working Paper 885, www.econ.kuleuven.ac.be/ew/academic/intecon/Degrauwe, 2003.

De Grauwe, Paul and Filip Camerman. 'How Big are the Big Multinational Companies?' www.econ.kuleuven.ac.be/ew/academic/intecon/Degrauwe, 2003.

Deardorff, Alan V. 'What Might Globalization's Critics Believe?' *The World Economy*, Vol. 26, No. 5 (May 2003), pp. 639–58.

Deininger, Klaus and Lyn Squire. 'A New Data Set Measuring Income Inequality'. *World Bank Economic Review*, Vol. 10, No. 3 (September 1996), pp. 565–92.

Demsetz, Harold. 'Information and Efficiency: Another Viewpoint'. *Journal of Law and Economics*, Vol. XII, No. 1 (1969).

Department for International Development. *Eliminating World Poverty: Making Globalization Work for the Poor*. White Paper on International Development, www.globalisation.gov.uk, December 2000.

De Soto, Hernando. *The Other Path: The Invisible Revolution in the Third World.* New York: Harper & Row, 1989.

Destler, I. M. and Peter J. Balint. *The New Politics of American Trade: Trade, Labor, and the Environment.* Washington DC: Institute for International Economics, 1999.

De Tocqueville, Alexis. *Democracy in America,* ed. Phillips Bradley. New York: Vintage Books, 1945 (first published 1848), Vols I and II.

Diamond, Jared. *Guns, Germs and Steel: The Fates of Human Societies.* New York and London: W. W. Norton, 1997.

Dikhanov, Yuri and Michael Ward. 'Measuring the Distribution of Global Income'. World Bank, 2000, mimeo.

Dobson, Wendy and Gary Clyde Hufbauer. *World Capital Markets: Challenge to the G-10.* Washington DC: Institute for International Economics, 2001.

Dollar, David and Aart Kraay. 'Growth is Good for the Poor'. Policy Research Working Paper No. 2587, World Bank, Washington DC, 2001.

Donahue, John D. and Joseph S. Nye Jr (eds). *Governance amid Bigger, Better Markets.* Washington DC: Brookings Institution, 2001.

Dore, Ronald. *Stock Market Capitalism: Welfare Capitalism – Japan and Germany versus the Anglo-Saxons.* Oxford: Oxford University Press, 2000.

Dornsbusch, Rudi. 'A Century of Unrivaled Prosperity'. In Ian Vasquez (ed.), *Global Fortune: The Stumble and Rise of World Capitalism.* Washington DC: Cato Institute, 2000, chapter 5.

Dornbusch, Rudi. 'Fewer Monies, Better Monies'. National Bureau of Economic Research Working Paper 8324, www.nber.org, June 2001.

Easterly, William. *The Elusive Quest for Growth: Economists' Adventures and Misadventures in the Tropics.* Cambridge, Massachusetts: MIT Press, 2001.

Easterly, William and Ross Levine. 'Tropics, Germs and Crops: How Endowments Influence Economic Development'. National Bureau of Economic Research Working Paper 9106, August 2002.

Ehrlich, Paul. *The Population Bomb.* New York: Ballantine Books, 1968.

Eichengreen, Barry. *Towards a New International Financial Architecture: A Practical Post-Asia Agenda.* Washington DC: Institute for International Economics, 1999.

Eichengreen, Barry. *Capital Flows and Crises.* Cambridge, Massachusetts and London: MIT Press, 2003.

Eichengreen, Barry and Michael D. Bordo. 'Crises Now and Then: What Lessons from the Last Era of Financial Globalization?' National Bureau of Economic Research Working Paper 8716, www.nber.org, January 2002.

Elliott, Larry and Dan Atkinson. *The Age of Insecurity.* London: Verso, 1998.

Engerman, Stanley L. 'The Slave Trade and British Capital Formation in the Eighteenth Century: A Comment on the Williams Thesis'. *Business History Review,* Vol. 46 (1972), pp. 430–43.

Esty, Daniel. 'Environmental Governance at the WTO: Outreach to Civil Society'. In Gary P. Sampson and W. Bradnee Chambers (eds), *Trade, Environment and the Millennium.* Tokyo: United Nations University, 1999, chapter 4.

Feenstra, Robert. 'Integration of Trade and Disintegration of Production in the Global Economy'. *Journal of Economic Perspectives,* Vol. 12 (1998), pp. 31–50.

Feldstein, Martin and C. Horioka. 'Domestic Savings and International Capital Flows'. *Economic Journal*, Vol. 90 (June 1980), pp. 314–29.

Findlay, Ronald. 'Globalization and the European Economy: Medieval Origins to the Industrial Revolution'. In Henryk Kierzkowski (ed.), *Europe and Globalization*. Basingstoke: Palgrave Macmillan, 2002, pp. 32–63.

Finger, J. Michael. 'The WTO's Special Burden on Less Developed Countries'. *Cato Journal*, Vol. 19, No. 3 (Winter 2000), pp. 425–37.

Fischer, Stanley. 'The International Financial System: Crises and Reform'. The Robbins Lectures, London School of Economics, October 2001, mimeo.

Fischer, Stanley. 'Financial Crises and Reform of the International Financial System'. National Bureau of Economic Research Working Paper 9297, October 2002.

Forrester, Viviane. *The Economic Horror*. Cambridge: Polity Press, 1999.

Frankel, Jeffrey and David Romer. 'Does Trade Cause Growth?' *American Economic Review*, June 1999.

Friedman, Thomas. *The Lexus and the Olive Tree*. London: HarperCollins, 2000.

Fukuyama, Francis. *The End of History and the Last Man*. London: Hamish Hamilton, 1992.

Gelb, Alan and associates. *Oil Windfalls: Blessing or Curse?* New York: Oxford University Press, for the World Bank, 1989.

Gellner, Ernest. *Nations and Nationalism*. Oxford: Basil Blackwell, 1983.

Giddens, Anthony. *The Third Way: The Renewal of Social Democracy*. Malden, Massachusetts: Polity Press, 1999.

Gilpin, Robert. *Global Political Economy: Understanding the International Economic Order*. Princeton: Princeton University Press, 2001.

Goklany, Indur M. 'The Globalization of Human Well-Being'. Policy Analysis No. 447. Cato Institute, Washington DC, 22 August 2002.

Golub, Stephen S. *Labor Costs and International Trade*. Washington DC: American Enterprise Institute for Public Policy Research, 1999.

Graham, Edward M. *Fighting the Wrong Enemy: Antiglobal Activists and Multinational Enterprises*. Washington DC. Institute for International Economics, 2000.

Gray, John. *False Dawn: The Delusions of Global Capitalism*. London: Granta, 1998.

Greider, Willam. *One World, Ready or Not: The Manic Logic of Global Capitalism*. New York: Touchstone, 1998.

Grossman, Gene and Alan Krueger. 'Economic Growth and the Environment'. National Bureau of Economic Research Working Paper 4634, February 1994.

Hardt, Michael and Antonio Negri. *Empire*. Cambridge, Massachusetts: Harvard University Press, 2000.

Harley. C. 1980. 'Transportation, the World Wheat Trade and the Kuznets Cycle, 1850–1913'. *Explorations in Economic History*, Vol. 17 (1980), pp. 218–50.

Hart, Oliver. *Firms, Contracts and Financial Structure*. Oxford: Clarendon Press, 1995.

Hausmann, Ricardo and Roberto Rigobon. 'An Alternative Interpretation of the "Resource Curse": Theory and Policy Implications'. National Bureau of Economic Research Working Paper 9424, December 2002.

Havel, Vaclav. *Summer Meditations*. New York: Alfred A. Knopf, 1992.

Hayek, Friedrich A. *The Road to Serfdom*. London: Routledge & Kegan Paul, 1944.

Hayek, Friedrich A. 'The Use of Knowledge in Society'. *American Economic Review*, Vol. 34 (1945), pp. 519–30.

Hayek, Friedrich A. *The Constitution of Liberty*. Chicago: University of Chicago Press, 1960.

Heckscher, Eli. *Mercantilism*. London: Allen & Unwin, 1955

Held, David and Anthony McGrew, David Goldblatt and Jonathan Perraton. *Global Transformations: Politics, Economics and Culture*. Cambridge: Polity Press, 1999.

Henderson, David. *Innocence and Design: The Influence of Economic Ideas on Policy*. Oxford: Basil Blackwell, 1986.

Henderson, David. *The Changing Fortunes of Economic Liberalism: Yesterday, Today and Tomorrow*. London: Institute of Economic Affairs, 1998.

Henderson, David. *The MAI Affair: A Story and its Lessons*. London: Royal Institute of International Affairs, 1999.

Henderson, David. *Anti-Liberalism 2000: The Rise of New Millennium Collectivism*. London: Institute of Economic Affairs, 2001.

Henderson, David. *Misguided Virtue: False Notions of Corporate Responsibility*. London: Institute of Economic Affairs, 2002.

Henry, Peter Blair. 'Capital Account Liberalization: The Cost of Capital, and Economic Growth'. National Bureau of Economic Research Working Paper 9488, February 2003.

Hertz, Noreena. *The Silent Takeover: Global Capitalism and the Death of Democracy*. London: William Heinemann, 2001.

Heston, Alan, Robert Summers and B. Aten. 'Penn World Table Version 6.0'. Center for International Comparisons at the University of Pennsylvania (CICUP), December 2001.

Hines, Colin. *Localization: A Global Manifesto*. London: Earthscan Publications, 2000.

Hirst, Paul and Grahame Thompson. *Globalization in Question: The International Economy and the Possibilities of Governance*. Second edition. Cambridge: Polity Press. 1999.

Hudec, Robert E. *Developing Countries in the GATT Legal System*. Thames Essay No. 50. Aldershot: Gower, for the Trade Policy Research Centre, 1987.

Hudec, Robert E. ' "Circumventing Democracy": The Political Morality of Trade Negotiations'. *New York University Journal of International Law and Politics* (1993), pp. 311–22. Reprinted in Hudec, *Essays on the Nature of International Trade Law*. London: Cameron May, 1999, chapter 7.

Huntingdon, Samuel P. *The Clash of Civilizations and the Remaking of World Order*. New York: Simon & Schuster, 1996.

Independent Evaluation Office of the International Monetary Fund. Report on Capital Account Crises in Brazil, Indonesia and South Korea. www.imf.org, August 2003.

International Financial Institution Advisory Commission (IFIAC). *Report*. Washington DC: United States Congress, 2000.

International Monetary Fund. *World Economic Outlook April 2002: Recessions and Recoveries*. Washington DC: 2002.

Irwin, Douglas A. *Against the Tide: An Intellectual History of Free Trade*. Princeton: Princeton University Press, 1996.

Irwin, Douglas A. 'Do We Need the WTO?' *Cato Journal*, Vol. 19, No. 3 (Winter 2000), pp. 351–7.

Irwin, Douglas A. *Free Trade under Fire*. Princeton: Princeton University Press, 2002.

Irwin, Douglas A. 'Did Import Substitution Promote Growth in the Late Nineteenth Century?' National Bureau of Economic Research, Working Paper 8751, February 2002.

Jackson, John H. 'The WTO "Constitution" and Proposed Reforms. Seven Mantras Revisited'. *Journal of International Economic Law*, 2001, pp. 67–78.

Jacobs, Jane. *Systems of Survival: A Dialogue on the Moral Foundations of Commerce and Politic*. New York: Vintage Books, 1992.

James, Harold. *The End of Globalization: Lessons from the Great Depression*. Cambridge, Massachusetts: Harvard University Press, 2001.

Jones, Eric L. *The European Miracle: Environments, Economies, and Geopolitics in the History of Europe and Asia*. Cambridge: Cambridge University Press, 1981, second edition 1988.

Jones, Eric L. *Growth Recurring: Economic Change in World History*. Ann Arbor: University of Michigan Press edition, 2000.

Jones, Eric L. *The Record of Global Economic Development*. Cheltenham: Edward Elgar, 2002.

Jones, Ronald W. *Globalization and the Theory of Input Trade*. Cambridge, Massachusetts: MIT Press, 2000.

Kaufmann, Daniel. 'Misrule of Law: Does the Evidence Challenge Conventions in Judiciary and Legal Reforms?' World Bank, draft, July 2001.

Kaul, Inge, Isabelle Grunberg and Marc A. Stern (eds). *Global Public Goods: International Cooperation in the 21st Century*. New York: Oxford University Press, for the United Nations Development Programme, 1999.

Keesing, Donald B. and Martin Wolf. *Textile Quotas against Developing Countries*. Thames Essay No. 23, London: Trade Policy Research Centre, 1980.

Kennedy, Paul. *The Rise and Fall of the Great Powers: Economic Change and Military Conflict from 15000 to 2000*. New York: Vintage Books, 1989.

Keynes, John Maynard. *The Economic Consequences of the Peace*. London: Macmillan 1919.

Kierzkowski, Henryk (ed.). *Europe and Globalization*. Basingstoke: Palgrave Macmillan, 2002.

King, Robert and Ross Levine. 'Finance, Entrepreneurship and Growth: Theory and Evidence'. *Journal of Monetary Economics*, 32 (December 1993).

Klein, Naomi. *No Logo*. London: Flamingo, 2000.

Kremer, Michael and Seema Jayachandran. 'Odious Debt'. National Bureau of Economic Research Working Paper 8953, May 2002.

Krueger, Anne O. *Liberalization Attempts and Consequences: Foreign Trade Regimes and Economic Development*, Vol. X. New York: Ballinger Publishing, for the National Bureau for Economic Research, 1978.

Krueger, Anne O. 'Trading Phobias: Governments, NGOs and the Multilateral System'. John Bonython Lecture, 10 October 2000. www.cis.org.au/JBL/JBL00.htm.

Krugman, Paul. 'Competitiveness: A Dangerous Obsession'. *Foreign Affairs*, Vol. 73 (March–April 1994), pp. 28–44.

Krugman, Paul. *Pop Internationalism*. Cambridge, Massachusetts and London: MIT Press, 1997.

Krugman, Paul. 'Ricardo's Difficult Idea: Why Intellectuals Don't Understand Comparative Advantage'. In Gary Cook (ed.), *The Economics and Politics of International Trade*, Vol. 2 of *Freedom and Trade*. London: Routledge, 1998.

Lal, Deepak. *The Poverty of 'Development Economics'*. Hobart Paper No. 16. London: Institute of Economic Affairs, second edition, 1997.

Lal, Deepak. *Unintended Consequences: The Impact of Factor Endowments, Culture and Politics on Long-Run Economic Performance*. Cambridge, Massachusetts: MIT Press, 1998.

Lal, Deepak and H. Myint. *The Political Economy of Poverty, Equity and Growth*. Oxford: Clarendon Press, 1996.

Landes, David. *The Unbound Prometheus: Technological Change and Industrial Development in Western Europe from 1750 to the Present*. Cambridge: Cambridge University Press, 1969.

Landes, David. *The Wealth and Poverty of Nations: Why Some are So Rich and Some So Poor*. London: Little Brown, 1998.

La Porta, Rafael, Florencio Lopez-de-Silanes, Cristian Pop-Eleches and Andrei Shleifer. 'The Guarantees of Freedom'. National Bureau of Economic Research Working Paper 8759, www.nber.org, February 2002.

Lawrence, Robert Z. and Matthew J. Slaughter. 'International Trade and American Wages in the 1980s: Giant Sucking Sound or Small Hiccup?' *Brookings Papers on Economic Activity*, No. 2 (1993), pp. 161–211.

Legrain, Philippe. *Open World: The Truth about Globalization*. London: Abacus, 2002.

Lenin, Vladimir I. 'The Impending Catastrophe and How to Combat it (1917)'. In *Lenin's Economic Writings*, ed. Meghnad Desai. Atlantic Highlands, New Jersey: Humanities Press International, 1989 (1917).

Lindert, Peter H. and Jeffrey G. Williamson. 'Does Globalization Make the World More Unequal?' Paper presented at the National Bureau of Economic Research conference on Globalization in Historical Perspective, Santa Barbara, California, 3–6 May 2001.

Lindert, Peter H. and Jeffrey G. Williamson. 'Globalization and Inequality: A Long History'. Paper prepared for the World Bank Annual Conference on Development Economics – Europe, Barcelona, 25–27 June 2001.

Lindsey, Brink. 'The Invisible Hand vs. the Dead Hand'. In Ian Vásquez (ed.), *Global Fortune: The Stumble and Rise of World Capitalism*. Washington DC: Cato Institute, 2000.

Lindsey, Brink. *Against the Dead Hand: The Uncertain Struggle for Global Capitalism*. Washington DC: John Wiley, 2002.

Lipsey, Robert E. and Fredrik Sjöholm. 'Foreign Direct Investment and Wages in Indonesian Manufacturing'. National Bureau of Economic Research Working Paper 8299, May 2001.

Little, Ian M. D. *Economic Development: Theory, Policy and International Relations.* New York: Basic Books, 1982.

Little, Ian M. D, Richard N. Cooper, W. Max Corden and Sarath Rajapatirana. *Boom, Crisis and Adjustment: The Macroeconomic Experience of Developing Countries.* Oxford and New York: Oxford University Press for the World Bank, 1993.

Little, Ian M. D., Tibor Scitovsky and Maurice Scott. *Industry and Trade in Some Developing Countries: A Comparative Study.* London: Oxford University Press, for the Organization for Economic Co-operation and Development, 1970.

Litvin, Daniel. *Empires of Profit: Commerce, Conquest and Corporate Responsibility.* London: Texere, 2003.

Lloyd, John. *The Protest Ethic: How the Anti-globalization Movement Challenges Social Democracy.* London: Demos, 2001.

Lomborg, Bjorn. *The Sceptical Environmentalist: Measuring the Real State of the World.* Cambridge: Cambridge University Press, 2001.

Lucas, Robert E. 'Why doesn't Capital Flow from Rich to Poor Countries?' *American Economic Review,* 80 (May 1980), pp. 92–6.

Luttwak, Edward. *Turbo Capitalism: Winners and Losers in the Global Economy.* London: Weidenfeld & Nicolson, 1998.

Macaulay, Thomas. 'On Mitford's History of Greece', *Knights Quarterley Magazine,* November 1824.

McMillan, John. *Reinventing the Bazaar: A Natural History of Markets.* New York: W. W. Norton, 2002.

McNeill, William H. *Plagues and People.* New York: Doubleday Anchor Books, 1977.

McNeill, William H. *The Pursuit of Power. Technology, Armed Force and Society since A.D. 1000.* Chicago: University of Chicago Press, 1982.

McNeill, William H. *The Global Condition: Conquerors, Catastrophes and Community.* Princeton: Princeton University Press, 1992.

Maddison, Angus. *Monitoring the World Economy, 1820–1992.* Paris: Development Centre of the Organization for Economic Co-operation and Development, 1995 and 1998.

Maddison, Angus. *The World Economy: A Millennial Perspective.* Paris: Development Centre of the Organization for Economic Co-operation and Development, 2001.

Mani, M. and D. Wheeler. 'In Search of Pollution Havens? Dirty Industry in the World Economy 1960–1995'. *Journal of Environment and Development,* Vol. 7, No. 3, 1998, pp. 215–47.

Maskus, Keith E. *Intellectual Property Rights in the Global Economy.* Washington DC: Institute for International Economics, 2000.

Mazur, Jay. 'Labor's New Internationalism'. *Foreign Affairs,* Vol. 79 (January/February 2000).

Messerlin, Patrick. *Measuring the Costs of Protection in Europe: European Commercial Policy in the 2000s.* Washington DC: Institute for International Economics, 2001.

Micklethwait, John and Adrian Wooldridge. *A Future Perfect: The Challenge and Hidden Promise of Globalization.* New York: Random House, 2000.

Milanovic, Branko. 'True World Income Distribution, 1988 and 1993: First Calculation Based on Household Surveys Alone'. World Bank, October 1999, mimeo.

Mokyr, Joel. *The Lever of Riches: Technological Creativity and Economic Progress.* Oxford: Oxford University Press, 1990.

Monbiot, George. *Captive State: The Corporate Takeover of Britain.* Basingstoke: Macmillan, 2000.

Monbiot, George, *The Age of Consent: A Manifesto for a New World Order.* London: HarperCollins, 2003.

Moore, Mark H. 'The Market versus the Forum'. In John D. Donahue and Joseph S. Nye Jr (eds), *Governance amid Bigger, Better Markets.* Washington DC: Brookings Institution, 2001, chapter 13.

Moore, Mike. *A World without Walls: Freedom, Development, Free Trade and Global Governance.* Cambridge: Cambridge University Press, 2003.

Moore, Stephen and Julian L. Simon. 'Twenty-Five Miraculous U.S. Trends of the Past 100 Years'. In Ian Vásquez (ed.), *Global Fortune: The Stumble and Rise of World Capitalism.* Washington DC: Cato Institute, 2000, chapter 4.

Moran, Theodore. *Foreign Direct Investment and Development: The New Policy Agenda for Developing Countries and Economies in Transition* (Washington DC: Institute for International Economics, 1998).

Moran, Theodore. *Beyond Sweatshops: Foreign Direct Investment and Globalization in Developing Countries.* Washington DC: Brookings Institution, 2002.

Norberg, Johan. *In Defence of Global Capitalism.* Stockholm: Timbro, 2001.

Nordhaus, William. 'Do Real Output and Real Wage Measures Capture Reality? The History of Lighting Suggests Not'. Cowles Foundation Discussion Paper 1078, September 1994.

North, Douglass C. *Structure and Change in Economic History.* New York: W. W. Norton, 1981.

North, Douglass C. 'Institutions, Transaction Costs, and the Rise of Merchant Empires'. In James D. Tracy (ed.), *The Political Economy of Merchant Empires: State Power and World Trade 1350–1750.* Cambridge: Cambridge University Press, 1991.

O'Brien, Richard. *Global Financial Integration: The End of Geography.* London: Royal Institute of International Affairs/Pinter, 1992.

Obstfeld, Maurice and Alan M. Taylor. 'Globalization and Capital Markets'. National Bureau of Economic Research Working Paper 8846, www.nber.org, March 2002.

Olson, Mancur. *The Logic of Collective Action.* Cambridge, Massachusetts: Harvard University Press, 1965.

Olson, Mancur. *The Rise and Decline of Nations: Economic Growth, Stagflation, and Social Rigidities.* New Haven, Connecticut: Yale University Press, 1982.

Olson, Mancur. 'Big Bills Left on the Sidewalk: Why Some Countries are Rich and Others Poor'. *Journal of Economic Perspectives,* Vol. 10 (Spring 1996), pp. 3–24.

Olson, Mancur. *Power and Prosperity: Outgrowing Communist and Capitalist Dictatorships.* New York: Basic Books, 2000.

Oneal, John and Bruce Russett. 'The Classical Liberals were Right: Democracy, Interdependence, and Conflict, 1950–1985'. *International Studies Quarterly,* 41 (June 1997), pp. 267–94.

Oneal, John and Bruce Russett. *Triangulating Peace: Democracy, Interdependence and International Organizations.* New York: W. W. Norton, 2000.

Orbinski, James. 'Health, Equity and Trade: A Failure in Global Governance'. In Gary P. Sampson (ed.), *The Role of the World Trade Organization in Global Governance.* Tokyo: United Nations University Press, 2001, chapter 11.

Organization for Economic Co-operation and Development. *Trade, Employment and Labour Standards.* Paris: OECD, 1996.

Organization for Economic Co-operation and Development. *Harmful Tax Competition: An Emerging Global Issue.* Paris: OECD, 1998.

Organization for Economic Co-operation and Development. *Electronic Commerce: Taxation Framework Conditions.* Paris: OECD, October 1998.

Organization for Economic Co-operation and Development. *Policy Competition for Foreign Direct Investment.* Paris: OECD, 2000.

Organization for Economic Co-operation and Development. *Economic Outlook 2003/1.* No. 73. Paris: OECD, June 2003.

Organization for Economic Co-operation and Development. *Revenue Statistics 1965–2001.* Paris: OECD, 2003.

O'Rourke, Kevin H. 'Europe and the Causes of Globalization, 1790 to 2000'. In Henryk Kierzkowski (ed.), *Europe and Globalization.* Basingstoke: Palgrave Macmillan, 2002, chapter 3.

O'Rourke, Kevin H. and Jeffrey G. Williamson. 'From Malthus to Ohlin: Trade, Growth and Distribution since 1500'. National Bureau of Economic Research Working Paper 8955, www.nber.org, May 2002.

Orwell, George. 'The Lion and the Unicorn' (1940). In Sonia Orwell and Ian Angus (eds), *George Orwell: The Collected Essays, Journalism and Letters,* Vol. 4. London: Penguin Books, 1970.

Ostry, Sylvia. 'Global Integration: Currents and Counter-Currents'. Walter Gordon Lecture, Massey College, University of Toronto, 23 May 2001.

Owen, Geoffrey. *From Empire to Europe: The Decline and Revival of British Industry since the Second World War.* London: HarperCollins, 1999.

Oxfam. *Rigged Rules and Double Standards: Trade, Globalization and the Fight against Poverty.* Oxford: Oxfam International, 2002, www.maketradefair.com.

Pogge, Thomas W. and Sanjay G. Reddy. 'Unknown: The Extent, Distribution and Trend of Global Income Poverty'. 16 July 2003, mimeo.

Polanyi, Karl. *The Great Transformation: The Political and Economic Origins of our Time.* Boston: Beacon Press, 1957 (first published 1944).

Pomeranz, Kenneth. *The Great Divergence: China, Europe and the Making of the Modern Economy.* Princeton and Oxford: Princeton University Press, 2000.

Potter, D., D. Goldblatt, M. Kiloh and P. Lewis (eds). *Democratization.* Cambridge: Polity Press, 1997.

Prasad, Ewar, Kenneth Rogoff, Shang-Jin Wei and M. Ayhan Kose. 'Effects of Financial Globalization on Developing Countries: Some Empirical Evidence'. www.imf.org, 17 March 2003, pp. 23–6.

Pritchett, Lant. 'Divergence, Big Time'. *Journal of Economic Perspectives,* Vol. 11, No. 3

(Summer 1997), pp. 3–17.

Progressive Policy Institute. 'America's Hidden Tax on the Poor: The Case for Reforming US Tariff Policy'. Washington DC, March 2002.

Radelet, Steven and Jeffrey D. Sachs. 'The East Asian Financial Crisis: Diagnosis, Remedies, Prospects'. *Brookings Papers on Economic Activity*, No. 1 (1998), pp. 1–90.

Ravallion, Martin. 'The Debate on Globalization, Poverty and Inequality: Why Measurement Matters'. World Bank, no date, www.worldbank.org.

Reinicke, Wolfgang H.. *Global Public Policy: Governing without Government*. Washington DC: Brookings Institution, 1998.

Righter, Rosemary. 'Free for All'. *Times Literary Supplement*, 26 September 2003.

Rodrik, Dani. *Has Globalization Gone Too Far?* Washington DC: Institute for International Economics, 1997.

Rodrik, Dani. *The New Global Economy: Making Openness Work*. Policy Essay No. 24. Baltimore: Johns Hopkins University Press, for the Overseas Development Council, 1998.

Rogoff, Kenneth. 'An Open Letter by Kenneth Rogoff to Joseph Stiglitz'. www.imf.org, 2 July 2002.

Rogoff, Kenneth. 'An Institution that Eases Financial Pain', *Financial Times*, 27 September 2002.

Rogoff, Kenneth. 'The IMF Strikes Back'. *Foreign Policy*, January/February 2003.

Rogoff, Kenneth. 'Moral Hazard in IMF Loans: How Big a Concern?' *Finance and Development*, Vol. 39, September 2002.

Rogoff, Kenneth and Jeromin Zettemeyer. 'Bankruptcy Procedures for Sovereigns: A History of Ideas, 1976–2001'. *IMF Staff Papers*, Vol. 49, No. 3, 2002, pp. 470–507.

Sachs, Jeffrey D. 'Do We Need an International Lender of Last Resort?' The Frank D. Graham Memorial Lecture presented at Princeton University, 1995, mimeo.

Sachs, Jeffrey D. 'Institutions Don't Rule: Direct Effects of Geography on Per Capita Income'. National Bureau of Economic Research Working Paper 9490, February 2003.

Sachs, Jeffrey D. and Andrew Warner. 'Natural Resource Abundance and Economic Growth'. Harvard Institute for International Development, November 1997.

Sala-I-Martin, Xavier. 'The Myth of Exploding Income Inequality in Europe and the World'. In Henryk Kierzkowski (ed.), *Europe and Globalization*. Basingstoke: Palgrave Macmillan, 2002, chapter 1.

Sala-I-Martin, Xavier. 'The Disturbing "Rise" of Global Income Inequality'. April 2002, mimeo.

Sala-I-Martin, Xavier. 'The World Distribution of Income (Estimated from Individual Country Distributions)'. May 2002, mimeo.

Sala-I-Martin, Xavier and Arvind Subramanian. 'Addressing the Natural Resource Curse: An Illustration from Nigeria'. May 2003, mimeo.

Sampson, Gary P. *Trade, Environment, and the WTO: The Post-Seattle Agenda*. Policy Essay No. 27. Baltimore: Johns Hopkins University Press, for the Overseas Development Council, 2000.

Sampson, Gary P. (ed.). *The Role of the World Trade Organization in Global Governance*.

Tokyo: United Nations University Press, 2001.

Sampson, Gary P. and W. Bradnee Chambers (eds). *Trade, Environment and the Millennium*. Tokyo: United Nations University, 1999.

Schumpeter, Joseph. *Capitalism, Socialism and Democracy*. New York: Harper & Row, 1976 (first published 1942).

Sen, Amartya. 'What is the Role of Legal and Judicial Reform in the Development Process?' Keynote Address at the Comprehensive Legal and Judicial Development Conference, World Bank, Washington DC, 5–7 June 2000.

Shleifer, Andrei. 'Will the Sovereign Debt Market Survive?' National Bureau of Economic Research Working Paper 9493, February 2003.

Smith, Adam. *An Inquiry into the Nature and Causes of the Wealth of Nations*. Oxford: Clarendon Press, 1976.

Smithers, Andrew and Stephen Wright. *Valuing Wall Street: Protecting Wealth in Turbulent Markets*. New York: McGraw-Hill, 2000.

Soros, George. *The Crisis of Global Capitalism*. New York: Little Brown, 1999.

Soros, George. *Open Society: Reforming Global Capitalism*. New York: Public Affairs, 2000.

Soros, George. *George Soros on Globalization*. New York: Public Affairs, 2002.

Srinivasan, T. N. *Eight Lectures on India's Economic Reforms*. New York: Oxford University Press, 2000.

Stiglitz, Joseph E. *Globalization and its Discontents*. London: Allen Lane, Penguin Press, 2002.

Stolper, Wolfgang and Paul A. Samuelson. 'Protection and Real Wages'. *Review of Economic Studies*, Vol. 9 (1941), pp. 58–73.

Talavera, Arturo Fontaine. 'Trends towards Globalization in Chile'. In Peter L. Berger and Samuel P. Huntingdon (eds), *Many Globalizations: Cultural Diversity in the Contemporary World*. Oxford: Oxford University Press, 2002.

Tanzi, Vito. 'Globalization and the Future of Social Protection'. IMF Working Paper, WP/00/12, January 2000, www.imf.org.

Tanzi, Vito and Ludger Schuknecht. *Public Spending in the 20th Century. A Global Perspective*. Cambridge: Cambridge University Press, 2000.

Taylor, Alan M. 'International Capital Mobility in History: The Saving–Investment Relationship'. National Bureau of Economic Research Working Paper 5743, www.nber.org, 1996.

Tiebout, Charles. 'A Pure Theory of Local Expenditures'. *Journal of Political Economy*, Chicago, Vol. 64 (1956), pp. 416–24.

Tracy, James D. (ed.). *The Political Economy of Merchant Empires: State Power and World Trade 1350–1750*. Cambridge: Cambridge University Press, 1991.

Turner, Adair. *Just Capital: The Liberal Economy*. London: Macmillan, 2001.

Twomey, Michael. *A Century of Foreign Investment in the Third World*. London: Routledge, 2000.

United Nations Conference on Trade and Development. *World Investment Report 2000: Cross-border Mergers and Acquisitions and Development*. New York: United Nations, 2000.

United Nations Conference on Trade and Development. *World Investment Report 2002: Transnational Corporations and Export Competitiveness*. New York and Geneva: United Nations, 2002.

United Nations Conference on Trade and Development. 'Are Transnationals Bigger than Countries?' TAD/INF/PR/47, 12 August 2002, www.unctad.org.

United Nations Development Programme. *Human Development Report 2001: Making New Technologies Work for Human Development*. New York: Oxford University Press, for the United Nations Development Programme, 2001.

United Nations Development Programme. *Human Development Report 2002: Deepening Democracy in a Fragmented World*. New York: Oxford University Press, for the United Nations Development Programme, 2002.

United Nations Development Programme. *Making Global Trade Work for People*. London: Earthscan Publications, 2003.

United Nations Development Programme. *Human Development Report 2003: Millennium Development Goals: A Compact among Nations to End Human Poverty*. New York: Oxford University Press, for the United Nations Development Programme, 2003.

Vargas Llosa, Mario. 'Liberalism in the New Millennium'. In Ian Vásquez (ed.), *Global Fortune: The Stumble and Rise of World Capitalism*. Washington DC: Cato Institute, 2000, chapter 1.

Vasquez, Ian (ed.). *Global Fortune: The Stumble and Rise of World Capitalism*. Washington DC: Cato Institute, 2000.

Wade, Robert. 'Winners and Losers'. *The Economist*, 26 April 2001.

Wade, Robert and Martin Wolf. 'Are Global Poverty and Inequality Getting Worse?' *Prospect*, March 2002, pp. 16–21.

Wheeler, D. 'Racing to the Bottom? Foreign Investment and Air Pollution in Developing Countries'. Policy Research Working Paper No. 2524, Development Research Group, World Bank, Washington DC, 2001.

Willett, Thomas D., Aida Budiman, Arthur Denzau, Gab-Je Jo, Cesar Ramos and John Thomas. 'The Falsification of Four Popular Hypotheses about the Asian Currency Crisis'. *The World Economy*, Vol. 27 (January 2004), pp. 25–44.

Williams, Eric. *Capitalism and Slavery*. Chapel Hill: University of North Carolina Press, 1944.

Williamson, Oliver. *The Economic Institutions of Capitalism*. New York: Free Press, 1985.

Williamson, Oliver. 'The New Institutional Economics: Taking Stock, Looking Ahead'. *Journal of Economic Literature*, September 2000, pp. 595–613.

Wilson, James Q. 'The Morality of Capitalism'. John Bonython Lecture, 15 October 1997, www.cis.org.au/JBL/JBL97.htm.

Wolf, Martin. *India's Exports*. New York: Oxford University Press, for the World Bank, 1982.

Wolf, Martin. 'Richard Cobden and the Democratic Peace'. Chapter 13 in Gary Cook (ed.), *The Economics and Politics of International Trade*, Vol. 2 of *Freedom and Trade*. London and New York: Routledge, 1998.

Wolf, Martin. 'Will the Nation State Survive Globalization?' *Foreign Affairs*, Vol. 80 (January–February 2001), pp. 178–90.

Wolf, Martin. 'What the World Needs from the Multilateral Trading System'. In Gary P. Sampson (ed.), *The Role of the World Trade Organization in Global Governance*. Tokyo: United Nations University Press, 2001, pp. 182–208.

Wolf, Martin. 'Nation, State and Globalization'. Orwell Lecture, delivered at Birkbeck College, London University, 25 April 2001.

Wolf, Martin. 'Countries Still Rule the World'. *Financial Times*, 6 February 2002.

Wolf, Martin. 'Is Globalization in Danger?' *The World Economy*, Festschrift in honour of Max Corden, Vol. 26, No. 4 (April 2003), pp. 393–411.

Wolf, Martin. 'The Morality of the Market'. *Foreign Policy*, September/October 2003, pp. 46–50.

Wood, Adrian. *North–South Trade, Employment and Inequality*. Oxford: Clarendon Press, 1994.

Wood, Adrian. 'Globalization and the Rise in Labour Market Inequalities'. *Economic Journal*, Vol. 108 (September 1998), pp. 1463–82.

World Bank. *World Development Report 1995: Workers in an Integrating World*. Oxford: Oxford University Press, for the World Bank, 1995.

World Bank. *World Development Report 2000/2001: Attacking Poverty*. Washington DC: World Bank, 2000.

World Bank. *Finance for Growth: Policy Choices in a Volatile World*. Washington DC: World Bank, 2001.

World Bank. *Global Economic Prospects and the Developing Countries 2002: Making Trade Work for the World's Poor*. Washington DC: World Bank, 2002.

World Bank. *Globalization, Growth & Poverty: Building an Inclusive World Economy*. Washington DC: World Bank, 2002.

World Bank. *Global Development Finance: Financing the Poorest Countries, Analysis and Summary Tables 2002*. Washington DC: World Bank, 2002.

World Bank. *World Development Indicators 2002*. Washington DC: World Bank, 2002.

World Bank. *Global Economic Prospects and the Developing Countries 2003: Investing to Unlock Global Opportunities*. Washington DC: World Bank, 2003.

World Bank. *World Development Report 2003: Sustainable Development in a Dynamic World: Transforming Institutions, Growth and Quality of Life*. New York: Oxford University Press, for the World Bank, 2003.

World Economic Forum. *The Global Competitiveness Report 2001–02*. New York: Oxford University Press, 2002.

World Institute for Development Economics Research. *World Income Inequality Database*. www.wider.unu.edu/wiid.

World Trade Organization. *Annual Report*. Geneva: WTO, 1998.

World Trade Organization. *WTO Policy Issues for Parliamentarians*. Geneva: WTO, 2001.

World Trade Organization. *International Trade Statistics 2002*. Geneva: WTO, 2002.

Wright, Robert. *Nonzero: The Logic of Human Destiny*. New York: Pantheon Books, 2000.

Wrong, Michaela. *In the Footsteps of Mr Kurtz: Living on the Brink of Disaster in the Congo.* London: Fourth Estate, 2000.

Yergin, Daniel and Joseph Stanislaw. *The Commanding Heights: The Battle between Government and the Marketplace that is Remaking the Modern World.* New York: Simon & Schuster, 1998.

Index